JUDGING EQUITY

T. Leigh Anenson analyzes the scope of judicial authority and discretion to recognize the equitable doctrine of unclean hands as a bar to actions seeking damages in the United States. Bringing an American perspective to the contentious conversation about law–equity fusion in other countries of the common law, Anenson provides a historical, doctrinal, and theoretical account of the defense, analyzes cases in the federal courts and across the fifty states, and places the issue of integration within a broader debate over the fusion of law and equity. Her analysis includes descriptive and normative accounts of the equitable maxim of unclean hands. This groundbreaking work, which clarifies conflicting case law and advances the idea of a principled fusion of law and equity, should be read by anyone interested in equity – its cultivation, preservation, and celebration.

T. LEIGH ANENSON is Professor of Business Law at the Robert H. Smith School of Business, University of Maryland, and Associate Director of the Center for the Study of Business Ethics, Regulation, and Crime. She is an internationally recognized scholar working in American equity law and related areas of remedies, private law, and jurisprudence. Her pioneering research has been building a foundation for equitable defenses in modern litigation.

Judging Equity

THE FUSION OF UNCLEAN HANDS IN U.S. LAW

T. LEIGH ANENSON

Robert H. Smith School of Business, University of Maryland

CAMBRIDGE
UNIVERSITY PRESS

CAMBRIDGE
UNIVERSITY PRESS

University Printing House, Cambridge CB2 8BS, United Kingdom

One Liberty Plaza, 20th Floor, New York, NY 10006, USA

477 Williamstown Road, Port Melbourne, VIC 3207, Australia

314–321, 3rd Floor, Plot 3, Splendor Forum, Jasola District Centre, New Delhi – 110025, India

79 Anson Road, #06–04/06, Singapore 079906

Cambridge University Press is part of the University of Cambridge.

It furthers the University's mission by disseminating knowledge in the pursuit of education, learning, and research at the highest international levels of excellence.

www.cambridge.org
Information on this title: www.cambridge.org/9781107160477
DOI: 10.1017/9781316675748

First published 2019

Printed in the United Kingdom by Clays Ltd, Elcograf S.p.A.

A catalogue record for this publication is available from the British Library.

Library of Congress Cataloging-in-Publication Data
NAMES: Anenson, T. Leigh, 1967– , author.
TITLE: Judging equity : the fusion of unclean hands in U.S. law / T. Leigh Anenson, Robert H. Smith School of Business, University of Maryland.
DESCRIPTION: Cambridge, United Kingdom ; New York, NY, USA : Cambridge University Press, 2018. | Includes index. | Based on author's thesis (doctoral - Monash University, Australia, 2017).
IDENTIFIERS: LCCN 2018023426 | ISBN 9781107160477 (hardback) | ISBN 9781316613603 (pbk.)
SUBJECTS: LCSH: Clean hands doctrine–United States.
CLASSIFICATION: LCC KF8880 .A96 2018 | DDC 347.73/72–dc23
LC record available at https://lccn.loc.gov/2018023426

ISBN 978-1-107-16047-7 Hardback

To my parents, for their love and kindness

Contents

Preface

This book proceeds from the conviction that American equity is a subject of law worthy of study. At a time when changes in the law are typically assumed to be made by legislatures, vast amounts of law continue to be created by judges. Equity is one such area of judge-made law. Its historically powerful role for the courts in fashioning reforms must never be forgotten. Too little attention has been given to equitable principles and practices in the United States. Equitable defenses, in particular, have largely gone unnoticed. This book is directed at one essential defense – unclean hands.

Judging Equity: The Fusion of Unclean Hands in U.S. Law discusses how the clean hands doctrine came alive and whether courts were warranted in bringing it to life. It focuses on the defense's widening scope and influence by tracing its expansion into legal remedies, including damages. It provides the background necessary to understand the defense, summarizes leading cases, and considers questions of what is and should be its definitive qualities. It seeks to explain the persistence and evolution of the problem of fusion, which concerns the viability and desirability of engaging equitable doctrines in legal cases or vice versa. Around the world, disputes and discussions about fusion are ongoing.

This book uses the experience of unclean hands to offer insight into the issue of fusion and suggests lessons it might offer for the future. Along with an examination of the defense itself, there is a more general discussion of equity, especially as it touches on the relations of equity and law. Doubtless some of the challenges inherent in combining exposition and analysis, critique and simplification, remain.

I have been working on this book officially since 2016 and unofficially almost my entire academic life. As a litigator, I was involved in several cases in which equitable defenses impacted the outcome. Yet I searched in vain for commentary on these equitable doctrines and their underlying philosophy. These controversies not only piqued my curiosity about the subject, but also instilled in me a firm belief that understanding equity is still crucially important. To this end, I am writing the book I wanted to have when I was an attorney.

Judging Equity: The Fusion of Unclean Hands in U.S. Law is meant for lawyers, judges, academics, and other members of the legal community. It should also engage anyone attracted to the workings of the law and the achievement of justice. In academia, especially, it should be of interest to scholars outside the United States working within systems that share our English inheritance of a common law legal system. Within the United States, it is my hope it will at least encourage others to dig into the topic of equity and further explore the territory that I have mapped out.

Acknowledgments

The author is indebted to many friends and colleagues, too many to mention, and a host of anonymous reviewers for their valuable comments and suggestions. I am also eternally grateful to the mentors on my academic journey, Larry DiMatteo and George Siedel, for their encouragement and guidance. This book stands on additional shoulders as well, including those of the many other scholars and researchers, both here and abroad, who have taught me so much.

This book would not have been written without the generous support of the Department of Business Law and Taxation, Monash University, including the advice and assistance of Paul Von Nessen, Rick Krever, and Abe Herzberg. Peter Mellor was exceedingly helpful as well. Portions of this book were written during my visiting scholarships and fellowships at the University of Cambridge, the University of Sydney, and the Australian National University. My appreciation to those universities and law faculties for their interest and critical take on the book's arguments. This book additionally benefited from the research assistance of Evan Llewellyn, Matthew Touton, and Faith Harrington.

Research for *Judging Equity: The Fusion of Unclean Hands in U.S. Law* developed through the preparation of a series of law review and journal articles on equitable defenses. Throughout the book, I draw substantially from this work. I express my appreciation to the editors and reviewers of "Announcing the 'Clean Hands' Doctrine," Vol. 51, *U.C. Davis Law Review* 1827–1890 (2018); "Equitable Defenses in the Age of Statutes," Vol. 37, *University of Texas Review of Litigation* 529–579 (2018); "Statutory Interpretation, Judicial Discretion, and Equitable Defenses," Vol. 79, *University of Pittsburgh Law Review* 1–59 (2017); "Limiting Legal Remedies: An Analysis of Unclean Hands," Vol. 99, *Kentucky Law Journal* 63–118 (2010); "Beyond Chafee: A Process-Based Theory of Unclean Hands," Vol. 47, *American Business Law Journal* 509–574 (2010); "Treating Equity like Law: A Post-Merger Justification of Unclean Hands," Vol. 45, *American Business Law Journal* 455–509 (2008).

Wilson Huhn inspired my interest in jurisprudence during law school. To him, I am thankful. I would also like to thank my partners at Reminger Co., L.P.A., who had the audacity to give me authority and otherwise involve me in several cases comprising equitable principles and doctrines. My fellow warriors include Mario Ciano, Bill Farrall, Nick Satullo, and Larry Sutter.

Last, but certainly not least, I enthusiastically acknowledge Matt Gallaway and his staff at Cambridge University Press for their superb editorial assistance. Their meticulous reading of the manuscript, copious comments, and corrections through many revisions strengthened it immensely.

1

Introduction

Equity, in America at least, has fallen on hard times. From antiquity to the end of the nineteenth century, equity was one of the enduring legal subjects.[1] By the mid-twentieth century, however, it had largely been forgotten in the United States. Contributing to its demise was the unification of law and equity courts and their procedures.[2] The study of equity was later relegated to a remedies course and scattered among the many legal topics in the contemporary law school

---

[1]   The regimes of law and equity began with the royal prerogative of English kings to do justice in any case between their subjects. Roger L. Severns, *Nineteenth Century Equity: A Study in Law Reform*, 12 CHI.-KENT L. REV. 81, 90–91 (1934). Over time, it became customary for the king to delegate his authority to administer justice to his secretary, the chancellor. William F. Walsh, *Equity Prior to the Chancellor's Court*, 17 GEO. L.J. 97, 100–06 (1929). The chancellor was the head of Chancery and a great officer in the nature of a secretary of state or prime minister. Garrard Glenn & Kenneth R. Redden, *Equity: A Visit to the Founding Fathers*, 31 VA. L. REV. 753, 761 (1945). The process of referring petitions to the chancellor was common at the time of Edward I, but it was Edward III in 1349 that confirmed the procedure and ordered the chancellor to base his decision on "Honesty, Equity, and Conscience." 1 JOHN NORTON POMEROY, A TREATISE ON EQUITY JURISPRUDENCE AS ADMINISTERED IN THE UNITED STATES OF AMERICA §§ 33–35, 38–40 (Spencer W. Symons ed., Bancroft-Whitney 5th ed. 1941). The High Court of Chancery emerged as a separate forum for the administration of equity in the fourteenth century. RALPH A. NEWMAN, EQUITY AND LAW: A COMPARATIVE STUDY 22–23 (1961); *see also* 1 FREDERICK POLLOCK & FREDERIC W. MAITLAND, HISTORY OF ENGLISH LAW 3 (2d ed. 1898) (explaining that Chancery was known at that time as the *Curia Cancellariae*). The court began as a marble table and chair at the upper end of Westminster Hall on the right hand side of the entryway, opposite to the King's Bench on the left. Glenn & Redden, *supra*, at 762 (citing 1 JOHN LORD CAMPBELL, LIVES OF THE LORD CHANCELLORS 206 (1878)). The rules that were administered in that court came to be known as equity due to derivation from the Latin *aequitas* or leveling. PHILIP S. JAMES, INTRODUCTION TO ENGLISH LAW 29 (8th ed. 1972). For a discussion of the historical evolution of the separate judicial systems, see ROSCOE POUND, THE SPIRIT OF THE COMMON LAW 27 (1921).

[2]   The Field Code in New York abolished common law forms and united law and equity in a simplified procedure in 1848. Stephen N. Subrin, *David Dudley Field and the Field Code: A Historical Analysis of an Earlier Procedural Vision*, 6 LAW & HIST. REV. 311, 314 (1988); discussion *infra* Chapter 4. It precipitated the merger in other states and eventually the federal

---

curriculum.[3] Not surprisingly, scholarship on American equitable principles waned in the wake of these phenomena.[4] Court confusion over equitable principles soon followed.[5] Consequently, while the merger of law and equity was billed as the triumph of equity,[6] it appeared to be nothing more than a caricature. Roscoe Pound was prescient when he claimed that "reform came too soon"; that is, before the integration of law and equity had been accomplished through the judicial method.[7]

But the world may be turning again. New federal and state cases have highlighted the enduring significance of equity. As such, American legal scholars are beginning to study and reflect on the subject that might herald the revival of one of England's most remarkable inventions.

This book addresses an important modern question about ancient equity jurisprudence. It investigates the availability and desirability of equitable defenses to prevent legal remedies, with a particular focus on the clean hands doctrine.

For centuries, judges have relied on their discretion when considering whether equitable defenses preclude actions seeking legal relief. As part of that process, courts have incorporated many equitable defenses into the law.[8] This trend is known

---

system. Subrin, *supra*. The formal separation of law and equity procedure in the federal system was not eliminated until 1938 when the Federal Rules of Civil Procedure went into effect. *See generally* Stephen N. Subrin, *How Equity Conquered Common Law: The Federal Rules of Civil Procedure in Historical Perspective*, 135 U. PA. L. REV. 909, 929 (1987). There is no current, comprehensive historical description of the fusion of law and equity in the United States. *See* George P. Smith II & Walter W. Nixon III, *La Dolce Vita: Law and Equity Merged at Last!*, 24 ARK. L. REV. 162, 176–77 nn.54–56 (1970) (surveying authorities and showing inconsistencies over which states belong to which classes of equity jurisdiction).

For an account of the virtually simultaneous reform effort underway in England culminating in the abolishment of the Court of Chancery, see, for example, Gunther A. Weiss, *The Enchantment of Codification in the CommonLaw World*, 25 YALE J. INT'L L. 435, 486–88 (2000) (discussing an 1828 speech by Lord Brougham as the catalyst for procedural change); Mr. Justice Lurton, *The Operation of the Reformed Equity Procedure in England*, 26 HARV. L. REV. 99, 100–01 (1912) (discussing the English Judicature Acts of 1873 and 1875).

3   *See* Edward D. Re, *Introduction* to SELECTED ESSAYS ON EQUITY xiv (Edward D. Re ed., 1955) ("[T]he elimination of a separate course in equity in many of the law schools in the United States has caused much that is truly valuable in the study of equity to be either completely lost or scattered to the point of useless dilution in various courses."); Douglas Laycock, *Remedies: Justice and the Bottom Line Introduction*, 27 REV. LITIG. 1, 7 (2007) (explaining that the prior courses in equity, damages, and restitution were combined into a single course in remedies (summarizing Douglas Laycock, *How Remedies Became a Field: A History*, 27 REV. LITIG. 161 (2008)) [hereinafter Laycock, *How Remedies Became a Field*].

4   T. Leigh Anenson, *Public Pensions and Fiduciary Law: A View from Equity*, 50 U. MICH. J.L. REF. 251–90 (2017); Zechariah Chafee, Jr., *Foreword* to SELECTED ESSAYS ON EQUITY, *supra* note 3, at iii ("The absence of a collection of leading articles on Equity has long been a serious lack among law books."); discussion *infra* Chapter 2.

5   *See* discussion *infra* Chapters 3–5.

6   *See* Douglas Laycock, *The Triumph of Equity*, 56 LAW & CONTEMP. PROBS. 53, 53 (1993); *infra* Chapters 2 and 3.

7   NEWMAN, *supra* note 1, at 53 (quoting Roscoe Pound, *The Etiquette of Justice* 3, in address before the Nebraska State Bar Association, Nov. 24, 1908).

8   *See* T. Leigh Anenson & Donald O. Mayer, *"Clean Hands" and the CEO: Equity as an Antidote for Excessive Compensation*, 12 U. PA. J. BUS. L. 947, 979–80 (2010); discussion *infra* Chapters 2 and 4.

as "fusion." And commonlaw legal systems throughout the world have experienced fusion – from the United States to England to Australia. This concept is noteworthy because it informs much of our jurisprudence: "The evolution of law is to a large extent the history of its absorption of equity."[9]

Despite this trend, some state and federal courts reject fusion. Historically, law and equity occupied carefully delineated spheres.[10] In that context, unclean hands – like

---

[9] NEWMAN, *supra* note 1, at 255.

[10] Early American courts were modeled upon the dual English system, with separate courts given jurisdiction to administer law and equity. *See, e.g.,* WILLIAM F. WALSH, OUTLINES OF THE HISTORY OF ENGLISH AND AMERICAN LAW 69–70 (1923); GEORGE TUCKER BISPHAM, PRINCIPLES OF EQUITY: A TREATISE ON THE SYSTEM OF JUSTICE ADMINISTERED IN COURTS OF CHANCERY 26 (Baker, Voorhis & Co., 11th ed. 1934) (advising that many state constitutions provided for the establishment of a separate equity court patterned after the High Court of Chancery in England). For a hundred years before the Revolution, however, equity had been bitterly attacked in a majority of the colonies. Charles Warren, *New Light on the History of the Federal Judiciary Act,* 37 HARV. L. REV. 49, 96 (1923); *see* Calvin Woodward, *Joseph Story and American Equity,* 45 WASH. & LEE L. REV. 623, 641 (1988) (explaining that equity was not popular because "one of the most common grievances in the colonies was the arbitrary and capricious behavior of Crown officials"). Massachusetts, not surprisingly, never had equity courts, and its trial court was not permitted to exercise equity power until 1870. FRANK AUGUST SCHUBERT, INTRODUCTION TO LAW AND THE LEGAL SYSTEM 12 (2014). Moreover, during the colonial period, chancery courts, common law courts, and legislatures had equity powers. *See* S.D. Wilson, *Courts of Chancery in the American Colonies,* 779, *in* 2 SELECT ESSAYS IN ANGLO-AMERICAN LEGAL HISTORY (AALS ed. 1908); Sidney G. Fisher, *The Administration of Equity Through Common Law Forms in Pennsylvania, id.* at 810. Professor Warren summarizes the status of fusion in 1787 when the Constitution was drafted:

> There were Courts of Chancery . . . in New York, South Carolina, Maryland, Virginia, and to some extent New Jersey; in Pennsylvania, Delaware and North Carolina, there were no such courts, though the common law courts had certain equity powers; in Connecticut and Rhode Island the Legislature exercised some powers of the Court of Chancery; in Massachusetts and New Hampshire, there were common law courts only, having a few very limited equity powers; Georgia had only common law courts.

Warren, *supra,* at 96; *see also* Charles T. McCormick, *The Fusion of Law and Equity in United States Courts,* 6 N.C. L. REV. 283, 284 (1928) ("[C]hancery and the admiralty retained their separate existence in most colonies, and even these failed to take root in some of the colonies."). At the time of the adoption of the Constitution in 1790, the majority of states administered equity in chancery courts as a system separate from the common law. *Id.* at 283–84. States entering the union also established chancery courts. HENRY M. UTLEY & BYRON M. CUTCHEON, MICHIGAN AS A PROVINCE, TERRITORY AND STATE: THE TWENTY-SIXTH MEMBER OF THE FEDERAL UNION 94–95 (1906) (outlining the creation and abolishment of Michigan's equity courts for a ten-year period from 1836–47). Therefore, equity had separate courts, judges, and procedures. Congress did not create separate national courts of law and equity in the federal system yet provided for different procedures for their administration. *See* McCormick, *supra,* at 284; Robert von Moschzisker, *Equity Jurisdiction in the Federal Courts,* 75 U. PA. L. REV. 287 (1927); *see also* Jesse G. Reyes, *The Swinging Pendulum of Equity: How History and Custom Shaped the Development of the Receivership Statute in Illinois,* 44 LOY. U. CHI. L.J. 1019, 1034 (2013) ("One of the leading Chancery lawyers of the period [after independence], Alexander Hamilton, was an outspoken proponent of equity jurisdiction in the federal courts.").

Most state systems gradually integrated law and equity within one court but allowed for their administration by separate procedural rules. *See* Wesley Newcomb Hohfeld, *The Relations*

other equitable defenses such as laches – was used almost exclusively to deny equitable relief.[11] But the law is not stagnant. Law and equity have also merged. Since the merger, judges have applied the clean hands doctrine to bar legal relief in both commonlaw and statutory actions.[12] Courts holding otherwise generally do so without citing any authority, by clinging to outdated case law predating the union of law and equity, or by misunderstanding the meaning of the merger.[13] In these jurisdictions, then, the merger was just a means of attaining freedom but not synonymous with it.

By studying discretionary limits on legal remedies, this book adds an American perspective to the current and contentious conversation about fusion in the Commonwealth.[14] The narrative provides a descriptive and normative account of

---

between Equity and Law, 11 MICH. L. REV. 537, 549 (1913) (relating the three versions of the administration of equity as two courts, two procedures such as in New Jersey, one court and two procedures like in Illinois and the federal system, and one court and one procedure as found in New York and California); McCormick, *supra* note, at 284 (explaining that thirty of forty-eight states had merged their courts and procedures by 1928); *supra* note 2. Some states did not merge law and equity until the twenty-first century. Arkansas merged its law and equity courts in 2000. John J. Watkins, *The Right to Trial by Jury in Arkansas After Merger of Law and Equity*, 24 U. ARK. LITTLE ROCK L. REV. 649, 649 (2002). Virginia did not merge its law and equity courts until 2012. Doug Rendleman, *The Triumph of Equity Revisited: The Stages of Equitable Discretion*, 15 NEV. L.J. 1397, 1402 (2016) [hereinafter Rendleman, *Stages of Equitable Discretion*].

Today, six states (Delaware, Illinois, New Jersey, South Carolina, Tennessee, Mississippi) preserve separate courts (or divisions) of law and equity. *See* T. Leigh Anenson, *Treating Equity Like Law: A Post-Merger Justification of Unclean Hands*, 45 AM. BUS. L.J. 455, 456 n.5 (2008) [hereinafter Anenson, *Treating Equity Like Law*]; *see also* Samuel L. Bray, The *System of Equitable Remedies*, 63 UCLA L. REV. 530, 537 (2016) (noting that Georgia distinguishes equity for trial and appellate jurisdiction and that Iowa has unified courts that administer what the state constitution calls "distinction and separate jurisdictions" for law and equity). South Carolina, for instance, has special masters-in-equity courts in certain counties which are a division of the circuit court. S.C. CODE ANN. § 14–11-10 *et seq.* Illinois separates law and equity in Cook County. *See Chancery Division*, CIR. CT. COOK COUNTY, (last visited Feb. 10, 2018) http://www.cookcountycourt.org/ABOUTTHECOURT/CountyDepartment/ChanceryDivi sion.aspx (noting that the Chancery Division of the Circuit Court of Cook County is established pursuant to General Order 1.2, 2.1 (b) [amended, effective Jan. 1, 2008] of the General Orders of the Circuit Court of Cook County and is divided into two sections: General Chancery Section and the Mortgage Foreclosure/Mechanics Lien Section); *see also* Roger L. Severns, *Equity and Fusion in Illinois*, 18 CHI.-KENT. L. REV. 333, 358 n.79 (1940) (surmising that in Cook County the designation of certain judges as chancellors for the term made the separation probably more complete there than elsewhere in the state). New Jersey has separate divisions of law and equity in the same court. *See* N.J. REV. STAT. § 4:3–1(a)(1) (2018). Delaware, Tennessee, and Mississippi continue to have courts of chancery. Del. Code Ann. tit. 10 § 341 (2014); Miss. Const. art. VI § 159; Tenn. Code Ann. § 16–11-101 (2018); *see also* Rendleman, *Stages of Equitable Discretion, supra*, at 1402 ("Delaware Chancery, the nation's premier business court, will be with us for the foreseeable future.").

[11] *See* discussion *infra* Chapters 3 and 4.
[12] *See* discussion *infra* Chapters 3 and 4.
[13] *See* discussion *infra* Chapters 3 and 4.
[14] *See* Keith Mason, *Fusion: Fallacy, Future or Finished?, in* EQUITY IN COMMERCIAL LAW 41, 75 (James Edelman & Simone Degeling eds., 2005) (Justice Keith Mason, New South Wales Court of Appeals) ("Debate about the fusion of law and Equity goes back for centuries.").

the equitable maxim of unclean hands. Its storyline clarifies the conflicting case law and advances the idea of a principled fusion of law and equity. The book's broader aim is to demonstrate a need for equity – its cultivation, preservation, and celebration.

1.1 OVERVIEW OF THE BOOK

This book addresses the following question: Can and should the equitable defense of unclean hands be available to bar legal relief including damages? *Yes.*

For hundreds of years, the defense of unclean hands has prevented recovery for equitable (and not legal) relief. In spite of the dirt on their hands, litigants could still be compensated in damages. Even the union of law and equity did not dislodge the defense from its confinement to equity actions. Fifty years ago, however, state and federal courts in the United States began to apply the defense regardless of the remedy requested. The doctrine now precludes a wide variety of common law and statutory claims.

America's break with tradition is a narrow axis upon which to engage the wider debate over the legitimacy of using once exclusively equitable principles in law. The movement of unclean hands across the law–equity divide provides evidence upon which to test the philosophical and practical foundations for and against fusion. Drawing attention to the use of the unclean hands defense in the United States also provides an in-depth look at a doctrine that has been discredited and disregarded. This book attempts to scrape off and refurbish the clean hands doctrine by demonstrating not only the defense's appropriateness in curtailing damages but also its continued importance today.

After introducing the clean hands doctrine, this book examines the corpus of cases incorporating unclean hands into the common and statutory law in the United States. It provides an extensive explanation of unclean hands in legal cases by looking more closely at the defense's doctrinal underpinnings. Describing the arguments and justifications in the debate over the legal status of unclean hands seeks to inform this divisive issue and aid its resolution. The availability of unclean hands in damages actions has not been the subject of sustained analysis at an appellate level in state and federal law. It remains unresolved in many jurisdictions, with other courts addressing the issue in error or through oversight. Judges have also expressed their frustration with the lack of doctrinal and theoretical scholarship

---

A conference on the interplay of common law and equity in modern commercial law was held in Sydney, Australia, in December 2004, culminating in a book of essays on the topic of fusion with case examples from England, Australia, New Zealand, and Canada. James Edelman & Simone Degeling, *Introduction* to EQUITY IN COMMERCIAL LAW, *supra*. Another conference, "Law and Equity: Fusion and Fission," was held more recently at St. Catharine's College, Cambridge.

considering the availability of unclean hands to bar legal remedies.[15] The book aims to end the arbitrariness and judicial extremes on the subject of unclean hands in an effort to unify this fragmented area of law.

Identifying the reasons behind the rules adopting or rejecting the clean hands doctrine at law, this research clarifies the meaning of the law–equity merger in federal and state civil procedure. It suggests that the unification did not prevent courts from adopting the defense in lawsuits seeking legal remedies on a case-by-case basis. It further directs courts to be sensitive to whether the application of the defense is consistent with its purposes and does not otherwise defeat the purposes of the asserted claim. Along with advocating substantive fusion on a principled basis, this book provides an alternative way of fusing the unclean hands defense as a matter of procedure. It further derives a decision-making framework for distinguishing substance from procedure going forward.

It additionally engages the debate over law–equity integration. During the centuries following the merger of law and equity, there has been a vigorous discussion about the relationship between these two traditions in the United States and the rest of the common law world.[16] These so-called fusion wars advance diverse views about the role of law and equity in the current legal framework.[17] Battlegrounds have been drawn on an array of subjects like property, remedies, choice of law, fiduciaries, and unjust enrichment.[18] This book includes the equitable doctrine of clean hands in that conversation.

The value of equity is up for fuller explication in American law. Equitable defenses are fundamental conceptions of equity jurisprudence.[19] Yet seldom are they the focus of study in the modern law school curriculum.[20] Attorneys who began

---

[15] *See, e.g.*, Unilogic, Inc. v. Burroughs Corp., 12 Cal. Rptr. 741, 745 (Cal. Ct. App. 1992) (commenting on the lack of relevant authorities and precedents in considering the availability of unclean hands to bar a legal claim).

[16] Beverley McLachlin, *Introduction* (Chief Justice, Canadian Supreme Court) ("[D]espite the passage of time, the fusion of law and equity remains a live issue today, subject to debate by academics, practitioners, and judges alike."), *in* EQUITY IN COMMERCIAL LAW, *supra* note 14, at vii, vii; Tiong Min Yeo, *Choice of Law for Equity* ("The extent of the fusion of the substantive rules of common law and equity remains a matter of great controversy today, and different legal systems in the common law tradition have adopted different approaches to this question."), *in* EQUITY IN COMMERCIAL LAW, *supra* note 14, at 147, 150.

[17] McLachlin, *supra* note 16, at vii (using the phrase "fusion wars" to refer to the discussion of the relationship of law and equity).

[18] *Id.* at vii; Mason, *supra* note 14, at 65 (explaining that in Australia, Canada, and New Zealand, the question of whether damages are appropriate for breach of an exclusively fiduciary duty has been a catalyst for discussion about the fusion of law and equity).

[19] *See* 1 DAN B. DOBBS, DOBBS LAW OF REMEDIES: DAMAGES-EQUITY-RESTITUTION § 2.10, 247–48 (2d ed. 1993) (discussing unclean hands, laches, and estoppel as a basis for refusing injunctive relief).

[20] *See* Jerome Frank, *Civil Law Influences on the Common Law – Some Reflections on "Comparative" and "Contrastive" Law*, 104 U. PA. L. REV. 887, 895 n.43 (1956) ("In several of our leading law schools there is now no course on 'equity.'"); Jack B. Weinstein & Eileen B. Hershenov, *The Effect of Equity on Mass Tort Law*, 1991 U. ILL. L. REV. 269, 272 (explaining that "equity was taught as a separate course until the 1950's"). *Compare* Robert S. Stevens, *A Brief on Behalf*

their legal education prior to the 1970s may recall that equitable defenses like unclean hands are typically used to prevent opportunism.[21] They may also remember that these maxims rest on sound moral principles such as prohibiting litigants from taking advantage of their own wrong and protecting the judicial system.[22] They may even recollect that doctrines like clean hands usually operate *ex post* rather than *ex ante* to allow judges discretion and flexibility in adjusting case outcomes.[23]

With a focus on the fusion of law and equity, this inquiry will analyze ancient equity in the modern context and "the abstention courts exercise under the short-hand phrase 'unclean hands.'"[24] Tracing the integration of unclean hands into damages actions provides an important opportunity to explore the defense itself as

---

of a Course in Equity, 8 J. LEGAL EDUC. 422, 422 (1955) (criticizing a trend of law schools that do not offer a separate course in equity), *with* Hohfeld, *supra* note 10, at 537–38 (agreeing with Maitland's view to eliminate a separate course in equity so as not to preserve the distinctiveness of equity). *See also* Doug Rendleman, *Remedies: A Guide for the Perplexed*, 57 ST. LOUIS U. L.J. 567, 572 (2013) [hereinafter Rendleman, *Remedies*] (noting that Virginia and Delaware continue to test equity on the bar exam).

[21] There are a variety of equitable defenses utilized in an almost infinite range of contexts. As such, any attempt to capture their essence is necessarily incomplete. Some simplification is useful, however, and the idea of opportunism probably best captures the spirit of the defenses discussed in this book. For opportunism as a general theory of equity, *see* Henry E. Smith, *Why Fiduciary Law Is Equitable*, in PHILOSOPHICAL FOUNDATIONS OF FIDUCIARY LAW 261 (Andrew S. Gold & Paul B. Miller eds., 2014) ("This chapter will argue that a functional theory of equity – of equity as a decision-making mode aimed at countering opportunism – captures the character of fiduciary law."). For remedies as correcting for party opportunism, *see* Mark P. Gergen, John M. Golden, & Henry E. Smith, *The Supreme Court's Accidental Revolution? The Test for Permanent Injunctions*, 112 COLUM. L. REV. 203, 237 (2012) ("A major theme in equity has been the need to correct for party opportunism and injunctions partake of this overarching purpose.") For equitable defenses aimed at the prevention of opportunism, *see* T. Leigh Anenson, *The Role of Equity in Employment Noncompetition Cases*, 42 AM. BUS. L.J. 1, 62–63 (2005) [hereinafter Anenson, *Role of Equity*] (discussing how equitable defenses prevent double standards and duplicity); Anenson & Mayer, *supra* note 8 (advocating the use of unclean hands to prevent company executives' unfair advantage-taking in their employment contracts). For another explanation of equitable defenses, *see* Sheelagh McCracken, *Marshalling: A Case Study in Complexity*, at 96–111, in PRIVATE PROPERTY AND REMEDIES (Russell Weaver & Francois Lichere eds., 2015) (theorizing equitable defenses in commercial law as mechanisms of financial risk allocation).

[22] *See* discussion *infra* Chapter 2 (explaining rationales of unclean hands); T. Leigh Anenson, *The Triumph of Equity: Equitable Estoppel in Modern Litigation*, 27 REV. LITIG. 377, 388 (2008) [hereinafter Anenson, *Triumph of Equity*] (explaining rationale for estoppel as doing unto others as you would have them do unto you).

[23] *See* Anenson, *Treating Equity Like Law*, *supra* note 10, at 508 (discussing the role of equitable defenses as a significant safety valve); *The Cleansing Power of Equity*, 11 RESEARCH@SMITH 4, 5 (Fall 2010) https://www.rhsmith.umd.edu/news/researchsmith-fall-2010 (remarking that equitable defenses operate *ex post* rather than *ex ante*) (reviewing Anenson & Mayer, *supra* note 8); *see also* Henry Smith, *The Equitable Dimension of Contract*, 45 SUFFOLK U. L. REV. 897, 907 (2012) (explaining *ex post* operation of equitable estoppel and unclean hands).

[24] Johnson v. Yellow Cab Transit Co., 321 U.S. 383, 387 (1944) (Frankfurter, J., and Roberts, J., dissenting).

well as the forgotten relationship between law and equity.[25] Therefore, this book advances the practice of equity and its seminal principles. It likewise influences theory by reducing the size of the substantial gap in our understanding of modern American equity.[26]

Investigating the muddle of opinions integrating equitable defenses into legal relief is difficult and time consuming. But doing so provides greater understanding of this outwardly chaotic and contested case law. It must be emphasized that equity has not been earmarked for separate study in the United States.[27] During the previous century, it failed to benefit from the laborious process of systemization undertaken in other areas of judge-made law.[28] Because much less preliminary work has been done on equitable doctrines than those of the common law, the task of restating its principles and precedents is even greater.

Clarifying the meaning of the merger enhances predictability by reducing mistakes in decisions and making them more understandable. These outcomes should enhance judicial legitimacy. Moreover, deriving a clear method of incorporating unclean hands into the law allows courts to focus attention on the equally arduous task of applying the defense. It should also enable better observation and comparison in developing principles of judicial discretion.[29] Further, it highlights the need for across-the-board research on unclean hands, and equitable defenses generally,

---

[25] Unclean hands originated in private law, and many of the Supreme Court decisions analyze the defense in that context. The equitable remedial rights doctrine in federal courts, which required federal courts to redress state-created rights with remedies determined by uniform federal equity jurisdiction, was neither preserved by the merger of law and equity nor saved by the *Erie* doctrine of the Rules of Decision Act. Stephen B. Burbank, *The Bitter with the Sweet: Tradition, History, and Limitations on Federal Judicial Power – A Case Study*, 75 NOTRE DAME L. REV. 1291, 1317 (2000) (citing Note, *Equitable Remedial Rights Doctrine: Past and Present*, 67 Harv. L. Rev. 836, 836 (1954)).

[26] *See, e.g.,* T. Leigh Anenson & Gideon Mark, *Inequitable Conduct in Retrospective: Understanding Unclean Hands in Patent Remedies*, 62 AM. U. L. REV. 1441, 1525 (2013) ("Equity is not lost, for it continues in a steady stream of precedents, but it has ceased being understood."); John R. Kroger, *Supreme Court Equity, 1789–1835, and the History of American Judging*, 34 HOUS. L. REV. 1425, 1427 (1998) (noting the lack of literature on Supreme Court equity jurisprudence and emphasizing that an appreciation of these equity decisions is indispensable to an understanding of the history of American judging).

[27] T. Leigh Anenson, *Announcing the "Clean Hands" Doctrine*, 51 U.C. DAVIS L. REV. 1827, 1830 (2018).

[28] In the early twentieth century, the legal community began to develop and clarify other subjects in the private law sphere through *Restatements of the Law. See* discussion *infra* Chapter 2, Section 2.6 (identifying which subject areas of the *Restatements* address the clean hands doctrine). The aim of the American Law Institute was to simplify the law to the rules and principles that are to guide the conduct of clients and litigants. *See, e.g.,* Harlan F. Stone, *Some Aspects of the Problem of Law Simplification*, 23 COLUM. L. REV. 319, 334–35 (1923).

[29] *See* Sarah M. R. Cravens, *Judging Discretion: Contexts for Understanding the Role of Judgment*, 64 U. MIAMI L. REV. 947, 950 (2010) (advising that discretion began receiving scholarly attention only since the late 1960s); Daniel A. Farber, *Taking Costs into Account: Mapping the Boundaries of Judicial and Agency Discretion*, 40 HARV. ENVTL. L. REV. 87, 134 (2016) ("Discretion occupies an oddly neglected place in Anglo-American legal thought.") (quoting

which is virtually nonexistent,[30] and may renew calls for a *Restatement of Remedies* (or Equity).[31] Finally, analyzing the relationship between equity and the law through the lens of unclean hands fosters scholarship in the law of obligations, remedies, and the federal courts.[32] Taken as a whole, this book seeks to enrich our larger social understanding of what medieval equity means in the modern era.

1.2 SUMMARY OF CHAPTERS

The following chapters explain and defend the recognition of the unclean hands defense in damages actions in the United States. After an initial outline of the defense, the book begins by offering a doctrinal account of the scope of authority and discretion to recognize equitable defenses that prevent recovery of legal relief for breaches of judge-made and statutory rights before turning to more theoretical matters.

Judge William A. Fletcher, *The Discretionary Constitution Institutional Remedies and Judicial Legitimacy*, 91 YALE L.J. 635, 641 (1982)); *see also* Rendleman, *Remedies, supra* note 20, at 578–79 ("Discretion in decision-making is a fertile field for inquiry. Careful scholars have published several well-researched and well-reasoned articles calling for discretion in equity."); *id.* at 579 n.57 (citing T. Leigh Anenson, *Beyond Chafee: A Process-Based Theory of Unclean Hands*, 47 AM. BUS. L.J. 509 (2010); Anenson & Mayer, *supra* note 8; T. Leigh Anenson, *Limiting Legal Remedies: An Analysis of Unclean Hands*, 99 KY. L.J. 63 (2011); Anenson, *Treating Equity Like Law, supra* note 10).

[30] *See* Anenson & Mark, *supra* note 26, at 1450–52, 1504–05, 1511–12 (endorsing a trans-substantive approach to understanding equitable remedies and defenses). My scholarship is the exception. It has studied the operation of one or more equitable defenses across state and federal statutory and common law. *See, e.g.*, T. Leigh Anenson, *Equitable Defenses in the Age of Statutes*, 37 REV. LITIG. 529 (2018) (evaluating the methodology of the U.S. Supreme Court in providing the scope of equitable defenses in federal legislation); T. Leigh Anenson, *Statutory Interpretation, Judicial Discretion, and Equitable Defenses*, 79 UNIV. PITT. L. REV. 1 (2017) (revealing an assumption of equitable defenses under silent statutes and analyzing issues of judicial authority and competence); Anenson & Mark, *supra* note 26 (examining the tradition of unclean hands in light of its evolution in patent law); T. Leigh Anenson, *From Theory to Practice: Analyzing Equitable Estoppel Under a Pluralistic Model of Law*, 11 LEWIS & CLARK L. REV. 633 (2007) (analyzing equitable estoppel); Anenson, *Role of Equity, supra* note 21, at 24–53 (explaining the function of assorted equitable defenses in unfair competition cases). Other scholars that have analyzed equitable defenses tend to focus on one subject such as contracts. *See generally* Emily L. Sherwin, *Law and Equity in Contract Enforcement*, 50 MD. L. REV. 253, 253–64 (1991) (explaining the purpose of equity in the context of contract enforcement); Edward Yorio, *A Defense of Equitable Defenses*, 51 OHIO ST. L.J. 1201, 1202 (1990) (exploring both positive and normative perspectives to defend equitable defenses); *see also* Anenson, *Triumph of Equity, supra* note 22, at 382 n.14 (listing equitable estoppel literature by subject matter).

[31] *See* Laycock, *How Remedies Became a Field, supra* note 3, at 266 ("In the late 1980s, the American Law Institute considered a *Restatement of Remedies*, which would have ensconced the field even more firmly in the legal establishment."); *see also id.* at 172 (explaining that there is a *Restatement of Restitution* that is considered part of the law of remedies).

[32] Equitable defenses are often associated with remedies, but they are also part of private law. Yet the American legal world divides remedies and private law into different domains, where they have developed more or less independently. As such, scholars with unique outlooks and techniques of appraisal tend to study one subject or the other.

The second chapter introduces the clean hands doctrine and provides an overview of it. It travels back in time and across the globe to identify the defense's origins. It traces the development of the unclean hands defense in American decisions as well as its discussion in American literature. The chapter also describes the defense's philosophical foundations and corresponding components.

The third chapter details the development of unclean hands as a defense to legal remedies. It reviews the reception of the doctrine in common law and statutory decisions across the United States and summarizes its status under federal and state law. It also exposes the underlying rationales for and against the absorption of unclean hands to better evaluate the idea of fusion and end the disparate treatment of the defense.

The fourth chapter focuses on the question of whether judges have power to fuse the clean hands doctrine in actions seeking damages. It reconsiders the purpose of the procedural union of law and equity. The unintended effect of the unification is that judges have relied on it to either automatically include or exclude the defense in legal actions. It reconciles these opposing rationales regarding the merger by proposing a new method to resolve the incorporation question. The compromise position suggests a case-by-case approach that is consonant with the text of the merger and the intent of the legislature.

The fifth chapter addresses the issue of whether the unclean hands defense should be available to bar legal relief. It situates the specific issue of remedial coherence for the clean hands doctrine, and equitable defenses generally, within the general debate on the relationship between law and equity that is being engaged in by academics, practitioners, and judges in England, Australia, New Zealand, and Canada. This chapter provides reasons to consider the defense's universal use in law or equity cases. It shows that the labels "law" and "equity" have become obstacles to decisions instead of guides and argues for a commonsense approach to the application of unclean hands that weighs its advantages and disadvantages in a particular case. It concludes that courts should cease discriminating against the equitable defense of unclean hands solely on account of the merger and begin treating equity like law.

The sixth chapter presents a process-based theory of unclean hands. It undertakes an innovative analysis to divide the concept of unclean hands along two dimensions: substance and procedure. This is both novel and significant because the doctrine is commonly assumed to have only a substantive side. The chapter examines the accumulating legacy of court decisions that invoke the defense to defend the litigation process. It demonstrates how judges in cases of fusion are shifting emphasis from the defense's rationale of preventing litigants from benefiting from their own wrong to protecting the court and the integrity of the law. The process-based theory integrates the defense across claims by focusing on its court-protection purpose. It also unifies the disparate treatment of the defense across jurisdictions by providing a procedural paradigm of incorporation. By rethinking the clean hands doctrine from a procedural perspective, the recommended framework not only clarifies the defense but also advances the assimilation of it into the law.

The book concludes by explaining that it is navigating a path of equity in American law by concentrating on the clean hands doctrine. Equity has been understudied and undertheorized. So this research helps ameliorate the imbalance in the literature on equity and promotes an awareness and understanding of a highly complicated and critical area of the law. It also furthers research on the defense by Zechariah Chafee that is still relied upon by courts and scholars worldwide.

2

Announcing the Clean Hands Doctrine

[A] universal rule guiding and regulating the action of equity courts in their interposition on behalf of suitors for any and every purpose, and in their administration of any and every species of relief.

– John Norton Pomeroy[1]

2.1 INTRODUCTION

The equitable doctrine of clean hands plays a vital role in protecting citizens and courts. From modest beginnings in ancient equity cases involving drunken promises and debauchery,[2] the defense now applies in both state and federal court litigation of a distinctly modern vintage.[3] Its coverage extends to entire categories of tort and contract law,[4] an ever-broadening range of statutory disputes,[5] and even to international human rights.[6] What is more, the defense

---

[1] 2 JOHN NORTON POMEROY, A TREATISE ON EQUITY JURISPRUDENCE AS ADMINISTERED IN THE UNITED STATES OF AMERICA § 397 (Spencer W. Symons ed., Bancroft-Whitney 5th ed. 1941) [hereinafter POMEROY'S EQUITY JURISPRUDENCE, FIFTH EDITION].

[2] Zechariah Chafee, Jr., *Coming into Equity with Clean Hands*, 47 MICH. L. REV. 877, 878 (1949) [hereinafter Chafee I] (noting its "humble beginnings in suits about contracts made under the influence of liquor or amorous philandering").

[3] *See* discussion *infra* Chapter 3.

[4] *See* discussion *infra* Chapter 3.

[5] *See* discussion *infra* Chapter 3; T. Leigh Anenson, *Statutory Interpretation, Judicial Discretion, and Equitable Defenses*, 79 UNIV. PITT. L. REV. 1, 1–59 (2017) [hereinafter Anenson, *Statutory Interpretation*] (revealing an assumption of equitable defenses under silent statutes and analyzing issues of judicial authority and competence).

[6] *See generally* Aleksandr Shapovalov, *Should a Requirement of "Clean Hands" Be a Prerequisite to the Exercise of Diplomatic Protection? Human Rights Implications of the International Law Commission's Debate*, 20 AM. U. INT'L L. REV. 829 (2005) (discussing unclean hands as a general principle of international law and its applicability in cases of diplomatic protection).

has taken on a life of its own. It is reproducing and multiplying into more distinctive doctrines, thus magnifying the defense's impact.[7]

"Unclean hands" is arguably the most powerful and least containable defense that came from ancient courts of equity. Broader and newer than other equitable defenses, discretionary dismissals for unclean hands are not limited to illegality, but extend to any inequitable, unconscionable, or bad-faith conduct that is connected to the case.[8] For reasons of court and party protection, judges have invoked unclean hands to preclude an assortment of equitable and increasingly legal remedies.[9]

This chapter offers an analysis of equitable defense of unclean hands whose existence and operation in the common and statutory law have been largely ignored, undervalued, or simply uncharted since the last century. Despite its popularity in the courts,[10] some scholars find the defense dubious at best and would eradicate the doctrine even from its historic home in equity jurisprudence.[11] Prior research on unclean hands divided the defense into topical areas of the law.[12] Consistent with this approach, the conclusion reached was that it lacked cohesion and shared properties.[13] This chapter sees things differently. It suggests a common language to help avoid compartmentalization along with a unified framework to provide a more precise way of understanding the defense. Advancing an overarching theory and structure of the defense should better clarify not only when the doctrine should be allowed, but also why it may be applied differently in different circumstances.

---

[7] The unclean hands defense has transformed into a number of different doctrines in intellectual property law. These include, among others, copyright misuse, patent misuse, and inequitable conduct in the patent process. Anenson, *Statutory Interpretation, supra* note 5, at 8 n.27 (listing doctrines derived from the unclean hands defense). The employee misconduct defense in state and federal law is said to stem from the doctrine as well. *Id.* The U.S. Supreme Court has also identified habeus corpus as an outgrowth of the clean hands doctrine. *See* Munaf v. Geren, 553 U.S. 674, 693 (2008). In addition, the California Supreme Court announced that the defense of recrimination in divorce law is a derivative of the unclean hands defense. DeBurgh v. DeBurgh, 250 P.2d 598, 605 (Cal. 1952).

[8] *See* discussion *infra* Chapter 6, Section 6.4.2 (comparing unclean hands to estoppel as well as to the legal doctrines of *in pari delicto* and fraud on the court); discussion *infra* Sections 2.6 and 2.7 (describing the clean hands doctrine).

[9] *See* discussion *infra* Section 2.8; discussion *infra* Chapter 3.

[10] *See* ZECHARIAH CHAFEE, JR., SOME PROBLEMS OF EQUITY 12 (1950) [hereinafter, CHAFEE, SOME PROBLEMS] (noting the "astonishing number" of cases decided under the doctrine of unclean hands); discussion *infra* Section 2.4.

[11] *See* discussion *infra* Chapter 5.

[12] Chafee examined eighteen different groups of cases considering unclean hands. *See* Chafee I, *supra* note 2, at 881; Zechariah Chafee, Jr., *Coming into Equity with Clean Hands*, 47 MICH. L. REV. 1065, 1091–92 (1949) [hereinafter Chafee II]; *infra* Section 2.6 and Chapter 6, Section 6.3.1 note. 20 (listing subjects).

[13] Chafee I, *supra* note 2, at 878 (concluding that unclean hands "is really a bundle of rules relating to quite diverse subjects").

Because English and American courts did not develop the idea of unclean hands until the late eighteenth century, it is one of the youngest equitable maxims.[14] Moreover, older doctrines are now known as "law" (not "equity")[15] or are routinely recognized in actions at law.[16] Unlike unclean hands, they were incorporated before the integration of law and equity courts and so were unaffected by it.[17] Perhaps due to its newness relative to the other doctrines, the defense remained exclusively a defense against equitable (not legal) actions at the time of the merger.[18] Despite the rhetoric of completing the union of law and equity,[19] procedural reform was initially interpreted by many courts to eternally bar this presumably substantive defense in legal cases.[20]

---

[14] Professor Chafee described it as "a child beside some other maxims ... which [were] mature in Shakespeare's day." CHAFEE, SOME PROBLEMS, *supra* note 10, at 5; *see also id.* at 2 (commenting that unclean hands "is a rather recent growth").

[15] Defenses like fraud, duress, illegality, unconscionability, and accommodation derived from equity but were converted to law and often are considered legal defenses. *See generally* James Barr Ames, *Specialty Contracts and Equitable Defences*, 9 HARV. L. REV. 49 (1895) (discussing how the former equitable defenses of fraud, illegality, failure of consideration, payment, accommodation, and duress were subsequently recognized at law in specialty contracts).

[16] Equitable defenses that retained their equitable designation but that were incorporated into the law include estoppel, *see* Kirk v. Hamilton, 102 U.S. 68 (1880) (adopting equitable estoppel into the common law); waiver, *see* USH Ventures v. Global Telesystems Group, Inc., 796 A.2d 7, 19 (Del. Super. Ct. 2000) (explaining that waiver has been used at law in contract suits); rescission, *see id.* at 18 (noting that rescission is "both a cause of action and a defense"); ratification, *see* Colish v. Brandywine Raceway Ass'n, 119 A.2d 887, 892 (Del. Super. Ct. 1955); and acquiescence, *see* DAN B. DOBBS, DOBBS LAW OF REMEDIES: DAMAGES-EQUITY-RESTITUTION 44 (2d ed. 1993) [hereinafter DOBBS LAW OF REMEDIES] (noting the invocation of acquiescence in purely legal cases).

[17] *E.g.*, William F. Walsh, *Is Equity Decadent?*, 22 MINN. L. REV. 479, 485 (1938) (explaining that equitable estoppel was "fully adopted" in courts of law by 1938). Integration was prompted by "[t]he perception that parallel court systems were applying substantially similar substantive rules of law under different procedural [processes]." Thomas O. Main, *Traditional Equity and Contemporary Procedure*, 78 WASH. L. REV. 429, 464 (2003); E.W. Hinton, *Equitable Defenses Under Modern Codes*, 18 MICH. L. REV. 717, 721 (1920) ("This development of an equitable cause of action into a legal cause of action, or into a defense to a legal action, has been fairly common in the later period of the common law."); *see also* William Searle Holdsworth, *Blackstone's Treatment of Equity*, 43 HARV. L. REV. 1, 7 (1929).

[18] *See* Original Great Am. Chocolate Chip Cookie Co. v. River Valley Cookies, Ltd., 970 F.2d 273, 281 (7th Cir. 1992) ("Unclean hands is a traditional defense to an action for equitable relief."); *see also* Hinton, *supra* note 17, at 719 ("[T]here were equitable defenses to equitable claims, where there were no similar defenses to corresponding legal claims.").

[19] *See* Charles E. Clark, *The Union of Law and Equity*, 25 COLUM. L. REV. 1, 2 (1925) ("The day will come when lawyers will cease to inquire whether a given rule be a rule of equity or a rule of common law ... " (quoting MAITLAND, EQUITY 20 (1910))); Roscoe Pound, *The Decadence of Equity*, 5 COLUM. L. REV. 20, 26 (1905) ("[A] complete absorption or blending of the two systems into one ... is now completely predicted by jurists.").

[20] *See* discussion *infra* Chapter 4. Chapter 6 proposes a procedural paradigm for incorporating the defense of unclean hands.

But times have changed. A number of state and federal courts no longer restrict unclean hands to equitable remedies or preserve the substantive version of the defense.[21]

With more than fifty years of decisions extending the unclean hands defense to bar cases seeking damages, this study is meant to take the measure of the defense. It has implications for theory and practice. The path of unclean hands in state and federal law affords a unique window into the defense and its application. It also provides a basis to assess the defense's appropriateness in damages action. The role of the clean hands doctrine in limiting legal relief has implications for the fusion of law and equity that has stimulated a worldwide discussion.[22]

2.2 OVERVIEW

To provide a backdrop for analyzing the fusion of the clean hands doctrine in actions seeking damages, this chapter sketches an outline of the defense. First, it depicts the origins of the doctrine in English and American law. Second, it traces the defense's development in the decisional law and literature in the United States. Third, via a close reading of state and federal cases, it defines and evaluates the key components of the defense along with the role of discretion. The chapter concludes that the equitable defense of unclean hands plays an important role in the law of remedies. Examining how judges extend the defense to damages should enhance understanding of this obscure and often impenetrable equitable principle in a way that appreciates the law as a coherent whole.

2.3 PHILOSOPHY OF EQUITY AND UNCLEAN HANDS

The familiar maxim of equity that "he [or she] who comes into equity must come with clean hands" is "one of the elementary and fundamental conceptions of equity jurisprudence."[23] Because the defense operates as a part of the whole of equity jurisprudence, arriving at a working definition of equity seems like a good place to begin. An exact expression of equity, however, does not come easy.[24]

---

[21] There are hundreds of cases now applying the defense against legal remedies. *See* discussion *infra* Chapter 3.

[22] *See* discussion *supra* Chapter 1 and *infra* Chapter 5.

[23] T. Leigh Anenson & Gideon Mark, *Inequitable Conduct in Retrospective: Understanding Unclean Hands in Patent Remedies*, 62 AM. U. L. REV. 1441, 1450 (2013) (quoting POMEROY'S EQUITY JURISPRUDENCE, FIFTH EDITION, *supra* note 1, § 397).

[24] *See* Samuel L. Bray, The *System of Equitable Remedies*, 63 UCLA L. REV. 530, 536 (2016) [hereinafter Bray, *System*] ("Equity means many different and overlapping things."); Hila Keren, *Undermining Justice: The Two Rises of Freedom of Contract and the Fall of Equity*, 2 CANADIAN J. COMP. & CONTEMP. L. 339, 391 (2016) (noting that "the legal tradition captured by the term equity is rich, diverse, and much contested among scholars.").

Our English heritage of equity is a system of rules that developed in a separate medieval court.[25] As history rolled along, equity intervened across vast areas of the law that defied simple summaries of its contents. Equity became a complex system. And "[c]omplex systems have many features."[26] "Equity," like "jurisdiction," is a "coat of many colors."[27] For this reason, academic writing has hesitated to offer or endorse a "just so" account of equity.[28] In fact, it is understandable that jurists most steeped in the vagaries of equity and well-versed in its multitude of doctrines and principles would insist that the subject is indescribable.[29] But some general theorizing is useful to set the stage for understanding unclean hands.

Equity can be seen as a system and a process,[30] along with other impressions.[31] The sense of equity as a system sees it as an interlocking web of precepts.[32] One of the earliest accounts grounded these ideas in fraud, accident, and things of confidence.[33] Contrast the foregoing focus on equity's internal identity with a relational model.[34] The process perspective stems from the instinct that equity is more than a

---

[25] For a discussion of the historical evolution of the separate judicial systems and the role of the chancellor, *see* T. Leigh Anenson, *Public Pensions and Fiduciary Law: A View from Equity*, 50 U. MICH. J.L. REF. 261 n.52 (2017) [hereinafter Anenson, *A View from Equity*]; T. Leigh Anenson, *The Triumph of Equity: Equitable Estoppel in Modern Litigation*, 27 REV. LITIG. 377, 378 n.4 (2008) [hereinafter Anenson, *Triumph of Equity*].

[26] P.G. Turner, *Equity and administration*, in EQUITY AND ADMINISTRATION 1, 5 (P.G. Turner ed., 2016).

[27] United States v. L.A. Tucker Truck Lines, Inc., 344 U.S. 33, 39 (1952) (Frankfurter, J., dissenting); *see* Bray, *System*, *supra* note 24, at 68 (calling equity jurisdiction an old and imprecise term).

[28] Keren, *supra* note 24, at 56 ("[A]s an old concept that survived centuries of use by different humans in a variety of countries and cultures, equity cannot possibly have a simple meaning.").

[29] *See* R.P. MEAGHER ET AL., MEAGHER, GUMMOW AND LEHANE'S EQUITY: DOCTRINES AND REMEDIES 3 (4th ed. 2002) [hereinafter MEAGHER, GUMMOW AND LEHANE'S EQUITY, FOURTH EDITION] ("Equity can be described but not defined. It is the body of law developed by the Court of Chancery in England before 1873."); John L. Garvey, *Some Aspects of the Merger of Law and Equity*, 10 CATH. U. L. REV. 59, 61 (1961) [hereinafter Garvey, *Some Aspects*] ("Probably no other term [equity] has so consistently evaded definition by legal writers.").

[30] *See generally* Philip A. Ryan, *Equity: System or Process?*, 45 GEO. L.J. 213, 215–17 (1957) (describing equity from different perspectives such as functional or historical); *infra* Chapter 5, Section 5.3.1.

[31] *See* T. Leigh Anenson, *Limiting Legal Remedies: An Analysis of Unclean Hands*, 99 KY. L.J. 63, 107 (2011) [hereinafter Anenson, *Limiting Legal Remedies*] ("[T]he post-merger trend of adopting unclean hands into the law establishes that courts are no longer satisfied that traditional differences in form support different treatment in substance."); Samuel L. Bray, *Form and Substance in the Fusion of Law and Equity* (UCLA Sch. of Law, Public Law Research Paper No. 17–07, 2016) (elaborating on what those two terms mean). *See generally* Turner, *Equity and administration*, *supra* note 26, at 4 (summarizing a series of essays explaining equity's facilitative role).

[32] *See* Ryan, *supra* note 30, at 214–15.

[33] Anenson, *A View from Equity*, *supra* note 25, at 261–62; *see* discussion *infra* notes 176–180.

[34] A later classification scheme described equity's structure as exclusive, auxiliary, and concurrent jurisdiction. MEAGHER, GUMMOW AND LEHANE'S EQUITY, FOURTH EDITION, *supra* note 29, at

recitation of its rules.[35] Rather, the process school of thought emphasizes equity's flexibility in maintaining the integrity of the law.[36] This perspective then emphasized not what it is but why and how it is.

Scholars contemplating equity often emphasize the traditional means by which ancient chancellors decided cases in contrast to judges of the common law.[37] A core concept of equity originated with the Aristotelian idea that the law would fail due to its generality.[38] The cleansing power of equity calls for *ex post* discretion by courts to prevent and remedy the problem.[39] It is the reason why many of its doctrines remain flexible.[40] The need for some level of open-endedness also tells us why standards, rather than rules, generally accompanied an equitable approach.[41] Certainly, the equitable model of decision making has been a

---

450. Because there is overlap between the categories, the tripartite scheme has not been entirely satisfactory. While this scheme classifies equity in relation to the common law, it still centers on the nature or content of equity rather than its purposes.

[35] The intuition was that a historical description of equitable doctrines and principles is incomplete. Ryan, *supra* note 30, at 217–23.

[36] *Id.* at 217 (advising of equity's "built-in dynamicism"). Blackstone described equity as the "soul" of the law. JOSEPH STORY, COMMENTARIES ON EQUITY JURISPRUDENCE AS ADMINISTERED IN ENGLAND AND AMERICA 6 (9th ed. 1866) (citing 3 WILLIAM BLACKSTONE, THE COMMENTARIES ON THE LAWS OF ENGLAND 222 (4th ed. 1876) by stating "[e]quity, in its true and genuine meaning, is the soul and spirit of all law; positive law is construed, and rational law is made, by it"). This comports with Maitland's justification of equitable intervention on the grounds that equity came not to destroy the law, but to fulfill it. JAMES W. EATON, HANDBOOK OF EQUITY JURISPRUDENCE 47 (1901) [hereinafter EATON ON EQUITY].

[37] *See generally* Doug Rendleman, *The Triumph of Equity Revisited: The Stages of Equitable Discretion*, 15 NEV. L.J. 1397, 1428–31 (2016).

[38] *See* Anenson, *Statutory Interpretation, supra* note 5, at 26–27. The concept of equity was based on the Aristotelian idea of *epikeia*, which recognized the impossibility of crafting laws to cover every contingency. RALPH A. NEWMAN, EQUITY AND LAW: A COMPARATIVE STUDY 13 (1961) [hereinafter NEWMAN, EQUITY AND LAW] ("Twenty-three centuries ago Aristotle said that equity is that idea of justice which contravenes the written law."); *see also* ST. THOMAS AQUINAS, SUMMA THEOLOGICA, pt. I-II, q. 96, art. 1, 2, & 6; pt. II-II, q. 120, art. 1 (stating that "since human actions, with which laws are concerned, are composed of contingent singulars and are innumerable in their diversity, it was not possible to lay down rules of law that would apply to every single case").

[39] Henry E. Smith, *Why Fiduciary Law Is Equitable*, in PHILOSOPHICAL FOUNDATIONS OF FIDUCIARY LAW 261, at 264–65 (Andrew S. Gold & Paul B. Miller eds., 2014) [hereinafter Smith, *Fiduciary Law*] (explaining that equity cannot be too predictable because opportunists will anticipate it and evade it as well as invent new ways of engaging in such behavior); *see also* T. Leigh Anenson, *Equitable Defenses in the Age of Statutes*, 37 REV. LITIG. 529, 564–66 (2018) [hereinafter Anenson, *Age of Statutes*] (discussing judicial discretion as a component of equitable defenses).

[40] *See* Anenson, *Age of Statutes, supra* note 39, at 549; *see also* Lionel Smith, *Fusion and Tradition*, in EQUITY IN COMMERCIAL LAW 19, 31 (James Edelman & Simone Degeling eds., 2005) [hereinafter Smith, *Fusion and Tradition*] (advising that the idea of discretion has deep historical roots in equity).

[41] *See* Anenson, *A View from Equity, supra* note 25, at 264 (explaining that equity also employed *ex ante* rules in the service of combatting opportunism); *see also* Anenson & Mark, *supra* note 23, at 1514–17 (discussing how rule-based precepts can be underinclusive for equitable doctrines aimed at preventing the unconscientious abuse of rights). The discretionary aspect of many

distinguishing mark of equity.[42] As Chafee explained, equity is a "way of looking at the administration of justice."[43]

In evaluating its doctrines and defenses, judges apply moral norms in highly contextualized situations.[44] Lawyers and laypersons alike consider "equity" to be a synonym for fairness.[45] Early equity tradition reflected the prevailing belief that litigants have ethical responsibilities that equity can help discharge.[46] After all, as a practical matter, equity historically was a source of new common law rules.[47]

Professor Lionel Smith reminds us that equity systematically enforced certain ethical ideals like good faith in contrast to the common law.[48] Unclean hands shares this interest.[49] There are other core values supporting equitable defenses including promoting fair play, protecting weaker parties, and preserving the integrity of the

> equitable doctrines, including defenses, is related to the discussion about the preferred form of the law as rules or standards (or something in between). *See generally* T. Leigh Anenson, *From Theory to Practice: Analyzing Equitable Estoppel Under a Pluralistic Model of Law*, 11 Lewis & Clark L. Rev. 633, at 642–43 (2007) [hereinafter Anenson, *Pluralistic Model*] (discussing rules and standards in the context of equitable doctrines).
>
> [42] *See* Anenson, *A View from Equity, supra* note 25, at 261; Emily L. Sherwin, *Law and Equity in Contract Enforcement*, 50 Md. L. Rev. 253, 307 (1991) ("The legal model of enforcement is conduct-oriented and rule-based. The equitable model is better suited to remedial goals and particularistic decisionmaking.").
>
> [43] Zechariah Chafee, Jr., *Foreword* to Selected Essays on Equity iii (Edward D. Re ed., 1955) [hereinafter Chafee, Selected Essays on Equity].
>
> [44] *See* Leonard J. Emmerglick, *A Century of New Equity*, 23 Tex. L. Rev. 244, 250 (1945) (commenting that equity courts "mainly clothed moral values with legal sanctions"); Anenson, *A View from Equity, supra* note 25, at 261 n.51 (explaining that early chancellors were church officials trained in Canon and moral law).
>
> [45] T. Leigh Anenson & Donald O. Mayer, *"Clean Hands" and the CEO: Equity as an Antidote for Excessive Compensation*, 12 U. Pa. J. Bus. L. 947, 975–96 (2010); *see* Snell's Principles of Equity 6 (Robert Megarry & P.V. Baker eds., 27th ed. 1973) [hereinafter Snell's Twenty-Seventh Edition] (noting that, in modern English statutes, provisions relating to what is "equitable" are usually construed to mean what is fair). For judicial correlation of equity with basic fairness, *see, for example*, Rauscher v. City of Lincoln, 691 N.W.2d 844, 852 (Neb. 2005) ("Equity is determined on a case-by-case basis when justice and fairness so require."); Clark II v. Teeven Holding Co., Inc., 625 A.2d 869, 878 (Del. Ch. 1992) ("The use of the term 'equitable principles' ... is merely equivalent to the words 'principles of fairness or justice.'").
>
> [46] Anenson & Mayer, *supra* note 45, at 1009; *see* Dezell v. Odell, 3 Hill 215, 225 (N.Y. Sup. Ct. 1842) ("It is a question of ethics.").
>
> [47] *See* Anenson & Mayer, *supra* note 45, at 1008 ("The experience of equity is evidence of this dynamic and reflective process. Over hundreds of years, equity has made inroads in the law and resulted in its modification and amenability to notions of fairness and justice."); Wesley Newcomb Hohfeld, *The Relations between Equity and Law*, 11 Mich. L. Rev. 537, 567 n.23 (1913) (explaining that equity resulted in "a liberalizing and modernizing of the law" (quoting Roscoe Pound, Address to the Law Association of Philadelphia: The Organization of Courts (Jan. 31, 1913))).
>
> [48] *See* Smith, *Fusion and Tradition, supra* note 40, at 32–36 (explaining differences in underlying moral norms like respect for other people's obligations and the justiciability of motive).
>
> [49] Pomeroy's Equity Jurisprudence, Fifth Edition, *supra* note 1, § 397 (stating the maxim "is based upon conscience and good faith").

justice system.[50] They rest on maxims obligating litigants to follow the golden rule or, like unclean hands and others, prevent them from taking advantage of their own wrong.[51] Equity is often associated with mercy as well.[52] Circumstances giving rise to the application of equitable principles are a mixed bag of manners, mores, and machinations.

It is not surprising that equity is often theorized in conscience-based terms.[53] Roscoe Pound famously explained that equity intervened to prevent an unconscientious use of rights.[54] Equitable defenses are often justified in this manner.[55]

---

[50] Anenson, *Pluralistic Model, supra* note 41, at 663.

[51] *See* T. Leigh Anenson, *Treating Equity Like Law: A Post-Merger Justification of Unclean Hands,* 45 AM. BUS. L.J. 455, 461 (2008) [hereinafter Anenson, *Treating Equity Like Law*] (relating rationales of unclean hands); Anenson, *Triumph of Equity, supra* note 25, at 388 (explaining rationale for estoppel as doing unto others as you would have them do unto you); Anenson, *Statutory Interpretation, supra* note 5, at 11 n.31 (describing doctrine of *in pari delicto* prevents parties to a common illegal scheme from profiting from their own wrongdoing); Stephen A. Smith, *Form and Substance in Equitable Remedies, in* DIVERGENCES IN PRIVATE LAW 321, 335 (Andrew Robertson & Michael Tilbury, eds. 2016) ("The clean hands bar is based on the same principles that underlie the traditional common law doctrine of illegality.").

[52] *See, e.g.,* Hecht Co. v. Bowles, 321 U.S. 321, 329–30 (1944) (explaining equity's qualities of mercy and practicality that allow for a nice adjustment to reconcile the public interest and private need); Martha C. Nussbaum, *Equity and Mercy,* 22 PHIL. & PUB. AFF. 83, 85 (1993); *see also* Emmerglick, *supra* 44, at 254 (grounding equity in the *epicia* of Aristotle and in the Roman *clementia* or "clemency").

[53] *See* Keren, *supra* note 24, at 347 ("[Equity is the] insistence that judicial discretion should be applied with conscience in mind, and that the legal outcome must deter exploitation of the law while promoting fairness, moral behavior, and social justice."). The notion of conscience (as well as whose conscience) has been a key in understanding equitable intervention through the ages. *See* DENNIS R. KLINCK, CONSCIENCE, EQUITY, AND THE COURT OF CHANCERY IN EARLY MODERN ENGLAND vii (2010) ("One cannot delve very far into judicial equity without encountering the notion of 'conscience.'"); Irit Samet, *What Conscience Can Do for Equity, in* JURISPRUDENCE: AN INTERNATIONAL JOURNAL OF LEGAL AND POLITICAL THOUGHT 32 (2012) (explaining that conscience in equity does the job of justifying liability and defining its border; *see also id.* at 20 (explaining that medieval conscience came from God and was therefore uniform). *See generally* Anenson, *Pluralistic Model, supra* note 41, at 660 (discussing the notion of conscience in equity). The maxim is grounded on the historical concept that a court of equity represents the collective conscience of the public. *See id.* (discussing the institutional idea of conscience in Chancery).

[54] Roscoe Pound, *The End of Law as Developed in Legal Rules and Doctrines,* 27 HARV. L. REV. 195, 226 (1914); *see also* MEAGHER, GUMMOW AND LEHANE'S EQUITY, FOURTH EDITION, *supra* note 29, at 451 (explaining that equity prevents the unconscientious use of legal rights); Tiong Min Yeo, *Choice of Law for Equity* (explaining how the "[u]nconscientiousness in the exercise of legal rights provides the reason for the intervention" of equity), *in* EQUITY IN COMMERCIAL LAW, *supra* note 40, at 147, 157; Anthony Mason, *Equity's Role in the Twentieth Century,* 8 KING'S C. L.J. 1 (1998) ("[E]quitable principles were shaped with a view to inhibiting unconscientious conduct and providing for relief against it.").

[55] *See* DOUG RENDLEMAN, COMPLEX LITIGATION: INJUNCTIONS, STRUCTURAL REMEDIES, AND CONTEMPT 269 (2010) [hereinafter RENDLEMAN, COMPLEX LITIGATION] (discussing equitable defenses and explaining that every edition of Pomeroy maintained that the Chancellor could refrain from granting relief on the ground that the conduct violated the court's conscience); Anenson & Mark, *supra* note 23, at 1450–51, 1522; Anenson, *Pluralistic Model, supra* note 41, at

More recent scholarship emphasizes equity's role as a second-order safety valve in combatting opportunism.[56] Equitable defenses like unclean hands partake of this attitude as well.[57]

To be sure, famous for its appeal to history and high-minded ethical ideals, equity should also be remembered for its practicality – its function. The "fossil records" of history and the "majesty got from ethical associations" do not provide a complete picture of equitable principles in American law.[58] The purposes of equity, and its defenses in particular, were to stop strategic behavior and safeguard the court.[59]

In this vein, the maxim of "he [or she] who comes into equity must come with clean hands" developed to "protect the court against the odium that would follow its interference to enable a party to profit by his own wrong-doing."[60] It follows that the defense serves two fundamental purposes. It protects judicial integrity and promotes justice.[61] The application of unclean hands protects judicial integrity "because allowing a plaintiff with unclean hands to recover in an action creates doubts as to the justice provided by the judicial system."[62] Thus, the court acts to protect itself and not the opposing party.[63] In this regard, it seems that the equitable defense serves an expressive function for courts.[64] Judges are guardians of the court's integrity

---

662 (outlining how estoppel prevented unconscionable conduct and withheld aid to the wrongdoer).

[56] *See* Dennis Klimchuk, *Equity and the Rule of Law, in* PRIVATE LAW AND THE RULE OF LAW 247, 247 (Lisa M. Austin & Dennis Klimchuk, eds., 2014) (describing equity as anti-opportunism in preventing the exploitation of the generality or strictness of the law).

[57] *See* discussion *supra* Chapter 1 n. 21 and accompanying text; *see also* Anenson, *Statutory Interpretation, supra* note 5, at 5–6 ("Famous for its appeal to history and high-minded ethical ideals, equity should also be remembered for its practicality – its function.").

[58] O.W. Holmes, *The Path of the Law,* 10 HARVARD L. REV. 457, 464 (1897).

[59] *See generally* Anenson & Mayer, *supra* note 45 (advocating the use of unclean hands to prevent company executives' unfair advantage taking in their employment contracts); *see also* Smith, *Fiduciary Law, supra* note 39, at 262–63 (asserting anti-opportunism as a general theory of equity); Mark P. Gergen, John M. Golden, & Henry E. Smith, *The Supreme Court's Accidental Revolution? The Test for Permanent Injunctions,* 112 COLUM. L. REV. 203, 237 (2012) (explaining injunctions as correcting for party opportunism). For court protection purpose, *see* HENRY L. McCLINTOCK, HANDBOOK OF THE PRINCIPLES OF EQUITY § 26, at 59–69 (2d ed. 1948) (discussing court protection purpose of unclean hands); discussion *infra* Chapter 6 (citing authorities).

[60] N. Pac. Lumber Co. v. Oliver, 596 P.2d 931, 939–40 (Or. 1979) (quoting McCLINTOCK, *supra* note 59, § 26, at 63 (1949)).

[61] *See* Maldonado v. Ford Motor Co., 719 N.W.2d 809, 818 (Mich. 2006); Manown v. Adams, 598 A.2d 821, 824–25 (Md. Ct. Spec. App. 1991), *rev'd on other grounds,* 615 A.2d 611, 612 (Md. 1992).

[62] Kendall-Jackson Winery Ltd. v. Superior Court, 90 Cal. Rptr.2d 743, 749 (Cal. Ct. App. 1999); *see also* Mas v. Coca-Cola Co., 163 F.2d 505, 511 (4th Cir. 1947).

[63] *See* Gaudiosi v. Mellon, 269 F.2d 873, 881 (3d Cir. 1959); Fibreboard Paper Prods. Corp. v. E. Bay Union of Machinists, 39 Cal. Rptr. 64, 96 (Cal. Ct. App. 1964).

[64] Anenson, *Statutory Interpretation, supra* note 5, at 42 (discussing unclean hands and other equitable defenses).

and conservators of equity's primary corrective ideal in maintaining the law's continuity and coherence.[65]

The clean hands doctrine promotes justice by preventing "a wrongdoer from enjoying the fruits of his [or her] transgression"[66] or, put differently, making the wrongdoer litigant "answer for his [or her] own misconduct in the action."[67] Similar to comparative negligence and other defenses used in actions seeking damages, courts contemplating unclean hands recognize that the fault of both parties is an important consideration in the judicial settlement of disputes.[68]

The objective of unclean hands to prevent unfair advantage taking by wrongdoers is said to rest on moral values such as *in delicto, tu quoque*, and even retribution.[69] The former *in delicto* norm concerns situations in which the claimant is involved or responsible for the same wrong as the respondent.[70] The latter retributive norm relates to settings in which the claimants' inequity is the reason they are denied the right to be heard.[71] The norm of *tu quoque* denies standing to attribute blame to one who also committed the same wrong regardless of the merits of the claim.[72]

---

[65] Anenson & Mayer, *supra* note 45, at 974 (commenting that the application of equitable defenses reinforces equity's function in maintaining law's integrity).

[66] Precision Instrument Mfg. Co. v. Auto. Maint. Mach. Co., 324 U.S. 806, 815 (1945); Keystone Driller Co. v. Gen. Excavator Co., 290 U.S. 240, 245 (1933); Fairway Developers, Inc. v. Marcum, 832 N.E.2d 581, 585 (Ind. Ct. App. 2005) ("The purpose of the unclean hands doctrine is to prevent a party from reaping benefits from his misconduct.").

[67] *Kendall-Jackson Winery*, 90 Cal.Rptr.2d at 748.

[68] See T. Leigh Anenson, *Beyond Chafee: A Process-Based Theory of Unclean Hands*, 47 AM. BUS. L.J. 509, 528 (2010) [hereinafter Anenson, *A Process-Based Theory*]. Chafee explained:

> [T]he clean hands maxim is not peculiar to equity, but is simply a picturesque phrase applied by equity judges to a general principle running through damage actions as well as suits for specific relief. This principle is that the plaintiff's fault is often an important element in the judicial settlement of disputes, as well as the defendant's fault.

Chafee II, *supra* note 12, at 1091–92.

[69] See Ori J. Herstein, *A Normative Theory of the Clean Hands Defense*, 17 LEGAL THEORY 171, 195–96, 199–200 (2011). The notion of punishment is anathema to equity. See Pappas v. Pappas, 320 A.2d 809, 811 (Conn. 1973) ("It is applied not by way of punishment but on considerations that make for the advancement of right and justice." (citing Johnson v. Yellow Cab Co., 321 U.S. 383, 387 (1944))); Andrew Burrows, *Remedial Coherence and Punitive Damages in Equity* (analyzing controversy over whether punitive damages are available in Australia for equitable wrongs and explaining that there is no notion of punishment operating under the labels or concepts of equity), *in* EQUITY IN COMMERCIAL LAW, *supra* note 40, at 381, 391–92. For a discussion of an early period when Chancery partook of a criminal nature where the remedy was punishment of the offenders, see Willard Barbour, *Some Aspects of Fifteenth Century Chancery*, 31 HARV. L. REV. 834, 856–57 (1918).

[70] See Herstein *supra* note 69, at 193–95 (claiming that unclean hands also embodies the moral norm *in delicto* that deals with wrongful provocation or inducement (i.e., "you started it" or "you made me do it" or "it is your fault")).

[71] See Herstein, *supra* note 69, at 199–200.

[72] *Id.* at 195; *id.* at 195–96 (reviewing philosophical literature ascribing moral value to *tu quoque*). Professor Nicholas Cornell recently argued that the defenses of unclean hands and unconscionability are both concepts in which the court denies relief to those who lack moral

Because the clean hands doctrine is personal to the plaintiff, courts often declare that it may not be invoked against third parties or subject to attribution. In other words, "it is irrelevant whether anyone other than the one seeking equitable relief acted with unclean hands."[73]

Reasonable people may disagree on which of the two primary policies of the clean hands doctrine are paramount or nested within others.[74] The two goals are also not entirely separable.[75] The maxim of unclean hands "derives from the unwillingness of a court of equity, as a court of conscience, to lend the aid of its extraordinary powers to a plaintiff who himself is guilty of reprehensible conduct in the controversy and thereby to endorse such behavior."[76]

In summary, the equitable defense of unclean hands depicts the values and reflects the logic of equity. It has lofty goals still relevant today. Modern trial judges, just like medieval Chancellors, use the defense to defend both litigants and courts.[77] This often-forgotten doctrine prevents hypocrisy and gamesmanship in the system of justice and safeguards the judiciary from approving unethical and illegal conduct.[78] As shown by its present application in countless cases, the doctrine of unclean hands continues to be legally and socially significant.[79]

Because the law (particularly equity) is reliant on the past,[80] the next section outlines the origins of the defense. The story of the clean hands doctrine begins several thousand miles across the Atlantic – and a few centuries from today.[81] Its birth coincided with the founding of the United States of America.[82] The principle on which it rests, however, dates many generations beyond.[83]

---

standing to complain. *See* Nicholas Cornell, *A Complainant-Oriented Approach to Unconscionability and Contract Law*, 164 U. PA. L. REV. 1131, 1163 (2016).

[73] Heidbreder v. Carton, 645 N.W.2d 355, 371 (Minn. 2002) (quotations omitted).

[74] *Compare* Anenson, *A Process-Based Theory, supra* note 68, at 526–41 (emphasizing court protection purpose of unclean hands), *with* Herstein, *supra* note 69, at 208 (expressing skepticism of the court protection justification of unclean hands but not ruling it out entirely). *See* discussion *infra* Chapter 6.

[75] Anenson, *A Process-Based Theory, supra* note 68, at 539.

[76] Union Pac. R.R. Co. v. Chicago & Nw. Ry. Co., 226 F. Supp. 400, 410 (N.D. Ill. 1964). *See also* CHAFEE, SOME PROBLEMS, *supra* note 10, at 1.

[77] *See* Anenson, *Statutory Interpretation, supra* note 5, at 6.

[78] *See* T. Leigh Anenson, *The Role of Equity in Employment Noncompetition Cases*, 42 AM. BUS. L.J. 1, 62–63 (2005) [hereinafter Anenson, *Role of Equity*] (discussing how equitable defenses prevent gamesmanship and hypocrisy at the expense of the court, the law, and other litigants).

[79] *See* Anenson, *Limiting Legal Remedies, supra* note 31, at 73–99 (identifying and reviewing unclean hands decisions resulting in ineligibility of legal relief); *infra* Chapter 3.

[80] *See* Richard A. Posner, *Past-Dependency, Pragmatism, and Critique of History in Adjudication and Legal Scholarship*, 67 U. CHI. L. REV. 573, 573 (2000) ("Law is the most historically oriented, or if you like the most backward-looking, the most 'past dependent,' of the professions.").

[81] *See* discussion *infra* Section 2.4.

[82] *See* CHAFEE, SOME PROBLEMS, *supra* note 10, at 5 ("[Unclean hands] is exactly as old as the United States Constitution.").

[83] *See* discussion *infra* Section 2.4.

2.4 ORIGINS OF THE UNCLEAN HANDS DEFENSE

The familiar maxim in equity of "he who comes into equity must come with clean hands" has served the justice system for more than three centuries. It is a British legacy. English barrister Richard Francis first coined a conception of the clean hands doctrine in his book *Maxims of Equity* published in 1728.[84] His version, derived from equity cases, articulated the standing doctrine as "[h]e [or she] that hath committed iniquity shall not have equity."[85]

Chief Baron Eyre of the English Court of Exchequer subsequently adopted the defense as "unclean hands" in *Dering v. Earl of Winchelsea* at the end of the eighteenth century.[86] Historically, the departments of Exchequer and Chancery conducted the civil service of England with Exchequer as the fiscal department and Chancery as the secretarial department.[87] Exchequer had equity powers.[88]

The general principle underpinning the clean hands doctrine dates to antiquity. Commentators have traced the genesis of unclean hands to Chinese customary law and to the Roman period of Justinian.[89] In civil law countries without a separate body of law called "equity," a kindred idea can be found in the recognition of wrongdoing for an abuse of right.[90] Therefore, this country has taken a few hundred years to digest all the equity it swallowed. And the change is irreversible. The next section does not so much attempt to rescue authentic English equity as to track its trajectory in America.

2.5 DEVELOPMENT OF THE DEFENSE IN AMERICAN DECISIONS

Courts have been shooting off decisions on this equitable doctrine like Roman candles since the American Revolution. There were approximately two hundred state and federal cases mentioning the clean hands doctrine before the Civil War

---

[84] *See* Roscoe Pound, *On Certain Maxims of Equity, in* CAMBRIDGE LEGAL ESSAYS WRITTEN IN HONOUR OF AND PRESENTED TO DOCTOR BOND, PROFESSOR BUCKLAND AND PROFESSOR KENNY 259, 263–64 (1926); *see also* Chafee I, *supra* note 2, at 881–82 (noting that the phrase was repeated in 1749 by "a gentleman of the Middle Temple" in his *Grounds and Rudiments of Law and Equity* and again in 1793 by Fonblanque).

[85] RICHARD FRANCIS, MAXIMS OF EQUITY 6 (Richmond: Sheppard and Pollard, Printers, 1st Am. ed. 1823) (1728) (second maxim). For a history and overview of the maxims of equity, *see generally* PETER W. YOUNG ET AL., ON EQUITY, §§ 3.1–3.9 (2009).

[86] Dering v. Earl of Winchelsea, (1787) 29 Eng. Rep. 1184, 1186; *see also* CHAFEE, SOME PROBLEMS, *supra* note 10, at 2 ("[Unclean hands] is exactly as old as the U.S. Constitution.").

[87] *See* FREDERIC W. MAITLAND, EQUITY: A COURSE OF LECTURES 2 (A.H. Chaytor & W.J. Whittaker eds., 2d ed. 1936).

[88] *See* PHILIP S. JAMES, Introduction to English Law 25 (8th ed. 1972) (explaining that Exchequer became the earliest of the common law courts and, over the course of time, acquired a wide jurisdiction in equity).

[89] *See* NEWMAN, EQUITY AND LAW, *supra* note 38, at 31, 250 n.19.

[90] Anenson, *A View from Equity, supra* note 25, at 262 n.60 (asserting that the prevention of an abuse of right is the motto of many equitable defenses).

and more than eight hundred cases before the turn of the twentieth century.[91] Today, despite its containment to mainly actions in equity, cases considering the doctrine already tally in the tens of thousands.[92]

The United States Supreme Court endorsed the doctrine of unclean hands early in our nation's history.[93] In fact, the Court has considered the defense in every decade but one since the founding of the country.[94] This means that judges were considering the clean hands doctrine during the major events shaping American history. The Supreme Court's opinions during the Industrial Revolution, for example, discussed unclean hands as a condition of equitable intervention and the discretion to refuse aid from "time immemorial."[95] By the twentieth century, the Supreme Court invoked unclean hands, explaining: "This is the doctrine of the highest court of England, and no court has laid it down with any greater stringency than the Supreme Court of the United States."[96] Around the same time, lower federal courts announced that "the [unclean hands] maxim is of so ancient an origin that extended analysis of its scope and effect would seem unnecessary."[97] The clean hands doctrine was well settled by the time of the Great Depression.[98]

The defense then became a "bone of bitter controversy" in at least four decisions after Pearl Harbor.[99] One of those decisions, *Precision Instrument Mfg. Co. v. Auto. Maint. Mach. Co.*, is still the leading case on the unclean hands defense throughout the country.[100] The Supreme Court explained the rationale of unclean hands: "That doctrine is rooted in the historical concept of court of equity as a vehicle for

---

[91] The data was generated by a Westlaw legal database search of "clean hands" or "unclean hands" in the database "all cases" on February 22, 2017.

[92] A Westlaw legal database search of "clean hands" or "unclean hands" in the database "all cases" on February 26, 2017, yielded more than 10,000 cases (that is the limit of the search engine).

[93] The United States Supreme Court first recognized the doctrine of unclean hands in 1795 in *Talbot v. Jansen*, 3 U.S. 133 (1795). By 1831, the Court referenced that the defense was "well settled." Cathcart v. Robinson, 30 U.S. 264, 276 (1831).

[94] A Westlaw database shows there are roughly one hundred United States Supreme Court cases concerning unclean hands.

[95] *See* Haffner v. Dobrinski, 215 U.S. 446, 450 (1910); Pope Mfg. Co. v. Gormully, 144 U.S. 224, 236 (1892).

[96] Clinton E. Worden & Co. v. Cal. Fig Syrup Co., 187 U.S. 516, 535 (1903) (quoting Cal. Fig Syrup Co. v. Frederick Stearns & Co. 73 F. 812, 817 (6th Cir. 1896)).

[97] Keystone Driller Co. v. Gen. Excavator Co., 62 F.2d 48, 50 (6th Cir. 1932).

[98] *See* Precision Instrument Mfg. Co. v. Auto. Maint. Mach. Co., 324 U.S. 806, 814 (1945) (explaining that the clean hands doctrine is "far more than a mere banality"); Olmstead v. United States, 277 U.S. 438, 483 (1928) (Brandeis, J., dissenting) (calling the unclean hands defense "settled").

[99] Chafee I, *supra* note 2, at 878.

[100] *See* DOUGLAS LAYCOCK, MODERN AMERICAN REMEDIES 938 (4th ed. 2010) [hereinafter, LAY-COCK, REMEDIES] (noting that the decision is the leading Supreme Court case on unclean hands). Moreover, *Precision Instrument* has been given precedential value by the Supreme Court in subsequent unclean hands cases. *See, e.g.*, S&E Contractors v. United States, 406 U.S. 1, 15 (1972) (citing *Precision Instrument*, 324 U.S. 806; Hazel-Atlas Glass Co. v. Hartford-Empire Co., 322 U.S. 238 (1944)). State courts likewise rely on the same decision in understanding and expanding unclean hands and related doctrines. *See, e.g.*, Kendall-Jackson Winery,

affirmatively enforcing the requirements of conscience and good faith. This presupposes a refusal on its part to be 'the abetter of iniquity.'"[101] In another seminal case, the Court declared:

> [T]hat whenever a party who, as actor, seeks to set the judicial machinery in motion and obtain some remedy, has violated conscience, or good faith, or other equitable principle, in his prior conduct, then the doors of the court will be shut against him in limine; the court will refuse to interfere on his behalf, to acknowledge his right, or to award him any remedy.[102]

State courts adopted the doctrine with similar alacrity. Five state supreme courts had cases concerning the defense of unclean hands in the post–Revolutionary War period before the nineteenth century.[103] Even prior to English recognition of the doctrine in *Dering v. Earl of Winchelsea*, the Superior Court of Connecticut in 1785 acknowledged the principle, although it did not use the phrase "clean hands" or "unclean hands."[104] The Supreme Court of Judicature of New Jersey was the earliest court in the United States to announce the maxim.[105] Citing Lord Kenyon for the idea that "those who come into a court of justice must come with clean hands," the court upheld a plea that a bond sued on was obtained by fraud.[106] Prophetically, the court relied on the defense in a law (not equity) case.[107] With more states entering the union by the mid-century mark, the defense of unclean hands continued its popularity in American jurisdictions.[108]

Ltd. v. Superior Court, 90 Cal. Rptr. 2d 743, 749 (Cal. Ct. App. 1999) (citing *Precision Instrument*, 324 U.S. 806 in extending the defense to legal remedies).

[101] Precision Instrument Mfg. Co. v. Auto. Maint. Mach. Co., 324 U.S. 806, 814 (1945) (quoting Bein v. Heath, 47 U.S. 228 (1848)).

[102] Keystone Driller Co. v. Gen. Excavator Co., 290 U.S. 240, 244–45 (1933).

[103] In certain cases, the defense was raised by counsel as then reported in court opinions. *See* Owens v. Whitaker, 1 Ky. 123, 140 (Ky. 1795); Moncrieff v. Goldsborough, 4 H. & McH. 281, 282 (Gen. Ct. Md. 1799); Mason v. Evans, 1 N.J.L. 182, 186 (N.J. 1793); Ward v. Webber, 1 Va. 274, 278 (Va. 1794). The General Court of Maryland was a precursor of sorts to its highest court today. There were also several state supreme court cases concerning unclean hands immediately thereafter as well. *See, e.g.*, Mitchell v. Smith, 4 Yeates 84, 84 (Pa. 1804); Barnard v. Crane, 1 Tyl. 457, 473 (Vt. 1802).

[104] Little v. Fowler, 1 Root 94, 94, 1785 WL 3 (Conn. Super. Ct. 1785).

[105] *See* Mason, 1 N.J.L. at 186.

[106] *Id.*

[107] *See id.* at 182–83 (action of debt on bond). The availability of fraud as a defense to actions at law had been subject to numerous conflicting decisions in the inferior federal courts. *See* Edwin H. Abbot, Jr., *Fraud as a Defense at Law in the Federal Courts*, 15 COLUM. L. REV. 489, 504 (1915); *see also* James W. Beatty, *Federal Procedure – Juries – Attacking Release for Fraud in Action at Law*, 53 MICH. L. REV. 288, 290 (1954) (discussing whether fraud is legal or equitable for purposes of jury trial).

[108] *See, e.g.*, Conrad v. Lindley, 2 Cal. 173, 175–76 (1852) (equating unclean hands defense with a lack of good faith in seeking specific performance of a contract); Charles William Luther, Note, *Plaintiff Granted Injunction Despite Unclean Hands*, 7 HASTINGS L.J. 92, 93 (1955–56) (noting that California courts readily adopted the clean hands doctrine at an early stage in their judicial history); *see also* Chafee I, *supra* note 2, at 878 (relating that "the maxim is involved in

Fast forward to the present, the coverage of unclean hands comprises myriad forms of misbehavior barring an assortment of state and federal claims.[109] The defense has also been the basis of other doctrines and morphed into more specific defenses in several fields.[110] Courts have additionally read the defense into state and federal legislation without the explicit approval of the legislature.[111]

2.6 DISCUSSION OF THE DEFENSE IN AMERICAN LITERATURE

With a notable exception in the middle of the twentieth century, the defense of unclean hands has been overlooked by legal scholars. This is true despite its significance to commercial and other relations since the inception of the country. Equitable defenses like unclean hands are universally available.[112] They potentially apply in every area of the law, common law and statute, and effectively prevent a remedy for a violation of the law. As such, courts can alter the value of rights by the liberal or restrictive interpretation and application of defenses that negate liability.

Before the twentieth century, there were fewer than a dozen law review articles mentioning the clean hands doctrine in the United States. Other than a one-sentence Note in the *Harvard Law Review*, these articles were devoted to particular areas of law dealing with subjects such as trademark, fraudulent conveyance, and bankruptcy.[113]

The advent of American equity treatises placed the defense of unclean hands within that subject matter and, accordingly, across subjects. Joseph Story and John Norton Pomeroy are the Mount Rushmore of equity scholars in the United States. Story began publishing his *Commentaries on Equity Jurisprudence* in 1839.[114]

scores of cases"); *cf.* Hohfeld, *supra* note 47, at 550 (noting maxim of unclean hands to be of "slight importance" compared to other equitable doctrines).

[109] *See* discussion *infra* Chapters 3–4.

[110] *See* Anenson & Mark, *supra* note 23 (tracking the defense of unclean hands to inequitable conduct); discussion *infra* Chapter 5.

[111] *See generally* Anenson, *Statutory Interpretation, supra* note 5, at 10–19 (identifying an assumption of equitable discretion to invoke unclean hands and other equitable defenses in legislation); discussion *infra* Chapter 5.

[112] *See, e.g.*, SARAH WORTHINGTON, EQUITY 34 (2d ed. 2006) (explaining that the doctrine potentially arises in the resolution of any dispute regardless of subject matter and effectively cancels existing legal rights); Anenson & Mark, *supra* note 23, at 1450.

[113] *See, e.g.*, Note, *Equity — No Relief to Wrong-Doer — Limits of Principle*, 5 HARV. L. REV. 151, 151 (1891); Note, *Property — Fraudulent Conveyance — Notice by Possession*, 11 HARV. L. REV. 554, 554 (1898); Note, *Trade-Marks — Assignability of Orchestra Name*, 11 HARV. L. REV. 131, 131 (1897).

[114] JOSEPH STORY, COMMENTARIES ON EQUITY JURISPRUDENCE AS ADMINISTERED IN ENGLAND AND AMERICA (1st ed. 1835–36) [hereinafter STORY'S COMMENTARIES, FIRST EDITION]. *See* Gary L. McDowell, *Joseph Story's Science of Equity*, 1979 SUP. CT. REV. 507 153, 156 (explaining that Story wrote his commentaries to cultivate equity as a science that was "completely fenced in by principle" in response to the codification movement where inherited English equity was "epitomized as obnoxious"); Lionel Smith, *Common Law and Equity in R3RUE*, 68 WASH. & LEE L. REV. 1185, 1188 (2011) [hereinafter, Smith, *Equity in*

The first ten editions made no specific mention of unclean hands.[115] Published in 1873, the eleventh edition referenced the doctrine in a footnote.[116] The fourteenth (and last) edition is the first time that the unclean hands defense gets attention above line in the text. Published in 1918 long after Story's death, this edition contains five sections on the unclean hands defense totaling six pages.[117]

Less than a decade after Story discovered the clean hands doctrine, American equity scholar John Pomeroy devoted eleven pages to the defense in his first edition of *Equity Jurisprudence* published in 1881.[118] His fifth and last edition, published in 1941, dedicates eight sections to the subject covering twenty-four pages.[119] Pomeroy portrays unclean hands as "a universal rule guiding and regulating the action of

R3RUE] (relating Story's work as part of a vocation to lead judges, rather than to follow them). At the time of publication, Story had been an Associate Justice of the United States Supreme Court for more than twenty years.

[115] *See* Chafee I, *supra* note 2, at 884. These books did, however, pay attention to other kindred maxims, such as: "He [or she] who seeks equity, must do equity." *Id.* The fourth edition of the treatise is the last edition in which Story actually worked. *Id.* 884 n.27; *see* JOSEPH STORY, COMMENTARIES ON EQUITY JURISPRUDENCE AS ADMINISTERED IN ENGLAND AND AMERICA (4th ed. 1846).

Other treatises during the same time period offer little or nothing on the clean hands doctrine. *See* Chafee I, *supra* note 2, at 884; *see also* HERBERT BROOM, SELECTION OF LEGAL MAXIMS xxv, xxvi (1845) (not referencing unclean hands). For example, Spence's equity treatise offered one sentence on the clean hands doctrine. GEORGE SPENCE, 1 EQUITABLE JURISDICTION OF THE COURT OF CHANCERY 422 n.f. (1st ed. 1846). Similarly, the original edition of Bispham's treatise outlined eight lines of text without any citation to the unclean hands defense. GEORGE TUCKER BISPHAM, PRINCIPLES OF EQUITY: A TREATISE ON THE SYSTEM OF JUSTICE ADMINISTERED IN COURTS OF CHANCERY 48–49 (1st ed. 1874). Bispham's second to last edition, published more than fifty years later, contains four pages on the maxim with ample citations along with additional references under implied trusts, specific performance, and injunctions. *Id.* at 70–73, 154, 605, 642 n.4, 719 n.5 (The Banks Law Publishing Co., 10th ed. 1925) [hereinafter BISPHAM, TENTH EDITION]. George Tucker Bispham was well known for his equity treatise as a senior professor in the Department of Law at the University of Pennsylvania. William Draper Lewis, *George Tucker Bispham*, 54 AM. L. REG. 718, 718 (1906).

[116] Chafee I, *supra* note 2, at 884.

[117] JOSEPH STORY, COMMENTARIES ON EQUITY JURISPRUDENCE AS ADMINISTERED IN ENGLAND AND AMERICA §§ 98–102 (W.H. Lyon ed., 14th ed. 1918) [hereinafter STORY'S COMMENTARIES, FOURTEENTH EDITION].

[118] *See* Rosalind Poll, Note, *"He Who Comes into Equity Must Come with Clean Hands,"* 32 B.U. L. REV. 66, 67 (1952); JOHN NORTON POMEROY, A TREATISE ON EQUITY JURISPRUDENCE, AS ADMINISTERED IN THE UNITED STATES OF AMERICA 432–43 (1st ed. 1881) (3 volumes). A book review of the third edition had this to say:

[T]he second edition in 1892, after the death of the author … It is difficult to overestimate the importance of this work, or the effect that it has had upon the development of equity jurisdiction in this country. At the time of appearance in 1881, few of the states had any large or consistent body of equity precedents in their reported cases.

H.T.L., Book Review, 19 HARV. L. REV. 481, 481 (1906); *see also id.* at 483 (claiming it is "one of the few masterpieces of our legal literature").

[119] 2 POMEROY'S EQUITY JURISPRUDENCE, FIFTH EDITION, *supra* note 1, §§ 397–404.

equity courts in their interposition on behalf of suitors for any and every purpose, and in their administration of any and every species of relief."[120]

Zechariah Chafee, Jr., a practitioner and Harvard law professor, was the first scholar to undertake a comprehensive analysis of the defense in the United States.[121] The Thomas M. Cooley Lectures that he delivered at the University of Michigan Law School in 1949 and his subsequent publications in the *Michigan Law Review* (and as a book) continue to be the primary source of the American experience with the equitable defense.[122] Without any sustained analysis of the defense in other countries, Chafee is still relied on as authoritative on the subject.[123]

---

[120] *Id.* at § 397. Although not focusing on the clean hands doctrine, other American literature to examine equity holistically and philosophically was also published in the middle of the twentieth century. *See, e.g.,* WILLIAM Q. DE FUNIAK, HANDBOOK OF MODERN EQUITY (2d ed. 1956); MCCLINTOCK, *supra* note 59; WILLIAM F. WALSH, A TREATISE ON EQUITY (1930); *see also* John L. Garvey, *Handbook of Modern Equity,* 8 CATH. U.L. REV. 51, 53 (1959) (book review) ("One is tempted to say that this and McClintock's hornbook are the only current American texts in the field, although the recent edition of Clark's work might cause some to quarrel with the statement."); *id.* ("Though the reviewers had only light praise for the original edition of this work, public response justified three printings in the six years that passed before the appearance of this second edition.").

[121] Zechariah Chafee, Jr., a practitioner and professor at the Harvard Law School, was a noted scholar of equity jurisprudence. *See generally* DONALD L. SMITH, ZECHARIAH CHAFEE, JR.: DEFENDER OF LIBERTY AND LAW (1986) (biography of Chafee). To my knowledge, he is also the last scholar to study unclean hands other than my recent work. *See* CHAFEE, SOME PROBLEMS, *supra* note 10, at iii–iv; *see also* Edgar N. Durfee, *Foreword* to *id.* at ix–xi.

[122] *See* CHAFEE, SOME PROBLEMS, *supra* note 10, at 5; Chafee I, *supra* note 2, at 877; Chafee II, *supra* note 12, at 1065; *see also* Chafee, SELECTED ESSAYS ON EQUITY, *supra* note 43, at iii, iv; *accord* Durfee, *supra* note 121, at ix–xi. He is most known for the Thomas M. Cooley Lectures Chafee delivered at the University of Michigan Law School in 1949 and later published in the *Michigan Law Review. See generally* Chafee I, *supra* note 2; Chafee II, *supra* note 12.

[123] Zechariah Chafee's work is the leading source of research on unclean hands in this country and abroad. *See, e.g.,* Scattaretico v. Puglisi, 799 N.E.2d 1258, 1261–62 n.14 (Mass. App. Ct. 2003) ("The indispensable writing on the subject by Professor Chafee . . ."); LAYCOCK, REMEDIES, *supra* note 100, at 938 (describing Chafee's as probably the "best treatment" of unclean hands). For international recognition of Chafee's analysis of unclean hands, *see* R.P. MEAGHER, W.M.C. GUMMOW, & J.R.F. LEHANE, EQUITY: DOCTRINES AND REMEDIES § 322, at 82 n.15 (3d ed. 1992) (noting Chafee's "important article" but disagreeing with its emphasis on illegality and unclean hands' operation at law).

There were a few student notes on the subject of unclean hands defense as well. *See, e.g.,* Poll, *supra* note 118; D.C.H., Case Comment, *Equity-Clean Hands-Iniquity of One Plaintiff Bars All,* 48 W. VA. L Q. 172, 173 (1941–42) (discussing unclean hands as a factor to be considered in the exercise of judicial discretion). In fact, twenty-five years before my research regarding the fusion of unclean hands at law, there was student interest in the topic. *See* William J. Lawrence, III, Note, *The Application of the Clean Hands Doctrine in Damage Actions,* 57 NOTRE DAME L. REV. 673, 673 (1982); *see also* Roger G. Rose, Note and Comment, *Equitable Defenses to Actions at Law,* 34 OR. L. REV. 55, 55 (1954) (discussing fusion of unclean hands in Oregon). Other scholarship, also primarily student notes, has been relegated to specific subject areas. *See, e.g.,* Kevin Mack, Note, *Reforming Inequitable Conduct to Improve Patent Quality: Cleansing Unclean Hands,* 21 BERKELEY TECH L.J. 147, 149 (2006); Dan Markel, Note, *Can Intellectual Property Law Regulate Behavior? A "Modest Proposal" for Weakening Unclean Hands,* 113 HARV. L. REV. 1503, 1503–04 (2000).

Writing in the next decade, Professor Ralph Newman analyzed unclean hands in portions of his comparative study of law and equity.[124] Newman also studied equity in the traditional trans-substantive manner, although he would be one of the last American scholars to do so.[125] After law school curricular changes began in earnest, any seminal work on equity would be examined under the label "remedies."[126] Dan Dobbs's book fits this description.[127] This text also addresses the defense of unclean hands and provides insights on the application of its elements.[128] The American Law Institute, analyzing case law for various *Restatements of the Law,* has discussed the defense within the separate contexts of contracts, torts, property, and, most recently, restitution.[129]

Practitioners may resort to encyclopedias such as *Corpus Juris Secundum* for simple (if not overly simplistic) summaries of the doctrine.[130] Certain state treatises contain a more rigorous analysis, but even they fail to synthesize the

---

[124] The book addressing the troublesome problem of fusion was the product of a grant by the *Evening Post.* Sheldon Tefft, *Equity and Law: A Comparative Study by Ralph A. Newman,* 15 J.L. EDUC. 231, 231 (1962) (reviewing Newman's book). It was supervised by an advisory board of distinguished scholars from the United States, Australia, Scotland, France, and Spain. Ralph Newman was a professor at Washington College of Law of American University and known for his hornbook on the *Law of Trusts.* Lee Silverstein, *Equity and Law: A Comparative Study by Ralph A. Newman,* 62 COLUM. L. REV. 193, 198 (1962) (reviewing Newman's book).

[125] *See* Anenson & Mark, *supra* note 23, at 1507–08 (explaining that equitable defenses have not been systematically studied in the last fifty years); *see also* Anenson, *Triumph of Equity, supra* note 25, at 438–39 (discussing the lack of contemporary American treatises on equity).

[126] *See* Douglas Laycock, *How Remedies Became a Field: A History,* 27 REV. LITIG. 161, 249–60 (2008))[hereinafter Laycock, *How Remedies Became a Field*] (discussing the law school movement away from an equity course and the new AALS section on Remedies that began in the 1970s which "undertook to help cement the modern remedies course in the curriculum"); discussion *supra* Chapter 1.

[127] DOBBS LAW OF REMEDIES, *supra* note 16. The original edition by Dobbs was the first treatise on the subject of remedies. Laycock, *How Remedies Became a Field, supra* note 126, at 261. Doug Laycock describes the treatise as "an invaluable resource that everyone in the field relies on . . . As the treatise ages, it is not so good for finding authoritative cases any more, but its analysis is still authoritative and it continues to answer questions for novices and old hands alike." *Id.* at 262. Recently, the treatise was updated and re-published by Caprice Roberts. DAN B. DOBBS & CAPRICE L. ROBERTS, DOBBS LAW OF REMEDIES: DAMAGES-EQUITY-RESTITUTION (3rd ed. 2018).

[128] DOBBS LAW OF REMEDIES, *supra* note 16, at 92.

[129] As an example, for the application of the unclean hands defense in tort law, *see* RESTATEMENT (SECOND) OF TORTS §§ 7, 76, 196 (AM. LAW. INST. 1965); RESTATEMENT (SECOND) OF TORTS § 693 (AM. LAW. INST. 1977); RESTATEMENT (SECOND) OF TORTS §§ 766, 766B, 768, 889, 894, 933 cmt. A, 940 (AM. LAW. INST. 1979). There is no reference to the defense in the third edition comprising specific subject matter. The defense can also be found in the Restatements of Agency, Employment, Trusts, Conflicts of Law, and Unfair Competition.

[130] *See, e.g.,* 30A CORPUS JURIS SECUNDUM *Equity* § 109 (2018); 27A AM. JUR. 2D *Equity* §§ 100 – 106 (2016). As discussed previously, Story and Pomeroy treatises provided a comprehensive treatment of equity in the early twentieth century; but even these books were geared to practitioners and concentrated on the technical aspects of equitable doctrines. *See* POMEROY'S EQUITY JURISPRUDENCE, FIFTH EDITION, *supra* note 1; STORY'S COMMENTARIES, FOURTEENTH EDITION, *supra* note 117.

defense in a comprehensive manner.[131] Consequently, the defense of unclean hands must be cobbled together from various subjects and often out-of-date resources.

The lack of attention to unclean hands is a symptom of greater events. The law-equity merger in state and federal courts and subsequent law school curricular changes, masked the evolution of equity.[132] In the late twentieth century, following the unification of courts and procedures, law schools transitioned from teaching a course in equity to a course in remedies (comprising both law and equity).[133] As a result, a considerable amount of equitable principles were lost in the transition.[134] No doubt due to their universal application to all subject matter, equitable defenses such as unclean hands went missing.[135] American scholars also stopped specializing in the subject of equity.[136]

Notwithstanding these developments, courts continued to recognize and even extend equitable principles, including defenses, long after judges and the bar ceased understanding them. Not surprisingly, without any guidance, certain courts have been inconsistent in how they define and determine the scope of equitable defenses.[137] In many disputes, equitable defenses as an appropriate basis for

---

[131] *See, e.g.,* 2 CALIFORNIA AFFIRMATIVE DEFENSES § 45:1 (2d ed. 2017); CORPORATE & COMMER-CIAL PRACTICE IN THE DELAWARE COURT OF CHANCERY § 11.07 (2017).

[132] Anenson, *A View from Equity, supra* note 25, at 272; discussion *supra* Chapter 1.

[133] Laycock, *How Remedies Became a Field, supra* note 126, at 249–60; Anenson, *Pluralistic Model, supra* note 41, at 647 ("Many practicing lawyers have graduated without the benefit of a comprehensive course in equity."); discussion *supra* Chapter 1.

[134] Edward D. Re, *Introduction* to SELECTED ESSAYS ON EQUITY, *supra* note 43, at xiv.

[135] Legal textbooks on remedies and associated subjects have continued to at least mention equitable defenses such as unclean hands. Although it is not clear how much time in class, if any, is devoted to the subject. LAYCOCK, REMEDIES, *supra* note 100, at 938–41.

[136] Anenson, *A View from Equity, supra* note 25, at 273 n.138 ("There is no comprehensive treatment of modern equity in American law."). By way of background, in the Commonwealth that shares the United States legal tradition, equity is the domain of private law scholars. Equity is a separate subject along with other areas of judge-made law: contracts, torts, and property. In the United States, equity sits somewhat uncomfortably between the fields of private law, jurisprudence, remedies, and increasingly, the federal courts. My research on equitable defenses aims to fill a critical gap in this area.

[137] *See generally* Anenson & Mark, *supra* note 23 (criticizing the Federal Circuit's definition of inequitable conduct derived from unclean hands); *see also* discussion *infra* Chapter 5. Many of the cases reaching the Supreme Court for decision involved circuit splits on the availability and application of equitable defenses. *E.g.,* Petrella v. Metro-Goldwyn-Mayer, Inc., 134 S. Ct. 1962, 1972 (2014) (involving the application of laches in copyright law). Moreover, the Supreme Court recently reversed the Federal Circuit, sitting en banc, which decided 6 to 5 that laches was available to bar damages under the Patent Act. *See* SCA Hygiene Prods. v. First Quality Baby Prods., 807 F.3d 1311, 1323–29 (Fed. Cir. 2015), *rev'd,* SCA Hygiene Prods. v. First Quality Baby Prods., 137 S. Ct. 954, 959–67 (2017). For a future issue, *see* Steven Ferrey, *Inverting the Law: Superfund Hazardous Substance Liability and Supreme Court Reversal of All Federal Circuits,* 33 WM. & MARY ENVTL. L. & POL'Y REV. 633, 669 (2009) (noting conflict in the Circuits over the availability of equitable defenses under certain CERCLA provisions).

argument have not been squarely presented to the courts.[138] Judicial opinions, as a result, neglect to provide a clear explanation of the merger and other issues because they have not properly characterized or evaluated the problem.[139] Therefore, before turning to the subject of fusion in later chapters, the next section aims to eliminate the doctrinal confusion by inventorying, reconciling, and coordinating cases on the equitable defense of unclean hands.

2.7 DEFINITION OF THE DEFENSE

Anything less than a "pure conscience" and "pure hands" may disqualify the litigant seeking the aid of equity under the clean hands doctrine.[140] To invoke the defense, courts generally require some form of illegal or unethical conduct to warrant dismissal.[141] Many courts also mandate that the unclean conduct have a connection to the case.[142] The "unclean" conduct and "connection to the litigation" components of the defense are explored in what follows along with the association between them.

2.7.1 *Unclean Conduct Component*

Any and all misfeasance that smacks of injustice may constitute unclean hands.[143] The English court in *Dering v. Earl of Winchelsea*[144] explained that

---

[138] *Id.*; discussion *infra* Chapters 3–4. In *Park 'n Fly v. Dollar Park & Fly*, for example, the Supreme Court found that federal court authority did not encompass a substantive challenge to the validity of the mark, but clarified that neither the court of appeals nor counsel relied on the power to grant or deny equitable relief to support the decision. 469 U.S. 189, 203 (1985).

[139] *Ibid.*; Anenson, *Age of Statutes*, *supra* note 39, at 533–34 (citing cases and other authorities).

[140] Manhattan Med. Co. v. Wood, 108 U.S. 218, 227 (1883) (describing the unclean hands defense in a trademark intellectual property case as "pure hands and pure conscience") (citation omitted); *see also* Buchannon v. Upshaw, 42 U.S. 56, 81 (1843) (argument of counsel) ("clean hands and pure heart"); United States v. Schooner Betsey, 8 U.S. 443, 444 (1807) (argument of counsel) ("pure heart" and "clean hands").

[141] Dobbs Law of Remedies, *supra* note 16, at 92–96 (illegal or unethical).

[142] 2 Pomeroy's Equity Jurisprudence, Fifth Edition, *supra* note 1, § 399, at 94–95 (discussing the limitations upon the principle); *id.* at 97 ("The dirt upon his [or her] hands must be his [or her] bad conduct in the transaction complained of."). *But see* Snell's Twenty-Seventh Edition, *supra* note 45, at 33 (noting that the "limitation was not recognised [in England] in the reign of Elizabeth I and her immediate successors and . . . has been lost sight of in some American jurisdictions.").

[143] *See, e.g.*, Keystone Driller Co. v. Gen. Excavator Co., 290 U.S. 240, 244–45 (1933) (stating the governing principle that courts are shut to parties whose prior conduct "has violated conscience, or good faith, or other equitable principle" (citation omitted)); Deweese v. Reinhard, 165 U.S. 386, 390 (1897).

[144] (1787) 29 Eng. Rep. 1184; Chafee I, *supra* note 2, at 882 (noting it is the first case articulating the doctrine of unclean hands).

it must be a depravity in the legal as well as the moral sense.[145] Nevertheless, actions that lack a proper equitable nature need not be illegal;[146] "inequitable," "unconscionable," or deriving from a "bad motive" will do.[147] Conduct that does not conform to "minimum ethical standards" may also satisfy the doctrine.[148]

So are there any limits on the kind of disqualifying behavior? One issue yielding different answers is whether the defense requires a particular mental state. Following the United States Supreme Court's reference to "any willful act" in one of its epic cases invoking the clean hands doctrine,[149] certain state and federal courts parrot that particular state of mind regardless of the subject matter of the lawsuit.[150] Like many cases, the Supreme Court's decisions demonstrate that one of the circumstances that may satisfy unclean hands is a specific intent to deceive.[151] But the Supreme Court never required it. The Supreme Court's opinions took account of actions as well.[152]

---

[145] *Id.*
[146] Precision Instrument Mfg. Co. v. Auto. Maint. Mach. Co., 324 U.S. 806, 815 (1945) ("[O]ne's misconduct need not necessarily have been of such a nature to be punishable as a crime or to justify legal proceedings of any character.").
[147] *See In re* Shewchuk Estate, 282 A.2d 307, 314 (Pa. 1971) (finding conduct not sufficiently unclean when inconsistent statements were not made with a selfish motive or for personal gain); Poll, *supra* note 118, at 67–68 (referencing early twentieth-century cases applying the clean hands doctrine in situations involving bad motive or immoral intent).
[148] *Precision Instrument,* 324 U.S. at 816 (justifying the application of unclean hands on the grounds that the petitioner's conduct did not conform to "minimum ethical standards"); *see also* Morton Salt Co. v. G.S. Suppiger Co., 314 U.S. 488, 492 (1942) (equity may rightly withhold its assistance from improper business practices); 4 CALLMANN ON UNFAIR COMPETITION, TRADEMARK & MONOPOLY § 23:14 (4th ed. 2001 Supp.) (noting the doctrine of unclean hands "is of special importance in unfair competition cases, for fairness in business ... is a common duty owed by all to all."); *cf.* Int'l News Serv. v. Associated Press, 248 U.S. 215, 245 (1918) (finding no unclean hands because conduct comports with industry standard). For an evaluation of equitable defenses, including unclean hands, as a remedy for unethical behavior, *see* Anenson & Mayer, *supra* note 45 and Anenson, *Role of Equity, supra* note 78.
[149] *Precision Instrument,* 324 U.S. at 815 ("Any willful act concerning the cause of action which rightfully can be said to transgress equitable standards of conduct is sufficient cause for the invocation of the maxim ..."); discussion *supra* Section 2.4.
[150] Weiss v. Smulders, 96 A.3d 1175, 1198 n.19 (Conn. 2014).
[151] *See Precision Instrument,* 324 U.S. at 814 (ruling that equity requires suitors to act fairly and without fraud or deceit); Hazel-Atlas Glass Co. v. Hartford-Empire Co., 322 U.S. 238, 251 (1944) (vacating a patent because it was obtained by fraud); Keystone Driller Co. v. Gen. Excavator Co., 290 U.S. 240, 247 (1933) (holding that equitable relief is unavailable for those that act fraudulently or not in good faith).
[152] For example, the Supreme Court's unclean hands decisions in *Keystone Driller Co.,* described the conduct as "wrongful acts." Keystone Driller Co. v. Gen. Excavator Co., 290 U.S. at 244–45.

In line with state law, what is inequitable,[153] unconscionable,[154] or lacking in good faith[155] has been a constant consideration of the Supreme Court in applying unclean hands.[156] While not necessarily inconsistent with the imposition of a particular mental state, the Court has also found conduct that is simply unfair to be unclean.[157]

The Supreme Court mentioned that a "willful act" is sufficient to invoke unclean hands, but it did not limit the defense to this single condition or cite any authority for the reference.[158] Presumably, the reference came from Story's formulation given

[153] Courts often describe unclean conduct as "inequitable conduct" in their decisions. *See, e.g.,* Heidbreder v. Carton, 645 N.W.2d 335, 371 (Minn. 2002); *In re* France, 186 S.W.3d 534, 551 (Tex. 2006); Fladeboe v. America Isuzu Motors, Inc., 58 Cal. Rptr. 3d 225, 235–36 (Cal. Ct. App. 2007); Neeme Sys. Sol. Inc. v. Spectrum Aeronautical LLC, 250 P.3d 1206, 1213 (Ariz. Ct. App. 2011) (quoting Smith v. Neely, 380 P.2d 148, 149 (Ariz. 1963)); Cornish Coll. of the Arts v. 1000 Va. Ltd. P'ship, 242 P.3d 1, 13 (Wash. Ct. App. 2010).

[154] Nat'l Fire Ins. Co. v. Thompson, 28 U.S. 331, 338 (1930) (declining to interfere based on an "unconscientious" attitude); Clarke v. White, 37 U.S. 178, 193 (1838) (stating that the doctrine applies only where the plaintiff comes with an "unaffected conscience").

[155] ABF Freight Sys. v. NLRB, 510 U.S. 317, 330 (1994) (Scalia and O'Connor, JJ., concurring) (finding "inequitableness or bad faith relative to matter in which he seeks relief" (quoting McCLINTOCK, *supra* note 59, § 26, at 63, n.75)); Sample v. Barnes, 55 U.S. 70, 74 (1852) ("[N]ever interfere in opposition to conscience or good faith"). The Supreme Court explained again in *Precision Instrument* that "[t]he doctrine is rooted in the historical concept of court of equity as a vehicle for affirmatively enforcing the requirements of conscience and good faith." Thus, the Court held that the defense "closes the door of a court of equity to one tainted with inequitableness or bad faith." *Precision Instrument Mfg. Co.*, 324 U.S. at 814 (quoting Bein v. Heath, 47 U.S. 228, 247 (1848)). Correspondingly, honesty and good faith typically negates unclean hands. Newton v. Consol. Gas Co., 258 U.S. 165, 175–76 (1922) (implying good faith excludes unclean hands).

[156] *See, e.g.,* Johnson v. Yellow Cab Transit Co., 321 U.S. 383, 392 (1944) ("We do not find here any 'unconscientious or inequitable attitude' on the part of the carrier." (quoting Int'l News Serv. v. Associated Press, 248 U.S. 215, 245 (1918))).

[157] Bein, 47 U.S. at 247 (declaring that the courts will never serve "one who has acted fraudulently, or who by deceit or any unfair means has gained an advantage") (cited by Kitchen v. Rayburn, 86 U.S. 254, 263 (1874) and Keystone Driller Co. v. Gen. Excavator Co., 290 U.S. 240, 245 (1933)); *accord* Kendall-Jackson Winery, Ltd. v. Superior Court, 90 Cal. Rptr. 2d 743, 754 (Cal. Ct. App. 1999) ("[I]t is an equitable rationale for refusing a plaintiff relief where principles of fairness dictate that the plaintiff should not recover, regardless of the merits of his claim . . . ."); STORY'S COMMENTARIES, FOURTEENTH EDITION, *supra* note 117, § 99 (commenting that an unfair transactions can constitute unclean hands even if within the law).

[158] Precision Instrument Mfg. Co. v. Auto. Maint. Mach. Co., 324 U.S. 806, 815 (1945) ("Any willful act concerning the cause of action which rightfully can be said to transgress equitable standards of conduct is sufficient cause for the invocation of the maxim . . ."). Before *Precision Instrument*, at least one Supreme Court decision addressing unclean hands used the term "willful" to indicate an absence of good faith. *See* Curtin v. Benson, 222 U.S. 78, 85–86 (1911) (indicating that unclean hands did not apply when the conduct was not willful, but rather an "honest assertion of rights"); *see also* Weiner v. Romley, 381 P.2d 581, 582–83 (Ariz. 1963) (declaring that the invocation of unclean hands requires willful misconduct as opposed to an honest mistake); Hartman v. Cohn, 38 A.2d 22, 25 (Pa. 1944) (holding that honest conduct, as opposed to willful conduct, will allow a party to seek equitable relief). Only a few other unclean hands decisions (out of an estimated one hundred decisions or so) by the Supreme

by some early American courts calling for willful conduct regarding the matter in litigation.[159] Various modern decisions have retained the willfulness criterion.[160] Certain contemporary courts have elevated the state of mind even further to an

Court even mention the term. *See* Clinton E. Worden & Co. v. Cal. Fig Syrup Co., 187 U.S. 516, 530 (1903). Congruently, the leading case on the defense of equitable estoppel required willfulness, but later American courts relaxed the requirement. *See* Anenson, *Pluralistic Model, supra* note 41, at 650.

Even by the 1980s, Prosser and Keaton advised that there was still no clear consensus on the meaning of any of the requisite mental states. PROSSER AND KEETON ON THE LAW OF TORTS § 8 (W. Page Keeton ed., 5th ed. 1984) (explaining that state of mind definitions diverged in authoritative treatises and in court opinions); *see also id.* (defining willfulness as between negligence and intentional conduct).

[159] STORY'S COMMENTARIES, FOURTEENTH EDITION, *supra* note 117, § 99 ("Any willful act in regard to a matter in litigation, which would be condemned and pronounced wrongful by honest and fair-minded men will be sufficient to make hands of the application unclean."); *cf.* JOSIAH WILLIAM SMITH, A MANUAL OF EQUITY JURISPRUDENCE § 36 at 29 (J. Trustram ed., 14th ed. 1889) (describing unclean hands in fraudulent transactions as "willful misconduct"). Story also described unconscionable conduct constituting unclean hands as "morally reprehensible as to known facts." STORY'S COMMENTARIES, FOURTEENTH EDITION, *supra* note 117, § 98; *see also* Danciger v. Stone, 187 F. 853, 858 (E.D. Okla. 1909) (explaining that "free and deliberate action with knowledge of the facts is sufficient" for unclean hands). Pomeroy does not mention a state of mind requirement in the text of the fourth edition of his treatise (published the same year as Story's fourteenth edition), but a case annotation uses "willful" in referring to the connection component of unclean hands. *See* 2 JOHN NORTON POMEROY WITH JOHN NORTON POMEROY, JR., A TREATISE ON EQUITY JURISPRUDENCE, AS ADMINISTERED IN THE UNITED STATES OF AMERICA § 399, at 741 n.1 (Bancroft-Whitney 4th ed. 1918) (annotation quoting *Lewis & Nelson's Appeal*, 67 Pa. 153, 166 (1870) (citing EDMUND H.T. SNELL, PRINCIPLES OF EQUITY 25 (London, Stevens & Haynes, 1st ed. 1868))). Pomeroy's earlier and later editions are the same. 1 JOHN NORTON POMEROY WITH JOHN NORTON POMEROY, JR., A TREATISE ON EQUITY JURISPRUDENCE, AS ADMINISTERED IN THE UNITED STATES OF AMERICA § 399, at 659 n.1 (Bancroft-Whitney 3rd ed. 1905); POMEROY'S EQUITY JURISPRUDENCE, FIFTH EDITION, *supra* note 1, § 399, at 95 n.7. The willful reference in many American courts can be tracked to the original edition of Snell's leading English treatise. *See, e.g.*, Yale Gas-Stove Co. v. Wilcox, 29 A. 303, 311 (Conn. 1894). The reference to willful misconduct in *Snell's* was removed in later editions by the twentieth century. For other courts espousing a willfulness criterion rely on *Precision Instrument, see* Stachnik v. Winkel, 230 N.W.2d 529, 534 (Mich. 1975), or for a passage from the *Corpus Juris Secundum* from the mid-twentieth century, *see* Seal v. Seal, 510 P.2d 167, 173 (Kan. 1973) (quoting 30A CORPUS JURIS SECUNDUM, *supra* note 130, § 95(a)) ("[W]illful conduct which is fraudulent, illegal, or unconscionable.")).

[160] *Compare* Queiroz v. Harvey, 205 P.2d 1120, 1122 (Ariz. 2009) (en banc) ("In *Weiner*, this Court held that when inequitable conduct was not 'willful,' unclean hands would not apply."), *and* Broome v. Broome, 75 So. 3d 1132, 1140 n.15 (Miss. Ct. App. 2011) ("The clean hands doctrine prevents a complaining party from obtaining equitable relief in court when he is guilty of willful misconduct in the transaction at issue."), *and* Shapiro v. Shapiro, 204 A.2d 266, 268 (Pa. 1964) ("Application of the unclean hands doctrine is confined to willful misconduct which concerns the particular matter in litigation."), *with* Saudi Basic Indus. Corp. v. ExxonMobil Corp., 401 F. Supp. 2d 383, 393–94 (D.N.J. 2005) (rejecting willfulness as criterion and noting number of decisions that allow "gross negligence," or "recklessness" to satisfy unclean hands).

intent to deceive.[161] It seems there is no current consensus, and Supreme Court cases appear expressly to the contrary.

In particular, the Supreme Court has declared that it is not essential that the unclean conduct be illegal or justify legal proceedings to invoke the defense and disqualify the remedy.[162] The Supreme Court's often-cited opinion in *Cathcart v. Robinson* by Chief Justice Marshall is clear that conduct constituting unclean hands need not meet the criteria for fraud or misrepresentation.[163] Lower state and federal courts are in accord.[164] Moreover, *Bein v. Heath*, relied on by the Court in subsequent decisions, seems to negate any requirement of a fraudulent intent.[165] Furthermore, the Supreme Court in *United States v. Marshall Silver Mining Co.*

[161] *See* Japan Telecom, Inc. v. Japan Telecom Am. Inc., 287 F.3d 866, 870 (9th Cir. 2002) ("Bad intent is the essence of the defense of unclean hands." (quoting Wells Fargo & Co. v. Stagecoach Props., Inc., 685 F.2d 302, 308 (9th Cir. 1982)); Shriner v. Sheehan, 773 N.E.2d 833, 848 (Ind. Ct. App. 2002) (listing intentional misconduct as an element of unclean hands); Locken v. Locken, 650 P.2d 803, 805 (Nev. 1982) ("[S]uch conduct, standing alone, absent an intent to deceive, does not amount to unclean hands."). There is no liability standard requiring intentional misconduct in federal decisions concerning the spoliation of evidence and other litigation misconduct often grounded in unclean hands. RENDLEMAN, COMPLEX LITIGATION, *supra* note 55, at 269; discussion *infra* Chapter 6 (discussing fabrication, destruction, and suppression of evidence).

[162] The Court explained in *Precision Instrument*, that "one's misconduct need not necessarily have been of such a nature as to be punishable as a crime or to justify legal proceedings of any character." 324 U.S. at 815.

[163] Cathcart v. Robinson, 30 U.S. 264, 267–77 (1831) (noting unclean hands is broader than contract defenses sufficient to justify rescission); *accord* POMEROY'S EQUITY JURISPRUDENCE, FIFTH EDITION, *supra* note 1, § 400 (advising that unclean hands includes concealment of important facts even if not actually fraudulent). The decision denied a request for the specific performance of a contract where the seller aided the buyer's mistake. *See generally Cathcart* at 281–82.

[164] *See, e.g.*, San Ann Tobacco Co., v. Hamm, 217 So. 2d 803, 810 (Ala. 1968) (finding that fraud or deceit that would amount to unclean hands did not need to be the same conduct as would constitute fraud or deceit under the common law); DeRosa v. Transamerica Title Ins. Co., 262 Cal. Rptr. 370, 373 (Cal. Ct. App. 1989) ("The doctrine does not require the party seeking relief to be guilty of fraud; it is sufficient if he merely acted unconscientiously."); DuPont v. DuPont, 85 A.2d 724, 725–26 (Del. Ch. 1951); *Stachnik*, 230 N.W.2d at 534 (stating that all elements of fraud need not be present to invoke the clean hands maxim to bar specific performance). *See generally* 30A CORPUS JURIS SECUNDUM, *supra* note 130, § 112 (citing cases).

[165] Bein v. Heath, 47 U.S. 228, 247 (1848) ("fraud[[]... *or any unfair means*" (emphasis added)) (cited by Kitchen v. Rayburn, 86 U.S. 254, 263 (1874) and Keystone Driller Co. v. Gen. Excavator Co., 290 U.S. 240 (1933)). Justice Brandeis's famous dissent in *Olmstead v. United States* declared that the principle of unclean hands has "long been settled" and referenced contract illegality cases that do not require scienter. 277 U.S. 438, 483 (1928) (Brandeis, J., dissenting) (citing McMullen v. Hoffman, 174 U.S. 639 (1899) (discussing history of contract illegality and explaining that there is no need for fraud, oppression, or corruption) and Hazelton v. Sheckells, 202 U.S. 71 (1906) (denying contract enforcement on grounds of illegality irrespective of intent)).

affirmed the dismissal of a land patent dispute for delay constituting unclean hands because the party was not free of fault or neglect, knowledge, and negligence.[166]

However, courts have hesitated to bar claims for unclean hands based solely on unreasonable conduct. Some decisions have avoided a legal determination as to whether mere negligence could constitute unclean hands by indicating that the defendant failed to cite any authority for the proposition.[167] Others are clear that negligent conduct does not amount to the defense.[168]

The fact that inequitable conduct constituting unclean hands often concerns fraud does not change its definition and validate a specific intent to deceive.[169] Supreme Court opinions describe unclean hands in the disjunctive as "fraud *or* any other type of inequitable conduct."[170] State courts similarly list bad motive as amounting to unclean hands as well as other circumstances.[171] Furthermore, unclean hands is a species of equitable (constructive) fraud that is broader than common law fraud.[172] Fraud in equity did not require intent – only acts

---

[166] See United States v. Marshall Silver Mining Co., 129 U.S. 579, 589 (1889). Similarly, in *Simmons v. Burlington, Cedar Rapids, & N. Ry. Co.*, 159 U.S. 278 (1895), the Supreme Court reversed the lower court and dismissed the cross bill in equity under the maxim of unclean hands because the lienholder had delayed in asserting his rights after reorganization. *Id.* at 291–92. Citing *Pomeroy*, the court held that acquiescence (which implies knowledge) is an important factor in obedience to the clean hands maxim. *See id.* at 291; *see also* Johnson v. Yellow Cab Transit Co., 321 U.S. 383, 403 (1944) (Frankfurter and Roberts, JJ., dissenting) (pronouncing that the unclean hands doctrine was established to prevent a violation of the law even if the plaintiff had no moral turpitude). For a lower court case finding that negligence can constitute unclean hands, see POM Wonderful LLC v. Coca Cola Co., 166 F. Supp.3d 1085, 1092 (C.D. Cal. 2016) (defining conduct component under the Lanham Act as wrongfulness or willfulness or gross negligence or bad faith).

[167] See Dollars Sys. Inc. v. Avcar Leasing Sys., Inc, 890 F.2d 165, 173 (9th Cir. 1989) (declaring that it was presented with no authority that negligent breach of contract in a franchise dispute constitutes unclean hands); Wolf & Klar Cos. v. Garner, 679 P.2d 258, 260 (N.M. 1984) (affirming the trial court's refusal of the unclean hands defense based on the plaintiff jeweler's negligent hiring and supervision of employee even though it could have avoided the loss).

[168] See Crick v. Starr, No. 08 MA 173, 2009 WL 4895270, at *17 (Ohio Ct. App. Dec. 9, 2009) (declaring that unclean hands is not mere negligence, ignorance, or inappropriateness).

[169] Poll, *supra* note 118, at 66 (explaining that the clean hands maxim embodies several other principles, such as: "No action arises out of fraud and deceit.").

[170] United States v. Dubilier Condenser Corp., 289 U.S. 178, 221 (1933) (Stone, J., dissenting) (patent case specifying "fraud *or* any other type of inequitable conduct" (emphasis added)).

[171] See, e.g., Johnson v. Freberg, 228 N.W. 159, 160 (Minn. 1929) (explaining that bad motive or conduct benefiting oneself or injuring others may constitute unclean hands).

[172] Eaton explains two kinds of fraud in equity: actual and constructive. "Actual fraud arises from facts and circumstances of imposition, and may be described as something said, done, or omitted by a person with the design of perpetrating what he must have known to be a positive fraud." EATON ON EQUITY, *supra* note 36, § 122, at 287. "Constructive fraud may be described as an act done or omitted, not with actual design to perpetrate positive fraud or injury upon other persons, but which, nevertheless, amounts to positive fraud, or is construed as a fraud by the court because of its detrimental effect upon public interests and public or private confidence." *Id.* §123.
    From the more general idea of fraud came more specific doctrines, such as contribution, which was at issue in the English case that first recognized the principle of unclean hands. *See*

inconsistent with fair dealing and good conscience."[173] Equitable fraud has no exact definition for the purpose of promoting deterrence.[174] Equity extended the ancient maxim that one should not profit from their own wrong to include situations in which it is hard to tell if one was profiting from their own wrong.[175] Activities regarded as fraudulent in equity were done without any intention to deceive or cheat.[176] The state of mind was simply irrelevant.[177] In certain situations, equity acted on simple negligence.[178]

MEAGHER, GUMMOW AND LEHANE'S EQUITY, FOURTH EDITION, *supra* note 29, at 450 (explaining that fraud is "[o]ne of the three pillars which support entire structure of equity jurisdiction, exclusive, auxiliary, concurrent"); *see also* Smith, *Fusion and Tradition*, *supra* note 40, at 25 n.34 (noting that the phrase equitable fraud in some periods covered all grounds of equitable intervention).

[173] *See* POMEROY'S EQUITY JURISPRUDENCE, FIFTH EDITION, *supra* note 1, § 399, at 99 n.17 ("Fraud, in equity, often consists in the unconscientious use of a legal advantage originally gained with innocent intent ..."); L.A. SHERIDAN, FRAUD IN EQUITY 210 (1952) (fraud remains "the residuary legatee of what offends the conscience"); 27 AM. JUR.2D *Equity* § 5 (2008) ("[F]raud in equity has a much broader connotation than at law and includes acts inconsistent with fair dealing and good conscience ...").

[174] STORY'S COMMENTARIES, FOURTEENTH EDITION, *supra* note 117, at 261 (advising that "[b]y disarming the parties of all legal sanction and protection, they suppress the temptations and encouragements which might otherwise be found too strong for their virtue."). It was the deterrence goal that the Supreme Court found dispositive when it refused to require a particular state of mind in *Pinter v. Dahl*, 486 U.S. 622, 633–34 (1988). In that case, the Court established the criteria for the clean hands doctrine's kindred legal defense of *in pari delicto* in dismissing statutory actions under the securities laws. *Id.* The securities claim at issue was a strict liability offense, and the plaintiff argued the defense was inappropriate. The Court disagreed. It held that the plaintiff's fault need not be either intentional or willful in order to establish a judge-made defense to a private action under the securities statutes. *Id.* It explained that "regardless of the degree of scienter, there may be circumstances in which the statutory goal of deterring illegal conduct is served more effectively by preclusion of suit than by recovery." *Id.* at 634; *see, e.g.*, Anenson, *Statutory Interpretation*, *supra* note 5, at 15 (analyzing the case among other cases involving equitable defenses); discussion *infra* Chapter 3 (discussing cases fusing unclean hands at law by analogy to legal defense of *in pari delicto*); Chapters 5 and 6 (discussing similarities and differences between unclean hands and *in pari delicto*).

[175] Smith, *Fiduciary Law*, *supra* note 39, at 273; *see also* Anenson, *A View from Equity*, *supra* note 25, at 265. The prevention of an abuse of right is the motto of many equitable defenses. *See* Anenson & Mark, *supra* note 23, at 1449–50 (explaining rationale of unclean hands); Anenson, *Pluralistic Model*, *supra* note 41, at 662 (describing one of the purposes of estoppel as withholding aid to a wrongdoer).

[176] *See* MEAGHER, GUMMOW AND LEHANE'S EQUITY, FOURTH EDITION, *supra* note 29, at 445 (equitable fraud is not just actual, intentional, premeditated fraud).

[177] *See* Anenson, *A View from Equity*, *supra* note 25, at 263 n.62 ("Moral culpability ... need not be proven to justify equitable fraud—it has a different role." (quoting JOHN GLOVER, EQUITY, RESTITUTION & FRAUD, § 1.6, at 8 (2004))); *see also* Anenson, *Pluralistic Model*, *supra* note 41, at 650 (examining the removal of reliance and relaxation of intent for equitable estoppel in light of certain core concerns of equity); Anenson, *Triumph of Equity*, *supra* note 25, at 390–91, 398–400 (same).

[178] Anenson & Mark, *supra* note 23, at 1467 n.161.

Sir Thomas More, the first Lord Chancellor drawn from the ranks of the common lawyer,[179] is said to have grounded the authority of the Chancery in not only fraud, but also accident and things of confidence.[180] These are the three general circumstances that moved the conscience of the Chancellor.[181] Because historic equity acted on "conscience,"[182] it could conceivably include all of the grounds for equity jurisdiction including innocent misrepresentation.[183]

In light of the foregoing, any fraud found in the facts of certain Supreme Court cases does not find support in their legal precedents or the equitable tradition of unclean hands. Given the totality of the Supreme Court decisions, along with the bulk of authority across the states, it seems the requisite level of cognition and culpability to disqualify a litigant is left to the discretion of the trial court. As a practical matter, however, cases that have been found to be sufficiently serious to amount to unclean hands tend to involve some level of cognition of a wrong, especially behavior that is intentional or done in bad faith.

2.7.2 Connection Component

Courts apply unclean hands only where the inequitable act has a connection to the matter in controversy.[184] In the words of Pomeroy: "The dirt on his [or her] hands

---

[179] *See* Anenson, *Triumph of Equity, supra* note 25, at 379 n.4 (explaining that Sir Thomas More was the first lawyer to be Lord Chancellor in 1529). Every chancellor from 1380 to 1488 was a church official. Thomas Edward Scrutton, *Roman Law Influence in Chancery, Church Courts, Admiralty, and Law Merchant,* in SELECT ESSAYS IN ANGLO-AMERICAN LEGAL HISTORY 208, 214–15 (Ass'n of Am. Law Schs. ed., 1907); *see also* Henry Arthur Hollond, *Some Early Chancellors,* 9 CAMBRIDGE L.J. 17, 23 (1945) (indicating that the position was held by laymen for only about twelve years during the fourteenth century).

[180] MEAGHER, GUMMOW AND LEHANE'S EQUITY, FOURTH EDITION, *supra* note 29, at 450.

[181] *See* Anenson, *A View from Equity, supra* note 25, at 261–62; *see also* STORY'S COMMENTARIES, FOURTEENTH EDITION, *supra* note 117, at 47 (explaining that the chancellor was the dispenser of the king's conscience); discussion *infra* Chapter 1.

[182] Helmut Coing, *English Equity and the Denunciatio Evangelica of the Canon Law,* 71 L.Q. REV. 223, 223 (1955) ("[T]he Court of Chancery is addressed as a 'Court of Conscience,' and the decisive question in most cases is whether defendant could have acted in good conscience as he [or she] did."); MEAGHER, GUMMOW AND LEHANE'S EQUITY, FOURTH EDITION, *supra* note 29, at 451 (explaining that equity prevents the unconscientious use of legal rights); *accord* Keystone Driller Co. v. Gen. Excavator Co., 290 U.S. 240, 245 (1933) ("A court of equity acts only when and as conscience commands . . .") (quoting Deweese v. Reinhard, 165 U.S. 386, 390 (1897))).

[183] WORTHINGTON, *supra* note 112, at 39–40; T. M. YEO, CHOICE OF LAW FOR EQUITABLE DOCTRINES 96 (2004); *see also* SHERIDAN, *supra* note 173, at 210 (explaining that innocent misrepresentation as a ground of equitable intervention was introduced late in the nineteenth century); SNELL'S PRINCIPLES OF EQUITY 431–32 (H. Gibson Rivington & A. Clifford Fountaine eds., 19th ed. 1925) [hereinafter SNELL'S NINETEENTH EDITION]. Given equity's recognition that bright lines cannot always be drawn among shadings of an almost infinitely varied human experience, it is not remarkable that courts failed to distinguish intentional from unintentional conduct in discerning unclean hands. *See* PROSSER AND KEETON ON THE LAW OF TORTS, *supra* note 158, § 8, at 33 (observing that intent is "one of the most basic, organizing concepts of legal thinking" as well as the "most often misunderstood").

[184] *See Keystone Driller,* 290 U.S. at 245 (explaining that the violations of conscience must affect the equitable relations between the parties concerning "something brought before the court for adjudication"). The doctrine of clean hands is generally defined as follows: "a court of equity

must be his [or her] bad conduct in the transaction complained of."[185] Certain cases have also recognized similar wrongdoing.[186] As analyzed in Section 2.3, judges employ the doctrine for purposes of preventing a private advantage and protecting the court.[187]

The connection condition of unclean hands formed the basis of the original English case of *Dering v. Earl of Winchelsea*.[188] In *Dering*, the court emphasized that the maxim is not invoked merely by establishing a "general depravity."[189] It ruled that there must be an "immediate and necessary" connection between the conduct said to make the plaintiff's hands unclean and the right claimed.[190]

Early American cases reiterated *Dering's* "immediate and necessary" language.[191] United States Supreme Court cases of unclean hands continue to require a relationship between the wrong and the remedy or right.[192] In fact, a twenty-first-century case by the Court addressing the defense reiterated Pomeroy's classic formulation that the wrongdoing must be "in the course of the transaction at issue."[193] But the unclean conduct need not be in the same transaction so long as

---

may deny relief to a party whose conduct has been inequitable, unfair, and deceitful, *but [the] doctrine applies only when the reprehensible conduct complained of pertains to the controversy at issue.*" *Unclean Hands Doctrine*, BLACK'S LAW DICTIONARY (6th ed. 1990) (emphasis added) (citations omitted).

[185] 2 POMEROY'S EQUITY JURISPRUDENCE, FIFTH EDITION, *supra* note 1, § 399. *But see* SNELL'S TWENTY-SEVENTH EDITION, *supra* note 45, at 33 (noting that the connection restriction is not recognized in some American jurisdictions or in England during the sixteenth century).

[186] Boca Raton Community Hosp., Inc. v. Tenet Healthcare Corp., 238 F.R.D. 679, 693–94 (S.D. Fla. 2006) (ruling that unclean hands may be available as a defense to legal relief under federal civil RICO claim for illegal pricing based on the plaintiff's illegal pricing in violation of the statute); discussion *infra* Chapter 3, Section 3.4, and Chapter 5.

[187] *See* discussion *supra* Section 2.3 (discussing two purposes of unclean hands); *accord* YOUNG ET AL., *supra* note 85, at 180–84 (discussing Australian and English law of unclean hands).

[188] (1787) 29 Eng. Rep. 1184 (recognizing the doctrine of unclean hands but denying its application on the ground that the alleged unclean acts lacked the requisite relation to the case).

[189] *Id.* at 1184–85.

[190] *Id.*

[191] *See, e.g.*, Bateman v. Fargason, 4 F. 32, 32 (C.C.W.D. Tenn. 1880); Shaver v. Heller & Merz Co., 108 F. 821 (8th Cir. 1901); FREDERICK S. WAITE, TREATISE ON EQUITY § 439, at 584 (1884) (citing cases from Pennsylvania and Tennessee). For modern cases endorsing the "immediate and necessary" language, *see* Ne. Women's Ctr., Inc. v. McMonagle, 868 F.2d 1342, 1354 (3d Cir. 1989).

[192] *See, e.g.*, ABF Freight Sys., Inc. v. NLRB, 510 U.S. 317, 329–30 (1994) (Scalia and O'Connor, JJ., concurring). In *Keystone*, the Supreme Court echoed *Dering's* "immediate and necessary" language and ruled that the wrongful acts "affect the equitable relations between the parties *in respect of something brought before the court for adjudication.*" Keystone Driller Co. v. Gen. Excavator Co., 290 U.S. 240, 245 (1933) (emphasis added). Again, the Court explained in *Precision Instrument* that the defense "closes the doors of a court of equity to one tainted with inequitableness or bad faith *relative to the matter in which he seeks relief.*" Precision Instrument Mfg. Co. v. Auto. Maint. Mach. Co., 324 U.S. 806, 814 (1945) (emphasis added).

[193] McKennon v. Nashville Banner Publ'g Co., 513 U.S. 352, 360 (1995) (citing POMEROY'S EQUITY JURISPRUDENCE, FIFTH EDITION, *supra* note 1, § 399).

the events are related.[194] Akin to fraud jurisprudence, it is sufficient if the dirty deed infects the issue before the court.[195]

Discussing the condition in the nineteenth century, Justice Brandeis emphasized that "[e]quity does not demand that its suitors shall have led blameless lives."[196] Discerning a "want of equity in the allegations and corresponding proof" as opposed to "the bad conduct in life and character of the complainant" is not exclusively factual but normative.[197]

Take the initial *Dering* case.[198] The case involved one surety seeking contribution from two other sureties. The former had been sued by the Crown to pay the debt of his brother, a customs collector. The plaintiff was one of three persons that had given a security for the performance of the collector's duties. The allegation of unclean hands by the defendants asserted that the plaintiff encouraged the collector (his brother) in gaming when he knew his brother lacked his own funds and was breaking the rules of the Treasury in his use of public funds.[199]

The court assumed the "evil example" of the plaintiff led the collector on and contributed to the missing public funds.[200] Yet still, it concluded that the facts did not constitute a defense.[201] By analogy to modern-day tort law and the principle of proximate cause, a judge might have said there was a factual connection but not a legal one. Presumably, the court declined the defense because it decided that the collector is responsible to fulfill his own duties regardless of outside pressure or encouragement.

Cases from the Supreme Court and lower state and federal courts regularly use risk language of "direct" versus "collateral, remote, indirect" in assessing the

---

[194] An example can be found in *Pond v. Insur. Co. of N. America*, 198 Cal. Rptr. 517, 521–23 (Cal. App. 1984), examined *infra* in Chapter 3, Section 3.4.1.1.

[195] *See* Conard v. Nicoll, 29 U.S. 291, 297 (1830) (explaining that "if the particular act sought to be avoided be not shown to be tainted with fraud, it cannot be affected by those other frauds, unless in some way or other it be connected with or form a part of them"); Samasko v. Davis, 64 A.2d 682, 685 (Conn. 1949) ("Where a plaintiff's [equitable] claim 'grows out of or depends on, or is inseparably connected with his own prior fraud, a court of equity will, in general, deny him any relief, and will leave him to whatever remedies and defenses at law he may have.'" (quoting Gest v. Gest, 167 A. 909, 912 (Conn. 1933))); Anenson & Mark, *supra* note 23, at 1497–98 (reviewing *Keystone Driller Co. v. Gen. Excavator Co.*, 290 U.S. 240, 244–46 (1933), and noting that although the inequitable conduct occurred as to only one patent, the Supreme Court affirmed the dismissal of all five patents for practical and procedural reasons).

[196] *See* Loughran v. Loughran, 292 U.S. 216, 229 (1934).

[197] *See* Clarke v. White, 37 U.S. 178, 193 (1838); *see also* RESTATEMENT (THIRD) OF RESTITUTION AND UNJUST ENRICHMENT § 63(e) (AM. LAW INST. 2011) ("Whether a particular misconduct is directly relevant or merely 'collateral' to the relief sought by the claimant will depend on the court's sense of fitting punishment in the case at hand.").

[198] Dering v. Earl of Winchelsea, (1787) 29 Eng. Rep. 1184, 1184.

[199] *Id.*

[200] *Id.* (relating that "this may all be true" and that the plaintiff might possibly have involved his brother in some way").

[201] *Id.* at 1185.

connection component.[202] In his iconic analysis of unclean hands, Chafee likewise posed the question as to the closeness of the connection as whether an illegal transaction is "central" or "collateral" to the litigated claim.[203] He concluded that the answer cannot be determined solely by the facts but by an analysis of underlying values.[204] It requires judgment. As analyzed earlier in this chapter, courts apply the doctrine for purposes of preventing a private advantage and/or public harm.[205] Similarly, Dobbs described the connection component of unclean hands as akin to a duty analysis.[206] From this vantage, a trial judge would have discretion to determine foreseeability and decide whether the unclean conduct is so closely related to the claim or case that it was within the scope of the risk.[207]

Cases (even within the same jurisdiction) are not uniform on whether the unclean conduct must result in harm or prejudice.[208] However, the weight of

[202] *See, e.g.*, Johnson v. Yellow Cab Transit Co., 321 U.S. 383, 390–93 (1944) (distinguishing collateral versus direct violation of federal criminal law); Loughran v. Loughran, 292 U.S. 126, 129 (1934) (employing the language of "collateral," and "indirect and remote" in reference to violation of law); Kendall-Jackson Winery Ltd. v. Superior Court, 90 Cal. Rptr.2d 743, 749 (Cal. Ct. App. 1999) (using direct versus indirect dichotomy); *see also* DOBBS LAW OF REMEDIES, *supra* note 16, §2.4(2) at 93 n.22 (citing Ne. Women's Ctr., Inc. v. McMonagle, 868 F.2d 1342, 1354 (3d Cir. 1989), *cert. denied*, 493 U.S. 901 (1989)).

[203] Chafee I, *supra* note 2, at 896–98 (examining suits to enforce illegal contracts in law and equity). After asking whether the main transaction is illegal, Chafee poses the following questions: Is the illegal transaction "central to the litigated claim"? Or is it collateral? *Id.* at 897–98.

[204] *Id.* at 898. Chafee commented on the difficulty courts have in determining the effect of unlawful acts that are completed. *Id.* at 896–98 (comparing relationship requirement issue in the equity case of *McMullen v. Hoffman*, 174 U.S. 639, 654 (1899) (seller resisted specific performance of a land contract because the buyer got the price as a bribe for political favors to a third person) with the law case of *Loughran v. Loughran*, 292 U.S. 216, 228 (1934)).

[205] *See* discussion *supra* Section 2.3 (discussing two purposes of unclean hands); *accord* YOUNG ET AL., *supra* note 85, at 180–84 (discussing Australian and English law of unclean hands).

[206] Dobbs theorized that the connection component of unclean hands is congruent if the wrongdoing was: (1) same kind of harm that the plaintiff intended or unreasonably risked and it resulted in (2) actual or threatened harm to the defendant (or group of persons which the defendant is identified with). DOBBS LAW OF REMEDIES, *supra* note 16, § 2.4(2), at 93.

[207] Professor Rendleman describes Dobbs's analysis as asking whether the plaintiff's misconduct is so closely related that it is within the scope of the risk. RENDLEMAN, COMPLEX LITIGATION, *supra* note 55, at 270. Dobbs also saw the case law as employing two different standards depending on the circumstances. DOBBS LAW OF REMEDIES, *supra* note 16, § 2.4(2) at 95. In some cases, he found that courts used a narrow formula. *See id.* They emphasize that "[w]hat is material is not that the plaintiff's hands are dirty, but that he dirties them in acquiring the right he now asserts . . ." *Id.* In other cases, he concluded that courts used a broad formula. *See id.* They simply ask whether the improper conduct "sufficiently affected the equitable relations between the parties." *Id.* Research in Chapter 6 *infra* further defends the idea of analyzing the relationship between the wrong and remedy under principles of proximity.

[208] *Compare* Belling v. Croter, 134 P.2d 532, 537 (Cal. Ct. App. 1943) ("'[U]nclean hands' principle is equally applicable to cases of intent to defraud as to those in which the intent ripened into accomplishment." (citing Tognazzi v. Wilhelm, 56 P.2d 1227 (Cal. 1936)), *with* Miller & Lux v. Enter. Canal & Land Co., 75 P. 770, 772 (Cal. 1904) ("[F]raud without injury is never

authority appears to favor application of the defense without it.[209] There are certainly cases of unclean hands in which the plaintiff has been unjustly enriched at the defendant's expense. As such, the extent of any unfair benefit can be considered in relation to the defendant's harm.[210] Nevertheless, courts typically do not require it. In *Morton Salt Co. v. G.S. Suppiger Co.*, for instance, the United States Supreme Court declared that the clean hands doctrine applies "regardless of whether the particular defendant has suffered from the misuse of the patent."[211]

While the original English and American cases *did* require proof of harm to the defendant,[212] later decisions did not. The prevailing view is that unclean hands applies even though the plaintiff has not injured anyone (including the defendant).[213] Just one example is the Delaware Court of Chancery decision in *Nakahara v. NS 1991 Am. Trust.*[214] Citing the Supreme Court decision in *Deweese v. Reinhard*, the chancellor rejected the idea of "no harm, no foul" and explained that "[e]quity does not reward those who act inequitably, even if it can be said that no tangible injury resulted."[215] As a result, courts have held that

---

available as a defense in equity."), *and* Jeong Soon v. Beckman, 44 Cal. Rptr. 190, 192 (Cal. Ct. App. 1965) (declaring that prejudice is required for unclean hands).

[209] *See, e.g.,* FLIR Sys., Inc. v. Sierra Media, Inc., 965 F. Supp. 2d 1184, 1194 (D. Or. 2013) ("[W]hile the Ninth Circuit has recognized that the extent of the harm caused by the plaintiff's misconduct is a highly relevant consideration, it has not held that a defendant asserting an unclean hands defense is *required* to demonstrate prejudice." (internal quotation marks and citation omitted) (emphasis added)).

[210] *See, e.g.,* Earle R. Hanson & Assoc. v. Farmers Coop. Creamery Co., 403 F.2d 65, 70 (8th Cir. 1968) ("The plaintiff may be denied relief .... where the result induced by his conduct will be unconscionable either in the benefit to himself or the injury to others."); *accord* RESTATEMENT (THIRD) OF RESTITUTION AND UNJUST ENRICHMENT, *supra* note 197, § 63(a) (discussing unclean hand as a defense to unjust enrichment).

[211] Morton Salt Co. v. G.S. Suppiger Co., 314 U.S. 488, 494 (1942) (affirming trial court dismissal of patent infringement complaint for want of equity under the clean hands doctrine).

[212] *See* Chafee I, *supra* note 2, at 881 (explaining that the early cases referenced by Francis were situations in which the applicant harmed the respondent); *id.* (noting that one of Francis's footnotes specifies that "[t]he iniquity must be done to the defendant himself" (citing FRANCIS, MAXIMS OF EQUITY, 6 n.(b) (4th ed.))). Some cases still require injury to the defendant in order to satisfy the clean hands doctrine. *See* Kostelnik v. Roberts, 680 S.W.2d 532, 535–36 (Tex. Ct. App. 1984) (holding that there is no connection between claimant's unclean hands and claim because the wrongful conduct complained of "must have been done to the defendant himself and not to some third party."). *But see* RESTATEMENT (THIRD) OF RESTITUTION AND UNJUST ENRICHMENT, *supra* note 197, § 63(f) (asserting the case fundamentally misstates the law)).

[213] *See* Green v. Higgins, 535 P.2d 446, 450 (Kan. 1975) (citing MCCLINTOCK, *supra* note 59, § 26 and cases from Arkansas and Washington); *see also* Yeiser v. Rogers, 108 A.2d 877, 878–79 (N.J. Super. Ct. App. Div. 1954), *aff'd* 116 A.2d 3 (N.J. 1955) (declaring that it is not the wrong accomplished but the wrong planned that matters when invoking unclean hands).

[214] 739 A.2d 770 (Del. Ch. 1998).

[215] *Id.* at 794–95 (denying litigation expenses for unclean hands even though satisfied contractual prerequisites (citing Deweese v. Reinhard, 165 U.S. 386, 390 (1897))).

misrepresentation and concealment of important facts, even though nonmaterial, constitutes unclean hands.[216]

A finding of unclean hands in the absence of detrimental reliance is especially noticeable if there has been an attempt to gain an advantage. Federal and state courts routinely hold that such circumstances satisfy the doctrine.[217] This includes when misconduct has the potential to interfere with the process of decision making.[218] As the Supreme Court pronounced in *Hazel-Atlas Glass Co. v. Hartford-Empire Co.*: "No fraud is more odious than an *attempt* to subvert the administration of justice."[219]

Another ordinary use of the defense is when the injury, whether actual or symbolic, is to the public interest. Consider again the United States Supreme Court. It has been particularly vigilant in safeguarding judicial and administrative processes as well as government contracting.[220] In *S&E Contractors, Inc. v. United States*, the Supreme Court endorsed the application of unclean hands.[221] It declared that "[c]ontracts with the United States – like patents – are matters concerning far more than the interest of the adverse parties; they entail the public interest."[222] The Court declared:

> Where a suit in equity concerns the public interest as well as the private interests of the litigants this doctrine assumes even wider and more significant proportions. For if an equity court properly uses the maxim to withhold its assistance in such a case it not only prevents a wrongdoer from enjoying the fruits of his transgression but averts an injury to the public.[223]

---

[216] *See* Turchi v. Salaman Media Partners, Ltd., No. 11268, 1990 Del. Ch. LEXIS 34, at *23 (Mar. 14, 1990), *aff'd sub nom.* Media v. Turchi, 597 A.2d 354 (Del. 1991); *see also* Portnoy v. Cryo-Cell Int'l, Inc., 940 A.2d 43, 81 n.206 (Del. Ch. 2008) ("Harm . . . is not strictly required for the doctrine of unclean hands to bar relief.").

[217] *See* Anenson & Mark, *supra* note 23, at 1472–84 (detailing how the Supreme Court's decisions applying unclean hands in intellectual property law do not require harm).

[218] *See id.* (detailing cases including Supreme Court inequitable conduct decisions).

[219] Hazel–Atlas Glass Co. v. Hartford–Empire Co., 322 U.S. 238, 246 (1944) (Roberts, J., dissenting) (emphasis added). *Precision Instrument* described the patentee's obligations as an "uncompromising duty [to the Patent Office] to report to it all facts concerning *possible* fraud or inequitableness underlying the applications in issue." *See* Precision Instrument Mfg. Co. v. Auto. Maint. Mach. Co., 324 U.S. 806, 818 (1945) (emphasis added). The patentee in *Keystone* adjudicated the validity of the patent in prior litigation without disclosure of the contract keeping secret the potential prior use. Keystone Driller Co. v. Gen. Excavator Co., 290 U.S. 240, 242 (1933).

[220] *See* Anenson & Mark, *supra* note 23, at 1474–75. The Supreme Court has also found the public interest vital in other areas of federal law. *See, e.g.,* Bevans v. United States, 80 U.S. 56, 62 (1872) (affirmed finding of unclean hands because public policy requiring strict accountability of receivers of public money).

[221] S&E Contractors, Inc. v. United States, 406 U.S. 1, 15 (1972).

[222] *Id.*

[223] *Id.* (quoting *Precision Instrument*, 324 U.S. at 815).

Lower courts have embraced the public interest under the doctrine of unclean hands as well.[224] In deterring violations of the law, they have refused to require private harm in dismissing statutory actions.[225] Private law cases in which the unclean conduct involved potential statutory violations additionally establish that possible public injury is sufficient grounds for unclean hands.[226] Courts are using the defense of unclean hands as an indirect method of deterring serious violations that were otherwise hard to obtain.[227] For this reason, private or even public harm is not a condition of dismissal if the conduct has the potential to encourage future violations.[228]

Chafee advised that the progression of unclean hands to include third-party protection occurred in the late nineteenth century.[229] Dobbs's commentary on unclean hands instructed its further extension to protect the public interest had taken hold by the early twentieth century.[230] Therefore, as evinced by a plethora of decisions, courts had carved out an exception to the injury requirement in the public interest.[231]

Notwithstanding, the Court of Appeals for the Federal Circuit recently reinvented unclean hands in patent law by requiring detrimental reliance on the basis of the same criterion found in common law fraud.[232] Again, though, unclean hands decisions from the Supreme Court and lower state and federal courts are clear that the defense is broader than fraud; it is beyond fraud.[233] Moreover, "equitable" rather than "common law" fraud is the appropriate comparison. Remember that the doctrine of unclean hands is considered part of the larger

---

[224] See 30A CORPUS JURIS SECUNDUM, *supra* note 130, § 116 (citing cases involving protection of the public interest).

[225] See, e.g., Mallis v. Bankers Tr. Co., 615 F.2d 68, 75–76 (2d Cir. 1980) (applying New York state law and holding that no injury is needed if there is harm to public policy); Thompson v. Orcutt, 777 A.2d 670, 674–81 (Conn. 2001) (noting an exception to private harm if the application of unclean hands furthers the public interest).

[226] See Anenson & Mark, *supra* note 23, at 1476–77 (citing cases).

[227] Chafee I, *supra* note 2, at 902 (analyzing unclean hands category of illegality decisions).

[228] In *Carrington*, cited in *Keystone*, for instance, applying the unclean hands defense promoted the deterrence function. Carrington v. Pratt, 59 U.S. 63, 66–68 (1855) (noting that the party acting in bad faith "would risk nothing" if the security was held valid to the extent of the loan).

[229] Chafee I, *supra* note 2, at 892 (discussing unclean hands expansion in the late 1800s to include third parties (citing cases)).

[230] DOBBS LAW OF REMEDIES, *supra* note 16, § 2.4(2), at 94–95 (criticizing cases of unclean hands for improper conduct not causing injury to the defendant).

[231] For cases in Australia not requiring harm to the defendant due to the paramount public interest, see YOUNG ET AL., *supra* note 85, at 183–84 (citing Kettles & Gas Appliance Ltd. v. Anthony Hordern & Sons Ltd., 35 SR (NSW) 108 (1934) and Angelides v. James Steadman Hendersons Sweets Ltd., 40 CLR 43 (1927)).

[232] Anenson & Mark, *supra* note 23, at 1484 (critiquing Therasense, Inc. v. Becton, Dickinson & Co., 649 F.3d 1276 (Fed. Cir. 2011)).

[233] See *id.*; discussion *supra* Section 2.7.1.

notion of constructive fraud that provided a basis for equitable intervention.[234] Traditionally, fraud in equity included agreements affecting public relations by interfering with legislative, executive, or judicial proceedings.[235] Equitable fraud did not require detrimental reliance, just as it did not require a specific intent to deceive.[236]

The fact that fraud in the broad sense can constitute unclean hands does not necessarily preclude a narrow approach in a given situation. A more conservative outlook could prevent relief if the dirty deed was absolutely essential by having the plaintiff plead it or rely on it to prove the claim. Using the language of tort law, "but for" the unclean conduct, could the applicant make out their case? If not, they have unclean hands. If so, they do not. (Under a wider perspective, they may still have unclean hands if there is a requisite connection.) The fraudulent conveyance scenario fits the bill.[237] To recover the property, the applicant must set forth the real reason for its conveyance in the first place.

Another cautious stance is when the unclean conduct negates an element of the claim. Thus, rather than arguing that circumstances exist that should qualify or preclude a claim, the defendant demonstrates that not all the elements of a plaintiff's claim have been made out. While there are cases whose fact patterns fit within these positions,[238] no court has mandated either restrictive view.[239] The surrounding circumstances notwithstanding, these are the easier cases concerning the clean hands doctrine.

---

[234] See discussion *supra* Section 2.7.1. Story advised that:

> It is not easy to give a definition of Fraud in the extensive signification in which that term is used in Courts of Equity; and it has been said that these Courts have, very wisely never laid down as a general proposition what shall constitute fraud, or any general rule beyond which they will not go upon the ground of fraud, lest other means of avoiding the Equity of the Courts should be found out.

STORY'S COMMENTARIES, FOURTEENTH EDITION, *supra* note 117, §186.

[235] See POMEROY'S EQUITY JURISPRUDENCE, FIFTH EDITION, *supra* note 1, § 399; SNELL'S NINE-TEENTH EDITION, *supra* note 183, at 441.

[236] In contrast to positive fraud that required an intent to deceive and reliance, Story explained that constructive fraud in equity included situations involving confidential relations, imbalances of power, and agreements against public policy (including abuses of judicial processes), and/or a mixture of them. See STORY'S COMMENTARIES, FIRST EDITION, *supra* note 114, §§ 258–59. Equity originated in the Middle Ages when the "might makes right" mentality predominated among kings and commoners. See Anenson, *Triumph of Equity*, *supra* note 25, at 384–85.

[237] See Health Maint. Network v. Blue Cross of So. Cal., 249 Cal. Rptr. 220, 232 (Cal. Ct. App. 1988) (commenting that the "clean hands" doctrine "is usually associated with the rule of law which precludes a grantor from recovering his property from a grantee when the conveyance is deemed a fraudulent one"); *see also* BISPHAM, TENTH EDITION, *supra* note 115, at 71 n.4 (citing cases from multiple states).

[238] Blain v. Doctor's Co., 272 Cal. Rptr. 250, 258–59 (Cal. Ct. App. 1990); *infra* notes 241–244 and Chapter 3, Section 3.4.1.1 and Chapter 6, Section 6.3.5.3.

[239] See *Blain*, 272 Cal. Rptr. at 258–59.

Courts are certainly more comfortable with Chafee's vision that entailed situations in which the plaintiffs' fault contributed to their own harm.[240] This corresponds to *Dering's* dicta that the unclean hands defense may be satisfied if the applicant for relief had bored a hole in the side of a ship that caused his goods to be thrown overboard to save the ship.[241] For a modern take, consider *Blain v. Doctor's Co.*[242] In this case, a doctor brought a legal malpractice action based on his attorney's bad advice to lie under oath. The court found lying constituted unclean hands, which was attributable to the doctor's own injuries for emotional distress and loss of work as a physician.[243] As such, the doctor lacked proof that the attorney's professional negligence had a causal connection to these injuries.[244]

More extreme decisions apply unclean hands to the same or similar conduct that does not cause or attempt to cause harm to the defendant. The litigants are not acting in concert, which might merit the application of the narrower doctrine of *in pari delicto*.[245] Nor does the traditional idea of equitable estoppel fit the fact patterns because there is no reliance on the inequitable conduct.[246] The most notable cases here involve unfair competition. Some of these cases, though, can be understood under the public interest exception to the connection component. When the plaintiff violates the same statute as the defendant, the public harm criterion satisfies the connection component. In a civil RICO case,[247] for instance, the court recognized the possibility of unclean hands to preclude legal relief where both parties allegedly engaged in illegal pricing.[248]

---

[240] *See* Chafee II, *supra* note 12, at 1091–92; discussion *supra* Section 2.3 note 59; *see also* Mullins v. Picklesimer, 317 S.W.3d 569, 577 (Ky. 2010) ("In a long and unbroken line of cases [the Kentucky Supreme Court] has refused relief to one, who has created by his fraudulent acts the situation from which he asks to be extricated.").

[241] Dering v. Earl of Winchelsea, (1787) 29 Eng. Rep. 1184, 1185 (announcing that such a person could not claim contribution from his fellow cargo-owners because he would be the author of the loss).

[242] 272 Cal. Rptr. 250 (Cal. Ct. App. 1990).

[243] *Id.* at 258–59.

[244] *Id.*

[245] The unclean hands defense and other kindred defenses like estoppel, illegality, or *in pari delicto* are not a complete match. *See* Anenson, *Role of Equity, supra* note 78, at 51–52 (explaining that unclean hands is broader in application than the defenses of equitable estoppel and waiver); Anenson, *A Process-Based Theory, supra* note 68, at 566–69 (comparing defenses of *in pari delicto* and unclean hands); *see* discussion *infra* Chapter 5, Section 5.3.1 and Chapter 6, Section 6.4.2.

[246] *See* sources cited *supra*, note 245.

[247] Boca Raton Community Hosp., Inc. v. Tenet Healthcare Corp., 238 F.R.D. 679 (S.D. Fla. 2006).

[248] *Id.* at 693–94 (denying plaintiff's renewed motion for class certification due in part to the potential availability of unclean hands as a defense to legal relief under federal civil RICO based on the plaintiff's illegal pricing in violation of the statute); *see also* Smith, *Form and Substance in Equitable Remedies, supra* note 51, at 336 (explaining that the kind of disqualifying behavior amounting to unclean hands in England need not be based on unconscionability (citing *Hubbard v. Vosper* (1972) 2 QB 84 (Eng.)) (Scientologists denied an injunction against defamatory publications due to their own deplorable activities)).

There are many decisions of deceptive trade practices in trademark law. In *Haagen-Dazs, Inc. v. Frusen Gladje, Ltd.*,[249] the plaintiff was barred from obtaining an injunction against the defendant's false designation of its ice cream as Swedish where the plaintiff's own labeling falsely suggests that its ice cream was from Scandinavia.[250] Some cases, however, are more tenuous in terms of the public interest. These cases do not involve breach of a statute. In *Unilogic, Inc. v. Burroughs Corp.*,[251] the plaintiff was held ineligible for damages for the conversion of software from a failed joint development project where the plaintiff was also guilty of conversion.[252]

Consider *UZ Engineered Prods. Co. v. Midwest Motor Supply Co., Inc. (Kimball-Midwest)* as well.[253] The case involved one competitor suing another for interference with its employment contracts, resulting in the loss of its sales force. Because the defendant company used a noncompete contract with identical terms, counsel for the plaintiff argued that equitable defenses, including unclean hands, precluded the defendant from challenging the validity of its employment agreements.[254] The appellate court agreed, although it announced the principle as equitable estoppel.[255] Because estoppel traditionally requires reliance on an inconsistency that was absent in this case, however, the better fit was unclean hands.[256]

These situations still can be loosely rationalized under the concept of preventing litigants from benefiting from their own wrong. The litigants lack standing under

---

[249] 493 F. Supp. 73 (S.D.N.Y. 1980).

[250] *Id.* at 74–76 (finding the plaintiff guilty of the same deceptive trade practices of which it accuses defendants); *see also* Chafee II, *supra* note 12, at 1076–77 (reviewing Clinton E. Worden & Co. v. Cal. Fig Syrup Co., 187 U.S. 516, 528 (1903) (refusing to aid "California Fig Syrup" that had no figs)). Other disputes involving trademarks have mandated that plaintiff's conduct must have injured the defendant. *See, e.g.*, Lawler v. Giliam, 569 F.2d 1283, 1293 n.7 (4th Cir. 1978). Mid-twentieth-century decisions involving statutory violations as constituting unclean hands have been justly criticized for strictly applying the defense of unclean hands to preclude a remedy without weighing or otherwise considering the policies of the claim. *See* Chafee I, *supra* note 2, at 878; Chafee II, *supra* note 12, at 1092; discussion *infra* Section 2.8.

[251] 12 Cal. Rptr. 741 2d (Cal. Ct. App. 1992).

[252] *Id.* at 743–45 (finding unclean hands available for the same conduct on which the plaintiff based their claim for relief).

[253] *See* UZ Engineered Prods. Co. v. Midwest Motor Supply Co., Inc. (Kimball-Midwest), 770 N.E.2d 1068, 1079–80 (Ohio Ct. App. 2001).

[254] *Id.* The author was trial and appellate counsel for UZ Engineered Prods. Co. in this case. *Id.* Kimball-Midwest not only executed the same covenants as UZ, but acknowledged and enforced them as well. Anenson, *Role of Equity, supra* note 78, at 21 (reviewing the case).

[255] Without discussing its elements or policies, the appellate court simply labeled the defense "estoppel." UZ Engineered Prods. Co., 770 N.E.2d at 1079–80; *see* Anenson, *Role of Equity, supra* note 78, at 54 n.253.

[256] Some courts have removed the reasonable reliance requirement of equitable estoppel in furtherance of other policies. *See* Anenson, *Pluralistic Model, supra* note 41, at 663–64; Anenson, *Triumph of Equity, supra* note 25, at 390–91. For a comparison of estoppel and unclean hands, *see* Anenson, *Role of Equity, supra* note 78, at 47–53. For other unfair competition cases involving unclean hands based on the same conduct, such as when both parties improperly stealing trade secrets or customers, *see* Chafee II, *supra* note 12, at 1082.

the clean hands doctrine by their hypocrisy in taking an identical stance to the one they are attempting to condemn. In other words, the claim may have merit, but the hypocrite does not deserve to raise it. As outlined in Section 2.3, it has been argued that the moral norm of *tu quoque*, among others, is embodied in the defense's normative structure.[257] This Latin tag means "you too" or can be understood by equivalent phrases like "look who's talking" or "the pot calling the kettle black."[258]

Generally, tort actions will be more remote than contract cases and lack the requisite link. This is due to the absence of a prior relationship between the parties. It is not surprising that the early descriptions of unclean hands associated it with transactions.[259] However, litigation involving fraud or other tortious conduct arising from a contractual or other prior relationship tends to be less tenuous and, as a result, more favorable for the application of the defense.[260]

Another question is whether the connection is assessed on the entire controversy or on a claim-by-claim basis.[261] Most courts separate the analysis without elaboration.[262] This seems correct. After all, the concept of clean hands arose, and had been applied repeatedly, before the proliferation of code pleading concluded at the federal level and in most states by the middle of the twentieth century.[263] The modern codes permitted an expanded scope to a single action. Technological advances during the same period meant that issues appeared in new and more complex combinations. Under the technical pleading requirements abolished by the Field Code and other Field-type statutes recognizing a liberal joinder of claims and defenses, there was simply no need to make such a determination.

If the connection component is to have any teeth, it makes sense that the defense of unclean hands should be analyzed according to the claim for relief rather than the entire cause of action. It should only prevent the claim to which the unclean conduct is related. The whole controversy should not stand or fall as a unity. Claims unaffected by the unclean conduct should remain.[264] Indeed, Pomeroy discussed the doctrine as refusing "all" relief but qualified the explanation "with reference to

---

[257] *See* Herstein, *supra* note 69, at 205.

[258] *Id.* at 192–93; *see* G. A. Cohen, *Casting the First Stone: Who Can, and Who Can't, Condemn the Terrorists?, in* Finding Oneself in the Other 115, 119 (Michael Otsuka ed., 2013); *see also id.* at 119 n.8 (explaining that the interpersonal dimension of moral utterances has been neglected in moral philosophy).

[259] 2 Pomeroy's Equity Jurisprudence, Fifth Edition, *supra* note 1, § 397, 399.

[260] *See, e.g.,* Unilogic, Inc. v. Burroughs Corp., 12 Cal. Rptr. 2d 741, 742–43 (Cal. Ct. App. 1992) (asserting claims in tort arising out of business dealings).

[261] The right to a jury trial has the same confusion. *See* Anenson, *Triumph of Equity, supra* note 25, at 412–21 (analyzing differences in state and federal law to jury trial of equitable defenses, including confusion over whether to classify by controversy or claim); Note, *The Right To Jury Trial Under Merged Procedures,* 65 Harv. L. Rev. 453, 455–57 (1952) (analyzing how courts judge the issue of jury trial either by action or issue).

[262] *See infra* note 268.

[263] *See supra* Chapter 1, Section 1.1 note 2.

[264] Anenson & Mark, *supra* note 23, at 1496–1502 (making argument for litigation claims and patent claims).

the subject matter or transaction in question."[265] This comports with the unclean hands' justificatory norm of retribution that punishment should be proportional to the wrong committed.[266]

In California, where courts have broadened the ambit of unclean hands, decisions are clear that the defense is applied in a granular fashion.[267] Courts carefully assess the viability of the defense by issue and do not lump all causes of action together in analyzing the appropriateness of its application.[268] Courts sometimes even narrow the inquiry further to decide between remedies to a single claim or use the doctrine to reduce (but not totally ban) the remedy.[269]

One United States Supreme Court decision, however, may appear to the contrary. It declared in *Manufacturers' Finance Co. v. McKey* that unclean hands denies relief *in toto*.[270] But the decision preceded the promulgation of the Federal Rules of Procedure providing for the liberal joinder of claims.[271] Since that time, lower federal courts have limited "the reach of the doctrine to only some of the claims."[272] Furthermore, under the related doctrine of fraud on the court stemming from the

---

[265] POMEROY'S EQUITY JURISPRUDENCE, FIFTH EDITION, *supra* note 1, § 397, at 91.

[266] Herstein, *supra* note 69, at 201–03; *supra* Section 2.3.

[267] *See* discussion *infra* Chapter 3, Section 3.4.1.1, and notes 268–269.

[268] Courts may apply the clean hands doctrine to preclude an entire lawsuit or to some claims and not others. *See* Murillo v. Rite Stuff Foods, Inc., 77 Cal. Rptr. 2d 12, 18 (Cal. Ct. App. 1998) (ruling that unclean hands bars wrongful discharge and contract claims but not sexual harassment); *see also* Ample Bright Dev., Ltd. v. Comis Int'l, 913 F. Supp. 2d 925, 940–41 (C.D. Cal. 2012) (refusing to apply the clean hands doctrine to promissory estoppel claim in part because the parties only raised the defense to declaratory judgment action); Blain v. Doctor's Co., 272 Cal. Rptr. 250, 258–59 (Cal. Ct. App. 1990) (making separate inquiries into the kinds of harm allegedly resulting from the professional negligence, emotional distress, and the inability to continue professional practice).

[269] *See* Anenson, *Statutory Interpretation*, *supra* note 5, at 38 (identifying the Supreme Court's new emphasis on equitable defenses as adjustment, rather than eradication, mechanisms (citing Petrella v. Metro-Goldwyn-Mayer, Inc., 134 S. Ct. 1962, 1978–79 (2014))); *accord* Salas v. Sierra Chem. Co., 327 P.3d 797, 812–13 (Cal. 2014), *cert. denied*, 135 S. Ct. 755 (2014) (holding that unclean hands could not be a complete defense to a statutory claim based on public policy but could guide the relief the court could fashion); Cortez v. Purolator Air Filtration Prods. Co., 999 P.2d 706, 716 (Cal. 2000) (ruling that "equitable defenses may not be asserted to wholly defeat a UCL claim (that is equitable)"); *infra* Section 2.8 and Chapter 5, Section 5.4.2. Unclean hands cases involving trademarks also recognize that the defense may bar legal and/or equitable relief in whole or in part. RESTATEMENT (THIRD) OF UNFAIR COMPETITION: PLAINTIFF'S MISCONDUCT § 32 (AM. LAW. INST. 1995) (March 2016 update).

[270] Mfrs.' Fin. Co. v. McKey, 294 U.S. 442, 451 (1935) (declaring that "the maxim, if applicable, required the district court to halt petitioner at the threshold and refuse it any relief whatsoever"). The Supreme Court alternatively held that no inequitable conduct was involved in the case. *Id.*

[271] *See* discussion *supra* Chapter 1 note 2 (discussing how the Federal Rules of Civil Procedure of 1938 joined law and equity processes in the federal system).

[272] New Valley Corp. v. Corp. Prop. Assocs. 2 & 3, 181 F.3d 517, 525 (3d Cir. 1999) ("As an equitable doctrine, application of unclean hands rests within the sound discretion of the trial court ... [T]he court has discretion to limit the reach of the doctrine to only some of the claims."). *See also* J.L. Cooper & Co. v. Anchor Sec. Co., 113 P.2d 845, 853–54 (Wash. 1941) ("Even proof of misconduct as to one part of a transaction will not necessarily deprive a party of equitable relief as to another part thereof.").

Supreme Court's unclean hands decision in *Hazel-Atlas Glass Co. v. Hartford-Empire Co.*,[273] courts regularly parcel the pleadings.[274]

An additional aspect of the connection component – timing – deserves attention. There is universal recognition of when to evaluate the requisite relationship between the conduct and the case (claim). As indicated earlier, courts are not in the business of assassinating a litigant's character in terms of their general behavior in life. Correspondingly, litigants are allowed to wash their once-dirty hands clean and maintain the lawsuit.[275]

Accordingly, the unclean hands defense does not apply unless there is a connection between the conduct and the case. In fact, the connection component of unclean hands has been the method by which courts typically constrain the defense.[276]

2.7.3 *Sliding Scale*

A trial court typically has discretion to consider the seriousness of the conduct and its relation to the case in tandem rather than determine each element in isolation. Specifically, in considering the clean hands doctrine, judges employ stricter rules of relatedness for inadvertence and allow a more liberal connection for increasing levels of cognition. Put differently, comparable to liability in tort,[277] courts tend to impose greater responsibility upon those whose conduct was intended to do harm rather than when they possess lesser states of mind.[278] In articulating unclean hands in trademark litigation, for instance, the Supreme Court held that if there is a willful

---

[273] 322 U.S. 238, 250–51 (1944).

[274] *See* discussion *infra* Chapter 5, Section 5.3.2.2.3 (comparing the doctrines of unclean hands and fraud on the court); Chapter 6, Section 6.4.2 (contrasting the doctrines of unclean hands and fraud on the court).

[275] *See, e.g.*, Gen. Elec. Co. v. Klein, 129 A.2d 250, 251 (Del. Ch. 1956) (ruling that a repentant sinner, especially where duly punished, is not unwelcome in equity); Howard v. Howard, 913 So.2d 1030, 1041–42 (Miss. Ct. App. 2005) (expressing the idea that unclean hands can be cleansed to allow the plaintiff to receive relief); Poll, *supra* note 118, at 72–75 (discussing cases denying the clean hands doctrine once the improper practice had ceased and its consequences dissipated).

[276] Anenson, *Treating Equity Like Law, supra* note 51, at 506; *see also* Anenson, *A Process-Based Theory, supra* note 68, at 516 ("While not universal, many courts also mandate that the unclean conduct have a connection to the case."); discussion *infra* Chapter 5, Section 5.4.4.

[277] *See* PROSSER AND KEETON ON THE LAW OF TORTS, *supra* note 158, § 8, at 35–37 (noting that courts have worked out a sliding scale). The doctrine of unclean hands has been described as "tortious," including conduct that is fraudulent, willful, and negligent. LAYCOCK, REMEDIES, *supra* note 100, at 938 (describing unclean hands as illegal or tortious conduct); *see* Thompson v. Orcutt, 777 A.2d 670, 674 (Conn. 2001) (suggesting unclean hands includes fraud and intentional, negligent, and innocent misrepresentation); *see also* Paul Finn, *Unconscionable Conduct*, 8 J. CONT. L. 37, 42 (1994) (considering equitable theories as developing a new breed of tort).

[278] Shinsaku Nagano v. McGrath, 187 F.2d 753, 758 (7th Cir. 1951) (pronouncing that it is not so much the effect of conduct, as the intent with which it is performed); Quieroz v. Harvey, 205 P.3d 1120, 1122 (Ariz. 2009) (en banc) (citing MacRae v. MacRae, 794 P. 280, 282–84 (Ariz. 1941)) (declaring that it is the moral intent of the party and not the actual injury done that is controlling in determining unclean hands).

false statement, it need not mislead.[279] Concomitantly, court opinions finding unclean hands for innocent misrepresentation generally show that the statement induced another to act to his or her detriment.[280] Accordingly, appellate courts rarely detach the components of the clean hands doctrine and deny the district court discretion to collectively discern them.[281]

The sliding scale approach makes it more difficult to trace the development of the doctrine with any exactitude or segregate its elements. The role of discretion, discussed in what follows, also adds to the complexity of the defense.

2.8 ROLE OF DISCRETION

Ancient equity practice and principle includes judicial consideration of the ethical ideals embodied in the defenses themselves as well as their subjugation to cases and other consequences, including statutory goals.[282] Because equitable defenses are discretionary in nature, history also directs the form of the defense as open textured.[283]

An often-repeated refrain in judicial decisions is that flexibility is a corollary to equitable defenses.[284] State and federal cases follow this view.[285] With unclean hands in particular, the Supreme Court warned against technical adherence to any formulae.[286] It has also declared that unclean hands

---

[279] Clinton E. Worden & Co. v. Cal. Fig Syrup Co., 187 U.S. 516, 531–32 (1903) (relying on English precedent cited with approval in Manhattan Med. Co. v. Wood, 108 U.S. 218, 225 (1883)).

[280] *See, e.g.,* Kackley v. Webber, 220 S.W.2d 587, 589 (Ky. 1949) ("[E]quity will not come to the aid of a party who has induced another to act to his detriment, even though the misrepresentations were innocently made.").

[281] *See* Anenson & Mark, *supra* note 23, at 1461–87 (criticizing the majority in *Therasense, Inc. v. Becton, Dickinson & Co.,* 649 F.3d 1276, 1292–93 (Fed. Cir. 2011) for changing the elements of inequitable conduct contrary to the tradition of unclean hands and removing them from the sliding scale).

[282] *Id.* at 1502–05; Thomas Geu, et al., *To Be or Not To Be Exclusive: Statutory Construction of the Charging Order in the Single Member LLC,* 9 DePaul Bus. & Comm. L.J. 83, 94 (2010) (considering codification of charging order derived from equity justified by equitable interpretation according to the policies of the statute).

[283] *See, e.g.,* Anenson & Mark, *supra* note 23, at 1502–05 (explaining the discretionary nature of unclean hands); Anenson, *Triumph of Equity, supra* note 25, at 404–05 (describing the discretionary nature of equitable estoppel).

[284] Precision Instrument Mfg. Co. v. Auto. Maint. Mach. Co., 324 U.S. 806, 815 (1945); *see* Johnson v. Yellow Cab Transit Co., 321 U.S. 383, 387 (1944) (repeating the explanation); *see also* Edward Yorio, *A Defense of Equitable Defenses,* 51 Ohio St. L.J. 1201, 1225–26 (1990) (noting flexibility and fairness benefits of equitable defenses); *cf.* Hecht Co. v. Bowles, 321 U.S. 321, 329 (1944) (stating that "[f]lexibility rather than rigidity" distinguishes equity).

[285] DeCecco v. Beach, 381 A.2d 543, 546 (Conn. 1977) (explaining that the clean hands maxim applies in the trial court's discretion and "is not one of absolutes").

[286] Keystone Driller Co. v. Gen. Excavator Co., 290 U.S. 240, 244–46 (1933) (declaring that the doctrine of unclean hands "is not bound by formula or restrained by any limitation that tends to trammel the free and just exercise of discretion," but is applied "upon consideration that make for the advancement of right and justice"). In *Hazel-Atlas,* the Court explained unclean hands

"necessarily gives wide range to the equity court's use of discretion in refusing to aid the unclean litigant."[287]

The original impetus for an equitable solution was that common law judges crafted their doctrines like glazed earthenware from a kiln.[288] Attempts to reform or remold such rules would cause them to scratch or even break. Historic equity, in response, emerged like molten glass from a furnace. Equitable doctrines could be spun, shaped, and stretched with an extraordinary degree of freedom.[289]

It bears repeating that the defense of unclean hands developed largely from the idea of equitable fraud designed to remedy the abuse of legal rights or other unfair advantage taking where elasticity was necessary to capture conduct that is hard to predict in advance.[290] In short, "equity was aiming at a moving target."[291] Seen as a safety valve, then, equitable defenses like unclean hands remained fuzzy around the edges.[292] Equitable doctrines provide "individualized justice ... illuminated by moral principles."[293] As discussed earlier, the inevitability of equitable discretion comes from Aristotle's insight was that no lawmaker could craft laws to cover every contingency and that discretion is needed to prevent the over- or under-inclusiveness of rules.[294]

---

as part of equitable relief that is "always been characterized by flexibility which enables it to meet new situations which demand equitable intervention, and to accord all the relief necessary to correct the particular injustices involved in these situations." Hazel-Atlas Glass Co. v. Hartford-Empire Co., 322 U.S. 238, 248 (1944).

[287] *Precision Instrument*, 324 U.S. at 815.

[288] Holdsworth, *supra* note 17, at 18–19 (discussing whether it was truly an intolerant attitude or the lack of power under existing procedures causing the injustices in the common law courts). The hardening of equity in the years before the merger received much criticism and was denounced as defeating the ultimate purpose of the legal system to provide just results. *See, e.g.,* Garvey, *Some Aspects, supra* note 29, at 63 ("[E]quity became just as legal, just as strict, as the common-law itself."); *see also* Harold Greville Hanbury, *The Field of Modern Equity, in* ESSAYS IN EQUITY 34 (1934) (commenting that despite the different epochs of flexibility and inflexibility of equity throughout history, "the stream of equity is, in reality, continuous throughout the ages").

[289] *See* Sherwin, *supra* note 42, at 307 (explaining that the equitable as opposed to the legal method of analysis is more individualistic); discussion *supra* Section 2.3.

[290] *See* Anenson & Mark, *supra* note 23, at 1484–85; Finn, *supra* note 277, at 37; discussion *supra* Section 2.7.

[291] Smith, *Fiduciary Law, supra* note 39, at 269; *see also* Anenson & Mayer, *supra* note 45, at 995 (discussing the contours of the clean hands doctrine and claiming that "[w]hat is 'unclean,' like what is fraud, necessitates some ambiguity to promote deterrence").

[292] *See* Anenson, *Triumph of Equity, supra* note 25, at 403–06 (describing the flexibility of equity and how estoppel has no exhaustive formula); Anenson, *Pluralistic Model, supra* note 41, at 651 (explaining the embryonic character of equitable doctrines); *see also* Gergen, Golden & Smith, *supra* note 59, at 237 (relating safety valve theory of equitable remedies).

[293] Ryan, *supra* note 30, at 217 (citing Emmerglick, *supra* note 44, at 254–55).

[294] *See* Anenson, *Triumph of Equity, supra* note 25, at 426 (explaining equitable defenses in relation to the Greek idea of *epikeia* (citing Anton-Hermann Chroust, *Aristotle's Conception of "Equity" (Epieikeia)*, 18 NOTRE DAME L. REV. 119, 125–26 (1942–43))); discussion *supra* Section 2.3 and *infra* Chapter 5, Section 5.4.3.

A leading international treatise on equity explains that "the phrase 'clean hands' will be of sufficiently imprecise import to permit application of the maxim to be tailored in each case very much *in personam.*"[295] For this reason, courts often define the maxim in the form of a tautology by equating unclean hands with equitable intervention.[296] The range of misbehaviors associated with the defense varies widely in terms of knowledge,[297] harm[298] or its foreseeability,[299] any admission of wrongdoing,[300] the effectiveness of lesser sanctions,[301] the nature of the relationship,[302] the role of the client as opposed to counsel,[303]

---

[295] MEAGHER, GUMMOW AND LEHANE'S EQUITY, FOURTH EDITION, *supra* note 29, at 451.

[296] *See* Merck & Co. v. SmithKline Beecham Pharms. Co., No. 15443-NC, 1999 Del. Ch. LEXIS 242, at *157–58 (Aug. 5, 1999) (stating inquiry as whether the party had "'transgressed equitable standards of conduct' in a way that might justify application of the unclean hands doctrine" (quoting Precision Instrument Mfg. Co. v. Auto. Maint. Mach. Co., 324 U.S. 806, 815 (1945))); Bellware v. Wolffis, 397 N.W.2d 861, 864 (Mich. Ct. App. 1996) ("Any willful act regarding cause of action which transgresses equitable standards of conduct is sufficient cause for the intervention of the clean hands doctrine.").

[297] *See, e.g.,* Bartlett v. Dunne, No. C.A. 89–3051, 1989 WL 1110258, at *3 (R.I. Super. Ct. Nov. 10, 1989) (emphasizing that the plaintiff's deception was willful).

[298] *See, for example,* Gaudiosi v. Mellon, 269 F.2d 873, 882 (3d Cir. 1959) (emphasis omitted), which quoted Judge Learned Hand's dissent in *Art Metal Works v. Abraham & Straus,* 70 F.2d 641, 646 (2d Cir. 1934) as follows:

> The doctrine [of unclean hands] is confessedly derived from the unwillingness of a court, originally and still nominally one of conscience, to give its peculiar relief to a suitor who in the very controversy has so conducted himself as to shock the moral sensibilities of the judge. It has nothing to do with the rights or liabilities of the parties; indeed the defendant who invokes it need not be damaged, and the court may even raise it sua sponte.

Gaudiosi, 269 F.2d at 882 (emphasis omitted).

[299] *See* Maldonado v. Ford Motor Co., 719 N.W.2d 809, 821–22 (Mich. 2006) (holding that a substantial likelihood of harm to the case is sufficient to invoke unclean hands). A pattern of misbehavior by the litigant could also help establish the requisite foreseeability of harm to the court system. *Id.* at 821; Pierce v. Heritage Props., Inc., 688 So.2d 1385, 1389 (Miss. 1997) (noting intentional nature, as well as the pattern of the plaintiff's conduct, which included deliberately providing false responses in three discovery mechanisms, should be considered in dismissal decision).

[300] *See, e.g.,* Smith v. Cessna Aircraft Co., 124 F.R.D. 103, 107–08 (D. Md. 1989) (admission of perjury).

[301] *See, e.g., Bartlett,* 1989 WL 1110258, at *3 (noting the alternative sanction of contempt available to address a party's unclean hands).

[302] A breach of fiduciary duties can constitute unclean hands. *See, e.g.,* Ross v. Moyer, 286 A.D.2d 610, 611 (N.Y. Ct. App. 2001); Jackson Law Office, P.C. v. Chappell, 37 S.W.3d 15, 26 (Tex. Ct. App. 2000).

[303] *See Maldonado,* 719 N.W.2d at 824 (considering the Supreme Court's comment in *Gentile v. State Bar of Nevada,* 501 U.S. 1030, 1074 (1991), that an attorney is an integral participant in the justice system and, therefore, the state can demand adherence to the precepts of the system in regulating their conduct); Jonathan M. Stern, *Untangling a Tangled Web Without Trial: Using the Court's Inherent Powers and Rules to Deny a Perjuring Litigant His Day in Court,* 66 J. AIR L. & COM. 1251, 1289 (2001) (stating that courts are less likely to dismiss the case when it is the lawyer (as opposed to the client) who commits misconduct); *see also* Rose v. Nat'l Auction Grp., Inc., 646 N.W.2d 455, 467 (Mich. 2002) (applying unclean hands despite reliance on expert advice since conduct "violate[d] basic ethical norms").

and the public interests.[304] The discretionary nature of the decision recognizes these varied phenomena.[305]

As indicated, one consideration is whether there is an alternative sanction to barring suit. In declining the defense despite proof of its dual components, judges will sometimes note that the danger posed by a party's dirty hands can be addressed another way.[306] Alternative sanctions could be outside the lawsuit or within it, such as applying a narrower defense like *in pari delicto*, illegality, or estoppel.[307] Courts are, or at least should be, conscious of the plaintiff's right to be heard by employing the least restrictive means of addressing the risk.[308] Applying the narrowest defense would also enhance clarity and coherence in an otherwise amorphous area of the law.[309]

Evaluating other mechanisms to prevent the plaintiff from taking advantage of their own wrong and protecting the court or public would seem necessary where there is a presumption against the application of the defense. The presumption-like phraseology limits the defense to "extraordinary," "disfavored," or "exceptional" cases.[310] Presumptions are familiar to equitable jurisprudence, although only a

---

[304] *See, e.g.*, Morton Salt Co. v. G.S. Suppiger Co., 314 U.S. 488, 492 (1942) (A court of equity "may appropriately withhold their aid where the plaintiff is using the right asserted contrary to the public interest."), *abrogated by* Ill. Tool Works Inc. v. Indep. Ink, Inc., 547 U.S. 28, 42–43 (2006) (concluding that a *per se* presumption of illegality for tying arrangements of patented products was no longer applicable given recent congressional amendments).

[305] *See, e.g.*, Kent Greenawalt, *Discretion and Judicial Decision: The Elusive Quest for the Fetters that Bind Judges*, 75 COLUM. L. REV. 359, 380 (1975) ("The obvious inappropriateness of denying discretion when a decision-maker must choose among an almost infinite number of alternatives on bases that are complex and yield uncertain conclusions.").

[306] In *Johnson v. Yellow Cab Transit Co.*, 321 U.S. 383, 387 (1944), a majority of the Supreme Court determined that the clean hands doctrine should not apply despite the potential violation of federal law because there were other ways to enforce the law and deter future violations. For state cases, *see* Bellino v. Bellino, No. A12–2319, 2013 WL 4045809 at *5 (Miss. Ct. App. Oct. 13, 2013) (indicating that respondent's removal as conservator would be a less drastic alternative remedy to barring suit under the clean hands doctrine); Bartlett v. Dunne, No. C.A. 89–3051, 1989 WL 1110258, at *3 (R.I. Super. Ct. Nov. 10, 1989) (finding litigant in contempt rather than precluding suit based on unclean hands).

[307] *See* discussion *infra* Chapter 5, Section 5.3.1 and Chapter 6, Section 6.4.2. All of these equitable defenses rest, at least in part, on the rationale of preventing wrongdoers from taking advantage of their own wrong. *Supra* Chapter 2, Section 2.3 note 51.

[308] *Accord* SAMANTHA HEPBURN, PRINCIPLES OF EQUITY AND TRUSTS, § 15.4, at 69–70 (2d ed. 2001) (outlining Australian law preference for the application of narrower defenses).

[309] *See* discussion *infra* Chapter 5, Section 5.4.2.

[310] Some jurisdictions narrow unclean hands and provide for its invocation only with prudence, *see* Milford Power Co. v. PDC Milford Power LLC, 866 A.2d 738, 748 (Del. Ch. 2004), reluctantly, *see* Farmers' Educ. & Coop. Union of Am. v. Farmers Educ. & Coop. Union of Am., 141 F. Supp. 820 (S.D. Iowa 1956), *aff'd sub nom.* Stover v. Farmers' Educ. & Coop. Union of Am., 150 F. Supp. 422 (S.D. Iowa 1957), *aff'd* 250 F.2d 809 (8th Cir. 1958), or in the exceptional case, *see* Markel v. Scovill Mfg. Co., 471 F. Supp. 1244, 1255 (W.D.N.Y.1979) ("[C]ourts are reluctant to apply the unclean hands doctrine in all but the most egregious situations.").

handful of jurisdictions use them for unclean hands.[311] In those courts that have adopted the parlance for the clean hands doctrine, the default position should assist courts in deciding close cases. Courts resolve doubts against the defense both in terms of determining its existence and in its application.[312] Applying the clean hands doctrine as a last resort is reminiscent of the evaluation for equitable relief for only those controversies that have no adequate remedy at law.[313]

The public policy criterion is particularly pronounced in equity and unclean hands.[314] Judges may expand or contract the unclean hands defense in the public interest.[315] Importantly, a critical part of the district court's discretion in determining unclean hands is to deny the defense and limit its application. At the time of the Supreme Court's inequitable conduct decisions and thereafter, a well-known

[311] The Supreme Court has resisted strong evidentiary presumptions for equitable relief, Gergen, Golden & Smith, *supra* note 59, at 219–30 (criticizing the Court's rejection of traditional evidentiary presumptions in determining equitable relief)), while maintaining a legal (interpretative) presumption of equity under silent statutes. Anenson, *Statutory Interpretation*, *supra* note 5, at 52–53.

[312] *See* Coca-Cola Co. v. Koke Co. of Amer., 254 U.S. 143, 145 (1920) (unclean hands is "scrutinized with a critical eye"). Certain jurisdictions have noted that the doctrine of unclean hands is not favored. *See* Schivarelli v. Chi. Transit Auth., 823 N.E.2d 158, 168 (Ill. Ct. App. 2005) ("The application of the unclean doctrine has not been favored by the [Illinois] courts."); Foursquare Tabernacle Church of God in Christ v. Dep't of Metro. Develop. of the Consol. City Of Indianapolis, 630 N.E.2d 1381 1385–86 (Ill. Ct. App. 1994) ("The doctrine is not favored by the courts and is applied with reluctance and scrutiny."); Butler v. Butler, 114 N.W.2d 595, 619 (Iowa 1962).

[313] *See* Anenson & Mark, *supra* note 23, at 1507 (explaining the Court's approach in *eBay v. MercExchange, L.L.C.*, 547 U.S. 388, 391 (2006) as developing mandatory reasoning requirements for the exercise of lower court discretion).

[314] *See, e.g.,* Robert S. Stevens, *A Brief on Behalf of a Course in Equity*, 8 J. LEGAL EDUC. 422, 424–25 (1955) (noting one of the factors to influence a decision in equity was that special consideration was given to the public interest); *supra* Section 2.7.2 (discussing public interest exception to connection component). Typically, a court will recite the public interest to expand the defense to find a connection yet restrict the defense pursuant to the public interest in the exercise of its residual discretion.

[315] For example, the Supreme Court has used the public interest doctrine to expand and contract equitable defenses. *See* Virginian Ry. Co. v. Sys. Fed'n, 300 U.S. 515, 552 (1937) ("Courts of equity may, and frequently do go much further both to give and withhold relief in furtherance of the public interest than they are accustomed to go when only private interests are involved."); Gene R. Shreve, *Federal Injunctions and the Public Interest*, 51 GEO. WASH. L. REV. 382, 382 (1983) ("The point [that equity courts may go further to give and withhold relief in the public interest] has been restated so often by federal courts that it has become an aphorism."). In endorsing unclean hands in patent law, the Supreme Court declared in *Precision Instrument Mfg. Co. v. Auto. Maint. Mach. Co.*: "Where a suit in equity concerns the public interest as well as the private interests of the litigants this doctrine assumes even wider and more significant proportions." Precision Instrument Mfg. Co. v. Auto. Maint. Mach. Co., 324 U.S. 806, 815 (1945); *supra* Section 2.6.2. Correspondingly, the Court relied on the public interest criterion to constrain the employee misconduct defense, derived from unclean hands, in statutory actions. In the employment law case of *McKennon v. Nashville Banner Publ'g Co.*, the Court explained that because the defense is founded on public policy, it may also be relaxed because of it. *See* McKennon v. Nashville Banner Publ'g Co., 513 U.S. 352, 360–61 (1995).

limitation on the doctrine was that courts would apply unclean hands only if it advanced and did not defeat the policies at issue in the case.[316] As a result, part of a trial court's discretion is to account for all the circumstances, including any mitigating factors, before deciding that unclean hands defeats a plaintiff's remedy.[317] Judges refuse the defense if they find the public interest outweighs its application in the case or it will otherwise work an inequitable result.[318] This inevitably involves a balancing process. While not uniform or always announced in the decision, courts can engage in two types of balancing. First, they compare the wrongdoing of the plaintiff and the defendant.[319] Second, they weigh and value the plaintiff's right against the wrong

---

[316] *See, e.g.,* Lyon v. Campbell, No. 01–1694, 2002 WL 470860, at *6 (4th Cir. Mar. 28, 2002) ("[E]ven if the district court might have been justified in applying the doctrine of unclean hands based on Lyon's false testimony, the court was not compelled to do so. Application of the doctrine of unclean hands is largely in the discretion of the district court."); *see also* Nakahara v. NS 1991 Am. Tr., 718 A.2d 518, 523 n.35 (Del. Ch. 1998) (citing cases refusing to apply unclean hands on public policy grounds); NEWMAN, EQUITY AND LAW, *supra* note 38, at 241–42 (citing cases).

[317] *See, e.g.,* Byron v. Clay, 867 F.2d 1049, 1051 (7th Cir. 1989) (Posner, J.) ("The doctrine of unclean hands ... gives recognition to the fact that equitable decrees may have effects on third parties – person who are not parties to a lawsuit, including taxpayers and members of the law abiding public – and so should not be entered without consideration of those effects."); *accord* YOUNG ET AL, *supra* note 85, at 183 (citing Australia, New Zealand, Hong Kong, and English cases).

[318] For federal cases, *see, for example,* Citizens Fin. Grp., Inc. v. Citizens Nat'l Bank of Evans City, 383 F.3d 110, 130 (3d Cir. 2004) ("We hold that the District Court's heavy reliance on the doctrine of unclean hands to justify its denial of injunctive relief improperly weighted the evidence to the exclusion of the merits of CNBEC's claim and the public interest, and constituted an abuse of discretion."); EEOC v. Recruit U.S.A., Inc., 939 F.2d 746, 753–55 (9th Cir. 1991) ("[T]he clean hands doctrine should not be strictly enforced when to do so would frustrate a substantial public interest. . . ."); Katiroll Co. v. Kati Roll & Platters, Inc., No. 10–3620 (GEB), 2011 U.S. Dist. LEXIS 61281, at *2 (D.N.J. June 8, 2011) ("[I]n a trademark infringement action, 'the court must show solicitude for the public in evaluating an unclean hands defense.'"); Fund of Funds, Ltd. v. First Am. Fund of Funds, Inc., 274 F. Supp. 517, 519 n.1 (S.D.N.Y. 1967) ("[T]he doctrine of unclean hands should not be applied since the central concern of the law of unfair competition in this case is protection of the public from confusion in the securities market."). For state cases, *see, for example,* Health Maint. Network v. Blue Cross of So. Cal., 249 Cal. Rptr. 220, 232 (Cal. Ct. App. 1988); Burnette v. Void, 509 A.2d 606, 608 (D.C. 1986). *See also* CORPORATE & COMMERCIAL PRACTICE IN THE DELAWARE COURT OF CHANCERY § 11.07[a] (2017) (listing cases).

[319] *See* Northbay Wellness Grp., Inc. v. Beyries, 789 F.3d 956, 960 (9th Cir. 2015) (explaining that the unclean hands defense requires balancing the alleged wrongdoing of the parties and weighing the right of the plaintiff against the plaintiff's transgression to foreclose the right); Dunlop-McCullen v. Local 1-S, AFL-CIO-CLC, 149 F.3d 85, 90 (2d Cir. 1998) (declaring that the "doctrine of unclean hands also may be relaxed if [the] defendant has been guilty of misconduct that is more unconscionable than that committed by [the] plaintiff" [internal quotation marks omitted]); JP Morgan Chase Bank, N.A. v. MGM IV, LLP, 2016 Ariz. App. Unpub. Westlaw 4249672, at *5 (Ariz. Ct. App. 2016) (citing Coleman v. Coleman, 61 P.2d 441, 443 (Ariz. 1936) (declaring that equitable relief may be warranted even for a party who acts inequitably when the other party is more culpable for its actions)); Sword v. Sweet, 92 P.3d 492, 501 (Idaho 2004) (ruling that the court has discretion to determine the relative conduct of both parties in applying the clean hands doctrine); *see also* Chafee I, *supra* note 2, at 904 (commenting that parties seem to fare better against the unclean hands defense when bringing tort rather than contract claims). Courts should not, however, confuse the defense of unclean

allegedly amounting to unclean hands.[320] Basically, in deciding the clean hands doctrine, they are identifying and reconciling competing interests in the case.[321]

A judge's residual discretion to deny the defense is a centuries-old condition. It is implicit in the application of equitable defenses and has been acknowledged explicitly in the state and federal courts.[322] Consequently, to continue the function of the clean hands doctrine, state and federal courts have retained its standard-like qualities and corresponding discretion.

2.9 CONCLUSION

In the United States, inquiries into equitable doctrines have been ad hoc and unsystematic.[323] There is not even a well-recognized taxonomy of equitable defenses.[324] A comprehensive analysis of the state and federal case law concerning the clean hands doctrine allows for an exhaustive assessment and systematic

---

hands and *in pari delicto*. See discussion *infra* Chapter 6, Section 6.4.2 (contrasting defenses). Weighing and comparing the parties conduct is equivalent to the balancing the equities criterion in determining whether to grant equitable relief. eBay Inc. v. MercExchange, L.L.C., 547 U.S. 388, 391 (2006) (articulating balancing the equities as one of a four-pronged approach to assessing equitable relief); *see also* Anenson, *Age of Statutes, supra* note 39, at 566–67 (outlining debate over the legitimacy of the balancing process for equitable remedies).

[320] *See* sources cited *supra*, note 319; Blain v. Doctor's Co., 272 Cal. Rptr. 250, 255 (Cal. Ct. App. 1990) (advising that analogies may be helpful, "but more significant is the way the effect given to the plaintiff's misconduct depends on the nature of his wrong and the nature of the defendant's wrong").

[321] In applying the clean hands doctrine to a legal malpractice action in *Blain v. Doctor's Co.*, 272 Cal. Rptr. 250 (Cal. Ct. App. 1990), for example, the court considered that denying the defense would deter attorneys from unsavory behavior. *Id.* at 258–59. Nevertheless, it determined that the societal interest in deterrence can be vindicated through criminal sanction or professional disciplinary proceedings. *Id.*

[322] *See* Anenson & Mark, *supra* note 23, at 1521 n.533 (listing federal and state cases). The discretion to deny unclean hands was evidenced in *Hazel-Atlas* where the Supreme Court justified its dismissal after noting there were "no intervening equities" that should change the outcome. Hazel-Atlas Glass Co. v. Hartford-Empire Co., 322 U.S. 238, 246 (1944). Additionally suggestive are the Court's patent misuse cases premised on the unclean hands doctrine that provided for discretion to limit the defense when the improper practice had been abandoned. *See* Poll, *supra* note 118, at 72–75 (discussing cases denying the clean hands doctrine once the improper practice had ceased and its consequences dissipated). More recent Supreme Court practice involving the application of unclean hands in other federal legislation has accounted for the discretion to deny the defense. The Supreme Court has similarly instructed the district courts to apply unclean hands' cousin – *in pari delicto* – only if barring recovery would not offend statutory policies. Pinter v. Dahl, 486 U.S. 622, 633 (1988).

[323] *See* discussion *supra* Chapter 1.

[324] *See* Anenson, *Triumph of Equity, supra* note 25, at 438–39 ("There has never been a book dedicated to equitable defenses."). The lack of clarity on equitable defenses has even been noted in the Commonwealth where equity still survives as a subject of study and lawyer specialization. *See* Smith, *Form and Substance in Equitable Remedies, supra* note 51, at 329 ("There is little agreement amongst writers or courts as to the number of traditional bars, their names or the borders between them."); *see also* Smith, *Fusion and Tradition, supra* note 40, at 29 n.48 (advising of England's Chancery Bar Association).

critique that is lacking for many theories of equity.[325] Moreover, because several courts of last resort (including the Supreme Court of the United States) have yet to address the issue of unclean hands at law after the union, the analysis should assist them in contemplating the extension of the defense to legal relief. The remainder of the chapters attempt to clarify the conflict and confusion in the cases and justify the incorporation of the defense into the law on positive and normative grounds.

---

[325] *See, e.g.,* Smith, *Equity in R3RUE, supra* note 114, at 1187–88 (commenting that equitable principles have suffered from a lack of systemization in comparison to the common law).

3

Examining the Cases

.

The clean hands doctrine ... ought not to be called a maxim of equity because it is by no means confined to equity.

– Zechariah Chafee, Jr.[1]

3.1 INTRODUCTION

This chapter focuses on the decisional law of the defense of unclean hands across the United States. In several opinions analyzed in what follows, state and federal courts considered the equitable defense as a bar to legal relief under a range of common law and statutory claims.

Many of these judges have held the law–equity line and refused to extend the clean hands doctrine to legal relief. This position corresponds to conventional wisdom. After all, while Chafee urged that the defense is not confined to equity, his analysis focused solely on the defense in cases seeking equitable remedies.[2] A long-standing authoritative treatise on the topic of remedies also advises that unclean hands is not available in damages and other so-called legal actions.[3]

Nevertheless, adjudications in state and federal courts evidence the expansion of the defense into matters of legal relief as well. Judges have found the clean hands doctrine available in private claims involving tort, contract, and property as well as statutes regulating racketeering and employment discrimination to intellectual

---

[1] Zechariah Chafee, Jr., *Coming into Equity with Clean Hands*, 47 MICH. L. REV. 877, 878 (1949) [hereinafter Chafee I].
[2] *See generally* Chafee I, *supra* note 1, at 885–906; Zechariah Chafee, Jr., *Coming into Equity with Clean Hands*, 47 MICH. L. REV. 1065–96 (1949).
[3] DAN B. DOBBS, DOBBS LAW OF REMEDIES: DAMAGES-EQUITY-RESTITUTION §2.4(2) at 68 (2nd ed. 1993) ("The most orthodox view of the unclean hands doctrine makes it an equitable defense, that is, one that can be raised to defeat an equitable remedy, but not one that defeats other remedies."); *see* discussion *supra* Chapter 2 (discussing Dobbs treatise).

property. Following the unanimous opinions of its lower courts, the California Supreme Court recently adopted the defense at law.[4] The Michigan Supreme Court has also recognized unclean hands and dismissed a damages action in a case of first impression.[5] Historically, though, other state supreme courts have limited its use to actions involving equitable relief. In the federal court system, the U.S. Supreme Court has not had occasion to address the viability of the clean hands doctrine to preclude damages. Therefore, the controversy over the legal status of unclean hands continues in the intermediate appellate and trial courts of state and federal jurisdictions.

A case-based analysis is an essential starting point before attempting to explain or even justify judicial action concerning fusion. Referring only to the sources of and constraints on judicial authority and discretion to extend the clean hands doctrine, any underlying political and theoretical presuppositions of a particular philosophy of law, would be like an announcer of a baseball game describing the field and the rules rather than providing an account of what the players are actually doing.

While certain courts have been cognizant of their equitable defense integration inquiry, the cases demonstrate that others are assuming the admittance (or exclusion) of these defenses at law. Judges have avoided larger questions of power and principle by focusing on individual equitable defense of unclean hands in each case. This should sound familiar. After all, courts do not write treatises but make decisions. But more direction in their approach is warranted. An explanation of why and how the clean hands doctrine is received into the law would assist in its consistent application and play a role in its justification.

To set the stage for answering questions of whether and how the defense should cross the law–equity border in the coming chapters, the following description tracks judicial action in state and federal cases.

3.2 OVERVIEW

Section 3.3 reviews court decisions that follow the conventional view that the equitable defense of unclean hands is limited to claims seeking equitable remedies. Section 3.4 explores the present decisional trend to consider the defense in cases seeking legal remedies. It studies how the cases are decided, how the precedents are used, and how the case law of unclean hands has evolved. It traces the incorporation process within and across state and federal jurisdictions.

Section 3.5 evaluates the future of unclean hands in light of the judicial justifications for and against the defense at law. It reveals how precedent and policy analysis dominate the thought processes of judges considering unclean hands and illustrates

---

[4] *See* Salas v. Sierra Chem. Co., 327 P.3d 797, 812–13 (Cal. 2014), *cert. denied*, 135 S. Ct. 755 (2014).
[5] *See* Maldonado v. Ford Motor Co., 719 N.W.2d 809, 818 (Mich. 2006).

how the complex interplay between human facts and abstract laws that confounded ancient English chancellors continue to challenge contemporary American judges. It suggests that rather than denying the defense in legal actions in reliance on its historical pedigree, the trend of absorbing the equitable defense of unclean hands into the law is likely to continue on the basis of policy.

The chapter concludes by placing unclean hands in its broader equitable context. The cases applying the defense in actions seeking legal remedies are important not only for what they say but also for what they represent. The laboratory that is unclean hands in damages actions could become a movement to eradicate the legal barrier to equity. To be sure, incorporating unclean hands into the law may help dissolve default notions of law and equity as unassailable symbols of an institution that has yet to grapple with its own coming of age.[6]

3.3 THE PAST: UNCLEAN HANDS EXCLUSIVE TO EQUITY

Before discussing the growing body of law that recognizes unclean hands in lawsuits seeking legal remedies and its implications for the future, this section surveys past court decisions rejecting unclean hands at law. Under these precedents, the defense is restricted to its traditional use in cases seeking equitable relief.

Two jurisdictions to deny unclean hands in a lawsuit seeking damages demonstrate a narrow outlook on the defense. In *Fremont Homes, Inc. v. Elmer*,[7] the Supreme Court of Wyoming supported its denial of the defense solely from precedent considering unclean hands to ban equitable relief.[8] Correspondingly, the District of Columbia Court of Appeals in *In re Barnes*[9] was persuaded to deny the defense because "we know of no authority for applying this 'maxim of equity' to a legal claim for money."[10] The Supreme Court of Utah refused to recognize the

---

[6] *See, e.g.*, Doug Rendleman, *The Trial Judge's Equitable Discretion Following* eBay v. MercExchange, 27 REV. LITIG. 63, 63 (2007) ("It would be salutary, I submit, for the profession to discard the nonfunctional terminology of separate legal and equitable discretion.").

[7] 974 P.2d 952 (Wyo. 1999).

[8] Fremont Homes, Inc. v. Elmer, 974 P.2d 952, 959 (Wyo. 1999) (lawsuit seeking damages for breach of employment contract). The Wyoming Supreme Court also cited Section 102 of the *Corpus Juris Secondum*, which misstated *DiMauro v. Pavia*, 492 F. Supp. 1051, 1068 (D.C. Conn. 1979). In considering the classic case of unclean hands to estop equitable relief, the *DiMauro* court instructed that unclean hands "may be invoked only to prevent affirmative relief." *Id.* The legal encyclopedia's version inserted the word "equitable" between "affirmative" and "relief." *See* 30A CORPUS JURIS SECUNDUM, *supra* note 130, § 102. The Supreme Court of Wyoming is the first and last appellate court for litigants.

[9] 754 A.2d 284, 288 n.6 (D.C. 2000).

[10] *In re* Estate of Barnes, 754 A.2d 284, 288 n.6 (D.C. 2000). D.C. precedent on this point stems from *Truitt v. Miller*, 407 A.2d 1073 (D.C. 1979), which relied on *Tarasi v. Pittsburgh Nat'l Bank* for the proposition that unclean hands will not defeat legal relief. *Id.* at 1079–80 (citing *Tarasi v. Pittsburgh Nat'l Bank*, 555 F.2d 1152, 1156–57 n.9 (3d Cir. 1977) (stating rule without authority)); *see also* First American Corp. v. Al-Nahyan, 17 F. Supp.2d 10, 29 (D.D.C. 1998)

clean hands doctrine as a bar to legal relief without citation to any authority.[11] State supreme courts in Connecticut,[12] Georgia,[13] Iowa,[14] Missouri,[15] and Pennsylvania[16] have reached similar conclusions, with other high courts in Minnesota,[17] North Dakota,[18] and New Jersey[19] suggesting an identical outcome.

("[U]nder D.C. law, unclean hands acts only as a defense to equitable, and not legal, actions.") (citing Truitt v. Miller, 407 A.2d 1073 (D.C. 1979)).

[11] Hill v. Estate of Allred, 216 P.3d 929, 935–36 (Utah 2009).

[12] *See* Weiss v. Smulders, 96 A.3d 1175, 1198 n.19 (Conn. 2014); *cf.* Samasko v. Davis, 64 A.2d 682, 685 (Conn. 1949) ("Where a plaintiff's [equitable] claim 'grows out of or depends upon or is inseparable connected with his own prior fraud, a court of equity will, in general, deny him any relief, and will leave him to whatever remedies and defenses at law he may have.'" (quoting Gest v. Gest, 167 A. 909, 912 (Conn. 1933)). Previously, three cases from its trial courts declared unclean hands available in actions at law and denied motions to strike the defense. *See* First Fairfield Funding, LLC v. Goldman, No. CV020465799S, 2003 WL 22708882, at *1 (Super. Ct. Conn. Nov. 3, 2003); Jesperson v. Ponichtera, 1990 WL 283884 at *1, No. CV88 0096615 S (Conn. Super. Jul 16, 1990); Robarge v. Patriot General Ins. Co., No. CV-91–0393211S, 1991 Conn. Super. LEXIS 2793, at *1 (Conn. Super. Ct. Dec. 4, 1991); *accord* Liberty Bank v. Holloway, No. CV92–0703852 S, 1993 WL 408314, at *1 (Conn. Super. Ct. Sept. 28, 1993) (laches) (citing *Jesperson*).

[13] Holmes v. Henderson, 549 S.E.2d 81, 81–82 n.1 (Ga. 2001) (citing Jones v. Douglas, 418 S.E.2d 19, 22–23 (Ga. 1992) (laches)).

[14] Ellwood v. Mid States Commodities, Inc., 404 N.W.2d 174, 184 (Iowa 1987); *see also* Sisson v. Janssen, 56 N.W.2d 30 (Iowa 1952) (equitable relief case) ("It is of course a doctrine which may be invoked only to prevent affirmative equitable relief.") (quoting Spitler v. Perry Town Lot & Improvement Co., 179 N.W. 69, 70 (Iowa 1920) (ruling without citation that unclean hands does not bar defenses, only affirmative equitable relief)); *cf.* Davenport Osteopathic Hosp. Ass'n v. Hosp. Service, 154 N.W.2d 153, 162 (Iowa 1967) (equitable defense of laches is not a defense to a legal action for breach of contract unless estoppel also exists).

[15] Russell v. White, 348 S.W.2d 548, 553 (Mo. 1964); *see also* Marvin E. Neiberg Real Estate Co. v. Taylor-Morley-Simon, 867 S.W.2d 618, 626 (Mo. Ct. App. 1993) (holding that the application of unclean hands is erroneous in an action at law for damages).

[16] Universal Builders, Inc. v. Moon Motor Lodge, Inc., 244 A.2d 10, 15 (Pa. 1968); *see also* Nedwidek v. Nedwidek, 92 A.2d 536, 537 (Pa. 1952) (discussing Pennsylvania's integration of law and equity in 1952).

[17] *See* Bieter Co. v. Blomquist, 848 F. Supp. 1446, 1450–51 (D. Minn. 1994) (noting that "Minnesota courts have not directly addressed the issue" but concluding that the Minnesota Supreme Court would not recognize unclean hands in an action for damages) (citing Thorem v. Thorem, 246 N.W. 674, 675 (Minn. 1933), Hagberg v. Colonial & Pacific Frigidways, Inc., 157 N.W.2d 33, 35 (Minn. 1968), and LaValle v. Kulkay, 277 N.W.2d 400, 403 n.3 (Minn. 1979))); *accord* Foy v. Klapmeier, 992 F.2d 774, 779 (8th Cir. 1993) (reaching the same conclusion under Minnesota law).

[18] Landers v. Biwer, 714 N.W.2d 476, 480 (N.D. 2006) ("A litigant seeking the remedy of specific performance is held to a higher standard than one merely seeking money damages, and to receive equity he must 'do equity' and must not come into court with 'unclean hands.'").

[19] Merchants Indem. Corp. v. Eggleston, 179 A.2d 505, 514 (N.J. 1962) (citing federal premerger precedent from the United States Supreme Court); *see also* Sprenger v. Trout, 866 A.2d 1035, 1045 (N.J. Super. A.D. 2005) (relying on Illinois precedent to bar unclean hands in consumer fraud action for damages due to an absence of authority in New Jersey). Recollect that New Jersey divides law and equity into separate divisions in a single court. *See supra* Chapter 1.

The state supreme courts of Maine,[20] Mississippi,[21] Virginia,[22] and West Virginia,[23] to name a few, have refused to permit the defense of laches in legal cases.[24] Laches shared the same premerger procedural posture as unclean hands,[25] suggesting they would deny the defense for the same reasons.[26]

The status of unclean hands is arguably an open question in Alabama.[27] While the Alabama Supreme Court in *San Ann Tobacco Co., Inc. v. Hamm* declared that unclean hands "may not constitute a defense at law," the decision predated the

---

[20] Strickland v. Cousens Realty, Inc., 484 A.2d 1006, 1008 (Me. 1984) (banning the equitable defense of laches in legal actions under code pleading).

[21] Aetna Ins. Co. v. Robertson, 94 So. 7, 28 (Miss. 1922):

> The rule that the enforcement of a right may be barred by laches is an application of the maxims, *vigilantibus, non dermientibus, subvenient leges,* he who seeks equity must come with clean hands . . . the defense of laches is peculiar to court of equity and is not pleadable in actions at law.

Mississippi is one of the states to retain separate courts of law and equity. *See* discussion *supra* Chapter 1 note 10.

[22] Portsmouth v. Chesapeake, 349 S.E.2d 351, 354 (Va. 1986) (ruling that a proceeding to enforce a legal right is not subject to the equitable defense of laches) *cited by* LBCMT 2007-C3 Seminole Trail, LLC v. Sheppard, No. 3:12CV00025, 2013 WL 3009319 at *5 (W.D. Va., June 17, 2013) (extending holding to the defense of unclean hands).

[23] Laurie v. Thomas, 294 S.E.2d 78, 80–81 (W. Va. 1982).

[24] The denial of laches in actions at law is the rule in many states. *See, e.g.,* Kodiak Elec. Ass'n, Inc. v. DeLaval Turbine, Inc., 694 P.2d 150 (Alaska 1984) (rejecting laches in legal action based on prevailing view and citing cases from Arkansas, California, Georgia, Minnesota, Missouri, and New Hampshire); Srebnick v. Lo-Law Transit Mgt., Inc., 557 N.E.2d 81, 85, 85 n.2 (Mass. App. Ct. 1990) (recognizing that "[p]rocedurally . . . equitable defenses may be raised in actions at law . . . laches is generally not available as a defense to a legal claim"). *But see* Moore v. Phillips, 627 P.2d 831, 835 (Kan. Ct. App. 1981) (citing McDaniel v. Messerschmidt, 382 P.2d 304 (Kan. 1963) (allowing equitable defense of laches in law actions)); Department of Banking and Finance of State of Neb. v. Wilken, 352 N.W.2d 145, 149 (Neb. 1984) (declaring laches available to defeat actions at law); Sutton v. Davis, 916 S.W.2d 937, 941 (Tenn. Ct. App. 1995) (stating that "laches may also bar purely legal claims").

[25] *See* John L. Garvey, *Some Aspects of the Merger of Law and Equity,* 10 CATH. U. L. REV. 59, 66 (1961); E.W. Hinton, *Equitable Defenses Under Modern Codes,* 18 MICH. L. REV. 717, 719 (1920).

[26] Robert J. Aalberts & T. Leigh Anenson, *Discretionary Limits on Statutes of Limitations: A Defense of Laches* (working paper, on file with author); *see also* USH Ventures v. Global Telesystems Group, Inc., 796 A.2d at 20 n.18 (Del. Super. 2000) ("It appears that in most Courts, laches cannot be asserted in an action at law."). However, the defense of laches has a substitute in the statute of limitations and may be displaced for that reason. Notes, *Displacement of the Doctrine of Laches by Statutes of Limitations – Crystallization of the Equitable Rule,* 79 U. PA. L. REV. 325, 341 (1931) (discussing issues of applicability with laches).

[27] 217 So.2d 803, 810 (Ala. 1968) (quoting Harton v. Little, 65 So. 9 51, 952 (Ala. 1914)). The quoted language, moreover, came from another equity case that did not address the issue of the application unclean hands in legal actions. *See generally Harton, supra.* Rather, the case concerned what conduct would constitute unclean hands. *See generally id.* The phrase was meant to explain that the fraud or deceit that would amount to unclean hands need not be the same conduct as would constitute fraud or deceit under the common law. *Id.* at 952–53.

state's merger of law and equity in 1973.[28] In addition, the highest courts in Oregon[29] and Maryland[30] agreed to address the adoptability issue but ultimately avoided it on appeal.[31]

The controversy concerning the common law recognition of unclean hands continues in the lower state courts.[32] Courts within New York[33] and Oregon[34] have reached different conclusions on the subject. Decisions from Texas,[35] Illinois,[36]

---

[28] *See* Wootten v. Ivey, 877 So.2d 585, 588 (Ala. 2003) (discussing merger of law and equity in 1973).

[29] Thompson v. Coughlin, 997 P.2d 191 (Ore. 2000).

[30] Adams v. Manown, 615 A.2d 611 (Md. 1992). Two dissenting justices would have denied the applicability of unclean hands to legal actions. *Id.* at 623 (citing premerger precedent from the court as well as the United States Supreme Court). Notably, Maryland did not complete the merger of law and equity procedure until 1984.

[31] Thompson v. Coughlin, 997 P.2d at 196 n.9; Adams v. Manown, 615 A.2d at 617.

[32] *See* General Dev. Corp. v. Binstein, 743 F. Supp. 1115, 1133–34 (D.N.J. 1990) (applying Florida, Connecticut, and Massachusetts law) ("Unclean hands is an equitable defense. This defense therefore is only applicable with respect to Plaintiff's claim for equitable relief[.]") (ruling unclean hands unavailable as a defense to claim for tortious interference seeking damages but applicable to request for injunctive relief); Sprenger v. Trout, 866 A.2d 1035, 1045 (N.J. Super. A.D. 2005) (relying on Illinois precedent to bar unclean hands in consumer fraud action for damages).

[33] *Compare* Mallis v. Bankers Trust Co., 615 F.2d 68 (2d Cir. 1980) (applying New York law) (unclean hands available to bar legal relief); Smith v. Long, 281 A.2d 897, 898 (N.Y. App. Div. 2001) (same), *with* Morrisania II Assoc. v. Harvey, 139 Misc.2d 651, 662 (N.Y. City Ct. 1988) (unclean hands inapplicable to legal claims) *and* Hasbro Bradley, Inc. v. Coopers & Lybrand, 128 A.D.2d 218, 220 (N.Y. App. Div. 1987) (same).

[34] *Compare* Kirkland v. Mannis, 639 P.2d 671 (Or. Ct. App. 1982) (applying unclean hands to legal action), *with* Beldt v. Beldt, 60 P.3d 1119, 1121 (Ore. App. Ct. 2003) (unclean hands unavailable in actions at law); Thompson v. Coughlin, 927 P.2d 146 (Ore. Ct. App. 1996) (same), *rev'd on other grounds*, 997 P.2d 191, 196 n.9 (Ore. 2000); *and* Gratreak v. N. Pacific Lumber Co., 609 P.2d 375 (Ore. App. Ct. 1980) (same). *See also* McKinley v. Weidner, 698 P.2d 983, 985–86 (Or. Ct. App. 1985) (acknowledging inconsistent decisions from the same court).

[35] *See* McMahan v. Greenwood, 108 S.W.3d 467, 494 (Tex. Ct. App. 2003); Steubner Realty 19, Ltd. v. Cravens Rd. 88, Ltd., 817 S.W.2d 160, 165–66 (Tex. Ct. App. 1991) (citing Ligon v. E.F. Hutton & Co., 428 S.W.2d 434, 437 (Tex. Ct. App. 1968) and Furr v. Hall, 553 S.W.2d 666, 672–73 (Tex. Ct. App. 1977)). Texas appellate courts have created an exception allowing unclean hands in law actions to the extent it works an estoppel. *See, e.g., Steubner Realty 19, Ltd., supra*, at 165. These courts also acknowledge a separate defense at law of "unclean acts" that involve a knowing and willful violation of state criminal law. *See* Shirvanian v. Defrates, No. 14-02-00447-CV, 2004 Tex. App. LEXIS 10426, at *41–44 (Tex. Ct. App. Nov. 18, 2004) (citing Ward v. Emmett, 37 S.W.3d 500, 503 (Tex. Ct. App. 2001)), *opinion withdrawn by, and substituted opinion on other grounds*, 161 S.W.3d 102 (Tex. Ct. App. 2004).

[36] *See* Chow v. Aegis Mortg. Corp., 286 F. Supp.2d 956, 964 (N.D. Ill. 2003) (applying Illinois law) ("Under Illinois law, unclean hands is an equitable remedy not applicable to claims for monetary relief.") (citing American National Bank & Trust v. Levy, 404 N.E.2d 946, 948 (Ill. Ct. App. 1980) ("Clearly, the equitable defense of unclean hands did not bar Hawthorn's action at law.")); Zahl v. Krupa, 850 N.E.2d 304, 309–310 (Ill. Ct. App. 2006); *cf.* Villiger v. City of Henry (Ill. Ct. App. 1977) (equitable defense of laches applies to both law and equity). Federal district courts in Illinois have allowed unclean hands in actions at law pursuant to federal law when legal and equitable claims are joined. *See* Urecal Corp. v. Masters, 413 F. Supp. 873, 876

North Carolina,[37] Ohio,[38] Arizona,[39] Colorado,[40] and Massachusetts[41] have also refused to assimilate the defense of unclean hands. In the federal courts, the District Court for the Northern District of Illinois[42] along with the Third Circuit Court of Appeals[43] likewise rejected the defense at law.

Consequently, notwithstanding postmerger criticism calling for the consideration of all equitable defenses to legal claims,[44] unclean hands has been traditionally dependent on equity jurisdiction.[45] But the customary reticence to recognize

(N.D. Ill. 1976) (diversity); Energizer Holdings, Inc. v. Duracell, Inc., No. 01 C 9720, 2002 WL 1067688, at *3 (N.D. Ill. May 28, 2002) (Lanham Act).

[37] Nat'l Mortg. Corp. v. American Title Ins. Co., 255 S.E.2d 622, 628–29 (N.C. Ct. App. 1979); Ekren v. K&E Real Estate Invest., LLC, No. 12 CVS 508, 215 WL 8199877 at *3 n.4 (Conn. Super. Ct. Nov. 12, 2015).

[38] *See, e.g.*, O'Brien v. Ohio State Univ., 859 N.E.2d 607, 607 n.3 (Ohio Ct. Cl. 2006) (unclean hands doctrine does not defeat legal claim for damages); Conklin v. Conklin, No. 14–77-7, 1978 Ohio App. LEXIS 9357, at *24 (Ohio Ct. App. Feb. 9, 1978) (rejecting unclean hands in an action at law because it is "strictly an equitable doctrine"); *see also* May v. May, 620 N.E.2d 317, 317 (Ohio C.P. 1993) (discussing Ohio history leading up the 1853 Code of Civil Procedure merging law and equity but noting that substantive distinctions still survive); *cf.* Smith v. Smith, 156 N.E.2d 113 (Ohio 1959) (equitable defense of laches does not apply to bar legal claim under merged procedures).

[39] *See* Tripati v. Arizona, 16 P.3d 783, 786 (Ariz. Ct. App. 2000); Ayer v. Gen. Dynamics Corp., 625 P.2d 913, 915 (Ariz. Ct. App. 1980).

[40] *See* Wilson v. Prentiss, 140 P.3d 288, 288 (Colo. Ct. App. 2006) ("The doctrine of unclean hands enables a defendant to raise an equitable defense to defeat equitable remedies, but not remedies at law.").

[41] Howe v. Fiduciary Trust Co., 2001 Mass. Super. LEXIS 135, at *30–31 (Mass. Super. Ct. Apr. 19, 2001).

[42] Lopez v. Autoserve, LLC, No. 05 C 3554, 2005 WL 3116053 (N.D. Ill. Nov. 17, 2005) (applying Illinois and federal law of unclean hands); *see also* Miller v. Beneficial Mgmt. Corp., 855 F. Supp. 691, 717 n.28 (D.N.J. 1994) (equating an employer's use of after-acquired evidence of an employee's misconduct under federal discrimination laws with the defense of unclean hands that the court presumed was restricted to equitable remedies). Another district court within the same circuit accepted the defense. *See* Columbus Regional Hosp. v. Patriot Medical Technologies, Inc., No. IP 01–1404-C K/H, 2004 WL 392938 at *7 (S.D. Ind. Feb 11, 2004) (also citing Federal Rules 2 & 8) (denying summary judgment on affirmative defense of unclean hands as a matter of federal law in a diversity case); Decatur Ventures, LLC v. Stapleton Ventures, Inc., No. 1:04-CV-0562-JDT-WTL Slip Copy, 2006 WL 1367436 at *4 (S.D. Ind. May 17, 2006) (also citing Federal Rules 2 & 8), *order amended*, No. 104CV-00562-JDT-WTL, 2006 WL 3305122 (S.D. Ind. Aug 16, 2006). The Seventh Circuit Court of Appeals held unclean hands available in a legal action. *See* Maltz v. Sax, 134 F.2d 2 (7th Cir. 1943) (applying unclean hands to bar an action for damages under the Sherman Anti-Trust Act).

[43] Tarasi v. Pittsburgh Nat'l Bank, 555 F.2d 1152, 1156–57 n.9 (3d Cir. 1977) (stating rule without authority).

[44] Zechariah Chafee logically concluded: "[T]he factors which divide judicial action from moral judgments seem to me the same whether the particular suit resembles what used to go on in chancery or what used to go on in the courts of common law." ZECHARIAH CHAFEE, JR., SOME PROBLEMS OF EQUITY 28 (1950) [hereinafter, CHAFEE, SOME PROBLEMS]; *see also* Edward Yorio, A *Defense of Equitable Defenses*, 51 OHIO ST. L.J. 1201, 1205–26 (1990) (summarizing criticisms of treating legal and equitable defenses differently).

[45] "Jurisdiction" does not generally refer to power over the subject matter, persons, or property but refers rather to equity jurisprudence. *E.g.*, WILLIAM Q. DE FUNIAK, HANDBOOK OF MODERN

unclean hands at law is changing. Courts recently have begun to absorb the defense. The next section details its integration into the law.

3.4 THE PRESENT: LEGAL DEVELOPMENT OF UNCLEAN HANDS

The following analysis traces the doctrinal development of unclean hands as a bar to legal relief in state and federal law.

3.4.1 *State Court Adoption of Unclean Hands*

Courts from six states have declared the doctrine of unclean hands available in an action at law.[46] Its absorption has occurred in dozens of cases from California, Oregon, Maryland, Michigan, New York, and Rhode Island.[47] All the incorporation decisions have been rendered by lower courts with the exception of Michigan and California. The Supreme Court of Michigan affirmed the dismissal of a case seeking damages in which the litigant's unclean hands amounted to litigation misconduct.[48] The Supreme Court of California recently recognized the defense in a statutory case seeking damages.[49]

EQUITY 37–39 (2d ed. 1956) (discussing differing definitions of "jurisdiction" as having either no power to act or having power to act but that it should not act); Henry Ingersoll, *Confusion of Law and Equity*, 21 YALE L.J. 58, 60–61 (1911) (explaining that jurisdiction of any case in equity does not depend upon an absence of a remedy at law). Such jurisprudence is conditioned on an equitable remedy.

[46] Federal courts sitting in diversity jurisdiction are divided on whether to use state or federal law to apply and/or define unclean hands in cases seeking legal relief. For federal courts with diversity jurisdiction applying a federal law of unclean hands, *see, for example*, Nature's Prods. Inc. v. Natrol, Inc., 990 F. Supp.2d 1307, 1317 (S.D. Fla. 2013); Big Lots Stores, Inc. v. Jaredco, Inc., 182 F. Supp.2d 644, 652–53 (S.D. Ohio 2002); *infra* Section 3.4.2. For federal courts with diversity jurisdiction applying a state law of unclean hands, *see* Gen-Probe, Inc. v. Amoco Corp., 926 F. Supp. 948, 952 (S.D. Cal. 1996) (applying California law of unclean hands in diversity case); Chow v. Aegis Mortg. Corp., 286 F. Supp.2d 956, 964 (N.D. Ill. 2003) (applying Illinois law of unclean hands); Bieter Co. v. Blomquist, 848 F. Supp. 1446, 1450–51 (D. Minn. 1994) (considering whether unclean hands is a valid defense to state law damage claims under Minnesota law); General Dev. Corp. v. Binstein, 743 F. Supp. 1115, 1133–34 (D.N.J. 1990) (applying Florida, Connecticut, and Massachusetts law of unclean hands). Because many courts have not acknowledged the source-of-law issue for unclean hands, it is often difficult to discern. In this section on state court adoption, I have included only federal courts that have clearly used a state law of unclean hands.

[47] While Kansas has no cases addressing the availability of unclean hands in actions at law, a court of appeals relied on the doctrine as a ground to apply the after-acquired evidence defense to bar damages in a contract claim for wrongful discharge. Gassman v. Evangelical Lutheran Good Samaritan Soc'y, 921 P.2d 224, 230 (Kan. Ct. App. 1996), *as modified by*, 933 P.2d 743 (Kan. 1997) (affirming adoption of after-acquired evidence doctrine without discussion of unclean hands).

[48] Maldonado v. Ford Motor Co., 719 N.W.2d at 818.

[49] Salas v. Sierra Chem. Co., 327 P.3d 797, 812–13 (Cal. 2014), *cert. denied*, 135 S. Ct. 755 (2014).

3.4.1.1 California

The story begins in the West. California received unclean hands as part of the state common law almost fifty years ago.[50] As the earliest state to adopt the defense at law, it has the most cases on the subject. Unlike Oregon and New York, discussed in what follows, California courts are unanimous.[51] The uniformity of its lower courts' decisions likely contributed to the defense's acceptance in the California Supreme Court without discussion.[52] California courts of appeal have considered unclean hands in both tort and contract actions.[53] Decisions have made the defense available to preclude conversion, malicious prosecution, and legal malpractice, as well as to bar the foreclosure of a mechanic's lien.[54] While certain opinions carefully considered the application question on a claim-by-claim basis, other opinions broadly echo its applicability in all cases.[55]

The process of integration began with *Fibreboard Paper Prods. Corp. v. East Bay Union of Machinists*.[56] In a case of "first impression," the appellate court questioned

---

[50] *See* Fibreboard Paper Prods. Corp. v. East Bay Union of Machinists, 39 Cal. Rptr. 64 (Cal. Ct. App. 1964).

[51] *See, e.g.*, Bio-Psychiatric-Toxicology Laboratory, Inc. v. Radcliff & West, 62 Cal. Rptr. 2d 853, 861 (Cal. Ct. App. 1997) ("In modern times the doctrine has been held applicable to suits for legal as well as equitable relief."); Vacco Industries, Inc. v. Van Den Berg, 6 Cal. Rptr. 2d 602, 612 (Cal. Ct. App. 1992) ("This is a principle which has application in a legal action as well as one in equity."); *see also* Al-Ibrahim v. Edde, 897 F. Supp. 620, 626 (D.D.C.1995) (applying California and Nevada law).

[52] *See* Salas v. Sierra Chem. Co., 327 P.3d 797, 812–13 (Cal. 2014), *cert. denied*, 135 S. Ct. 755 (2014).

[53] Camp v. Jeffer, Mangels, Butler & Marmaro, 41 Cal. Rptr. 2d 329 (Cal. Ct. App. 1995) ("In California, the doctrine of unclean hands may apply to legal as well as equitable claims . . . and to both tort and contract remedies.").

[54] *See* Unilogic, Inc. v. Burroughs Corp., 12 Cal. Rptr. 741 (Cal. Ct. App. 1992) (conversion); Pond v. Insur. Co. of N. America, 198 Cal. Rptr. 517, 522 (Cal. App. 1984) (malicious prosecution); Blain v. Doctor's Co., 272 Cal. Rptr. 250 (Cal. Ct. App. 1990) (legal malpractice); Burton v. Sosinsky, 250 Cal. Rptr. 33, 41 (Cal. Ct. App. 1988) ("California has taken the position that this defense is available in a legal action."); *see also id.* ("Although no case directly on point has been located, we see no reason why a successful defense of unclean hands should not bar the foreclosure of the mechanics' lien.").

[55] *Compare* Gen-Probe, Inc. v. Amoco Corp., Inc., 926 F. Supp. 948, 952 (S.D. Cal. 1996) (applying California law) (declaring the defense available to bar legal claims conversion claims in reliance on *Unilogic, Inc. v. Burroughs Corp.*), *with* Alan Klarik Enterprises, Inc. v. Viva Optique, Inc., No. B179607, 2006 WL 2423552 at *5 (Cal. Ct. App. Aug. 23, 2006) ("unclean hands applies not only to actions seeking equitable relief, but applies as well today as a defense to legal actions"); Travel America, Inc. v. Camp Coast To Coast, Inc., Nos. G028513, G028738, 2003 WL 558563 at *4 (Cal. Ct. App. Feb. 27, 2003) (unclean hands operates as a bar to the entire lawsuit asserting legal and equitable claims); Kendall-Jackson Winery, Ltd. v. Superior Court, 90 Cal. Rptr. 2d 743, 749 (Cal. Ct. App. 1999) ("The defense is available in legal as well as equitable actions.").

[56] 39 Cal. Rptr. 64 (Cal. Ct. App. 1964).

whether the equitable defense of unclean hands applies as a defense to a legal action.[57] It answered the question positively.[58] The court of appeals relied on language from prior California Supreme Court cases interpreting the merger of law and equity.[59] While unclean hands was not at issue, these decisions declared that "under the system of code pleading equitable defenses ... may be set up in actions at law."[60] Similar to the original English case of *Dering v. Earl of Winchelsea*,[61] the court of appeals in *Fibreboard Paper Prods. Corp.*, however, did not actually apply the defense because it found a lack of evidence to satisfy the doctrine's definitional elements.[62]

Goldstein v. Lees[63] followed *Fibreboard's* ruling that unclean hands is available in a claim for damages.[64] It then applied the doctrine to deny an attorney recovery for services rendered in violation of professional ethics rules.[65] *Pond v. Insur. Co. of No. America*[66] also followed *Fibreboard* in applying unclean hands to bar a claim for malicious prosecution.[67] The malicious prosecution cause of action in *Pond* was predicated on an unsuccessful indemnity suit filed by an insurer against an insurance agent arising out of a wrongful death action.[68] The agent knowingly withheld critical evidence and made other misrepresentations relevant to the insurer's defense

---

[57] *Id.* at 96. The court cited two prior California appellate court cases. *Id.* at 96–97. *A.I. Gage Plumbing Supply Co. v. Local 300 of the Internat. Hod Carriers, Building & Common Laborers Union of America*, 20 Cal. Rptr. 860 (Cal. Ct. App. 1962) indicated that unclean hands was available to deny the right to seek damages but did not find that the conduct constituted unclean hands and did not disclose whether any contention was made before the reviewing court that the defense was inapplicable. *Morrison v. Willhoit*, 145 P.2d 707 (Cal. Ct. App. 1944) dealt generally with the use of equitable principles in a legal demand and did not address the issue of unclean hands.

[58] *Id.* at 97–98 (declaring unclean hands available at law but refusing to dismiss the case because the plaintiff's alleged unclean conduct of contract breach and fraudulent misrepresentation was "not directed to the 'transaction' before the court in the instant case").

[59] *Id.* (citing Carpentier v. City of Oakland, 30 Cal. 439, 442 1866 WL 766 (Cal. 1866) (fraud) and Terry Trading Corp. v. Barsky, 292 P. 474, 478 (Cal. 1930) (accounting)).

[60] Terry Trading Corp. v. Barsky, 292 P. at 478.

[61] Dering v. Earl of Winchelsea, (1787) 29 Eng. Rep. 1184, 1185.

[62] The court determined there was no connection between the plaintiff's claim in tort and the defendant's alleged breach of contract and fraudulent misrepresentation. *Id.* at 98. "It would amount to a straining of the doctrine to hold that defendants found escape liability for tort because Fibreboard breached its contract or because it was guilty of fraudulent misrepresentations." *Id.* at 97.

[63] 120 Cal. Rptr. 253 (Cal. Ct. App. 1975).

[64] *Id.* at 255.

[65] *Id.* at 255 n.2 (Cal. Ct. App. 1975) (relying on unclean hands as alternative holding).

[66] 198 Cal. Rptr. 517 (Cal. App. 1984).

[67] *Id.* at 522.

[68] *Id.* at 521–23. The procedural history of the case is as follows: Insurer defended insured in wrongful death action under reservation of rights. *Id.* at 519. Insured filed declaratory judgment action against insurer. *Id.* Insurer filed cross-complaint against the agent who issued policy, alleging his actions weakened its position and caused it to settle the original personal injury lawsuit. *Id.*

in the underlying litigation that caused it to settle.[69] Because the agent's nondisclosures would have changed the outcome of the indemnity suit upon which he predicated his malicious prosecution claim, the court of appeals agreed with the trial court and barred his action for damages.[70]

Unilogic, Inc. v. Burroughs Corp.[71] further extended the application of unclean hands to a conversion claim.[72] The case involved a business dispute with both sides claiming various tort and contract violations arising out of a failed joint project to develop new technology.[73] Unilogic alleged that Burroughs tortiously converted its new technology.[74] Burroughs claimed unclean hands based on Unilogic's failure to return certain proprietary software upon termination of the joint development project as well as its use of the software in attempting to sell products to Burroughs's competitors.[75]

In considering the availability of unclean hands to bar the legal claim of conversion, the court found there was "scant authority on the subject."[76] It noted that *Pond* and *Goldstein* cited *Fibreboard* with approval for the general proposition that "[t]he unclean hands doctrine is not confined to equitable actions, but is also available in legal actions."[77] It then affirmed the trial court's decision to apply the defense because "Unilogic has not provided us with any reason, based on policy or otherwise, for holding that the unclean hands defense is never available in a legal action for conversion."[78]

---

[69] *Id.* at 519–20, 521–23. The court explained:

> The coverage issue in the defense of the wrongful death case was whether the lower pilot minimums were the ones agreed upon, an issue left ambiguous by Pond's conduct. It was upon this basis that the first suit was settled and INA's detriment incurred, largely a result of Pond's nondisclosures and misrepresentations.

Id. at 522.

[70] *Id.* at 522–23 (calling the agent's conduct in bringing the malicious prosecution action the "classic 'chutzpah'"). The court of appeals alternatively held that summary judgment was appropriate because the insurer relied on the good-faith advice of counsel negating the element of an absence of probable cause. *Id.* at 520–21.

[71] 12 Cal. Rptr. 741 (Cal. Ct. App. 1992).

[72] *Id.* at 745.

[73] *Id.* at 743.

[74] *Id.* at 743–44.

[75] *Id.*

[76] *Id.* at 745.

[77] *Id.* at 745 (citing Goldstein v. Lees, 120 Cal. Rptr. 253, 254 n.2 (Cal. App. 1975) ("The unclean hands doctrine is not confined to equitable actions, but is also available in legal actions.") and Pond v. Insur. Co. of N. America, 198 Cal. Rptr. 517, 522 (Cal. App. 1984) ("The doctrine [of unclean hands] is not restricted, however, to defense of suits in equity, but applies as well to suits at law.")). *Unilogic* also reviewed the recognition of the defense in Blain v. Doctor's Co., 272 Cal. Rptr. 250 (Cal. Ct. App. 1990), discussed *infra*, to bar a legal malpractice action. *Id.*

[78] *Id.* at 745. Citing both *Fibreboard* and *Unilogic*, the district court in Gen-Probe, Inc. v. Amoco Corp., Inc. applied California law and declared the defense available to bar legal claims in general and conversion claims in particular. F. Supp. 948, 952 (S.D. Cal. 1996) (applying California law). In Gen-Probe, Inc., two cases were pending before the court involving a business dispute over the ownership of a patent. *Id.* at 950. Gen-Probe, Inc. was seeking to

Another line of California authority supporting the adoption of unclean hands began in *Blain v. Doctor's Co.*[79] Without discussing *Fibreboard* or its progeny, the court of appeals in *Blain* applied the defense to bar a legal malpractice action arising out of a medical malpractice lawsuit.[80] The client brought the claim against his attorney after relying on his counsel's instruction to lie at his deposition.[81] In determining whether the perjury should constitute unclean hands, the court disregarded the application issue and focused on the policies of the doctrine.[82] Quoting Chafee, the court explained that the unclean hands standard "gets most of its qualities in a given group of cases from the substantive law of the particular subject."[83] It then analyzed two out-of-state legal malpractice cases from Oregon and Pennsylvania arising from criminal convictions before affirming the trial court's dismissal on grounds of unclean hands.[84]

The Pennsylvania case of *Feld and Sons, Inc. v. Pechner, Dorfman, Wolfee, Rounick, & Cabot,*[85] reviewed by the *Blain* court, applied a general principle of *in pari delicto.*[86]

---

expedite and consolidate discovery with the related case set for trial, where it was the defendant in order to better prepare its unclean hands defense. *Id.* The basis of its defense was the party opponent's filing of the related lawsuit with competitor funding. *Id.* at 951. While the court questioned whether the filing of a lawsuit could ever constitute unclean hands in the same case, it ultimately rejected the use of unclean hands because it found the funding issue unrelated to the specific issues in the complaint. *Id.* at 952.

[79] 272 Cal. Rptr. 250 (Cal. Ct. App. 1990).

[80] *Id.* at 255 (affirming dismissal on a finding that the unclean hands defense precluded physician's damages for emotional distress and loss of ability to practice medicine).

[81] *Id.* at 252.

[82] Blain v. Doctor's Co., 272 Cal. Rptr. at 254–55; *accord* London v. Marco, 229 P.2d. 401, 401 (Cal. Ct. App. 1951) (injunction) (misleading statements made to the court constitutes unclean hands); *In re* Marriage of Lazaro, No. A107473, 2005 WL 1332102 at *3 (Cal. Ct. App. June 6, 2005) (finding that presenting false testimony in a court proceeding in equity goes to the core of the unclean hands doctrine).

[83] Blain v. Doctor's Co., 272 Cal. Rptr. at 255.

[84] *Id.* at 258–59 (citing Kirkland v. Mannis, 639 P.2d 671 (Or. Ct. App. 1982) and Feld and Sons, Inc. v. Pechner, Dorfman, Wolfee, Rounick, & Cabot, 458 A.2d 545, 551–52 (Pa. Super. Ct. 1983)). The *Blain* court found the cases persuasive but differentiated them on the basis that recovery may have softened the effect of the penal sanction. *Id.* at 258.

[85] 458 A.2d 545 (Pa. Super. Ct. 1983).

[86] *See id.* at 551–52 (sustaining demurrers to the bulk of compensatory and punitive damages claims for malpractice and emotional distress); *see also id.* at 552–55 (denying the defense and allowing the action to proceed with respect to the claim for attorney fees on policy grounds). The Pennsylvania Superior Court in *Feld and Sons, Inc. v. Pechner, Dorfman, Wolfee, Rounick, & Cabot,* justified their application of *in pari delicto*:

> Were we to aid appellants – confessed perjurers – in their attempt to recover compensatory and punitive damages in excess of $250,000, we should indeed "suffer [the law] to be prostituted." For we should reward appellants, with a great deal of money, for their criminal conduct; we should soften the blow of the fines and sentences imposed upon them; and we should encourage others to believe that if they committed crimes on their lawyers' advice, and were caught, they too might sue their lawyers and be similarly rewarded.

Id. at 551–52.

The Oregon case of *Kirkland v. Mannis*[87] analyzed in *Blain* used unclean hands without discussion of its application in an action for damages.[88]

3.4.1.2 Oregon

Contrary to *Kirkland v. Mannis*, other Oregon appellate court decisions have reached the opposite conclusion.[89] In *McKinley v. Weidner*,[90] the same court had a chance to reconcile *Kirkland* with its prior ruling in *Gratreak v. N. Pacific Lumber Co.*[91]

In *Gratreak*, decided before the distinction between law and equity had been abolished in Oregon, the court rejected the defense of unclean hands in a legal action.[92] *Gratreak* distinguished the California Court of Appeals reading of the California merger in *Fibreboard* because it found Oregon's merger did not allow unclean hands.[93] *Kirkland* was arguably decided under the new *Oregon*

---

[87] 639 P.2d 671 (Or. Ct. App. 1982). The same court later acknowledged that it had erroneously relied solely on equity cases in applying unclean hands to a legal action. McKinley v. Weidner, 698 P.2d 983, 985 n.1 (Or. Ct. App. 1985).

[88] Kirkland v. Mannis, 639 P.2d at 671–73. In *Kirkland*, a prisoner claimed malpractice against his former criminal defense attorney because the attorney allegedly manufactured a story for his defense that formed the basis of his testimony. *Id.* at 671–72. Based on his acknowledged perjury, the court of appeals affirmed the trial court's dismissal on the basis of unclean hands. *Id.* at 673.

[89] Thompson v. Coughlin, 927 P.2d 146 (Ore. Ct. App. 1996), *rev'd on other grounds*, 997 P.2d 191, 196 n.9 (Ore. 2000) (unclean hands unavailable in actions at law); Gratreak v. N. Pacific Lumber Co., 609 P.2d 375 (Ore. App. Ct. 1980) (same); Beldt v. Beldt, 60 P.3d 1119, 1121 (Ore. App. Ct. 2003) (same).

Laches has also been denied in legal actions by the Supreme Court of Oregon. Corvallis Sand & Gravel Co. v. State Land Bd., 439 P.2d 575, 578 (Ore. 1968) (declaring its decision as the "prevailing view" and citing cases from New Jersey, Rhode Island, Arkansas, and Michigan). *See generally* Note & Comment, *Equitable Defenses to Actions at Law*, 34 Ore. L. Rev. 55 (1955) (reviewing conflicting authority under Oregon law regarding the application of unclean hands to legal actions).

[90] 698 P.2d 983, 985 (Or. Ct. App. 1985).

[91] 609 P.2d 375 (Ore. App. Ct. 1980).

[92] 609 P.2d at 378 n.7; *see also* OR. REV. STAT. § 11.020. In *Gratreak*, a former employee brought suit against his former employer claiming damages for tortious interference with his employment contract with a new employer. 609 P.2d at 376. The employer defended the case on the grounds that its conduct was justified under a valid restrictive covenant and presumably sought a declaratory judgment to that effect. *Id.* at 376–77. The employee responded to the employer's request to declare the restrictive covenant valid by seeking to foreclose the defense on grounds of unclean hands. *Id.* at 377; *cf.* T. Leigh Anenson, *Litigation Between Competitors with Mirror Restrictive Covenants: A Formula for Prosecution*, 10 STAN. J.L. BUS. & FIN. 1 (2005) (discussing UZ Engineered Prods. Co. v. Midwest Motor Supply Co., 770 N.E.2d 1068 (Ohio Ct. App. 2001), *appeal not allowed*, 766 N.E.2d 1002 (Ohio 2002) (precluding challenge to validity of a noncompete agreement based on the defense of estoppel under a similar procedural posture)).

[93] *Gratreak*, 609 P.2d at 378; *accord* Ellwood v. Mid States Commodities, Inc., 404 N.W.2d 174, 184 (Iowa 1987) (denying unclean hands at law despite the anomalous result that the same conduct may be a legal defense by another name).

Rules of Civil Procedure abolishing all procedural distinctions between law and equity.[94] As such, the two decisions would be consistent if the court chose to interpret the new civil rules as allowing unclean hands as a defense at law.[95] The court of appeals in *McKinley*, however, chose not to square its prior opinions in this manner. Instead, it held that *Kirkland's* reliance on unclean hands was misplaced and that *in pari delicto* should have been used to reach the same result.[96]

The Oregon Supreme Court subsequently granted *certiorari* to decide the application of unclean hands in a different case but decided the appeal on other grounds.[97]

3.4.1.3 Maryland

Like Oregon, the highest court in Maryland also circumvented the issue of availability of unclean hands in legal actions.[98] An intermediate appellate court in *Manown v. Adams*,[99] however, found the defense applicable to an action at law despite its equitable roots.[100]

The legal action in *Manown* requested repayment for a series of loans.[101] Adams filed the action to recover the funds, and Manown asserted unclean hands because Adams failed to list the transfer of assets in his bankruptcy proceeding and divorce action.[102] Essentially, Manown claimed that Adams defrauded both his wife and his creditors by hiding assets in Manown's name and perjured himself in the process.[103] Adams did not contest Manown's allegations but instead asserted that unclean hands is immaterial in an action at law.[104]

The appellate court disagreed.[105] It emphasized that unclean hands served to protect the court and to suppress illegal and fraudulent transactions.[106]

---

[94] McKinley v. Weidner, 698 P.2d at 985; *see also* ORE. R. CIV. PR. 2: "There shall be one form of action known as a civil action. All procedural distinctions between actions at law and suits in equity are hereby abolished, except for those distinctions specifically provided for by these rules, by statute, or by the Constitution of this state."

[95] 698 P.2d at 985.

[96] *Id.* at 985–86.

[97] Thompson v. Coughlin, 997 P.2d 191, 196 n.9 (Ore. 2000).

[98] Adams v. Manown, 615 A.2d 611, 617 (Md. 1992).

[99] 598 A.2d 821 (Md. Ct. Spec. App. 1991), *rev'd on other grounds*, 615 A.2d 611, 612 (Md. 1992).

[100] *Id.* at 826–27.

[101] *Id.* at 824.

[102] *Id.* One of the alleged loans included down payment on a house that Adams also did not claim any interest in his bankruptcy schedule. *Id.*

[103] *Id.* at 825.

[104] *Id.*

[105] *Id.* at 826. While the court of appeals accepted the trial court's ruling that unclean hands was applicable in the case, it ultimately reversed because it found the trial court erred in giving the issue of unclean hands to the jury. *Id.*; *cf.* Unilogic, Inc. v. Burroughs Corp., 12 Cal. Rptr. 741, 746–47 (Cal. Ct. App. 1992) (trial court did not err in having jury consider unclean hands defense when legal claim and equitable defense involved interrelated facts).

[106] 598 A.2d at 824–25.

The court then found such purposes to be furthered by the application of unclean hands in the case at bar.[107] It also relied on two cases from the high court in Maryland that applied the legal defense of *in pari delicto* as authority for the rule that unclean hands may be invoked to bar suits "at law and in equity."[108] The appellate court reasoned that *in pari delicto* is "merely a cognate principle to the clean hands doctrine," which justified the analogy.[109] The court additionally held that the "general trend" of merging procedures at law and equity supported its decision.[110]

As discussed previously, the Maryland Court of Appeals[111] eschewed making a decision on the basis of the clean hands doctrine on further appeal and found instead that the bankruptcy trustee was the real party in interest.[112] The dissent criticized the unannounced shifting of doctrinal focus.[113] These justices opined that the code merger was procedural only.[114] Referencing premerger precedent from Maryland and the United States Supreme Court, they concluded that unclean hands applies only in equity.[115]

---

[107] The court described court protection as "the idea being that judicial integrity is endangered when judicial powers are interposed to aid persons whose very presence before a court is the result of some fraud or inequity." *Id.* at 824; *see also* WinMark Ltd. P'ship v. Miles & Stockbridge, 693 A.2d 824, 834 (Md. 1997) ("'The clean hands doctrine is not applied for the protection of the parties nor as a punishment to the wrongdoer; rather, the doctrine is intended to protect the courts from having to endorse or reward inequitable conduct'"). The court of appeals also determined that deterring fraud is best accomplished by leaving the parties without remedy against each other. 598 A.2d at 825 (citing Roman v. Mali, 42 Md. 513, 533–34, 1875 WL 6172 at *12 (Md. 1875) ("The suppression of such illegal and fraudulent transactions is far more likely, in general, to be accomplished by leaving the parties without remedy against each other, and thus introducing a preventative check, than by enforcing them at the instance of one of the parties to the fraud[.]")); *see also* Bland v. Larsen, 627 A.2d 79, 85 (Md. Ct. Spec. App. 1993) (quoting *Manown, supra*).

[108] 598 A.2d at 825 (citing Messick v. Smith, 69 A.2d 478 (Md. 1949) and Shirks Motor Express Corp. v. Forster Transfer & Rigging Co., 133 A.2d 59 (Md. 1957)).

[109] 598 A.2d at 826 n.6.

[110] *Id.* at 826–27 (citing Md. Rule 2–301 (1991)). Relying in part on concerns over a jury trial, another Maryland appellate court had a contrary interpretation of the procedural unification in finding that laches may not be raised as a defense to a legal claim. *See* Smith v. Gehring, 496 A.2d 317, 322–23 (Md. App. 1985) (distinguishing between equitable affirmative relief and purely equitable defenses and holding that the procedural rules merging law and equity "do not extend to the elimination of distinctions between what defenses may be available to a legal claim as opposed to an equitable claim").

[111] Like New York, Maryland's court of last resort is called the "court of appeals."

[112] Adams v. Manown, 615 A.2d at 617; *accord* Universal Builders, Inc. v. Moon Motor Lodge, Inc., 244 A.2d 10, 15 (Pa. 1968) (refusing to apply unclean hands in part because it would penalize innocent creditors in bankruptcy).

[113] Adams v. Manown, 615 A.2d 611, 622 (Md. 1992) (Chasanow, J., joined by Bell, J., dissenting).

[114] *Id.* at 623.

[115] *Id.*

3.4.1.4 New York

Similar to the Maryland appellate decision of *Manown v. Adams,* two courts applying New York law found unclean hands applicable to legal relief by reference to the defense of *in pari delicto.*[116]

In *Smith v. Long,*[117] a New York appellate court allowed the defense of unclean hands to a legal claim when the conduct alleged a fraud on the government.[118] The plaintiffs sought damages for the failure to transfer stock under a buy-back agreement arising out of the formation of a corporation gone awry.[119] The plaintiffs had transferred their stock to one of the defendants after the Small Business Administration (SBA) denied their application for a minority business enterprise due in part to their ownership percentages.[120] The defendants asserted the claim should be barred under the doctrine of unclean hands because the plaintiffs had perpetrated a fraud on the SBA.[121] In reversing summary judgment to the plaintiff, the intermediate court of appeals declared that unclean hands was available in "law or equity."[122] Because the parties were allegedly accomplices in the same scheme, the court then defined the defense according to the parallel defense *in pari delicto.*[123] Subsequent decisions decided under New York law have followed *Smith* and barred legal claims on the basis of unclean hands without discussion of the application issue.[124]

Applying New York law before the decision in *Smith* and its progeny, the Second Circuit Court of Appeals also considered unclean hands to bar claims for legal relief

---

[116] Mallis v. Bankers Trust Co., 615 F.2d 68, 75 (2d Cir. 1980); Smith v. Long, 281 A.D.2d 897, 898 (N.Y. App. Div. 2001).

[117] 281 A.D.2d 897 (N.Y. App. Div. 2001).

[118] *Id.* at 898.

[119] *Id.* The plaintiffs sought specific performance and damages, *id.,* raising the question of whether the court considered its power to invoke unclean hands as a matter of resolving the requested legal relief under the equitable clean-up doctrine. *See generally* A. Leo Levin, *Equitable Clean-Up and the Jury,* 100 U. PA. L. REV. 320 (1951); John E. Sanchez, *Jury Trials in Hybrid and Non-Hybrid Actions: The Equitable Clean-Up Doctrine in the Guise of Separability and Other Analytical Problems,* 38 DEPAUL L. REV. 627 (1989). Other cases that appear to allow unclean hands at law concerned both legal and equitable relief. *See* Big Lots Stores, Inc. v. Jaredco, Inc., 182 F. Supp.2d 644, 652 (S.D. Ohio 2002); Urecal Corp. v. Masters, 413 F. Supp. 873, 876 (N.D. Ill. 1976).

[120] Smith v. Long, 281 A.D.2d at 897. The plaintiffs had also previously had problems with SBA loans. *Id.*

[121] *Id.* at 898.

[122] *Id.* The appellate held there was an issue of fact whether one of the plaintiffs executed the agreement to perpetrate a fraud on the SBA. *Id.*

[123] *Id.* at 898.

[124] *See* Craig v. Bank of New York, 169 F. Supp.2d 202, 210 (S.D.N.Y. 2001) (holding unclean hands bars breach of fiduciary duty and breach of contract claims under New York law); Bistricer v. Bistricer, 659 F. Supp. 215, 217 (E.D.N.Y. 1987) (indicating that unclean hands is available in legal action alleging breach of contract and fraud and noting that "both parties have treated the defense as applying to the claims under New York law"); *see also* Welch v. DiBlasi, 289 A.D.2d 964, 964 (N.Y. App. Div. 2001) (finding insufficient evidence of unclean hands without discussing its applicability due to the nature of the requested relief).

when the parties engaged in illegal activities.[125] In *Mallis v. Bankers Trust Co.*,[126] the plaintiffs brought an action under state and federal law to recover losses suffered from advancing money for the purchase of securities as a result of alleged misrepresentations by the defendant.[127] The defendant claimed that the plaintiffs also violated various state and federal laws in the securities transaction.[128] The court of appeals considered the defense of unclean hands against the pendant state common law claims of fraud and negligent misrepresentation.[129] It used the term *in pari delicto* in considering whether the same conduct barred the federal securities law claim.[130] Perhaps because the court equated two defenses,[131] it did not address the applicability of unclean hands to legal remedies and cited as support only cases applying the doctrine to bar equitable relief.[132]

In contrast to *Smith v. Long* and *Mallis v. Bankers Trust Co.*, other New York courts have rejected unclean hands as a defense in actions at law.[133] Thus, akin to Oregon,[134] New York cases are divided on the legal incorporation of unclean hands after the merger.[135]

[125] *See* Mallis v. Bankers Trust Co., 615 F.2d 68, 75–76 (2d Cir. 1980).

[126] 615 F.2d 68 (2d Cir. 1980).

[127] *Id.* at 69.

[128] *Id.* at 75. The defendant claimed that the plaintiffs agreement to advance funds for the purchase of securities violated the state statute prohibiting usury. *Id.* The defendant additionally asserted that the plaintiff falsely characterized the purpose of the loan in violation of federal law. *Id.*

[129] *Id.* at 75–76.

[130] The court ultimately found insufficient evidence of the defense because the plaintiffs' alleged unclean conduct had no connection to the subject matter of the litigation, did not cause injury, and was not equal in guilt to the defendant. *Id.* at 75.

[131] *See* Furman v. Furman, 178 Misc. 582, 586–87 (N.Y. Sup. Ct. 1941), *aff'd*, 262 A.D. 512, *aff'd*, 40 N.E.2d 643 (res judicata bars subsequent legal action based upon adjudication of unclean hands in prior equity suit because unclean hands has element of equal guilt and corresponds to *in pari delicto* defense at law). For cases differentiating unclean hands and *in pari delicto*, *see* discussion *infra* Chapters 5 and 6.

[132] Mallis v. Bankers Trust Co., 615 F.2d at 75.

[133] *See, e.g.*, Aetna Cas. and Sur. Co. v. Aniero Concrete Co., Inc., 404 F.3d 566, 607 (2d Cir. 2005) (applying New York law) ("Unclean hands is an equitable defense to equitable claims. Because [defendant-counter claimant] seeks damages in an action at law, Aetna cannot avail itself of unclean hands as a defense.") (citations omitted); In re Gulf Oil/Cities Service Tender Litigation, 725 F. Supp. 712, 742 (S.D.N.Y. 1989) (applying New York law); Manshion Joho Center Co. v. Manshion Joho Center, Inc., 24 A.D.3d 189, 190 (N.Y. App. Div. 2005) ("The doctrine of unclean hands is an equitable defense that is unavailable in an action exclusively for damages") (citing Hasbro Bradley, Inc. v. Coopers & Lybrand, 128 A.D.2d 218, 220 (N.Y. App. Div. 1987) ("nor can it invoke the equitable defense of unclean hands in this action exclusively at law")); Pecorella v. Greater Buffalo Press, Inc., 107 A.D.2d 1064, 1064 486 N.Y.S.2d 562, 563 (N.Y. App. Div. 1985); Morrisania II Assoc. v. Harvey, 139 Misc.2d 651, 662 (N.Y. City Ct. 1988).

[134] *See* discussion *supra* Section 3.4.1.2.

[135] The courts of New York returned to enforcing the distinction between law and equity in the pleadings even after the Field Code's abolishment of the distinction between actions at law and suits in equity. Ellen E. Sward, *A History of the Civil Trial in the United States*, 51 KAN. L. REV. 347, 385 (2003).

3.4.1.5 Michigan

Rather than ruling the merger does not prevent the universal use of unclean hands in law and equity remedies like the cases described from courts in California, Oregon, Maryland, and New York, Michigan courts have created an exception to the rule that unclean hands is inapplicable to legal claims in order to protect the court's ability to do justice in the present case.[136] Put simply, regardless of the relief requested, Michigan recognizes unclean hands on the basis of litigation misconduct in the case before the court.[137] In contrast to the Maryland case of *Manown v. Adams* and the California case of *Blain v. Doctor's Co.*[138] (involving perjury in previous litigation) or the New York case of *Smith v. Long*[139] (concerning other conduct possibly intended to defraud a government body), Michigan's accommodation for unclean hands in damages actions is more closely connected to the court protection purpose of the defense.[140] Michigan courts have justified the departure from precedent precluding unclean hands in legal actions under their inherent authority.[141]

In *Cummings v. Wayne Cty.*,[142] the court of appeals affirmed the trial court's decision to dismiss the case seeking monetary damages because the plaintiff in a personal injury case attempted to extort favorable evidence by threats and resorted to vandalism during the trial.[143] Finding that such flagrant misconduct of witness tampering posed a danger to the judicial process, the trial court found it had inherent authority to dismiss under the doctrine of unclean hands.[144] The appellate court agreed.[145]

The Michigan Court of Appeals distinguished a prior decision that denied unclean hands in actions at law for the reason that substantive distinctions survived the procedural merger.[146] Citing *Buchanan Home & Auto Supply Co., Inc.*

---

[136] *See, e.g.,* Maldonado v. Ford Motor Co., 719 N.W.2d 809, 818 (Mich. 2006).

[137] *Id.*

[138] 272 Cal. Rptr. 250 (Cal. Ct. App. 1990).

[139] 281 A.D.2d 897 (N.Y. App. Div. 2001).

[140] *See* discussion *supra* Chapter 6 (proposing four-phase procedural analysis for the legal incorporation of unclean hands by examining cases predicating the defense on (1) misconduct in the present litigation that potentially interferes with the process; (2) misconduct outside the present case that potentially interferes with the process; (3) misconduct in prior litigation that has no potential to interfere with the process; and, finally, (4) nonlitigation misconduct with no potential to interfere with the process) (citing cases).

[141] *See, e.g.,* Maldonado v. Ford Motor Co., 719 N.W.2d 809, 818 (Mich. 2006); Cummings v. Wayne Cty., 533 N.W.2d 13, 14 (Mich. Ct. App. 1995).

[142] 533 N.W.2d 13 (Mich. Ct. App. 1995).

[143] *Id.* at 13–15.

[144] *Id.* at 14.

[145] *Id.* (reviewing trial court dismissal under an abuse-of-discretion standard); *see also id.* (noting the civil rules permitting the court to dismiss an action for lack of progress and for discovery abuses).

[146] *Id.; see also* Clarke v. Brunswick Corp., 211 N.W.2d 101, 102–03 (1973) (denying both estoppel and unclean hands); *cf.* Grigg v. Robinson Furniture Co., 260 N.W.2d 898, 903 (Mich. Ct.

v. Firestone Tire & Rubber Co.,[147] it declared: "We do not believe that the [substantive-procedural] distinction prevents a court of law from invoking the 'clean hands doctrine' when litigation misconduct constitutes an abuse of the judicial process itself and not just a matter of inequity between the parties."[148] The court emphasized that the doctrine of unclean hands "applies not only for the protection of the parties but also for the protection of the court."[149]

It then quoted from *Hazel-Atlas Glass Co. v. Hartford-Empire Co.*,[150] where the United States Supreme Court invoked the historic power of equity to set aside a fraudulently begotten judgment:[151] "Tampering with the administration of justice . . . is a wrong against the institutions set up to protect and safeguard the public, institutions in which fraud cannot complacently be tolerated consistently with the good order of society."[152] The majority opinion in *Hazel-Atlas Glass Co.* did not discuss "unclean hands" as such,[153] but its ruling emphasized the same fundamental purpose of the doctrine by refusing to aid a litigant who had perpetrated "a deliberately planned and carefully executed scheme to defraud not only the Patent Office but the Circuit Court of Appeals."[154] The Michigan Court of Appeals in *Cummings* also cited *Precision Instrument Mfg. Co. v. Auto. Maint. Mach. Co.*,[155] a subsequent decision of the United States Supreme Court that specifically applied the doctrine of unclean hands in a suit in equity involving perjury in the patent process.[156]

App. 1978) (discussing the application of a different equitable defense than clean hands, the court explained: "At least since 1963, equitable and legal claims may be joined in a common complaint and equitable defenses may defeat legal claims.").

[147] 544 F. Supp. 242 (D.S.C. 1981). *Buchanan Home & Auto Supply Co., Inc.* applied unclean hands as a matter of federal law and is discussed *infra* at Chapter 3.4.2.

[148] *Cummings*, 533 N.W.2d at 14 (citing *Buchanan, supra*, at 244).

[149] *Id.* at 15.

[150] 322 U.S. 238, 246 (1944).

[151] *Id.* at 245 (explaining the facts before it "demands the exercise of the historic power of equity to set aside fraudulently begotten judgments").

[152] 533 N.W.2d at 14 (quoting *Hazel-Atlas Glass Co., supra*).

[153] *See* discussion *infra* Chapter 6 (noting that *Hazel-Atlas Glass Co.* decision is the seminal case for the doctrine of "fraud on the court"). Ironically, because the circumstances suggested that Hazel-Atlas Glass Co. knew about the fraud and benefited from it, the three justices in dissent raised the issue of unclean hands and preferred to have the district court resolve the dispute. 322 U.S. at 260–61, 270 (Roberts, J., dissenting, joined by Reed, J. and Frankfurter, J.); *see also id.* at 271 (Stone, C.J, concurring in the result).

[154] *Id.* at 245 (emphasizing that the fraud concerned more than the litigants). Hartford-Empire had manufactured evidence to obtain approval of a patent and prove its subsequent infringement. *Id.* at 240–41.

[155] Precision Instrument Mfg. Co. v. Auto. Maint. Mach. Co., 324 U.S. 806 (1945).

[156] *See Cummings*, 533 N.W.2d at 14; *Precision Instrument Mfg. Co., supra*, at 814–15, 819; *see also* Chapter 2 (discussing *Precision Instrument Mfg. Co.*). The appellate court in *Cummings* also relied on the Supreme Court's decision in *Roadway Express, Inc. v. Piper*, 447 U.S. 752, 764–65 (1980) that recognized the inherent power of courts to sanction litigation misconduct. *Cummings*, 533 N.W.2d at 14.

The *Cummings* decision has been followed in other appellate cases in Michigan.[157] In fact, the case was eventually cited with approval by the Supreme Court of Michigan in *Maldonado v. Ford Motor Co.*[158] The *Maldonado* court upheld the dismissal of a legal action alleging employment discrimination based on a party and her counsel's pretrial publicity of evidence intended to taint the jury pool.[159] Quoting *Cummings*, the Michigan Supreme Court announced the universal applicability of unclean hands based on litigation misconduct:

> The authority to dismiss a lawsuit for litigant misconduct is a creature of the "clean hands doctrine" and, despite its origins, is applicable to both equitable and legal damages claims ... The authority is rooted in a court's fundamental interest in protecting its own integrity and that of the judicial process ... The "clean hands doctrine" applies not only for the protection of the parties but also for the protection of the court.[160]

The Michigan Supreme Court rooted the trial court's dismissal power in its judicial authority under the state constitution.[161]

3.4.1.6 Rhode Island

Unlike Michigan, where the issue of fusion reached the state's highest court, a Rhode Island opinion allowing unclean hands to be pled against legal claims occurred at the trial level.[162] Matching other state courts incorporating the defense

---

[157] *See, e.g.,* Elite Publishing v. Wendover, No. 248971, 2004 WL 2533364 (Mich. Ct. App. Nov. 9, 2004) (relying on *Cummings* to uphold a trial court's authority to dismiss a lawsuit under the doctrine of unclean hands); *see also* Bygrave v. Van Reken, No. 218048, 2001 WL 672375 at *3 (Mich. Ct. App. May 4, 2001) (extending *Cummings* to include monetary sanctions not just dismissal); Beagele v. GMC, 2004 WL 2480484 at *1 (Mich. Ct. App. 2004) (same); Prince v. MacDonald, 602 N.W.2d 834, 836 (Mich. Ct. App. 1999) (extending the *Cummings* line of precedent without mentioning "unclean hands" for filing bad faith bankruptcy petition to delay proceedings).

[158] 719 N.W.2d 809 (Mich. 2006); *see also id.* at 817 n.15. *Contra* Russell v. White, 348 S.W.2d 548, 553 (Mo. 1964) (refusing to recognize unclean hands in a damages action and reversing trial court dismissal based on perjury).

[159] 719 N.W.2d at 826. The plaintiff and her counsel had repeatedly publicized evidence ruled inadmissible at trial. *See id.* at 811–16. The decision in *Maldonado v. Ford Motor Co.* was 4–3. The three dissenting judges found the dismissal of the case violated the plaintiff's right to free speech. *Id.* at 826–37 (Cavanaugh, J., dissenting) (Weaver and Kelly, JJ., concurring). One of the judges in a separate dissent also found there was no legal foundation for the dismissal. *Id.* at 837 (Weaver, J., dissenting).

[160] *Id.* at 818 (internal citations omitted) (quoting Cummings v. Wayne Co., 533 N.W.2d 13, 15 (1995), citing Buchanan Home & Auto Supply Co., Inc. v. Firestone Tire & Rubber Co., 544 F. Supp. 242, 244–245 (D.S.C., 1981)).

[161] *Id.* at 818–19; *see also id.* at 810. Consistent with *Maldonado*, courts around the country have remedied various kinds of litigation misconduct regardless of the relief requested under the doctrine of "fraud on the court." *See* discussion *infra* Chapters 5 and 6. Use of this doctrine obviates the need to address the effect of the consolidation of law and equity procedures on the defense of unclean hands.

[162] Bartlett v. Dunne, No. C.A. 89–3051, 1989 WL 1110258 (R.I. Super. Nov 10, 1989).

into the law, the ruling relied on the federal district court decision in *Buchanan Home & Auto Supply Co., Inc.*[163] as persuasive authority.[164]

The Rhode Island Superior Court decision in *Bartlett v. Dunne*[165] found that perjury warranted dismissal of a negligence claim for damages pursuant to unclean hands.[166] During the trial, plaintiff lied under oath regarding his alcohol consumption prior to the accident.[167] Because the court found that the "Plaintiff's deception is willful and it strikes at the very heart of the judiciary," it determined that a finding of contempt was insufficient and instead invoked unclean hands to dismiss the action.[168]

3.4.2 *Federal Court Adoption of Unclean Hands*

Federal courts have applied unclean hands to legal actions as a matter of federal law in both federal question and diversity cases.[169] As in state court jurisprudence,[170] some of the courts applied the defense without consideration of its application at law.[171] The following discussion analyzes federal court of appeals and district court decisions from the Fourth, Fifth, and Ninth Circuits as well as district court decisions from the Sixth, Seventh, and Eleventh Circuits.

3.4.2.1 Eleventh Circuit

A federal decision considering the applicability of unclean hands at law comes from the Eleventh Circuit. In *Boca Raton Community Hosp., Inc. v. Tenet Healthcare Corp.*,[172] the District Court for the Southern District of Florida denied the plaintiff's

---

[163] 544 F. Supp. 242 (D.S.C. 1981).

[164] Bartlett v. Dunne, 1989 WL 1110258, at *3; Cummings v. Wayne Cty., 533 N.W.2d 13, 14 (Mich. Ct. App. 1995) (citing *Buchanan Home, supra*, at 244).

[165] No. C.A. 89–3051, 1989 WL 1110258 (R.I. Super. Nov 10, 1989).

[166] *Id.* at *3; *accord* Smith v. Cessna Aircraft Co., 124 F.R.D. 103, 105–07 (D. Md. 1989) (pretrial perjury subject to unclean hands). For a discussion of *Smith, see infra* Chapter 6.

[167] *See* Bartlett v. Dunne, 1989 WL 1110258, at *2.

[168] 1989 WL 1110258, at *2–3.

[169] Some courts are not even clear upon which law (federal or state) they rely to either apply and/or define unclean hands. For instance, a New York district court sitting in diversity in *Gala Jewelry, Inc. v. Harring* appears to follow federal law. It declared that "[T]he law of this circuit restricts the 'unclean hands' doctrine to suits in equity, thereby categorically defeating defendant's attempted defense in this suit at law." No. 05 Civ. 7713(GEL), 2006 WL 3734202 at *2 n.3 (S.D.N.Y. Dec. 18, 2006) (quoting Aetna Cas. and Sur. Co. v. Aniero Concrete Co., Inc., 404 F.3d 566, 607 (2d Cir. 2005)). It also cited a federal decision from the U.S. Supreme Court. *See id.* (citing Keystone Driller Co. v. General Excavator Co., 290 U.S. 240, 245 (1933)). However, the Second Circuit decision actually applied New York law to determine the applicability of unclean hands to actions at law. *See Aetna Cas. and Sur. Co., supra.*

[170] *See* Mallis v. Bankers Trust Co., 615 F.2d 68 (2d Cir. 1980) (applying New York law); Blain v. Doctor's Co., 272 Cal. Rptr. 250 (Cal. Ct. App. 1990); Kirkland v. Mannis, 639 P.2d 671 (Or. Ct. App. 1982).

[171] *See, e.g.,* Big Lots Stores, Inc. v. Jaredco, Inc., 182 F. Supp.2d 644, 652 (S.D. Ohio 2002).

[172] No. 0580183CIV-SEITZ, 2006 WL 3716908 (S.D. Fla. Dec. 07, 2006).

renewed motion for class certification due in part to the potential availability of unclean hands as a defense to legal relief.[173]

Boca sued Tenet for federal civil Racketeer Influenced and Corrupt Organizations Act (RICO) violations due to its charging practices.[174] Tenet claimed unclean hands based on Boca's own charging practices.[175] In concluding that the viability of Tenet's unclean hands defense was "more than a mere possibility," thus justifying an order to deny class certification, the district court reviewed recent decisions from the Eleventh Circuit.[176] "Although not definitive," the district court found that the Eleventh Circuit's pronouncements on this issue in *Sikes v. Teleline, Inc.*,[177] and *Official Committee of Unsecured Creditors v. Edwards*,[178] "indicated that it would be receptive to Tenet's argument."[179] The court noted that in *Sikes*, the Eleventh Circuit suggested that civil RICO claims based on illegal gambling were rare because "plaintiffs may be barred from bringing such a claim by the 'unclean hands' doctrine."[180] Moreover, citing a decision that applied the defense of *in pari delicto* (corresponding to rulings from the courts of Maryland and New York), the district court relied on *Edwards*, wherein the Eleventh Circuit held that this related defense applies in civil RICO actions.[181] Furthermore, (similar to the rationale of the lower courts in California and Connecticut), the district court dismissed Boca's argument that the "Eleventh Circuit has never found the availability of [an unclean hands] defense to a civil RICO claim," with the rejoinder that "it is equally clear that the Eleventh Circuit has not held otherwise."[182] In light of the foregoing, the court ruled unclean hands a viable defense to a civil RICO claim for damages.[183]

---

[173] *Id.* at *15.

[174] *See id.* at *14.

[175] *See id.*

[176] *Id.* at *16.

[177] 281 F.3d 1350 (11th Cir. 2002).

[178] 437 F.3d 1145 (11th Cir. 2006).

[179] Boca Raton Community Hosp., Inc. v. Tenet Healthcare Corp., 2006 WL 3716908, at *16.

[180] *Id.* (quoting Sikes v. Teleline, Inc., 281 F.3d at 1366 n.41).

[181] *Id.* (quoting Official Committee of Unsecured Creditors v. Edwards, 437 F.3d. at 1155–56); *see also* Mallis v. Bankers Trust Co., 615 F.2d 68, 75–76 (2d Cir. 1980) (unclean hands considered to bar legal relief for state law claims and *in pari delicto* considered to bar the same conduct under the federal securities law claim); Manown v. Adams, 598 A.2d 821, 825–26 (Md. Ct. Spec. App. 1991), *rev'd on other grounds*, 615 A.2d 611, 612 (Md. 1992) (relying on *in pari delicto* to justify the application of unclean hands); Smith v. Long, 281 A.D.2d 897, 898 (N.Y. App. Div. 2001) (using *in pari delicto* interchangeably with unclean hands without discussion of any difference between them).

[182] *Boca Raton Community Hosp., Inc.*, 2006 WL 3716908, at *16; *see also* Unilogic, Inc. v. Burroughs Corp., 12 Cal. Rptr. 741 (Cal. Ct. App. 1992); First Fairfield Funding, LLC v. Goldman, No. CV020465799S, 2003 WL 22708882, at *1 (Super. Ct. Conn. Nov. 3, 2003).

[183] *Boca Raton Community Hosp., Inc.*, 2006 WL 3716908, at *16; *cf.* CGC Holding Company, LLC v. Hutchens, No. 11-CV-01012-RBJ-KLM, 2016 WL 3078986 at *5 (D. Colo. April 29, 2016) (commenting that there is "no definitive law at the circuit court level as to whether the equitable defense of 'unclean hands' could bar a civil RICO damages suit, and that such appellate law as does exist is mixed").

3.4.2.2 Fourth Circuit

The most widely cited opinion of unclean hands as a viable defense at law is *Buchanan Home & Auto Supply Co., Inc. v. Firestone Tire & Rubber Co.*[184] Sitting in diversity, the District Court for the District of South Carolina applied the doctrine to defeat claimed damages for warranty, tort, and contract violations.[185] A dealership sued Firestone for damages related to customer dissatisfaction with defects in a brand of its tires. Specifically, the plaintiff claimed it did not receive sufficient compensation for replacing and adjusting the unserviceable tires under the terms of its dealership agreement.[186]

Firestone paid the dealer a handling fee for each tire replaced and adjusted to account for its time replacing and adjusting tires.[187] The dealer also received billing credit as reimbursement for the cost of the replacement tire taken from its inventory.[188] Receipt of the handling fee and billing credit was conditioned on the return of the replaced tire along with an adjustment form signed by the customer.[189]

The dealership, however, admitted to a scheme of defrauding Firestone out of thousands of dollars by falsifying and forging the adjustment forms.[190] The forms would also be necessary for Firestone to defend against the dealer's claims because recovery would require a determination of how many legitimate warranty claims the plaintiff had to process.[191]

---

[184] Buchanan Home & Auto Supply Co., Inc. v. Firestone Tire & Rubber Co., 544 F. Supp. 242 (D.S.C. 1981), *cited in, e.g.*, Cummings v. Wayne Cty., 533 N.W.2d 13, 14 (Mich. Ct. App. 1995) (citing *Buchanan Home, supra*, at 244); Bartlett v. Dunne, No. C.A. 89-3051, 1989 WL 1110258 at *3 (R.I. Super. Nov 10, 1989) (same).

[185] Buchanan Home & Auto Supply Co., Inc., 544 F. Supp. at 245. The *Buchanan Home* opinion was authored by Judge Robert F. Chapman, who is now a Circuit Judge on the Fourth Circuit Court of Appeals. Despite diversity jurisdiction, the district court cited the federal rules and decisions for the proposition that unclean hands applies to bar legal relief. *See id.* at 245–47. So while it did not address the choice of law issue, the district court viewed the question of application as a matter of federal procedural law under the *Erie* Doctrine.
    The Fourth Circuit Court of Appeals relied on Maryland law to define unclean hands in an action between business partners. Lyon v. Campbell, 217 F.3d 839, 2000 WL 991650 at *3 (4th Cir. 2000) (first appeal) (applying Maryland law) (unpublished opinion) (reversing trial court's application of unclean hands for failing to disclose a conflict of interest in the potential sale as not sufficiently related to the breach of fiduciary duty claim to warrant application of the doctrine) (citing Manown v. Adams, 598 A.2d 821 (Md. Ct. Spec. App. 1991), *rev'd on other grounds*, 615 A.2d 611, 612 (Md. 1992)); Lyon v. Campbell, 33 Fed. Appx. 659, 665 (4th Cir. 2002) (second appeal) (applying Maryland law) (affirming trial court decision to impose equitable relief of constructive trust and to deny unclean hands based on false trial testimony because it was collateral to the main issues in the case).

[186] *Id.* at 246.

[187] *Id.* at 244.

[188] *Id.*

[189] *Id.*

[190] *Id.* at 245.

[191] *Id.* at 246.

In granting Firestone's motion to dismiss the complaint on grounds of unclean hands, the district court emphasized that the overriding reason for the defense is to protect the integrity of the court.[192] Because the dealership's presence in the courtroom suggested a danger to the administration of justice, the district court applied the defense and barred its claims for monetary relief.[193]

In reaching its conclusion that manufacturing evidence constitutes unclean hands, the district court drew an analogy to *Mas v. Coca-Cola Co.*,[194] in which the Fourth Circuit Court of Appeals applied unclean hands pursuant to its equity jurisdiction.[195] In *Mas*, the federal appellate court stated:

> No court of equity [or court of law in this instance] ought to listen to a man whose very presence suggests danger to the administration of justice and whose past conduct affecting the matter in litigation would cast doubt upon the ability of the court to ascertain from him the truth with respect thereto.[196]

As to its decision to apply unclean hands at law, the district court declared that "rights not suited for protection at equity should not be protected at law."[197] It also noted that Chafee and other twentieth-century commentators had called for the end to any distinction between law and equity after the integration.[198] It explained, "Court opinions and commentaries since the procedural merger of law and equity in 1938 have expressed the view that the clean hands doctrine embodies a general principle equally applicable to damage actions."[199]

While the "court opinions" referenced by the district court are not directly on point, they do embody the idea of equal application of unclean hands in principle. For example, in *Union Pac. R. Co. v. Chicago & N. W. Ry. Co.*,[200] the District Court of Illinois boldly proclaimed that "The clean hands maxim is not peculiar to equity, but expresses a general principle equally applicable to damage actions."[201] However, the case concerned only equitable relief. In making the statement, the

---

[192] *Id.* at 247.
[193] *Id.*
[194] 163 F.2d 505 (4th Cir. 1947).
[195] *Buchanan Home & Auto Supply Co., Inc.*, 544 F. Supp. at 245 (citing Mas v. Coca-Cola Co., 163 F.2d at 511). The plaintiff in *Mas* used forged documents and perjured testimony in a failed attempt to establish priority of invention before the Patent Office. *Id.* at 507; *see also* Universal Builders, Inc. v. Moon Motor Lodge, Inc., 244 A.2d 10, 15 (Pa. 1968) (citing *Mas* for the proposition that manufacturing evidence in the existing case constitutes unclean hands).
[196] Mas v. Coca-Cola Co., 163 F.2d at 511; *see also* Mas v. Coca-Cola Co., 198 F.2d 380, 381 (4th Cir. 1952) (upholding dismissal of patent action at law for damages, following dismissal on the ground of "unclean hands" of equitable suit involving same patent).
[197] *Buchanan Home & Auto Supply Co., Inc.*, 544 F. Supp. at 245.
[198] *Id.*
[199] *Id.*
[200] 226 F. Supp. 400 (D.C. Ill. 1964).
[201] *Id.* (citing CHAFEE, SOME PROBLEMS, *supra* note 44, at 94).

court was attempting to justify its analogy to a case seeking damages that involved an illegal contract made in violation of the securities laws.[202]

Additionally, the Fourth Circuit Court of Appeals decision in *Tempo Music, Inc. v. Myers*,[203] cited in *Buchanan Home*, arguably did not apply unclean hands to bar the legal claim asserted.[204] The case concerned a violation of federal copyright law, and the appellate court invoked unclean hands to defeat the request for equitable relief and equitable estoppel to estop the damages claim.[205] The district court in *Buchanan Home*, however, found *Tempo Music* to stand for the proposition that unclean hands applies "whether designated as the principle underlying clean hands or as equitable estoppel."[206]

Citing *Buchanan Home*, another district court within the jurisdiction of the Fourth Circuit dismissed a damages claim pursuant to unclean hands.[207] The District Court of Maryland in *Smith v. Cessna Aircraft Co.*[208] invoked the defense after the plaintiff lied during his deposition regarding his tax returns.[209] Among other damages, the plaintiff sought compensation for the income he lost recuperating from injuries resulting from the crash of his plane.[210] Because the plaintiff's pretrial perjury adversely affected an accurate assessment of potential liability, the court dismissed the claim relating to his lost income.[211]

---

[202] *See id.* (citing A. C. Frost & Co. v. Coeur d'Alene Mines Corp., 312 U.S. 38, 43 (1941)).

[203] 407 F.2d 503, 507–08 (4th Cir. 1969).

[204] *Buchanan Home & Auto Supply Co., Inc.*, 544 F. Supp. at 245.

[205] Tempo Music, Inc. v. Myers, 407 F.2d at 507, 508 n.8 (applying unclean hands when infringer requested list of copyrighted songs from owner that owner neglected to supply).

[206] *Buchanan Home & Auto Supply Co., Inc.*, 544 F. Supp. at 245 (*Tempo Music* "justified application of the clean hands principle to the damages portion of the suit by stating that principles of equitable estoppel would apply to deny the plaintiff its right to plead and prove the copyright infringement"); *accord* Metro Publ'g, Ltd. v. San Jose Mercury News, Inc., 861 F. Supp. 870, 880 (N.D. Cal. 1994) (citing *Buchanan Home* and *Tempo Music* as authority to apply clean hands to damages claims).

[207] *See* Smith v. Cessna Aircraft Co., 124 F.R.D. 103, 105–07 (D. Md. 1989); *see also* Stratton v. Sacks, 99 B.R. 686, 964 (D. Md. 1989) ("Although the clean hands doctrine is an equitable principle, *see* Mas v. Coca Cola Co., 163 F.2d 505, 507–08 (4th Cir. 1947), it has been applied by a district court in this Circuit to defeat an action at law. Buchanan Home & Auto Supply Co., Inc. v. Firestone Tire & Rubber Co., Inc., 544 F. Supp. 242, 245, 247 (D.S.C. 1981)."); McGovern v. Deutsche Post Global Mail, Ltd., No. Civ. JFM-04-0060, 2004 WL 1764088 at *10 n.6 (D. Md. Aug. 4, 2004) (noting in dicta that "[t]he clean hands doctrine originated in the courts of equity but now extends to actions at law.").

[208] 124 F.R.D. 103 (D. Md. 1989) (dismissing damages claim related to lost income).

[209] *Id.* at 105–07.

[210] *Id.*

[211] *Id.* at 105–07 (citing Buchanan Home & Auto Supply Co., Inc. v. Firestone Tire & Rubber Co., 544 F. Supp. 242, 246 (D.S.C. 1981) (plaintiff's fraud in submitting falsified adjustment forms to defendant "hopelessly obscure[d] any possibility of accurately resolving" validity of plaintiff's claim)). The court further explained that "the fact that the fraud and perjury are discovered before trial does not vitiate the taint upon the litigation process as a whole." *Id.*

3.4.2.3 Ninth Circuit

Notwithstanding its somewhat limited precedential foundation, the logic of *Buchanan Home* has been persuasive to federal courts in California that have relied on it and *Tempo Music, Inc.* in applying the equitable doctrine of unclean hands to bar actions for legal damages. Most of these decisions arose in claims under federal intellectual property law or state unfair competition law.[212] In copyright cases, unclean hands has even evolved into a special defense of "copyright misuse."[213]

The Ninth Circuit Court of Appeals in *Supermarket of Homes, Inc. v. San Fernando Valley Bd. of Realtors*[214] cited Fourth Circuit precedent in announcing that a legal action for copyright infringement may be barred by unclean hands where the copyright holder misused the copyright.[215] The District Court for the Northern District of California in *Metro Publ'g, Ltd. v. San Jose Mercury News, Inc.*[216] followed *Supermarket* in finding that unclean hands barred claims for damages on trademark infringement and dilution claims.[217] The district court also noted the decisions from the Fourth Circuit in support of its decision and quoted the following passage from *Buchanan Home*:

> Court opinions and commentaries since the procedural merger of law and equity in 1938 have expressed the view that the clean hands doctrine embodies a general principle equally applicable to damage actions, and that rights not suited for protection in equity should not be protected at law.[218]

---

[212] *See, e.g.*, McCormick v. Cohn, No. CV 90–0323 H, 1992 WL 687291, at *3 (S.D. Cal. July 31, 1992) (action for damages due to copyright infringement, trademark infringement, and unfair competition barred by unclean hands).

[213] *See* Sega Enterprises Ltd. v. Accolade, Inc., 785 F. Supp. 1392, 1399 (N.D. Cal.1992) ("The defense of copyright misuse is a form of unclean hands."), *aff'd in part, rev'd in part on other grounds*, 977 F.2d 1510 (9th Cir. 1992); Magnuson v. Video Yesteryear, No. C-92–4049 DLJ, 1994 WL 508826, at *5 (N.D. Cal. September 09, 1994), *aff'd in part, rev'd in part by on other grounds*, 85 F.3d 1424 (9th Cir. Jun 11, 1996) ("[Unclean hands] operates to deprive a copyright owner from asserting infringement and asking for damages when the infringement occurred by the claimant's dereliction of duty.") (citing *Supermarket*).

[214] 786 F.2d 1400 (9th Cir. 1986).

[215] *Id.* at 1408 (citing Tempo Music, Inc. v. Myers, 407 F.2d 503, 507 (4th Cir. 1969); Buchanan Home & Auto Supply Co., Inc. v. Firestone Tire & Rubber Co., 544 F. Supp. 242, 245 (D.S.C. 1981)). The court did not apply the defense because it found the facts did not constitute unclean hands. *Id.*

[216] 861 F. Supp. 870 (N.D. Cal. 1994).

[217] *Id.* at 880.

[218] *Id.* (quoting Buchanan Home & Auto Supply Co., Inc. v. Firestone Tire & Rubber Co., 544 F. Supp. 242, 245 (D.S.C.1981) (footnotes omitted)); *see also id.* (citing Tempo Music, Inc. v. Myers, 407 F.2d 503, 507, 507 n.8 (4th Cir. 1969) (barring legal recovery due to unclean hands where alleged infringer sought copyright holder's assistance to avoid infringing copyright and holder failed to assist)).

In addition to borrowing cases from the Fourth Circuit to apply unclean hands at law, Ninth Circuit precedent has had spillover effects in other federal circuits.[219]

3.4.2.4 Seventh Circuit

The District Court for the Northern District of Illinois in *Urecal Corp. v. Masters*[220] followed the Ninth Circuit decision in *Hall v. Wright*.[221] In a diversity action involving unfair competition, the *Urecal* court invoked the doctrine of unclean hands to bar both legal and equitable remedies.[222] Aware of the adoption issue in damages actions, the court explained that the federal rules left intact a distinction between law and equity only for purposes of determining the right to trial by jury.[223]

Urecal Corp. has been unanimously approved in other cases when legal and equitable relief is joined.[224] For instance, another Illinois district court in *Energizer Holdings, Inc. v. Duracell, Inc.*,[225] applied *Urecal* as authority to address unclean hands in a claim under the Lanham Act seeking both money damages and equitable relief.[226] *Urecal's* holding, however, has not been extended to cases solely seeking damages.[227]

---

[219] *See* Alcatel USA, Inc. v. DGI Techs., Inc., 166 F.3d 772, 792 n.80 (5th Cir. 1999) (explaining that the "copyright misuse" doctrine "has its historical roots in the unclean hands defense") (citing *Supermarket*).

[220] 413 F. Supp. 873 (N.D. Ill. 1976).

[221] *Id.* at 876. The district court reasoned: "In an unfair competition action like the case at bar, where equitable and legal claims are joined, the doctrine of 'clean hands,' if indicated by the facts, should preclude recovery on both claims." *Id.* (citing Hall v. Wright, 240 F.2d 787 (9th Cir. 1957) (affirming application of unclean hands)).

[222] *Id.* at 874; *see also id.* at 876 (alternatively holding there was insufficient proof of damages). Despite the state law claims, the court applied unclean hands as a matter of federal law. *Cf.* Am. Nat'l Bank & Trust Co. of Chicago, 404 N.E.2d 946, 948–49 (Ill. Ct. App. 1980) (citing premerger precedent of the U.S. Supreme Court to deny the defense in actions at law).

[223] Urecal Corp. v. Masters, 413 F. Supp. at 874 (citing Rogers v. Loether, 467 F.2d 1110, 1119 (7th Cir. 1972) (determining right to jury trial for compensatory damages under the Civil Rights Act of 1967)).

[224] Rauland Borg Corp. v. TCS Management Group, Inc., No. 93 C 6096, 1995 WL 242292, at *12–14 (N.D. Ill. April 24, 1995) (denying summary judgment on unclean hands asserted to bar right to injunctive relief or damages); Parkman & Weston Associates, Ltd. v. Ebenezer African Methodist Episcopal Church, No. 01 C 9839, 2003 WL 22287358, at *6 (N.D. Ill. Sept. 30, 2003) ("[I]n certain situations the clean hands doctrine may bar a claim at law for damages . . . For example, 'where equitable and legal claims are joined, the doctrine of 'clean hands,' if indicated by the facts, should preclude recovery on both claims.'") (internal citations omitted).

[225] No. 01 C 9720, 2002 WL 1067688 (N.D. Ill. May 28, 2002).

[226] *See id.* at *3. Other cases are in accord for Lanham Act claims, although they deny the defense for reasons other than its application at law. *See* Alpo Petfoods, Inc. v. Ralston Purina Co., 720 F. Supp. 194 (D.D.C. 1989), *aff'd in part and rev'd in part on other grounds*, 913 F.2d 958, 970 (D.C. Cir. 1990) ("The defense of unclean hands is available in an action brought under the Lanham Act seeking equitable and monetary relief."); Am. Home Prods. Corp. v. Johnson & Johnson, 654 F. Supp. 568, 590–92 (S.D.N.Y. 1987) (Lanham Act) (citing *Urecal*) (concluding that injunctive relief should not be denied based on unclean hands in light of public interest in the prevention of false and misleading advertising and precluding trial on damages for the reason that lost sales, profits, and good will could not be proven with any degree of reliability).

[227] *See* Lopez v. Autoserve, LLC, No. 05 C 3554, 2005 WL 3116053 (N.D. Ill. Nov. 17, 2005) (applying Illinois and federal law of unclean hands) (striking affirmative defense of unclean

At least one decision from the Seventh Circuit interpreting the federal rules appears to disagree and deem unclean hands available in actions exclusively seeking damages.[228] Soon after the merger, in fact, the court of appeals applied unclean hands to bar an action for damages under the Sherman Anti-Trust Act.[229] Citing Rule 2 of the Federal Rules of Civil Procedure, the court stated in *Maltz v. Sax*,[230] "As to unclean hands: the maxims of equity are available as defenses in actions at law."[231]

While the court has not addressed unclean hands since *Maltz*, the Seventh Circuit has indicated a willingness to continue this precedent. In *Byron v. Clay*,[232] for example, Judge Posner noted that while unclean hands is traditionally applicable to legal claims under the "clean up" doctrine in cases seeking both legal and equitable relief,[233] it should perhaps no longer be limited to equitable suits after the merger of law and equity.[234] He explained that even before the merger, *in pari delicto*, a corresponding doctrine to unclean hands barred damages if the plaintiff was as culpable as the defendant.[235]

Judge Posner's comments in *Maksym v. Loesch*[236] that considered the application of the purely equitable defense of laches at law were also telling:

> Not only is there a long tradition of applying equitable defenses in cases at law –
> indeed, fraud itself is an equitable defense typically interposed in suits at law for
> breach of contract – but with the merger of law and equity (Fed. R. Civ. P. 2) there
> is no longer a good reason to distinguish between the legal and equitable character
> of defenses, save as the distinction may bear on matters unaffected by the merger,
> such as the right to trial by jury in cases at law, a right preserved in federal courts by
> the Seventh Amendment . . .[237]

Relying on the meaning of the merger as announced in *Maltz* and *Byron*, district courts in Indiana have held all equitable defenses – including unclean hands – available at law.[238]

hands to bar violations of state and federal statutory employment law because the complaint
sought only legal damages).

[228] Maltz v. Sax, 134 F.2d 2 (7th Cir. 1943).

[229] *Maltz*, 134 F.2d at 5.

[230] 134 F.2d 2 (7th Cir. 1943) (citing 28 U.S.C.A. § 398 and Rule 2 of the Rules of Civil Procedure, 28 U.S.C.A. following section 723c).

[231] *Id.* at 5.

[232] 867 F.2d 1049 (7th Cir. 1989) (Posner, J.).

[233] *Id.* at 1052 (citing Medtronic, Inc. v. Intermedics, Inc., 725 F.2d 440, 442–43 (7th Cir. 1984) (Posner, J.)).

[234] *Id.* at 1053.

[235] *Id.* (citing Holman v. Johnson, 1 Cowp. 341, 98 Eng. Rep. 1120 (K.B.1775) (Mansfield, C.J.)).

[236] 937 F.2d 1237 (7th Cir. 1991) (Posner, J.).

[237] *Id.* at 1248 (ultimately determining that laches would not apply to legal relief under Illinois law).

[238] *See* Columbus Regional Hosp. v. Patriot Medical Technologies, Inc., No. IP 01–1404-C K/H, 2004 WL 392938 at *7 (S.D. Ind. Feb 11, 2004) (also citing Federal Rules 2 & 8) (denying

3.4.2.5 Sixth Circuit

Consistent with the decisions from the district courts in Illinois, the United States District Court for the Southern District of Ohio in *Big Lots Stores, Inc. v. Jaredco, Inc.*,[239] also indicated that unclean hands is available to bar a claim for damages in a business dispute requesting both legal and equitable relief.[240] Moreover, similar to the Northern District of Illinois in *Urecal Corp. v. Masters*,[241] the court relied on federal law to define unclean hands in a diversity case.[242] In contrast to *Urecal Corp.*, however, it did not explicitly discuss the extension of the defense to legal claims.[243]

In *Big Lots Stores, Inc.*, a creditor sued a debt collection agency, asserting state law claims for breach of confidentiality contract and conversion of customer accounts.[244] The agency claimed unclean hands barred the lawsuit on two grounds.[245] First, it contended that the creditor fraudulently attempted to induce it to begin performance of the proposed agreement for purchase of uncollected checks.[246] Second, it alleged that the creditor engaged in litigation misconduct by various activities that amounted to suborning perjury.[247] The court did not discuss the defense's application to legal claims but instead held that there was insufficient evidence to establish the defense.[248] The court also found the perjury claims to be "tangential" to the central issue in the case regarding breach of contract.[249]

---

summary judgment on affirmative defense of unclean hands as a matter of federal law in a diversity case); *see also* Decatur Ventures, LLC v. Stapleton Ventures, Inc., No. 1:04-CV-0562-JDT-WTL Slip Copy, 2006 WL 1367436 at *4 (S.D. Ind. May 17, 2006) (also citing Federal Rules 2 & 8), *order amended*, No. 104CV-00562-JDT-WTL, 2006 WL 3305122 (S.D. Ind. Aug. 16, 2006).

[239] 182 F. Supp.2d 644 (S.D. Ohio 2002).

[240] *Id.* at 653.

[241] 413 F. Supp. 873, 876 (N.D. Ill. 1976).

[242] 182 F. Supp.2d at 652–53. The court relied on precedent from United States Supreme Court, see Precision Instrument Mfg. Co. v. Auto. Maint. Mach. Co., 324 U.S. 806, 814 (1945) to define unclean hands and cited case law from the Sixth Circuit, see Kearney & Trecker Corp. v. Cincinnati Milacron Inc., 562 F.2d 365, 371 (6th Cir. 1977) to establish its burden of proof. *Id.* at 652. *But see id.* at 644 (West Headnotes stating that unclean hands was decided as a matter of Ohio law).

[243] *See id.* at 651.

[244] *See id.*

[245] *See id.* at 652–53.

[246] *See id.* at 653.

[247] *See id.* (alleging activities as obtaining a temporary restraining order, preparing false affidavits, and exchanging debt forgiveness for friendly affidavits).

[248] *See id.* at 654.

[249] *See id.* at 653 n.2 (noting that the litigation misconduct claims, at most, go to damages).

3.4.2.6 Fifth Circuit

The Fifth Circuit Court of Appeals in *Kuehnert v. Texstar Corp.*[250] permitted unclean hands to bar a tippee from recovering losses against an insider/tipper for providing false information in federal securities litigation.[251] Unlike the Seventh Circuit opinion considering unclean hands in another federal statutory action in *Maltz v. Sax,*[252] the Fifth Circuit made no mention of the merger of law and equity or any potential barrier to application of the equitable defense of unclean hands due to the law–equity distinction.[253] It focused exclusively on whether the application of unclean hands and the defense of *in pari delicto* were consonant with the policies of federal securities statute.[254] Like *Mallis v. Bankers Trust Co.*, the court of appeals used the defenses without discussion of any difference between them.[255]

Consequently, within the federal and state court systems, cases are incorporating the unclean hands defense into the common law and legislation through a combination of utility, intuition, and oversight. As addressed in what follows, a close examination of existing precedents also exposes the possibility for even broader application of the doctrine in the future.

3.5 THE FUTURE: FROM PEDIGREE TO POLICY

Sections 3.3 and 3.4 described the continuing conflict in the cases concerning the merger and its effect on the incorporation of unclean hands into the law. This

---

[250] 412 F.2d 700 (5th Cir. 1969).

[251] *Id.* at 704.

[252] 134 F.2d 2 (7th Cir. 1943) (citing 28 U.S.C.A. § 398 and Rule 2 of the Rules of Civil Procedure, 28 U.S.C.A. following section 723c).

[253] 412 F.2d at 703–05.

[254] *See id.* The majority explained: "The question must be one of policy: which decision will have the better consequences in promoting the objective of the securities laws by increasing the protection to be afforded the investing public." *Id.* at 704; *see also id.* at 703, 703 n.6 (citing cases establishing the availability of unclean hands in SEC proxy requirements and labor disputes). The dissent disagreed with the application of unclean hands on policy grounds. *See id.* at 705 (Godbold, J., dissenting); *accord* Nathanson v. Weis, Voisin, Cannon, Inc., 325 F. Supp. 50, 53 (D.C.N.Y. 1971); *see also* E.F. Hutton v. Berns, 682 F.2d 173, 176 n. 6 (8th Cir. 1982) (collecting securities law violation cases that either allow or deny the *in pari delicto* defense). Hence, the court divided solely on whether barring the lawsuit pursuant to unclean hands would promote the purposes of the federal securities statute. *See* Zygmunt J.B. Plater, *Statutory Violations and Equitable Discretion*, 70 CALIF. L. REV. 524 (1982) (suggesting courts have less remedial discretion in statutory versus common law or constitutional causes of action). For an analysis of the Supreme Court's *in pari delicto* cases in securities law, see T. Leigh Anenson, *Statutory Interpretation, Judicial Discretion, and Equitable Defenses*, 79 UNIV. PITT. L. REV. 1, 15 (2017) [hereinafter Anenson, *Statutory Interpretation*].

[255] *See* Kuehnert v. Texstar Corp. 412 F.2d at 704–05. *But see* Nathanson v. Weis, Voisin, Cannon, Inc., 325 F. Supp. at 52 (referencing the issue in *Kuehnert* as the application of *in pari delicto*). In *Mallis v. Bankers Trust Co.*, 615 F.2d 68 (2d Cir. 1980), however, the Second Circuit Court of Appeals considered unclean hands only against the pendant state claims.

section moves beyond an examination of the results to explore more thoroughly the reasons behind the emergent body of decisional rules incorporating unclean hands into the law and the principles upon which they stand. Understanding the premises of the precedents considering unclean hands provides inspiration for the future of the defense in damages or other legal actions.[256]

Significantly, decisions denying the defense at law have been made without the citation to any authority at all.[257] Certain courts citing decisional law also relied on opinions that predated the merger of law and equity[258] or that otherwise were not on point.[259] Moreover, cases rejecting the defense in damages actions are distinguishable because they contain qualifying language and have been subject to alternative holdings. For example, a review of those decisions denying the defense at law reveals some hesitancy in the holdings. Words such as "generally,"[260] "usually,"[261] or "traditionally"[262] precede the rule of denial. Hence, the Delaware Superior Court explained in *USH Ventures v. Global Telesystems Group, Inc.* that "[t]he defense of

---

[256] *See* Frederick Schauer, *Do Cases Make Bad Law?*, 73 U. CHI. L. REV. 883, 889–90 (Summer 2006) (discussing how the reasons for rules announced in decisions may have normative weight and constrain future decisions); *see also* Peter M. Tiersma, *The Textualization of Precedent*, 82 NOTRE DAME L. REV. 1187 (2007) (describing the textualization of the common law and the greater interpretative constraints on those who apply it).

[257] *See, e.g.*, General Dev. Corp. v. Binstein, 743 F. Supp. 1115, 1133–34 (D.N.J. 1990) (applying Florida, Connecticut, and Massachusetts law); Wilson v. Prentiss, 140 P.3d 288, 288 (Colo. Ct. App. 2006); Spitler v. Perry Town Lot & Improvement Co., 179 N.W. 69, 70 (Iowa 1920) (ruling without citation that unclean hands does not bar defenses, only affirmative equitable relief); Marvin E. Neiberg Real Estate Co. v. Taylor-Morley-Simon, 867 S.W.2d 618, 626 (Mo. Ct. App. 1993); Hasbro Bradley, Inc. v. Coopers & Lybrand, 128 A.D.2d 218, 220 (N.Y. App. Div. 1987); *see also* Am. Nat'l Bank & Trust Co. of Chicago v. Levy, 404 N.E.2d 946, 949 (Ill. Ct. App. 1980) ("Clearly, the equitable defense of unclean hands did not bar Hawthorn's action at law."); *cf.* Rodriquez v. Dicoa Corp., 318 So.2d 442 (Fla. Ct. App. 1975) (declaring there is "no authority is required" in reversing equitable attachment in legal action).

[258] *See* Merchants Indem. Corp. v. Eggleston, 179 A.2d 505, 514 (N.J. 1962) (citing federal premerger precedent from the United States Supreme Court).

[259] *See* discussion *supra* Section 3.3 (analyzing Wyoming decision denying unclean hands from precedent considering the defense to ban equitable relief and discussing Alabama case relying on purported decisional law to deny unclean hands in a damages action based on precedent that did not address the issue).

[260] Russell v. White, 348 S.W.2d 548, 553 (Mo. 1964) (discussing the "inapplicability of the doctrine *generally* in cases at law") (emphasis added); Universal Builders, Inc. v. Moon Motor Lodge, Inc., 244 A.2d 10, 15 (Pa. 1968) ("[I]t *generally* has been held that the doctrine operates only to deny equitable, and not legal, remedies.") (emphasis added); *see also* Clark v. Amoco Prod. Co., 794 F.2d 967 (5th Cir. 1986) (laches is "usually" available only in suits in equity); Sandobal v. Armour & Co., 429 F.2d 249, 256 (8th Cir. 1970) (laches is "rarely" invoked in an action at law).

[261] DiMauro v. Pavia, 492 F. Supp. 1051, 1068 (D.C. Conn. 1979) ("The principle of unclean hands is usually applied only to prevent affirmative relief . . .") (emphasis added).

[262] Nature's Prods. Inc. v. Natrol, Inc., 990 F. Supp.2d 1307, 1317 (S.D. Fla. 2013) ("The unclean hands doctrine traditionally only applies to equitable relief and does not bar a plaintiff from recovery of damages.").

'unclean hands' is *generally* inappropriate for legal remedies."[263] While the use of such conditional terms may express a willingness to find favor in the doctrine's application at law in the future, it also provides grounds for the court to create a policy exception like the *Cummings* and *Maldonado* courts in Michigan.[264] For instance, the District Court for the Southern District of New York in *Gala Jewelry, Inc. v. Harring*[265] struck an unclean hands defense to damages claims but appeared willing to explore opportunities of its application in the future: "Even if, as defendant insists, there may be exceptions to that rule where circumstances and justice require, ... this case presents no such exceptional circumstance."[266]

Another possible ground of distinction is hedging in the form of alternative holdings.[267] Such additional, independent reasons are frequently found in the decisions denying the defense in cases of legal relief. These include the failure to satisfy the elements of unclean hands[268] or that its application would be inconsistent with the policies or equities in the case.[269] Even cases refusing the defense against legal remedies exclusively due to its equitable origin can be explained on other grounds.[270]

Furthermore, the changing rationale in cases applying the defense in legal cases suggests less resistance to unclean hands in the future.[271] Indeed, despite the chaotic jurisprudence, the most promising aspect of the judicial reasoning process seems to

---

[263] USH Ventures v. Global Telesystems Group, Inc., 796 A.2d 7, 20 n.16 (Del. Super. 2000).

[264] *See* Maldonado v. Ford Motor Co., 719 N.W.2d 809, 818 (Mich. 2006) (creating exception to general rule against unclean hands in cases seeking legal relief on grounds of court protection); Cummings v. Wayne Cty., 533 N.W.2d 13 (Mich. Ct. App. 1995) (same).

[265] No. 05 Civ. 7713(GEL), 2006 WL 3734202 (S.D.N.Y. Dec. 18, 2006) (granting motion to strike unclean hands defense to damages claims for breach of contract, negligence, and conversion).

[266] *Id.* at *2 n.3 (citing *Keystone*, 290 U.S. at 245–46).

[267] *See* Weiss v. Smulders, 96 A.3d 1175, 1198 n.19 (Conn. 2014); Ellwood v. Mid States Commodities, Inc., 404 N.W.2d 174, 184 (Iowa 1987) (alternative holding). The courts *applying* the doctrine of unclean hands to bar legal relief have also found other grounds to support their decision. *See* Urecal Corp. v. Masters, 413 F. Supp. 873, 876 (N.D. Ill. 1976) (alternatively holding there was insufficient proof of damages even if unclean hands did not apply to bar legal relief).

[268] Courts typically find there is no connection between the case and the unclean conduct, see Karpierz v. Easley, 68 S.W.3d 565, 572 (Mo. Ct. App. 2002); Hasbro Bradley, Inc. v. Coopers & Lybrand, 128 A.D.2d 218, 220 (N.Y. App. Div. 1987); Birk v. Jackson, 75 S.W.2d 918, 920 (Tex. Ct. App. 1934), or that the conduct does not rise to the level of unclean hands, see Beldt v. Beldt, 60 P.3d 1119, 1122 (Ore. App. Ct. 2003). *See also* discussion *infra* Chapter 5.

[269] *See, e.g.*, Billes v. Bailey, 555 A.2d 460, 463 (D.C. 1989); Universal Builders, Inc. v. Moon Motor Lodge, Inc., 244 A.2d 10, 15 (Pa. 1968) (finding unclean hands inapplicable to legal claims as one of three alternative holdings).

[270] *See generally* Swisher v. Swisher, 124 S.W.3d 477 (Mo. Ct. App. 2003).

[271] One might read the Supreme Court's laches decision in *Petrella v. Metro-Goldwyn-Mayer, Inc.*, 134 S. Ct. 1962, 1967 (2014) to indicate a resistance to expanding equitable defenses across the boundary of law and equity. Nevertheless, the decision's rationale was specific to copyright regulation. *See* discussion *supra* note 206.

be a shift in attitude.[272] Many of the postmerger cases rejecting unclean hands did so without precedential support actually denying the defense in actions for damages.[273] The courts relied on an absence of authority applying the doctrine to legal claims and cited only equitable relief cases applying unclean hands.[274] Now, courts like *Unilogic* in California are making the opposite assumption.[275] Rather than requiring counsel to find cases that apply the defense at law, these courts mandate opposing counsel to find cases specifically rejecting it.[276] If none exist, the defense of unclean hands is available to defeat legal relief.[277]

Even courts following the law–equity distinction to dictate the denial of unclean hands in actions at law have found ways to invoke the defense by expanding the categories on both sides of the "equitable action or relief" equals "equitable defense" equation.[278] Courts apply unclean hands (or other equity-dependent doctrines) by construing the case or claim to be equitable in nature as opposed to origin.[279]

---

[272] *See* USH Ventures v. Global Telesystems Group, Inc., 796 A.2d 7, 19 (Del. Super. 2000) ("Courts of law have become increasingly flexible and have abandoned the worship of formalism and technicality that spawned the development of the split system of law and equity in England.").

[273] *See, e.g.,* Tarasi v. Pittsburgh Nat'l Bank, 555 F.2d 1152, 1156–57 n.9 (3d Cir. 1977) (stating rule without authority); Hill v. Estate of Allred, 216 P.3d 929, 935–36 (Utah 2009) (same); discussion *supra* Section 3.3.

[274] *See* Freemont Homes, Inc. v. Elmer, 974 P.2d 952, 959 (Wyo. 1999) (supporting denial of the defense solely from precedent considering unclean hands to ban equitable relief); *In re* Estate of Barnes, 754 A.2d 284, 288 n.6 (D.C. 2000) (denying unclean hands because "we know of no authority for applying this 'maxim of equity' to a legal claim for money"); discussion *supra* Section 3.3; *cf.* Keith Mason, *Fusion: Fallacy, Future or Finished?, in* EQUITY IN COMMERCIAL LAW 41, 72 (James Edelman & Simone Degeling eds., 2005) ("Chancery's unwillingness to award damages during the early nineteenth century was seen by some writers at the time to have been jurisdictional, in the sense of establishing an absence of power." (citing P.M. MCDERMOTT, EQUITABLE DAMAGES (Butterworths, Sydney, 1994)).

[275] *See* Boca Raton Community Hosp., Inc. v. Tenet Healthcare Corp., No. 0580183CIV-SEITZ, 2006 WL 3716908 (S.D. Fla. Dec. 7, 2006); Unilogic, Inc. v. Burroughs Corp., 12 Cal. Rptr. 741, 745 (Cal. Ct. App. 1992); *accord* Burton v. Sosinsky, 250 Cal. Rptr. 33, 41 (Cal. Ct. App. 1988) ("Although no case directly on point has been located, we see no reason why a successful defense of unclean hands should not bar the foreclosure of the mechanics' lien.").

[276] *See Boca Raton Community Hosp., Inc.,* 2006 WL 3716908, at *16; *Unilogic, Inc.,* 12 Cal. Rptr. at 745; *First Fairfield Funding, LLC,* 2003 WL 22708882, at *1.

[277] *Ibid.* Trial courts in Connecticut also followed the same rationale, see First Fairfield Funding, LLC v. Goldman, No. CV020465799S, 2003 WL 22708882, at *1 (Super. Ct. Conn. Nov. 3, 2003), before the Connecticut Supreme Court reasserted that the clean hands doctrine is only a creature of equitable relief. Weiss v. Smulders, 96 A.3d 1175, 1198 n.19 (Conn. 2014) ("[T]he equitable defense of unclean hands bars only equitable relief.").

[278] *See* discussion *infra* Chapter 5.

[279] *See* Sender v. Mann, 423 F. Supp.2d 1155, 1167–68 (D. Colo. 2006) (applying Colorado law) (finding bankruptcy trustee's fraudulent conveyance claims were equitable in nature and subject to unclean hands even though trustee only sought money damages); *see also* Corvallis Sand & Gravel Co. v. State Land Bd., 439 P.2d 575, 578 (Or. 1968) (reviewing case determining that quo warranto was equitable in nature despite being denominated as an action at law under the statute for the purpose of applying laches); C&K Engineering Contractors v. Amber Steel Co., 587 P.2d 1136, 1138–41 (Cal. 1978) (evaluating promissory estoppel for purposes of

This penumbra phenomenon can be seen in opinions referencing "quasi" equitable relief,[280] or, in contradistinction, "purely"[281] or "strictly"[282] legal rights.

Whether the foregoing circumstances reflect a changing attitude or not, it is enough to observe that a handful of states across the country have begun the process of assimilation.[283] An increasing number of federal courts have also applied the defense to bar legal claims.[284] In incorporating unclean hands into the law, courts focus their reasoning on the purpose of the merger statutes and rules.[285] They also use other authoritative sources of interpretation such as precedent in accepting that unclean hands can be considered in legal cases. For instance, courts ruling on cases of first impression are applying unclean hands at law by analogy to decisions recognizing comparable unclean conduct against equitable remedies[286] or against

determining the right to trial by jury); Philpott v. Super. Court in and for Los Angeles Cty., 36 P.2d 635, 640–41 (Cal. 1934) (discussing confusion with quasi-contract that originated in law but that is equitable in nature). _See generally_ SNELL'S PRINCIPLES OF EQUITY 6 (Robert Megarry & P.V. Baker eds., 27th ed. 1973) (discussing dual meaning of "equity"). As outlined _infra_ in Chapter 5, in many cases, it is difficult to discern the origin of the equitable claim or relief due to its mixed heritage.

[280] Ashley v. Boyle's Famous Corned Beef Co., 66 F.3d 164, 169 (8th Cir. 1995); Maksym v. Loesch, 937 F.2d 1237, 1248 (7th Cir. 1991) (laches); _see also_ Russell v. Casebolt, 384 S.W.2d 548, 553 (Mo. 1964) ("wholly or partially in equity").

[281] _Ashley_, 66 F.3d at 169; _Maksym_, 937 F.2d at 1248; _Corvallis Sand_, 439 P.2d at 578 (quo warranto).

[282] Am Nat'l Bank & Trust Co. of Chicago v. Levy, 39 Ill. Dec. 355, 357 (Ill. App. Ct. 1980) (unclean hands); _see also_ Clark v. Amoco Prod. Co., 794 F.2d 967, 971 (5th Cir. 1986) (laches).

[283] _See_ discussion _supra_ Section 3.4.1.

[284] _See_ discussion _supra_ Section 3.4.2.

[285] _See_ discussion _infra_ Chapter 4. A number of the opinions incorporating unclean hands into the law do not appear to acknowledge the historical distinction between the different kinds of equitable defenses based on their premerger pleading practices. _See, e.g.,_ Jesperson v. Ponichtera, 1990 WL 283884 at *1, No. CV88 0096615 S (Conn. Super. July 16, 1990) ("Another recognized principle is that equitable defenses may be interposed against actions at law.") (citing 1 AM. JUR. 2D § 7).

[286] _See_ discussion of cases _infra_ in Chapter 5. In reaching its conclusion that falsifying and forging evidence constitutes unclean hands in _Buchanan Home_, 544 F. Supp. 242 (D.S.C. 1981), the district court drew an analogy to _Mas v. Coca-Cola Co._, 163 F.2d 505 (4th Cir. 1947), in which the Fourth Circuit Court of Appeals applied unclean hands pursuant to its equity jurisdiction. _Mas_, 198 F.2d at 511; _see also_ Mas v. Coca-Cola Co., 198 F.2d 380, 381 (4th Cir. 1952) ("One who has had the door of a court of equity closed in his face because of his fraud may not have relief by the simple device of beginning again and labeling his suit an action at law for damages."); _see also_ Stratton v. Sacks, 99 B.R. 686, 964 (D. Md. 1989) ("Although the clean hands doctrine is an equitable principle, see Mas v. Coca Cola Co., 163 F.2d 505, 507–08 (4th Cir. 1947), it has been applied by a district court in this Circuit to defeat an action at law. Buchanan Home & Auto Supply Co., Inc. v. Firestone Tire & Rubber Co., 544 F. Supp. 242, 245, 247 (D.S.C. 1981)."). The Second Circuit Court of Appeals in _Mallis v. Bankers Trust Co._, 615 F.2d 68 (2d Cir. 1980), considered unclean hands against legal remedies and cited as support cases applying the doctrine to bar equitable relief. _Id._ at 75 (citing Weiss v. Mayflower Doughnut Corp., 135 N.E.2d 208, 210 (N.Y. 1956) and citing, _e.g._, National Distillers Corp. v. Seyopp Corp., 214 N.E.2d 361, 362–63 (N.Y. 1966)).

legal remedies although through kindred equitable defenses like *in pari delicto*[287] or equitable estoppel.[288] But the most persuasive principle seems to be policy.[289]

Courts are engaging in implicit and explicit policy analysis in incorporating unclean hands into the law.[290] An indirect policy-oriented approach is evident from the fact that some courts cite decisions allowing analogous legal and fully fused equitable defenses against legal relief, as well as cases applying unclean hands to equitable relief.[291] Justifying the application of unclean hands in damages actions by relying on the defense's use in equity cases levels the fictional severity or superiority

[287] See discussion *infra* Chapter 5, Section 5.3.2.2.1. As discussed *supra* Section 3.4, courts have also used the terms *in pari delicto* and unclean hands synonymously or relied on the similarity between them in justifying the availability of unclean hands in legal cases. *See, e.g.*, Blain v. Doctor's Co., 272 Cal. Rptr. 250 (Cal. Ct. App. 1990) (recognizing unclean hands at law by relying on the Pennsylvania case of Feld and Sons, Inc. v. Pechner, Dorfman, Wolfee, Rounick, & Cabot, 458 A.2d 545, 551–52 (Pa. Super. Ct. 1983) that applied a general legal principle of *in pari delicto*); Manown v. Adams, 598 A.2d 821, 825 n.6 (Md. Ct. Spec. App. 1991) (equating unclean hands and *in pari delicto* defenses), *rev'd on other grounds*, 615 A.2d 611, 612 (Md. 1992); Smith v. Long, 281 A.D.2d 897, 898 (N.Y. App. Div. 2001) (holding unclean hands applicable to legal relief by reference to the defense of *in pari delicto* and declaring unclean hands available in "law or equity"); Boca Raton Community Hosp., Inc. v. Tenet Healthcare Corp., No. 0580183CIV-SEITZ, 2006 WL 3716908 at *16 (S.D. Fla. Dec. 07, 2006) (relying on precedent applying the legal defense of *in pari delicto*). *But see* Russell v. White, 348 S.W.2d 548, 553 (Mo. 1964) (willing to apply illegality or against public policy but not unclean hands); Truitt v. Miller, 407 A.2d 1073, 1079–80 (D.C. 1979) (denying unclean hands defense in action at law despite noting its similarity to *in pari delicto*); Ellwood v. Mid States Commodities, Inc., 404 N.W.2d 174, 184 (Iowa 1987) (same). Judge Posner's dictum in *Byron v. Clay* also compared unclean hands and *in pari delicto* in concluding that unclean hands should no longer be limited to equitable actions. 867 F.2d 1049, 1052 (7th Cir. 1989). For a comparison of the defenses of unclean hands and *in pari delicto*, see *infra* Chapter 5.

[288] See discussion *infra* Chapter 5, Section 5.3.2.2.2. For cases, see, for example, Tempo Music, Inc. v. Myers, 407 F.2d 503, 507–08 (4th Cir. 1969); Buchanan Home & Auto Supply Co., Inc. v. Firestone Tire & Rubber Co., 544 F. Supp. 242, 245 (D.S.C. 1981). For the conversion of laches into an estoppel in order to apply the defense at law, see, for example, Davenport Osteopathic Hosp. Ass'n v. Hosp. Service, 154 N.W. 153, 162 (Iowa 1967); Moore v. Phillips, 627 P.2d 831, 835 (Kan. Ct. App. 1981); Maksym v. Loesch, 937 F.2d 1237, 1248 (7th Cir. 1991) ("It is really a doctrine of estoppel rather than a substitute for a statute of limitations."). In other countries that share the same common law heritage, there is discussion over the fusion of legal and equitable principles and doctrines by analogy. Anthony Mason, *Fusion, in* EQUITY IN COMMERCIAL LAW, *supra* note 274, at 11, 12.

[289] See discussion *infra* Chapter 5 (making a normative case for the availability of the clean hands doctrine against legal remedies on a case by case basis); *accord* T. Leigh Anenson, *From Theory to Practice: Analyzing Equitable Estoppel Under a Pluralistic Model of Law*, 11 LEWIS & CLARK L. REV. 633, 660 (2007) [hereinafter Anenson, *Pluralistic Model*] (suggesting that policy analysis be the preferred method of interpretation in equitable estoppel cases); *see also id.* at 659 (noting that equity has come to be regarded as public policy and that both equity and public policy promote the same purpose of change based on modern morality).

[290] See WILSON HUHN, THE FIVE TYPES OF LEGAL ARGUMENT 54 (2002) (tracing policy analysis to the "'ends-means'" philosophy of teleology) (citing ARISTOTLE, NICOMACHEAN ETHICS 3 (Oswald Trans. 1962)).

[291] HUHN, *supra* note 290, at 120 (explaining that deeming another decision a "precedent" based on a similarity in values is a form of policy analysis); *see* discussion *infra* Chapter 5.

between legal and equitable forms of relief.[292] These analogies also acknowledge equivalency between not only the conduct supporting these legal and equitable defenses but also the interests and purposes served by them.[293] In particular, by matching the kinds of conduct deserving dismissal in these decisions with unclean hands, courts are making a value judgment that litigants (and courts) should be treated the same in legal and equitable actions.[294] Courts are understandably moving toward coherence.

In addition to achieving policy objectives through the precedential form of analysis,[295] courts have also declared their policy preferences directly. In adopting unclean hands in legal cases, for example, the Superior Court of Connecticut concluded, "The integrity of the court is no less worthy of protection in actions at law, than in actions in equity."[296] The district court in *Buchanan Home and Auto Supply Co., Inc. v. Firestone Tire and Rubber Co.* likewise invoked unclean hands against claims for legal relief because "rights not suited for protection at equity

---

[292] CHAFEE, SOME PROBLEMS, *supra* note 44, at 29; Garvey, *supra* note 25, at 67–68; William J. Lawrence, III, Note, *The Application of the Clean Hands Doctrine in Damage Actions*, 57 NOTRE DAME L. REV. 673, 681 (1982) (calling for recognition of unclean hands in cases seeking legal relief because damages are often as severe as equitable remedies); *see* discussion *infra* Chapter 5, Section 5.3.2.3.

[293] HUHN, *supra* note 290, at 120 (explaining that judicial opinions become precedents by a matching of facts and/or values). Justice Cardozo found the practice of drawing analogies to the facts of the case without also considering the values involved incomplete: "Some judges seldom get beyond that process in any case. Their notion of their duty is to match the colors of the case at hand against the colors of many sample cases spread out upon their desk. The sample nearest in shade supplies the applicable rule." BENJAMIN N. CARDOZO, THE NATURE OF THE JUDICIAL PROCESS 20 (1921) [hereinafter CARDOZO, JUDICIAL PROCESS].

[294] Lionel Smith, *Fusion and Tradition* ("This goal [of treating like cases alike] is part of the rule of law, but only, I think, because it is rational to treat like cases alike, and if the law is not rational it loses it normative force."), *in* EQUITY IN COMMERCIAL LAW, *supra* note 274, 19, 23. Case analysis depends on what points of similarity and dissimilarity are deemed important. HUHN, *supra* note 290, at 120; *see also* Anenson, *Pluralistic Model, supra* note 289, at 611 ("The technique of developing grounds of decision based on reported judicial experience is an art."). How the judge answers the question of importance determines whether the prior decisional rule will be distinguished or applied. *See* STEVEN J. BURTON, AN INTRODUCTION TO LAW AND LEGAL REASONING 83 (1985); *see also* John Dickinson, *The Law Behind the Law II*, 29 Colum. L. Rev. 285, 290 (1929) (discussing the value judgments made by judges when choosing one analogy over another).

[295] Wilson Huhn presents the types of legal argument under his proposed pluralistic model of law as a "system" of legal reasoning techniques because they are interrelated. HUHN, *supra* note 290, at 81–82. In a single argument, one may utilize multiple arguments at the same time and in such a way that they may be distinguishable from each other. *Id.* (characterizing them as a cable rather than a chain).

[296] First Fairfield Funding, LLC v. Goldman, No. CV020465799S, 2003 WL 22708882 at *1 (Super. Ct. Conn. Nov. 3, 2003). As discussed *supra*, the Supreme Court of Connecticut held the law-equity line to limit the unclean hands defense to equitable relief. Weiss v. Smulders, 96 A.3d 1175, 1198 n.19 (Conn. 2014).

should not be protected at law."[297] In fact, it is the unity of facts and values between legal defenses and unclean hands that caused Professor Chafee's comment that the defense "ought not be called a maxim of equity because it is by no means confined to equity."[298]

The failure in many jurisdictions to consult equitable theories like unclean hands in legal cases that redress the same interests threatens to create inconsistencies across these analogous areas and endangers the overall capacity of the law to treat similarly situated parties the same.[299] The postmerger trend of adopting unclean hands into the law establishes that courts are no longer satisfied that traditional differences in form[300] support different treatment in substance.[301] What was equal in fact is becoming equal in law.[302] To be sure, courts seem less likely to ignore the outcome inconsistencies associated with the unequal treatment of unclean hands when the interests at stake are their own.[303] Thus, discrimination against unclean hands in legal cases is doubtful when the application of the defense achieves a targeted and

---

[297] *Buchanan Home*, 544 F. Supp. 242, 245 (D.S.C. 1981); *accord* Metro Publ'g, Ltd. v. San Jose Mercury News, Inc., 861 F. Supp. 870, 880 (N.D. Cal. 1994) (quoting *Buchanan Home*).

[298] Chafee I, *supra* note 1, at 878 (quoted in Messick v. Smith, 69 A.2d 478, 481 (Md. 1949)).

[299] *Accord* James Edelman & Simone Degeling, *Introduction* to EQUITY IN COMMERCIAL LAW, *supra* note 274, at 1 (advocating structural approach to the fusion of legal and equitable principles and doctrines in other common law countries); Mason, *Fusion, supra* note 288, at 15 ("There is no place for the inconsistent treatment of cases."); *see also* Mark P. Gergen, *Tortious Interference: How It Is Engulfing Commercial Law, Why This Is Not Entirely Bad, and a Prudential Response*, 38 ARIZ. L. REV. 1175, 1220–23 (1996) (noting the importance of identifying and reconciling the justifications underlying other ancillary bodies of law). Failing to account for similar policies and purposes in deciding cases is especially pernicious given that the historical differences in form have been eradicated with the merger of law and equity in most jurisdictions. Indeed, the doctrine of *stare decisis* embodies the ideal that like cases be treated alike. HUHN, *supra* note 290, at 16; *id.* at 41–43 (precedent supports the stability and predictability of law as a guide to future action).

[300] *See* William Searle Holdsworth, *The Relation of the Equity Administered by the Common Law Judges to the Equity Administered by the Chancellor*, 26 YALE L. REV. 1, 25–28 (1916) (discussing how the different remedies were a conflict in substantive rights and duties of citizens, but not a conflict in the form of the rules themselves); 1 AUSTIN WAKEMAN SCOTT, THE LAW OF TRUSTS § 1 (2d ed. 1956) ("There is no conflict in form . . . ; there is only a conflict in substance.").

[301] *See* Philpott v. Super. Court in and for Los Angeles Cty., 36 P.2d 635, 637 (Cal. 1934) (discussing the "parity of law and reason which governs both species of courts") (citing II COOLEY'S BLACKSTONE §436 at 1181–82 (4th ed.)).

[302] The "structural" approach to legal analysis that involves inferring rules from the relationship among ancillary doctrines was popularized by Philip Bobbitt, a Constitutional scholar, as one of six heuristic devices ("modalities") of interpreting the Constitution. PHILIP BOBBITT, CONSTITUTIONAL INTERPRETATION (1991). Wilson Huhn articulated a pluralist model of analysis that may be applied to all areas of the law and described Bobbit's structural, ethical, and prudential methods of legal reasoning as "policy" arguments consisting of a predictive portion and a value judgment. *See* Wilson R. Huhn, *Teaching Legal Analysis Using a Pluralistic Model of Law*, 36 GONZ. L. REV. 433, 456 (2000–01); BOBBIT, *supra*, at 12–13.

[303] *See* discussion *infra* Chapter 6 (citing cases illustrating that courts often consider the court protection policy paramount in applying unclean hands at law); *see also* Chafee I, *supra* note 1, at 895 (discussing the overall policy behind unclean hands is that "a court of justice should be very reluctant to do injustice").

immediate instrumental aim of court protection rather than merely furthering the overall, albeit more abstract, objectives of justice, fairness, and equality.[304] The recent decisions in Michigan, creating a policy-based exception to the conventional prohibition against unclean hands at law when litigation misconduct obstructs the judicial function, illustrates this phenomenon.[305]

Perhaps courts are still drawn to equity because it seems less possible (and rewarding) to approach the world through the myth of objectivity.[306] As in art or literature, similitude is often more revealing than verisimilitude.[307] Judges turn to equity and discretionary defenses like unclean hands to draw meaning from the bombardments of experience. With its malleability, ingenuity,

---

[304] *See* discussion *infra* Chapter 6 (proposing process-based theory of unclean hands where application at law is based on sliding scale between court and party protection); *see also* Anenson, *Pluralistic Model, supra* note 289, at 662–63 (listing similar policies for courts to create exceptions to the elements of equitable estoppel); *cf.* HUHN, *supra* note 290, at 135 (describing the range of policies as abstract values, instrumental concerns, or targeted societal goals).

[305] For conduct considered unclean hands that interferes with the judicial mission by tainting the jury pool, see Maldonado v. Ford Motor Co., 719 N.W.2d 809, 818 (Mich. 2006) or obstructing witness testimony, see Cummings v. Wayne Cty., 533 N.W.2d 13, 14 (Mich. Ct. App. 1995). *See also* discussion *infra* Chapter 6, Section 6.3.5.1 (citing similar cases from other states).

[306] *See* Morton J. Horwitz, *The Changing Common Law*, 9 DALHOUSIE L.J. 55, 62–63 (1984) (discussing the realist attack on the intellectual foundations of conceptualism and formalism); Nim Razook, *Obeying Common Law*, 46 AM. BUS. L.J. 55, 70 (2009) (discussing how realist scholars like Frank, Llewellyn, and Holmes saw their role as one of refuting legal determinism); *see also* HUHN, *supra* note 290, at 10–11 ("[The] rules of law do not describe objective truth, they reflect subjective intentions."); *accord* Edgar N. Durfee, *Foreword* to CHAFEE, SOME PROBLEMS, *supra* note 44, at x (commenting that Zechariah Chafee, Jr., a practitioner, professor, and scholar of equity jurisprudence, looked at law as a "kit of tools" to repair, sharpen, or redesign). Justice Cardozo described the diverse and opposing values served by law in attempting to do justice:

> The reconciliation of the irreconcilable, the merger of antithesis, the synthesis of opposites these are the great problems of the law .... We fancy ourselves to be dealing with some ultra-modern controversy, the product of the clash of interests in an industrial society. The problem is laid bare, and at its core are the ancient mysteries crying out for understanding.

BENJAMIN N. CARDOZO, THE PARADOXES OF LEGAL SCIENCE 4 (1928); *see also* O.W. Holmes, *The Path of the Law*, 10 HARVARD L. REV. 457, 467-68 (1897). (urging educators to train lawyers to consider the "social advantage" of the rule and to educate them to see that "they were taking sides upon debatable and often burning questions").

[307] In literary terms, a version of verisimilitude is where the reader is willing to suspend disbelief. *See* Robert P. Ashley, *What Makes a Good Novel*, THE ENGLISH JOURNAL 590, 596–98 (May 1971) (discussing Samuel Coleridge's version of verisimilitude); *see also* STANFORD ENCYCLOPEDIA OF PHILOSOPHY (2007) (noting that the literary idea of verisimilitude has been applied in the philosophical context). In legal parlance, verisimilitude could be equated to legal fictions like the labels "law" and "equity." *Cf.* Frederic M. Bloom, *Jurisdiction's Noble Lie*, 61 STAN. L. REV. 971 (2009) (characterizing the fixed and unyielding nature of jurisdiction as a noble lie in that it does not actually deceive); L.L. Fuller, *Legal Fictions*, 25 ILL. L. REV. 363, 367 (1930) ("For a fiction is distinguished from a lie by the fact that it is not intended to deceive.").

immediacy, and complexity, the doctrine of clean hands provides a fresh way to make sense of the world.[308]

Be it equity or law, however, the nature of jurisprudence is that it "often accretes by fragments, taking shape mosaically – its import visible only when one stands back and sees it whole."[309] "But the stories it tells may be no more than metaphors."[310] It is notable that both for and against use of the defense at law, decisions have been made without expressly considering the meaning of the merger.[311] Other opinions are ambiguous as to whether they are making new law and extending unclean hands to legal relief or are merely a remnant of the ancient equitable clean-up doctrine.[312]

---

[308] The equitable defense of unclean hands has been most recently suggested as a supplement to the regulatory regime in an effort to reduce or remedy excessive executive compensation. *See* Anenson & Mayer, *supra* note 8 (explaining unclean hands as a defense to contract law and outlining its use in the executive pay context). It has also been the basis for understanding the defense of inequitable conduct in patent law. *See* Anenson & Mark, *supra* note 26 (providing retrospective account of inequitable conduct based on unclean hands). Equity in general has been used to understand alternative dispute resolution, see Jacqueline M. Nolan-Haley, *The Merger of Law and Mediation: Lessons from Equity Jurisprudence and Roscoe Pound*, 6 Cardozo J. Conflict Resol. 57 (2004), administrative law, see Charles E. Clark, *The Handmaid of Justice*, 23 Wash. U. L.Q. 297, 303 (1938), and presidential powers, see Eric A. White, Note, *Examining Presidential Power Through the Rubric of Equity*, 108 Mich. L. Rev. 113 (2009). *Cf.* Anenson, *Pluralistic Model, supra* note 289, at 669 (concluding that the invocation of equitable estoppel enables juridical actors to create magic – what Pound called "juristic chemistry" – in resolving cases (quoting Roscoe Pound, *The Theory of Judicial Decision*, 36 Harv. L. Rev. 641, 643 (1923)) [hereinafter, Pound, *Theory*].

[309] Deborah Tall & John D'Agata, *The Lyric Essay*, Seneca Rev., http://www.hws.edu/senecareview/lyricessay.aspx (last visited June 30, 2018). What Helen Vendler says of the lyric poem is true of jurisprudence: "It depends on gaps … It is suggestive rather than exhaustive." *Id.* Another literary reference squares with the idea of common law making: "It might move by association, leaping from one path of thought to another by way of imagery or connotation, advancing by juxtaposition or sidewinding logic." *Id.* (describing the lyric essay as a genre of literature). As Holmes put it, through jurisprudence we might hope "to connect … with the universe and catch an echo of the infinite." Holmes, *supra* note 306, at 998.

[310] Tall & D'Agata, *supra* note 309.

[311] For courts applying unclean hands without discussion of its application to legal relief, see Mallis v. Bankers Trust Co., 615 F.2d 68 (2d Cir. 1980); Kuehnert v. Texstar Corp., 412 F.2d 700, 704 (5th Cir. 1969); Blain v. Doctor's Co., 272 Cal. Rptr. 250, 258–59 (Cal. Ct. App. 1990); Kirkland v. Mannis, 639 P.2d 671, 673 (Or. Ct. App. 1982), *discredited in* McKinley v. Weidner, 698 P.2d 983, 985 n.1 (Or. Ct. App. 1985); *see also* A.I. Gage Plumbing Supply Co. v. Local 300 of the Internat. Hod Carriers, Building & Common Laborers Union of America, 20 Cal. Rptr. 860 (Cal. Ct. App. 1962) (considering unclean hands in damages action without discussing the merger of law and equity), *cited in* Fibreboard Paper Prods. Corp. v. East Bay Union of Machinists, 39 Cal. Rptr. 64, 96 (Cal. Ct. App. 1964). Courts precluding unclean hands in actions at law tend to rely on premerger precedent or none at all. *See, e.g.,* General Dev. Corp. v. Binstein, 743 F. Supp. 1115, 1133–34 (D.N.J. 1990) (applying Florida, Connecticut and Massachusetts law); Wilson v. Prentiss, 140 P.3d 288, 288 (Colo. Ct. App. 2006); Marvin E. Neiberg Real Estate Co. v. Taylor-Morley-Simon, 867 S.W.2d 618, 626 (Mo. Ct. App. 1993); Hasbro Bradley, Inc. v. Coopers & Lybrand, 128 A.D.2d 218, 220 (N.Y. App. Div. 1987).

[312] *See* Big Lots Stores, Inc. v. Jaredco, Inc., 182 F. Supp.2d 644, 652 (S.D. Ohio 2002); Urecal Corp. v. Masters, 413 F. Supp. 873, 876 (N.D. Ill. 1976); *see also* Judith Resnik, *Constricting*

Lower federal courts in diversity actions do not consider the choice of state or federal law for the application and/or definition of unclean hands.[313] Nor do they seem to address their source of authority to apply unclean hands in statutory versus common law causes of action.[314] Significantly, these unanswered questions as to sources of law hold importance for the constitutional doctrines of separation of powers and federalism.[315]

The fact that some courts have not directly addressed the issue of incorporation (or related issues) involving unclean hands is perhaps a consequence of the omission of equity from the standard law school curriculum.[316] As a result, lawyers often advocate doctrines of law and equity without consciousness of the historic boundary between them.[317] The confusion surrounding some of these decisions is possibly also reflective of the lack of guidance from the courts of last resort.[318] Only in California

---

Remedies: The Rehnquist Judiciary, Congress, and Federal Power, 78 IND. L.J. 223, 254 (2003) (discussing the ambiguity left by the decision of *Grupo Mexicano de Desarrollo, S.A. v. Alliance Bond Fund, Inc.*, 527 U.S. 308 (1999) regarding the availability of equitable relief when both legal and equitable remedies are pled and whether the issue should be determined by discerning if equity "predominates" or alternatively, if it is "ancillary" or "incidental" to the legal relief claimed).

[313] *See* discussion *infra* Chapter 4, Section 4.2.2.

[314] *See* Kuehnert v. Texstar Corp., 412 F.2d 700, 704 (5th Cir. 1969) (finding application of unclean hands furthers the purposes of the statute); Bieter Co. v. Blomquist, 848 F. Supp. 1446, 1450–51 (D. Minn. 1994) (deciding the applicability of unclean hands in statutory cause of action per the policies of the statute). *See generally* Anenson, *Statutory Interpretation, supra* note 254 (identifying an unstated assumption of equitable defenses under silent statutes and analyzing possible bases for it).

[315] *See* discussion *infra* Chapter 6, Section 6.3.6 note 1408 (analyzing how the source of authority to invoke unclean hands has implications for the horizontal and vertical structures of our government); *see also id.* (discussing potential differences in implied power between the state and federal benches) (citing Judith S. Kaye, *State Courts at the Dawn of the New Century: Common Law Courts Reading Statutes and Constitutions*, 70 N.Y.U. L. REV. 1 (1995)).

[316] *See* discussion *supra* Chapters 1 and 2.

[317] Professor Laycock cites two cases to make the point that "judges and lawyers no longer understand what such references mean." Douglas Laycock, *The Triumph of Equity*, 56 LAW & CONTEMP. PROBS. 53, 81 (1993) [hereinafter Laycock, *Triumph of Equity*] (citing Mertens v. Hewitt Associates, 61 U.S.L.W. 4510, 4513 (June 1, 1993) and *In re* De Laurentiis Entertainment Group, Inc., 963 F.2d 1269, 1272 (9th Cir. 1992) (misdescribing quasi-contract as an equitable remedy)). Applying precedent that bans pure discretionary equitable defenses like unclean hands or laches, courts have erroneously banned fully incorporated equitable defenses like estoppel. *See* Howe v. Fiduciary Trust Co., 2001 Mass. Super. LEXIS 135, at *30–31 (Mass. Super. Ct. Apr. 19, 2001); Clarke v. Brunswick Corp., 211 N.W.2d 101, 102–03 (Mich. Ct. App. 1973); Russell v. Casebolt, 384 S.W.2d 548, 553 (Mo. 1964). While this oversight may initially appear to contribute to the fusion of law and equity, see Mason, *Fusion: Fallacy, Future or Finished?, supra* note 274, at 65, it actually adds to the lack of coherence and consistency in the law and undermines its development.

[318] *See* discussion *supra* Section 3.4 and *infra* Chapter 4. *See also* Robert J. Goldman, *Evolution of the Inequitable Conduct Defense in Patent Litigation*, 7 HARV. J.L. & TECH. 37, 67 (1993) ("Over a period of 37 years, various circuits experimented with three different standards of materiality and two different standards of intent.") (discussing the inequitable conduct defense derived from unclean hands before the creation of the Federal Circuit Court of Appeals). The

and Michigan has a high court accepted unclean hands.[319] The former decision expanded the defense to damages and yet constricted it in a statutory cause of action.[320] The latter decision applies the defense to legal relief in a potentially narrow class of cases involving litigation misconduct.[321] The United States Supreme Court has not taken a position on unclean hands during the seventy-five-year period following the consolidation of procedures in the federal system.[322] With the legal status of unclean hands unsettled in most federal and state jurisdictions, it is time for more courts to begin a conversation about the merger and what it now means for the defense of unclean hands. Notably, the fusion of unclean hands into claims for legal relief will likely have implications for other equitable defenses like laches that traditionally were exclusive to equity.[323]

lack of guidance from state supreme courts could be both a cause of the confusion in the lower courts and a consequence of the lack of education and training on equitable principles and doctrines. Notably, the U.S. Supreme Court has made errors in its decisions regarding what theories are historically equitable. John H. Langbein, *What ERISA Means By Equitable: The Supreme Court's Trail of Error in* Russell, Mertens, *and* Great-West, 103 COLUM. L. REV. 1317, 1351–54 (2003) (criticizing historical errors of the U.S. Supreme Court concerning what theories arose in equity in ERISA litigation); discussion *infra* Section 5.3.2.4 (discussing court difficulties in determining what is equity from law); *see also* Laycock, *How Remedies Became a Field*, *supra* note 13, at 168 (citing the Supreme Court's confusion over the tests for permanent and preliminary injunctions in *eBay Inc. v. MercExchange, L.L.C.*, 547 U.S. 388 (2006), as "a spectacular example of the confusion that can result from litigating a remedies issue without a remedies specialist").

[319] *See* discussion *supra* Section 3.4.

[320] *See* Salas v. Sierra Chem. Co., 327 P.3d 797, 812–13 (Cal. 2014), *cert. denied*, 135 S. Ct. 755 (2014).

[321] *See* Maldonado v. Ford Motor Co., 719 N.W.2d 809, 818 (Mich. 2006).

[322] The Supreme Court has not considered the issue of unclean hands despite expressly incorporating other equitable defenses like estoppel into legal actions even prior to the federal merger of law and equity in the 1938 *Federal Rules of Civil Procedure*. *See* Kirk v. Hamilton, 102 U.S. 68, 78 (1880) (declaring that "there would seem no reason why its application should be restricted in courts of law").

[323] *See* discussion *supra* Section 3.3. The Supreme Court had the opportunity to resolve the fusion debate over the equitable defense of laches in the context of Indian land claims but avoided it and ruled on other grounds. *See* Oneida County v. Oneida Indian Nation, 470 U.S. 226, 244 (1985) (discussing but not deciding whether equitable defense of laches applies to bar legal relief). *Compare* City of Sherrill v. Oneida Indian Nation, 544 U.S. 197 (2005) (invoking laches to bar equitable relief). The Second Circuit later adopted laches at law. *See* Cayuga Indian Nation of New York v. Pataki, 413 F.3d 266, 273 (2005). The legal adoption of laches in the area of Indian land claims has been the focus of scholarly attention. *See, e.g.*, Kathryn E. Fort, *The New Laches: Creating Title Where None Existed*, 16 GEO. MASON L. REV. 357 (2009). In the statutory area of copyright law, the Supreme Court preserved the traditional boundaries of laches. T. Leigh Anenson, *Equitable Defenses in the Age of Statutes*, 37 REV. LITIG. 529, 547–48 (2018) (examining the Court's 6–3 split on the issue of whether laches can block damages in *Petrella v. Metro-Goldwyn-Mayer, Inc.*, 134 S. Ct. 1962, 1967 (2014)). A way to explain the majority opinion in *Petrella* is that laches was preempted by the passage of the statute of limitations because the Court found the defense to undermine the legislative goals of certainty and uniformity. *Petrella*, at 1967 ("Courts are not at liberty to jettison Congress' judgment on the timeliness of suit."). The Court seemed to draw a negative inference against laches from the statutory provisions providing for a long duration of the copyright term, a short

A century ago, Roscoe Pound feared the disappearance of equity in a merged system.[324] Since then, scholars have debated the merits of more or less equitable principles and procedures in our unified systems.[325] But there has been consistent recognition by the legal community that the labels "law" and "equity" should cease to determine the outcome of cases where appropriate.[326] At minimum, my research on this subject aims to extend that reasoning to the equitable defense of unclean hands.

Critics may complain of unclean hands on its own merits – that the defense may encourage judges to go off on an uncharted course through interlocking webs of idea, circumstance, and language.[327] With any discretionary decision, there is the possibility of uncertain and inconsistent outcomes.[328] But before condemning the defense in this manner, courts should first expose unclean hands to the whole of law

time to sue for infringement, as well as a ceiling on damages. Anenson, *Statutory Interpretation, supra* note 254, at 17, 50 n.233 (reviewing the case). The Court recently extended *Petrella*'s holding in copyright law to patent law. SCA Hygiene Prods. v. First Quality Baby Prods., 137 S. Ct. 954, 959 (2017).

[324] *See* Roscoe Pound, *The Decadence of Equity*, 5 COLUM. L. REV. 20, 35 (1905) [hereinafter Pound, *Decadence of Equity*].

[325] *Compare* Main, *supra* note 17, at 495–514 (calling for more equity-like civil procedures); Stephen N. Subrin, *How Equity Conquered Common Law: The Federal Rules of Civil Procedure in Historical Perspective*, 135 U. PA. L. REV. 909, 975–1002 (1987) (arguing for less equity-like civil processes).

[326] *See, e.g.,* Douglas Laycock, *The Death of the Irreparable Injury Rule*, 103 HARV. L. REV. 687, 693 (1990) [hereinafter Laycock, *Death*]; Zechariah Chafee, Jr., *Foreword* to SELECTED ESSAYS ON EQUITY iii–iv (Edward D. Re ed., 1955); Laycock, *Triumph of Equity, supra* note 317, at 78; Pound, *Decadence of Equity, supra* note 324, at 35; *see also* RALPH A. NEWMAN, EQUITY AND LAW: A COMPARATIVE STUDY 29–30 (1961); Garvey, *supra* note 25, at 67. Certain judges agree with legal scholars on this point. *See* discussion *infra* Chapter 5, Section 5.3.2.3 (quoting Chancellor Quillen of the Delaware Court of Chancery) and *supra* Chapter 3 (quoting Federal Circuit Judge Posner).

[327] *See, e.g.,* HENRY L. MCCLINTOCK, HANDBOOK OF THE PRINCIPLES OF EQUITY § 26, 29 (1936) (noting that the "brevity and generality" of the maxims of equity "prevent them from having much utility" in predicting court action in a certain situation); discussion *infra* Chapter 5; *cf.* CARDOZO, JUDICIAL PROCESS, *supra* note 293, at 23 (quoting MONROE SMITH, JURISPRUDENCE 21 (1909)):

> The rules and principles of case law have never been treated as final truths, but as working hypotheses, continually retested in those great laboratories of the law, the courts of justice. Every new case is an experiment; and if the accepted rule which seems applicable yields a result which is felt to be unjust, the rule is reconsidered. It may not be modified at once, for the attempt to do absolute justice in every single case would make the development and maintenance of general rules impossible; but if a rule continues to work injustice, it will eventually be reformulated. The principles themselves are continually retested; for if the rules derived from a principle do not work well, the principle itself must ultimately be re-examined.

[328] Smith, *supra* note 294, at 38 (noting that uncertainty and inconsistency are two different vices of discretion). Notably, the lack of reconciliation between relevant legal and equitable bodies of law is also detrimental to the certainty and predictability of law. *See* T. Leigh Anenson, *Creating Conflicts of Interest: Litigation as Interference with the Attorney–Client Relationship*, 43 AM. BUS. L.J. 173, 205 (2006); Gergen, *supra* note 299, at 1221–22.

and not deprive litigants of its utility in an entire class of cases where they are seeking legal relief.[329] The experiential process of precedent moves legal precepts from the abstract to the particular and *placed*.[330] Eliminating an arbitrary and irrational legal barrier to unclean hands – a doctrine that is by turns formal and experimental, discursive and fragmentary – will allow courts to build, at the intersection of appearing law and disappearing equity, a defense that may account for and preserve the integrity of both.[331]

3.6 CONCLUSION

The merger of law and equity may not have remade the world of civil procedure, but it changed the terms of discourse sufficiently that expectations have been simultaneously raised and dashed.[332] Even the Herculean efforts of scholars have not been able to write

---

[329] See Smith, *supra* note 294, at 38 (discussing the relationship between equity and law and noting that discretion is not necessarily an injustice); *see also* discussion *infra* Chapter 6 (noting that attempting to eradicate unclean hands from our case law is not within the realm of reality as lawyers are asserting it and courts are listening). In addition to litigant protection by preventing opportunism, the defense of unclean hands also serves the interests of the court in providing a fair and impartial administration of justice. *See generally id.* (discussing a purpose of unclean hands as court protection and proposing a process-based theory of application); discussion *supra* Chapter 2.

[330] Wilson Huhn's insight was that standards evolve into rules through the use of formalistic analogies that identify the factual similarities in the cases that apply the standard. *See* Wilson R. Huhn, *The Stages of Legal Reasoning: Formalism, Analogy and Realism*, 48 VILL. L. REV. 305, 378–79 (2003). Rules evolve into standards through the use of realistic analogies that identify the interests justifying exceptions to the rule. *Id.* at 307 (proposing that precedent bridges the transition between formalism and realism and vice versa); *see also* Anenson, *Pluralistic Model, supra* note 289, at 643–51 (illustrating the phenomena in cases considering the equitable defense of estoppel).

[331] See Steve Hedley, *Rival Taxonomies Within Obligations: Is There a Problem?* ("A certain amount of theoretical incoherence is necessary price to pay for allowing both common law and equity to develop; allowing both to develop is necessary if they are not to become irrelevant to the needs of today."), *in* EQUITY IN COMMERCIAL LAW, *supra* note 288, at 77, 87. Professor Emily Sherwin reminds us that there is restraint in the common law construction process. Emily Sherwin, *A Defense of Analogical Reasoning in Law*, 66 U. CHI. L. REV. 1179 (1999) (explaining the benefits of judge-made law as providing numerous data for decision making, representing the collaborative efforts of judges over time, correcting the biases that might lead judges to discount the force of precedent, and exerting a conservative force in the law to change at a gradual pace); *see also* Anenson, *Pluralistic Model, supra* note 289, at 660 (discussing how equitable defenses are "built brick by brick on the backs of numerous judges bound by past precedents in saying what the law is – one case at a time"); Amy Coney Barrett, *Stare Decisis and Due Process*, U. COLO. L. REV. 1011, 1072 (Summer 2003) ("Allowing an issue to be hashed out multiple times compensates for the imperfections – the very humanness – in the process of decisionmaking. It allows the courts to see a more complete picture before rushing to judgment.").

[332] See Stephen B. Burbank, *The Bitter with the Sweet: Tradition, History, and Limitations on Federal Judicial Power – A Case Study*, 75 NOTRE DAME L. REV. 1291, 1292 (2000) ("It did not take long after Professor Chayes celebrated the 'triumph of equity' in public law litigation to

the labels "law" and "equity" into nonexistence.[333] And in the ensuing confusion over the status of unclean hands at law, conflicting decisions rule the day.[334]

This chapter has analyzed past and present adjudications of unclean hands that may have implications for its future. The digression into court decisions is an effort to explain the doctrinal role of the defense in legal cases. Assessing these episodes of legal adoption additionally helps to diagnose the impasse about the meaning of the merger in state and federal civil procedure that is at the heart of the debate over the legal incorporation of unclean hands. To be sure, the foregoing case-based analysis shows how competing concepts of "law" and "equity" crash into each other, leaving behind the smoking wreckage of dogma. The continued reliance on fictions developed during a long-obsolete form of judicial organization is the very antithesis of the time-honored tradition of equity in law.[335]

Understandably, law–equity talk will be abandoned when new arguments are sufficiently established to stand on their own.[336] Yet judges must be receptive to the idea of unclean hands at law for these new notions to take root. Roscoe Pound advised that decisional rules will not change until the picture of the law also changes in the minds of judges.[337] Unfortunately, given the number of cases rejecting or accepting unclean hands at law without discussion, the depiction of unclean hands

---

recognize that the announcement was premature – part prophecy, partly unfulfilled –at least if equity meant what he thought or hoped it meant.") (citing Abram Chayes, *The Role of the Judge in Public Law Litigation*, 89 HARV. L. REV. 1281, 1292 (1976)); *accord* James Edelman, *A "Fusion Fallacy" Fallacy*, 119 L.Q. REV. 375, 378 (2003) ("'[T]he dream has been a long time coming.' It seems, in Australia at least, that the dream still has some time to come.") (quoting Justice Mason of the New South Wales Court of Appeals in reference to Maitland's prophesy); *see also* Smith, *supra* note 294, at 26 n.37 (citing Mansfield and Blackstone as passionate advocates of substantive fusion).

[333] As discussed *supra* Section 3.5, Zechariah Chafee, among others, and more recently, Douglas Laycock have advocated the removal of the labels "law" and "equity" since unification. *Accord* ANDREW BURROWS, FUSING COMMON LAW AND EQUITY: REMEDIES, RESTITUTION & REFORM 44 (Hochelaga Lectures 2001, Hong Kong, 2002) (asserting "to see the two strands of authority, at law and in equity, moulded into a coherent whole"); Andrew Burrows, *We Do This at Common Law But That in Equity*, 22 OXFORD J. LEGAL STUD. 1 (2002); *see also* Smith, *supra* note 294, at 22 (noting that "terminological fusion, non-substantive in itself, is liable to lead to substantive fusion").

[334] *See* discussion *supra* Sections 3.3 and 3.4; *cf.* Mason, *Fusion* (noting confused state of equity in Australia due to lack of principled fusion), *supra* note 288, at 14.

[335] *See, e.g.,* Wesley Newcomb Hohfeld, *The Relations between Equity and Law*, 11 MICH. L. REV. 537, 567 n.23 (1913) (explaining that equity resulted in "a liberalizing and modernizing of the law" (quoting Pound)); Mason, *Fusion: Fallacy, Future or Finished?, supra* note 274, at 74 (commenting that "the Court of Chancery flowered 'to soften and mollify the Extremity of the Law'" (quoting Lord Ellesmere in his claim for equity's supremacy over Lord Coke's common law before James I)).

[336] Laycock, *Death, supra* note 326; *see also* CARDOZO, JUDICIAL PROCESS, *supra* note 293, at 35 (stating that the justification of judicial decisions ultimately depends on the judgment of lawyers).

[337] *See* Pound, *Theory, supra* note 308, at 660–61; *accord* Hohfeld, *supra* note 335, at 557 (noting how modes of thought and language may perpetuate the old dual system long after the merger of law and equity).

in legal cases seems to be gathering "more dust than light."[338] Surveying the legal landscape through the lens of unclean hands is meant to spotlight the debate to enable an accurate view of the defense that will (hopefully) stimulate contemplation over its social utility in the future.

Equity is hard law.[339] The surprising absence of scholarly commentary on the fusion of equitable defenses has surely contributed to the differing decisional law of unclean hands in cases seeking legal relief.[340] With the issue *sui generis* in many jurisdictions, the doctrinal analysis provided in this chapter may be a reference for those courts that find themselves suspended between progress and tradition, unable to move authoritatively in either direction.[341] Of course, the hermeneutic delay of our case law system means that whether unclean hands is a dinosaur or a phoenix can only be known in the fullness of time.[342] The foregoing case-based analysis is intended to enable an informed choice through the full exploration of the methodological stances of modern jurists who, like ancient chancellors, devote their energies and compassion to the search for just solutions.

---

[338] Studebaker Corp. v. Gittlin, 360 F.2d 692, 698 (2d Cir. 1966) (Friendly, J.) (discussing the irreparable injury rule of remedies). It would be better that courts address the matter of unclean hands at law directly and correctly. *See* NEWMAN, *supra* note 326, at 261 (noting that the indirect method of adoption is a form of common law resistance to the expansion of equity that retards wider acceptance of the doctrine).

[339] The difficulty of equity is recognized even in those countries that continue a strong equity tradition. Justice Gummow of the High Court of Australia explained that "[e]quity is hard law, even to those who have spent much of their professional lives wrestling with it." William Gummow, *Conclusion* to EQUITY IN COMMERCIAL LAW, *supra* note 288, at 515, 518. Disputes raising equitable theories tend to be legally and factually complex. The complicated nature of cases raising equitable issues is due in part to the historical content of the rules themselves as well as their foundation in philosophy. *See infra* Chapter 5, Section 5.3.2.4..

[340] Professor Samuel Bray has also taken up the topic. *See generally* Samuel L. Bray, *A Little Bit of Laches Goes a Long Way: Notes on Petrella v. Metro-Goldwyn-Mayer, Inc.*, 67 VAND. L. REV EN BANC, 1, 15 (2014).

[341] *See* Mason, *Fusion: Fallacy, Future or Finished?*, *supra* note 274, at 61 (commenting on the influence of judges and academics on the issue of fusion and the progress of the law); Karl N. Llewellyn, Paul Gewirtz, & Michael Ansaldi, *The Case Law System in America*, 88 COLUM. L. REV. 989, 991 (1988) (discussing Llewellyn's confidence that legal scholarship can contribute to the improvement of doctrine). Even in those jurisdictions that have a single precedent rejecting unclean hands in cases seeking legal relief, courts should reconsider its application at law. *See* Barrett, *supra* note 331, at 1072–74 (proposing that the precedential value of "thin" versus "thick" precedent is different in that "[i]t is the existence of the line of cases, not any one case, that gives a proposition its force").

[342] Dennis Patterson, *The Pseudo-Debate over Default Rules in Contract Law*, 3 S. CAL. INTER-DISC. L.J. 235, 272 (1993) ("Lawyers have always recognized the effects of 'hermeneutic delay' – that is, the meaning of today's precedent can only be known in the fullness of time."). Of course, there is the remote possibility of legislative correction explicating that unclean hands is available against causes of action seeking legal relief. Even the regulation of industries or other events, however, typically fails to explicate whether and when equitable defenses are available. *See* Anenson, *Statutory Interpretation*, *supra* note 254, at 8.

4

Interpreting the Merger

How absurd for us to go on until the year 2000 obliging judges and lawyers to climb over a
barrier which was put up by historical accident in 14th century England and built higher by
the eagerness of three extinct courts to keep as much business as possible in their own hands,
so that these hands might be full of fees!

— Zechariah Chafee, Jr.[1]

4.1 INTRODUCTION

The New York Field Code of 1848 marked the beginning of the end of a split system
of law and equity in this country.[2] The merger sparked a revolution culminating in
the Federal Rules of Civil Procedure almost one hundred years later.[3] Following the
unification in many states, the federal rules called for one form of action to which all
defenses – legal and equitable – could be pled.[4] This declaration reunited law and

---

[1] Zechariah Chafee, Jr., *Foreword* to SELECTED ESSAYS ON EQUITY iii, iv (Edward D. Re
    ed., 1955).
[2] Credit for the reform is given to David Dudley Field and his promulgation of the Field Code in
    New York that abolished common law forms and united law and equity in a simplified
    procedure in 1848. *See generally* Mildred Coe & Lewis Morse, *Chronology of the Development
    of the David Dudley Field Code*, 27 CORNELL L.Q. 238 (1942); *supra* Chapter 1. A proliferation
    of procedural codes soon followed in the other states and territories. *See* CHARLES E. CLARK,
    HANDBOOK OF THE LAW OF CODE PLEADING 19–20 (1928). The jurisdictions that did not
    model the procedural merger of law and equity on the New York Field Code amended their
    pleading rules to allow the assertion of equitable defenses in actions at law. *Id.*
[3] The 1938 Federal Rules of Civil Procedure were promulgated by the Supreme Court pursuant
    to Congressional authority. RALPH A. NEWMAN, EQUITY AND LAW: A COMPARATIVE STUDY 51
    (1961). Federal reform resulted in "essentially the same reforms" as the states. *Id.; see also*
    Samuel L. Bray, The *System of Equitable Remedies*, 63 UCLA L. REV. 530, 539 (2016) (relating
    that federal fusion of procedure was a long process that began with the Judiciary Act of 1789).
[4] Armistead Dobie, *The Federal Rules of Civil Procedure*, 25 VA. L. REV. 261 (1939); *see also* FED.
    R. CIV. P. 2; *supra* Chapter 1.

equity after five centuries of separation.[5] It was heralded as the "triumph of equity" that leveled jurisdictional and procedural barriers to the pursuit of substantive justice.[6]

In surveying American jurisprudence since that time, Douglas Laycock declared in his article "The Triumph of Equity" that the war between law and equity was over.[7] He explained how features once associated exclusively with equity had been absorbed in all areas of the law: remedies, procedure, and substance.[8]

While cautioning that distinctions still exist in theory as well as in practice, Laycock's principal point was to recast the debate between law and equity as simply a dialogue about the law.[9] Like Roscoe Pound,[10] Zechariah Chafee,[11] and other advocates of equity since unification,[12] he maintained that the content and application of a particular law in any given controversy should not depend on the historical happenstance of whether it originated in law or equity.[13] Because the historic boundary between law and equity was accidental and not functional, functional choices about the role of discretion, the method of adjudication, or an award of damages or specific performance should be considered outwardly and independently on their merits.[14]

This chapter advances Professor Laycock's thesis by studying postmerger precedent and the problems persisting in the adoption of the equitable defense of unclean hands. While the war *is* over for most equitable defenses that have been incorporated into the common law, the doctrine of unclean hands has yet to triumph. For this defense, a battle is still waging on the front lines of the courts, where antiquated distinctions are neither gone in theory nor forgotten in practice. Notwithstanding

---

[5]   Equity and law began in one system but were gradually split into two systems in the fourteenth century. *See* NEWMAN, *supra* note 3, at 22–23; George Burton Adams, *The Origin of English Equity*, 16 COLUM. L. REV. 87 (1916), *reprinted in* SELECTED ESSAYS ON EQUITY, *supra* note 1, at 5 ("Common Law and Equity originated together as one undifferentiated system in the effort of the king to carry out his duty of furnishing security and justice . . ."). The split was the result of power struggles between the English barons and the king. *See* William F. Walsh, *Equity Prior to the Chancellor's Court*, 17 GEO. L.J. 97, 100–06 (1929).

[6]   Many of the procedures adopted under the unified rules were products of equity. *See, e.g.,* Stephen N. Subrin, *How Equity Conquered Common Law: The Federal Rules of Civil Procedure in Historical Perspective*, 135 U. PA. L. REV. 909, 973–74 (1987). The rules also mandated that when a conflict arises between law and equity, equity wins. *See, e.g.,* Thomas O. Main, *Traditional Equity and Contemporary Procedure*, 78 WASH. L. REV. 429, 464 (2003).

[7]   Douglas Laycock, *The Triumph of Equity*, 56 LAW & CONTEMP. PROBS. 53, 53 (1993) [hereinafter Laycock, *Triumph of Equity*].

[8]   *See id.* at 54.

[9]   *See id.* at 78.

[10] *See* Roscoe Pound, *The Decadence of Equity*, 5 COLUM. L. REV. 20, 35 (1905).

[11] *See, e.g.,* Chafee, *supra* note 1, at iii–iv.

[12] *See* NEWMAN, *supra* note 3, at 29–30; John L. Garvey, *Some Aspects of the Merger of Law and Equity*, 10 CATH. U. L. REV. 59, 67 (1961).

[13] Laycock, *Triumph of Equity*, *supra* note 7, at 71; *see also* USH Ventures v. Global Telesystems Group, Inc., 796 A.2d 7, 14 (Del. Super. Ct. 2000) (describing Laycock as an "integrationist").

[14] Laycock, *Triumph of Equity*, *supra* note 7, at 78.

the merger of law and equity, a majority of courts deny the application of unclean hands in actions at law.

This chapter questions the jurisprudential objections to the adoption of unclean hands and aspires to change both reasons and results. It reconsiders the purpose of the procedural union and its unintended effect in court decisions that have either included or excluded the defense in damages actions. This chapter not only examines these opposing rationales regarding the merger but also reconciles them by proposing a new method to resolve the incorporation question. The compromise position suggests a case-by-case approach that is consonant with the text of the merger and the intent of the legislature(s). The goal is to provide a fresh look at a complex and important issue that courts can convert into practical, doctrinal application.

4.2 OVERVIEW

Section 4.3 discusses the premerger pleading of unclean hands under the dual court systems before the merger. Section 4.4 reviews the postmerger recognition of unclean hands at law in state and federal courts. Part 4.5 explains the meaning of the merger and how its misconception has mired the absorption of unclean hands into the law. The chapter concludes that judges should recognize their inherent power to absorb unclean hands in cases seeking legal remedies and cease the overt and unconscious prejudice against the defense.

4.3 PREMERGER PLEADING OF UNCLEAN HANDS

When courts administered law and equity in separate judicial systems before the merger, litigants pled unclean hands exclusively as a defense to an action for equitable affirmative relief in the court of chancery.[15] Equitable affirmative relief was that relief asserted in equity to defend against an action at law.[16] The defense of estoppel, for instance, was a form of affirmative relief.[17] The successful invocation of equitable estoppel in a court of chancery resulted in an injunction against a

---

[15] For a discussion of the general operation of the two systems, see FREDERICK WILLIAM MAIT-LAND, EQUITY AND THE FORMS OF ACTION 17 (Chayton ed. 1909); Willard Barbour, *Some Aspects of Fifteenth Century Chancery*, 31 HARV. L. REV. 834, 834 (1918).

[16] *See, e.g.,* SNELL'S PRINCIPLES OF EQUITY 12 (Robert Megarry & P.V. Baker eds., 27th ed. 1973) ("A plaintiff who had obtained a judgment in his favour in a court of law might be prevented from enforcing it by a 'common injunction' granted by the Court of Chancery, because in the opinion of the latter court he had obtained the judgment unfairly.").

[17] *See* Horn v. Cole, 51 N.H. 287, 290–91 (N.H. 1868) (listing two examples of estoppel against an action for trover of personal property and for writ of entry to land); T. Leigh Anenson, *The Triumph of Equity: Equitable Estoppel in Modern Litigation*, 27 REV. LITIG. 377, 384–87 (2008) [hereinafter Anenson, *Triumph of Equity*]; *see also* DOUGLAS LAYCOCK, MODERN AMERICAN REMEDIES 930 (4th ed. 2010) [hereinafter, LAYCOCK, REMEDIES] (citing fraud as another example).

common law action or judgment.[18] In contrast, chancellors invoked unclean hands only to defeat equitable relief (against the equitable action).[19] It was an equitable defense to equitable claims; it was not a defense to legal claims.[20] Other defenses like laches shared the same procedural posture.[21]

At the time of the merger, these "true" or "purely" equitable defenses continued to be used in the nature of affirmative equitable defenses as distinguished from defensive affirmative equitable actions.[22] Many other doctrines originating in equity, however, had been either converted to the legal realm and considered law or regularly applied in legal actions. In fact, the perception that parallel court systems were applying similar substantive rules under different procedural processes prompted integration.[23] The Supreme Court of California explained the equitable penetration of the common law:

> The distinction between strict law and equity is never in any country a permanent distinction. Law and equity are in continual progression, and the former is constantly gaining ground upon the latter. A great part of what is now strict law was formerly considered as equity, and the equitable decisions of this age will unavoidably be ranked under the strict law of the next.[24]

Defenses like fraud, duress, illegality, unconscionability, and accommodation derived from equity but were converted to law and often considered legal defenses.[25]

---

[18] *See* Horn v. Cole, 51 N.H. 287, 289–90 (N.H. 1868); Fleming James, Jr., *Right to a Jury Trial in Civil Actions*, 72 YALE L.J. 655, 679–81 (1963); *see also* 1A JOHN NORTON POMEROY, A TREATISE ON EQUITY JURISPRUDENCE AS ADMINISTERED IN THE UNITED STATES OF AMERICA §§ 181, 231 (Spencer W. Symons ed., Bancroft-Whitney 5th ed. 1941) [hereinafter POMEROY'S EQUITY JURISPRUDENCE, FIFTH EDITION] (explaining that the chancellor enjoined either the common law proceedings or the enforcement of the judgment).

[19] *See* Original Great Am. Chocolate Chip Cookie Co. v. River Valley Cookies, Ltd., 970 F.2d 273, 281 (7th Cir. 1992) (Posner, J.) ("Unclean hands is a traditional defense to an action for equitable relief."); Garvey, *supra* note 12, at 66.

[20] E.W. Hinton, *Equitable Defenses Under Modern Codes*, 18 MICH. L. REV. 717, 719 (1920) ("[T]here were equitable defenses to equitable claims, where there were no similar defense to corresponding legal claims.").

[21] *See, e.g.*, State ex rel. Comm. for the Referendum of Lorain Ordinance No. 77–01 v. Lorain Cty. Bd. of Elections, 774 N.E.2d 239, 247 (Ohio 2002) (discussing equitable doctrine of laches); *supra* Chapter 3.

[22] *See, e.g.*, Hinton, *supra* note 20, at 721 ("This development of an equitable cause of action into a legal cause of action, or into a defense to a legal action has been fairly common in the later period of the common law.").

[23] *See* William Searle Holdsworth, *Blackstone's Treatment of Equity*, 43 HARV. L. REV. 1, 7 (1929).

[24] Spect v. Spect, 26 P. 203, 205 (Cal. 1891) (quoting Lord Redesdale).

[25] *See* James Barr Ames, *Specialty Contracts and Equitable Defences*, 9 HARV. L. REV. 49 (1895) (discussing how the former equitable defenses of fraud, illegality, failure of consideration, payment, accommodation, and duress were subsequently recognized at law in specialty contracts); *see also* 3 POMEROY'S EQUITY JURISPRUDENCE, FIFTH EDITION, *supra* note 18, §§ 872–974a (discussing the contribution of equity to the law of fraud). "Originating in Equity as a form of relief against the harshness of penal bonds, [unconscionability] has been employed by courts to deny enforcement to harsh and unreasonable contract terms." Leasing Service Corp.

Others retained their equitable designation but were routinely recognized in actions at law.[26] Such equitable defenses included estoppel,[27] waiver,[28] rescission,[29] ratification,[30] and acquiescence.[31] Consequently, over hundreds of years, equity had made inroads in the law and resulted in its modification and amenability to notions of fairness and justice.[32]

4.4 POSTMERGER STATUS OF UNCLEAN HANDS

The advent of code pleading was said to complete the union of law and equity.[33] By calling for only "one form of action,"[34] jurists anticipated that the various legislatures recognized and approved the historical trend of absorbing equitable principles in all cases.[35]

---

v. Justice, 673 F.2d 70, 71 (2d Cir. 1982); *see also* U.C.C. § 2–302 (1990) (making unconscionability available at law or in equity).

[26] T. Leigh Anenson & Donald O. Mayer, *"Clean Hands" and the CEO: Equity as an Antidote for Excessive Compensation*, 12 U. PA. J. BUS. L. 947, 979–80 (2010).

[27] *See, e.g.*, Kirk v. Hamilton, 102 U.S. 68 (1880) (adopting equitable estoppel into the common law); *see also* William F. Walsh, *Is Equity Decadent?*, 22 MINN. L. REV. 479, 485 (1938) [hereinafter, Walsh, *Is Equity Decadent?*] (explaining that equitable estoppel was "fully adopted" in courts of law by 1938). There are various kinds of estoppel defenses besides equitable estoppel. *See* Anenson, *Triumph of Equity*, *supra* note 17, at 394–98 (comparing modern operation of equitable estoppel, judicial estoppel and quasi-estoppel).

[28] *See, e.g.*, USH Ventures v. Global Telesystems Group, Inc., 796 A.2d 7, 19 (Del. Super. Ct. 2000) ("Waiver has been, for some time, used at law as a valid defense to contract suits."); *cf.* LAYCOCK, REMEDIES, *supra* note 17, at 907 ("I have never been able to find out whether waiver originated in law or equity, but it no longer matters.").

[29] *See* 12A C.J.S. *Cancellation of Instruments* § 4 (1980); *see also* USH Ventures, 796 A.2d at 18 (noting that rescission is both a cause of action and a defense).

[30] *See, e.g.*, Colish v. Brandywine Raceway Ass'n, 119 A.2d 887, 892 (Del. Super. Ct. 1955). *See generally* 1 POMEROY'S EQUITY JURISPRUDENCE, FIFTH EDITION, *supra* note 18, § 69 (discussing ratification).

[31] *See* DAN B. DOBBS, DOBBS LAW OF REMEDIES: DAMAGES-EQUITY-RESTITUTION 44 (2nd ed. 1993) (discussing the invocation of acquiescence in purely legal cases).

[32] *See* Anenson & Mayer, *supra* note 26, at 979–80 (relating equitable defenses that developed in contract law); *see also* Oliver Wendell Holmes, *Early English Equity*, 1 L.Q. REV. 162, 162–63 (1885) (discussing substantive doctrines developed in chancery).

[33] *See* Charles E. Clark, *The Union of Law and Equity*, 25 COLUM. L. REV. 1, 10 (1925) [hereinafter Clark, *Union of Law and Equity*] ("The union of law and equity is justly considered to be the fundamental principle of the Code reform.").

[34] FED. R. CIV. P. 2 ("There shall be one form of action to be known as 'civil action.'").

[35] *See* discussion *supra* Chapter 3. *Compare* Ellen E. Sward, *A History of the Civil Trial in the United States*, 51 KAN. L. REV. 347, 385 (2003) (discussing how the original drafters of the Field Code intended to abolish "not only the forms but the 'inherent' distinction" between law and equity (quoting Clark, *Union of Law and Equity*, *supra* note 33, at 3)), *with* T.A. GREEN, A GENERAL TREATISE ON PLEADING AND PRACTICE IN CIVIL PROCEEDINGS AT LAW AND IN EQUITY UNDER THE CODE SYSTEM 51–52 (St. Louis, Mo., W.J. Gilbert 1879) (advising that the "substance of [common law and equitable actions] remains unchanged and wholly unchangeable, and cannot be united, fused or commingled into one by any human legislation").

4.4.1 *Procedural Union: Automatic Denial of Unclean Hands at Law*

The federal and state legislatures, however, limited the consolidation to the courts and their procedures.[36] The merger did not eliminate substantive differences between law and equity.[37] Substantive (as opposed to procedural) matters presumably include remedies and defenses asserted in response to them.[38] Because unclean hands was pled solely to defend against equitable remedies and had not yet been incorporated into law, most courts read the *procedural* union of law and equity to exclude the defense.[39] Under this interpretation, the historic distinction between the two kinds of equitable defenses survived the union of law and equity.[40]

Equitable defenses that were previously defensive affirmative equitable actions became viable defenses in legal actions. Affirmative equitable defenses did not. In this regard, Roscoe Pound's prediction at the turn of the twentieth century came true.[41] He feared we would lose (and confuse) equitable rules and principles after

---

[36] *See, e.g.*, NEWMAN, *supra* note 3, at 50–51. The fusion of law and equity under federal law was restricted to procedure with the Enabling Act providing that "said rules shall neither abridge, enlarge, nor modify the substantive rights of any litigant." *Id.* at 51 ("Like the field code, the reforms were directed exclusively to the procedural problem."); *see also id.* at 50 n.1 (discussing that the New York "legislative mandate to the Commissioners was reform in procedure – not alteration of the substantive rules of equity or the common law"). A leading treatise at the time of the federal merger stated that "the change … is one of procedure rather than remedy." BARRON & HOLTZOFF, FEDERAL PRACTICE AND PROCEDURE § 141 at 614 (1950).

[37] *See* Walsh, *Is Equity Decadent?*, *supra* note 27, at 480 ("Law and equity are simply brought together by code merger so that all relief, legal and equitable, may be applied in a single action without any change either of law or equity[.]"); *see also* Evans v. Mason, 308 P.2d 245, 248 (Ariz. 1957) ("The merger of these divisions of jurisprudence is a procedural one, and the substantive distinctions between equitable and legal remedies remain substantially unchanged."); Rodriguez v. Dicoa Corp., 318 So.2d 442 (Fla. Dist. Ct. App. 1975) ("No authority is required to support the statement that while our rules of procedure have been changed to substantially eliminate all distinctions between common law and equitable actions, the basic distinction between equity and law actions has been preserved."); Caudill v. Little, 293 S.W.2d 881 (Ky. Ct. App. 1956) ("While our new Civil Rules of Practice and Procedure abolish distinctions between a suit in equity and an action at law and provide that there shall be but one form of action, … the Rules do not affect the distinctions or rights of adjudication as between equity and law[.]").

[38] *E.g.*, 1–2 MOORE'S FEDERAL PRACTICE § 2.05 at 31–32 (2003) ("[T]here is no procedural barrier to the assertion of equitable defenses to legal claims"); Walsh, *Is Equity Decadent?*, *supra* note 27, at 489 ("Equitable defenses do not become legal defenses under Code merger."); *see also* WILLIAM Q. DE FUNIAK, HANDBOOK OF MODERN EQUITY § 8, at 15–17 (2d ed. 1956) (noting unification of law and equity in the United States was a merger of procedure and not substance). For a discussion of how Blackstone's paradigm of substance and procedure marginalized the law-equity distinction and facilitated the merger, see Main, *supra* note 6, at 453–64.

[39] *See* discussion *supra* Chapter 3.

[40] USH Ventures v. Global Telesystems Group, Inc., 796 A.2d 7, 20 (Del. Super. Ct. 2000). For a discussion of the same interpretation of equitable defenses given to the English procedural form, see Raymond Evershed, *Is Equity Past Child-Bearing?*, 1 SYDNEY L. REV. 1, 4 (1953).

[41] *See* Pound, *supra* note 10, at 35 (predicting the decline of equity after the fusion of courts and procedures).

the fusion of law and equity.[42] Newer equitable doctrines such as unclean hands got lost in the translation of the merger.[43]

As outlined in Chapter 3, several state supreme courts have denied unclean hands in lawsuits seeking damages due to its premerger status as an exclusively equitable defense. Other high courts indicated that they would reach the same result. Additionally, lower courts in a handful of states have uniformly found the defense unavailable to bar damages.

4.4.2 *Substantive Adjustment: Automatic Adoption of Unclean Hands at Law*

Based on an opposing interpretation of the merger, however, certain state and federal courts have begun to adopt unclean hands uniformly to legal and equitable relief. As chronicled in Chapter 3, lower courts from the states of California, Oregon, Maryland, New York, and Rhode Island have declared the doctrine of unclean hands available in actions at law.[44] Recently, the Supreme Court of California recognized the unclean hands defense in a damages action.[45] The Supreme Court of Michigan also approved a limited application of the doctrine against legal claims.[46] Furthermore, federal courts from the Fourth, Fifth, Sixth, Seventh, Ninth, and Eleventh Circuits have found unclean hands to be a viable defense in legal actions.[47]

---

[42] Pound, *supra* note 10, at 29.

[43] Robert S. Stevens, *A Plea for the Extension of Equitable Principles and Remedies*, 41 CORNELL L.Q. 351, 352, 354 (1956) (outlining textual debate regarding the definition of "equitable defenses"); *see also* Hinton, *supra* note 20, at 725 (discussing the three different views of pleading former equitable claims).

[44] An observation from the Nebraska Supreme Court on the equitable defense of laches indicates that it may apply clean hands to bar legal relief:

> The defense of laches is an equitable one ... The commonlaw rule is that equitable defenses cannot be used to defeat an action at law based upon contract; however, we have not accepted that position, but, on the contrary, we have held that any defense, whether it be legal or equitable, may be set up in any case.

Department of Banking and Finance of State of Neb. v. Wilken, 352 N.W.2d 145, 149 (Neb.1984); *see also* Marmo v. IBP, Inc., 2005 WL 675807, at *3 (D. Neb. Feb. 01, 2005) (applying Nebraska law) (relying on *Wilken* to declare the defense of unclean hands applicable to legal claims).

[45] *See* Salas v. Sierra Chem. Co., 327 P.3d 797, 812–13 (Cal. 2014), *cert. denied*, 135 S.Ct. 755 (2014); *supra* Chapter 3, Section 3.4.1.1.

[46] Maldonado v. Ford Motor Co., 719 N.W.2d 809, 818 (Mich. 2006); *supra* Chapter 3, Section 3.4.1.5. As discussed *infra* Chapter 6, the application of the unclean hands doctrine to legal actions in Michigan is limited to cases involving litigation misconduct that is potentially prejudicial to the fair administration of justice.

[47] When sitting in diversity, some federal courts have applied unclean hands to legal actions as a matter of federal law without discussion. *See, e.g.*, Urecal Corp. v. Masters, 413 F. Supp. 873, 874–76 (N.D. Ill. 1976); Buchanan Home & Auto Supply Co., Inc. v. Firestone Tire & Rubber Co., 544 F. Supp. 242, 244–45 (D.S.C. 1981); Columbus Regional Hosp. v. Patriot Medical

Certain opinions use a plain-language interpretation of the words "equitable defenses" that the merger codes and rules mention can be pled in actions at law.[48] State courts in California and Connecticut, in fact, bolster their conclusion by utilizing their own supreme court precedents declaring "equitable defenses" available at law in cases other than unclean hands.[49]

For instance, in *Fibreboard Paper Prods. Corp. v. East Bay Union of Machinists*,[50] a California Court of Appeals relied on language from prior California Supreme Court cases interpreting the merger of law and equity.[51] While unclean hands was not at issue, those decisions declared that "under the system of code pleading equitable defenses . . . may be set up in actions at law."[52] Similar to California, Connecticut trial courts have relied on the broad language of a case from that state's supreme court to hold unclean hands applicable to legal claims.[53] The trial courts have found it "well settled that equitable defenses or claims may be raised in an action at law."[54]

Technologies, Inc., No. IP 01–1404-C K/H, 2004 WL 392938, at *7 (S.D. Ind. Feb 11, 2004). *Contra* Chapter 3, *supra* Section 3.4.1.1 n. 46 (citing cases); *infra* Chapter 6, Section 6.3.4.

[48] *See* Fibreboard Paper Prods. Corp. v. East Bay Union of Machinists, 39 Cal. Rptr. 64, 89 (Cal. Ct. App. 1964); Jesperson v. Ponichtera, No. CV88 0096615 S, 1990 WL 283884, at *1 (Conn. Super. Ct. Jul 16, 1990); *see also* Gratreak v. N. Pacific Lumber Co., 609 P.2d 375, 379 (Or. Ct App. 1980) (Thorton, J., dissenting) (finding unclean hands applicable at law pursuant to statutory merger language of equitable "matters").

[49] *See Fibreboard*, 39 Cal. Rptr. at 97; First Fairfield Funding, LLC v. Goldman, No. CV020465799S, 2003 WL 22708882, at *1 (Conn. Super Ct. Nov. 3, 2003).

[50] 39 Cal. Rptr. 64.

[51] *Id.* at 97 (citing Carpentier v. City of Oakland, 30 Cal. 439, 442 1866 WL 766 (Cal. 1866) (fraud) and Terry Trading Corp. v. Barsky, 292 P. 474, 478 (Cal. 1930) (accounting)).

[52] Terry Trading Corp. v. Barsky, 292 P. 474, 478 (Cal. 1930). In Carpentier v. City of Oakland, 30 Cal. 439 (Cal. 1866), the court stated:

> Under our system of practice, a defendant is allowed to set up as many defences as he may have, regardless of the question as to whether they are of a legal or equitable nature, because the distinction which exists under the common law system between actions at law and suits in equity and the forms thereof have been abolished.

Id. at 442. However, a later case from the Supreme Court of California considering the right to trial by jury found that "cases legal and equitable have not been consolidated . . . the distinction between law and equity is as naked and broad as ever." Philpott v. Super. Court in and for Los Angeles Cty., 36 P.2d 635, 636–37 (Cal. 1934); *see also* County of Los Angeles v. City of Alhambra, 165 Cal. Rptr. 440, 449 (Cal. 1980) (finding laches only available in equity).

[53] *See First Fairfield*, 2003 WL 22708882, at *1 (citing Kerin v. Udolf, 334 A.2d 434, 437 (Conn. 1973) (citing Conn. Gen. Stat. § 52–1) (granting equitable relief to the defendant who claimed to have deposited the money in the mail in suit for default on a note)); Robarge v. Patriot General Ins. Co., No. CV-91–0393211S, 1991 Conn. Super. LEXIS 2793, at *1 (Conn. Super. Ct. Dec. 4, 1991) (mistakenly using the wrong case name); *see also* Hubley Mfg. & Supply Co. v. Ives, 70 A. 615, 615 (Conn. 1908) (discussing the "fundamental purpose" of the Practice Act of 1879 was so that "legal and equitable rights of the parties may be enforced and protected in one action").

[54] *First Fairfield*, 2003 WL 22708882, at *1; Jesperson v. Ponichtera, No. CV88 0096615 S, 1990 WL 283884, at *1 (Conn. Super. Ct. Jul 16, 1990). The court in *Jesperson* additionally cited *Grigg v. Robinson Furniture Co.*, 260 N.W.2d 898, 903 (Mich. Ct. App. 1978) ("equitable defenses can defeat legal claims") as persuasive authority for the proposition that equitable

Another textual debate about the meaning of the merger and its assimilation of unclean hands at law occurred within an appellate court in Oregon. In *Gratreak v. N. Pacific Lumber Co.*,[55] the majority decision denied the applicability of unclean hands in a legal action despite a statutory provision countenancing "equitable defenses" or "matters" to be pled in legal actions.[56] The court held that unclean hands was a "doctrine" and not a "defense" under the statute.[57] The dissent disagreed. It determined that the defense was included in the merger statute, which permitted the pleading of any equitable "matter."[58]

Instead of parsing the language of the merger, some courts announce that the intent of the integration was to include all equitable defenses. For example, citing Rule 2 of the Federal Rules of Civil Procedure, the Seventh Circuit Court of Appeals allowed unclean hands to bar an action for damages under the Sherman Anti-Trust Act in *Maltz v. Sax*.[59] The court declared: "As to unclean hands: the maxims of equity are available as defenses in actions at law."[60] Relying on the meaning of the merger as announced in *Maltz*, district courts in Indiana have held all equitable defenses – including unclean hands – available at law.[61] Notably, all of these cases fail to recognize (by ignorance or design) the substantive differences in chancery between the defenses.[62]

---

defenses may defeat legal claims. *Jesperson*, 1990 WL 283884, at *1. *Grigg*, like *Kerin v. Udolf*, 334 A.2d 434 (Conn. 1973), did not involve the defense of unclean hands. An additional two federal district court cases from Connecticut cited by the *Jesperson* court neither discussed the adoption question nor found the proof offered sustained the defense. *See* Burndy Corp. v. Teledyne Industries, Inc., 584 F. Supp. 656, 663 (D. Conn. 1984); Matthies v. Seymour Mfg. Co., 23 F.R.D. 64, 93–96 (D. Conn. 1958) (applying Connecticut law), *overruled on other grounds*, 270 F.2d 365 (2d Cir. 1959). The Supreme Court of Connecticut has since corrected the lower court decisions. *See* Weiss v. Smulders, 96 A.3d 1175, 1198 n.19 (Conn. 2014) (ruling that the unclean hands defense is not available to bar legal relief).

[55] 609 P.2d 375 (Or. Ct. App. 1980).

[56] *Id.* at 378 (citing OR. REV. STAT. § 16.460(2)).

[57] *Id.* The majority decision also distinguished the California Court of Appeals decision in *Fibreboard* because it found Oregon's legislature did not intend for the merger to include the defense of unclean hands. *Id.*; discussion *supra* Chapter 3, Section 3.4.1.2.

[58] *Id.* at 379 (Thorton, J., dissenting). The dissent also noted the anomalous result of the majority's holding. In *N. Pacific Lumber Co. v. Oliver*, 596 P.2d 931, 944 (Or. 1979), the Oregon Supreme Court had previously barred enforcement of the same noncompete agreement on the basis of unclean hands under its equitable jurisdiction.

[59] 134 F.2d 2, 5 (7th Cir. 1943) (citing 28 U.S.C.A. § 398; Rule 2 of the Rules of Civil Procedure, 28 U.S.C.A. following section 723c).

[60] *Id.*

[61] *See* discussion *supra* Chapter 3, Section 3.4.2.4 & note 238 (citing cases). Lower district courts in Illinois, however, appear to disagree. *See* Lopez v. Autoserve, LLC, No. 05 C 3554, 2005 WL 3116053 (N.D. Ill. Nov. 17, 2005) (applying Illinois and federal law of unclean hands) (refusing to recognize the defense of unclean hands because the case involved only legal damages).

[62] *See* discussion *supra* Section 4.3. While not stated directly, some courts intimate that a difference in application to legal and equitable remedies does not constitute a difference in substance.

Accordingly, the controversy concerning unclean hands centers on the meaning of the merger. Each position points to legislative prerogatives that mandate the defense's reception or denial. Many courts insist the union denies the defense; other courts assert the merger demands its application. The next section explains why both interpretations are wrong.

4.5 MEANING OF THE MERGER

The folly of the debate over the adoption of unclean hands is revealed in the defense of it. As discussed, each side of the controversy concerning the applicability of unclean hands in actions at law cites the unification of law and equity as authority for its position.

Some courts assert the code requires the adoption of unclean hands.[63] Other courts declare the merger dictates the denial of the defense.[64] They maintain the "procedural" union of law and equity bans the "substantive" reception of unclean hands.[65] Neither position is correct. Code pleading neither precludes nor demands the applicability of the equitable defense of unclean hands in every case at law. Instead, the better view of the merger is that it does not prohibit courts from considering the defense on a case-by-case basis.

The "procedural" merger did not mandate an all-or-nothing approach but a middle path. The integration of law and equity took a neutral position regarding the assertion of "purely" equitable defenses in actions at law. By making the distinction between law and equity irrelevant, it permits the application of equity like any other new principle of law.

This compromise position is consistent with the text of many codes and civil rules that allow "equitable defenses" to be pled in a single action.[66] At the same time, it recognizes the traditional pleading practices in chancery between "affirmative relief" and "true" defenses.[67]

This interpretation also reconciles the legislative intent in providing a "procedural" union as acknowledged by precedent with the general purpose to continue (or at least not to thwart) the custom of equitable adoption. True, the procedural consolidation eliminated the bifurcated system but kept the substantive status quo.[68] Yet the simple fact that the effect of integration made certain equitable

---

[63] *See* discussion *supra* Section 4.4.2.

[64] *See* discussion *supra* Section 4.4.1.

[65] *See, e.g.*, Russell v. Casebolt, 348 S.W.2d 548, 553 (Mo. 1964).

[66] Federal Rule of Civil Procedure 2 allows a court to try legal, equitable, and admiralty issues in the same action, effectively "eliminat[ing] any procedural impediment to interposing all relevant defenses." 1–2 MOORE'S FEDERAL PRACTICE § 2.05 at 31–32 (2003). In addition, Federal Rule of Civil Procedure 8(e)(2) permits a party to assert as many defenses "as the party has regardless of... whether based on legal, equitable, or maritime grounds."

[67] *See* discussion *supra* Section 4.3.

[68] *See* discussion *supra* Section 4.4.1.

defenses available at law under existing practice does not mean that the union *forever* forbade other equitable defenses like unclean hands.

The texts of the code(s) and rules certainly do not specify such an untenable conclusion.[69] Nor would they, considering the result would reverse the trend of absorbing equity into law.[70] As such, reading legislative silence to condition unclean hands on equity jurisdiction would defy tradition, impede the progress of incorporating equity into law, and be otherwise incompatible with a consolidated system.

While the point is a subtle one, clarifying the meaning of the merger removes legislative or other textual barriers to the application of unclean hands in actions at law. It eliminates the myth that the merger mandated either the inclusion or exclusion of unclean hands. It did not halt the process of integration and cast the division of law and equity in stone. Rather, the fusion of law and equity freed courts. Judges are free to consider the reception of unclean hands on historical, structural, doctrinal, ethical, and/or prudential grounds.[71] But freedom means choice, and choice – even under the best of circumstances – can be difficult. Therefore, the next chapter considers the clean hands doctrine in the context of the conversation for and against the fusion of law and equity.

4.6 CONCLUSION

The promulgation of the procedural codes and rules signaled the beginning of the end of separate systems of law and equity in this country. The time has come to end the beginning of unification. Courts should stop discriminating between law and equity and start treating equity like law.

The question of whether the equitable defense of unclean hands should be absorbed into the common law is really a debate about the law. It is an issue about whether a particular defense is available against a particular claim or

[69] *See, e.g.,* FED. R. CIV. P. 2.

[70] *See* discussion *supra* Section 4.3. A Maryland appellate court in *Manown v. Adams* also found the defense applicable to an action at law in part due to the "general trend" of merging procedures at law and equity. 598 A.2d 821, 826–27 (Md. Ct. Spec. App. 1991), *rev'd on other grounds*, 615 A.2d 611, 612 (Md. 1992) (citing MD. CODE ANN., § 2–301 (1991)).

[71] *See generally* PHILIP BOBBITT, CONSTITUTIONAL INTERPRETATION (1991) (popularizing pluralistic approach to legal analysis by identifying six heuristic devices of interpreting the Constitution); *see also* William N. Eskridge, Jr. & Philip P. Frickey, *Statutory Interpretation as Practical Reasoning*, 42 STAN. L. REV. 321, 322 (1990) (outlining analogous model of statutory interpretation). For articles adapting Bobbitt's forms of argument to private law, see T. Leigh Anenson, *Creating Conflicts of Interest: Litigation as Interference with the Attorney–Client Relationship*, 43 AM. BUS. L.J. 173, 203–05 (2006) (tort law); Mark P. Gergen, *Tortious Interference: How It Is Engulfing Commercial Law, Why This Is Not Entirely Bad, and a Prudential Response*, 38 ARIZ. L. REV. 1175, 1178 n.16 (1996) (tort law); Dennis Patterson, *The Pseudo-Debate over Default Rules in Contract Law*, 3 S. CAL. INTERDISC. L.J. 235, 235 (1993) (contract law).

category of claims under the circumstances of the case. It is a decision about how best to achieve justice.

The union of law and equity was not meant to halt the process of integration. Rather, the message of the merger was equality. If a defense that once applied in equity is no longer valued in society, it should not be preserved simply by force of tradition. The defense should be abrogated or modified as any other rule of law through the legitimate methodologies of jurisprudence. Similarly, if a defense formerly applied only in equity advances the end of the law in light of the legal relief claimed, it should not be rejected because it once fell within the realm of ancient equity. The defense should be evaluated like any other and adopted (or not) for those reasons.

Of course, the evolution of equity would benefit if the reasons given for adoption or exclusion were accurate or within a range of relevant choices. In this regard, discontinuing the debate that the merger is an all-or-nothing proposition is important. The admittedly "procedural" union of law and equity did not mandate or forbid the application of unclean hands. After the merger, as before, courts can consider the defense to bar legal remedies. As such, the conflict in the cases on this point is a pseudo-debate of sorts, signifying nothing.

Persisting with outmoded anachronisms of law and equity in order to determine the availability of unclean hands is to chase ghosts and leave courts in a constant state of epistemic failure. It also limits the legal reasoning process of judges to formulations designed in the dark days of the common law. Adherence to the labels of law and equity additionally diverts judicial resources from the true interests at stake and deprives the law of its ability to meet the needs of an ever-changing society. Distinctions between legal and equitable defenses are dead. They were buried with the merger. It is time for courts to begin writing their obituary.

5

Framing the Fusion Debate

One of the chief troubles with the frequent preoccupation of judges with the question of [equity] jurisdiction is that it makes them slide over the more important questions of wisdom and fairness that ought to receive careful attention.

– Zechariah Chafee, Jr.[1]

5.1 INTRODUCTION

Despite the confusion over the union of law and equity, equity-based doctrines have been surprisingly resilient in state and federal jurisprudence. With respect to equitable defenses, in particular, they are not gone but alive and even expanding beyond their traditional boundaries to all kinds of remedies.[2] As demonstrated in previous chapters, the clean hands doctrine is the poster child for equitable inroads into common law and legislation.[3] Equity paradoxically provides an entrée to the past and a gateway to the future.[4] If the common law and, increasingly, legislation marks the boundary of our duties to one another in modern civilization, then equity remains the frontier.[5]

---

[1] Zechariah Chafee, Jr., Some Problems of Equity 303–04 (1950) [hereinafter, Chafee, Some Problems].

[2] *See, e.g.*, T. Leigh Anenson, *Statutory Interpretation, Judicial Discretion, and Equitable Defenses*, 79 Univ. Pitt. L. Rev. 1 (2017) [hereinafter Anenson, *Statutory Interpretation*].

[3] *See* discussion and cases cited *supra* Chapter 3.

[4] T. Leigh Anenson & Gideon Mark, *Inequitable Conduct in Retrospective: Understanding Unclean Hands in Patent Remedies*, 62 Am. U. L. Rev. 1441, 1505 (2013) ("The remarkable duality found in equitable principles ensures they are grounded in the past, while simultaneously looking to the future.").

[5] 1 John Norton Pomeroy, A Treatise on Equity Jurisprudence as Administered in the United States of America § 67 (Spencer W. Symons ed., Bancroft-Whitney 5th ed. 1941) [hereinafter Pomeroy's Equity Jurisprudence, Fifth Edition] (discussing how equitable principles have "an inherent capacity of expansion, so as to keep abreast of each succeeding

History and moral philosophy, however, do not provide a complete picture of equitable defenses in state and federal law.[6] If Holmes was right that "[t]he law embodies the story of a nation's development," then American equity would still be telling England's story.[7] But that is clearly not the case. Over time, equity in the new world launched on its own destiny. As such, the defense of unclean hands is a good place to engage the conversation concerning the law–equity interface and the use of equitable defenses to bar legal relief. It also affords an opportunity to respond to the defense's critics.

5.2 OVERVIEW

The last chapter found that the law–equity merger allowed courts to consider whether to integrate the defense of unclean hands to preclude legal relief. This chapter asks whether they should. It answers the issue in the affirmative.

After an exegesis into the meaning of equity, Section 5.3 outlines the conversation for and against fusion to see how the defense of unclean hands fares in light of this debate. Section 5.4 then reappraises the defense.

5.3 DEBATING FUSION

Extending unclean hands to damages actions is one of many issues in the ongoing dialogue about the relationship between law and equity. The debate over fusion is undergoing a renaissance in the United States.[8] What was once a quintessentially "pro-fusion" atmosphere is quickly becoming a "no-fusion" environment.[9] Before

---

generation and age."); *see also* Paul Finn, *Unconscionable Conduct*, 8 J. Cont. L. 37, 39 (1994) [hereinafter Finn, *Unconscionable Conduct*] (explaining how the equitable concept of unconscionable conduct in Australian law applies just beyond the boundaries of contract and tort).

[6] O.W. Holmes, *The Path of the Law*, 10 Harvard L. Rev. 457, 464 (1897) [hereinafter Holmes, *The Path of the Law*] (speaking of the "fossil records" of history and the "majesty got from ethical associations").

[7] Oliver Wendell Holmes, The Common Law 1 (1881), *cited in* Paul Finn, *Statutes and the Common Law*, 22 U.W. Austl. L. Rev. 7, 9 (1992) (speaking of Australia until 1963).

[8] There was discussion of fusion since the merger of law and equity, *see, for example*, Charles T. McCormick, *The Fusion of Law and Equity in United States Courts*, 6 N.C. L. Rev. 283, 285 (1928) (commenting on the premerger debate of whether the Constitution prohibited Congress from consolidating law and equity under federal law), but there is recently a renewed interest in the United States. The Remedies Section of the Academy of American Law Schools (AALS) sponsored a panel discussion on federal equity at the 2016 Annual Conference. The same section of the Southeastern Academy of Law Schools is sponsoring a workshop on the fusion of law and equity in August 2017.

[9] After the merger(s) of law and equity, the general consensus seemed to be pro-fusion. *See* discussion *supra* Chapter 3. Characteristically, the most recent research has taken an antifusion stance. *See generally* Henry Smith, *Fusing the Equitable Function in Private Law*, at 173, 173, *in* Private Law in the 21st Century (Kit Barker, Karen Fairweather, & Ross Grantham eds., 2017) [hereinafter Smith, *Fusing the Equitable Function*] ("This paper will present a functionalist case for skepticism about substantive fusion."). *See generally* Samuel L. Bray, The *System*

analyzing the arguments in favor of extending exclusively equitable doctrines with those against, the next section arrives at a working definition of equity and discusses its implications for fusion.

5.3.1 *Arriving at a Working Definition of Equity*

In the twentieth century, the merger(s) of law and equity inspired conversations about what equity is or could be.[10] The conversation continues today. Two predominant views of equity emerged in the United States at the time that state and federal courts were unifying their courts and procedures. Is it a system or process?[11] As considered in Chapter 2, the system model focused on the historical practices, while the process model more or less looked at equity's overall objective in supplying deficiencies in the common law.[12] The process perspective was more amenable to the fusion of legal and equitable doctrines.

The latter image of equity seemingly held sway over the legal community until the present day. It certainly lingered past the mid-century mark. Equity as a process of adjustment had implications for fusion. Indeed, the decidedly pro-fusion stance began at a time of great change in almost every aspect of American life. One might expect that equity's inherent adaptability would be seen as an asset.[13] As such, equity was perceived as a positive, creative force in the law.[14]

Later, of course, it was felt that courts went too far in their law making.[15] A time of retrenchment and reflection followed. The call for restricting equitable principles

---

of Equitable Remedies, 63 UCLA L. REV. 530, 537 (2016) [hereinafter Bray, *System*] (expressing an antifusion attitude).

[10] *See, e.g.*, Ralph A. Newman, *The Hidden Equity: An Analysis of the Moral Content of the Principles of Equity*, 19 HASTINGS L.J. 147, 147 (1967) [hereinafter, Newman, *The Hidden Equity*] ("In the common law system we are not only uncertain as to just what equity is, but as to just what to do with it, whatever it may be.").

[11] Philip A. Ryan, *Equity: System or Process?*, 45 GEO. L.J. 213, 215–17 (1957) (describing equity from different perspectives such as functional or historical).

[12] *See* discussion *supra* Chapter 2, Section 2.3; GEORGE TUCKER BISPHAM, PRINCIPLES OF EQUITY: A TREATISE ON THE SYSTEM OF JUSTICE ADMINISTERED IN COURTS OF CHANCERY 10 (2d ed. 1878) (explaining that equity supplied deficiencies by recognizing rights unknown to the common law and by enforcing common law rights).

[13] *See generally* Garrard Glenn & Kenneth R. Redden, *Equity: A Visit to the Founding Fathers*, 31 VA. L. REV. 753, 759–63 (1945) (reviewing the history of equity to demonstrate that the traditional theory of the equitable process can help solve modern problems); Newman, *The Hidden Equity*, *supra* note 10, at 147 (describing and endorsing equity as a creative force in the law).

[14] *See* Sidney Post Simpson, *Fifty Years of American Equity*, 50 HARV. L. REV. 171, 179–81 (1937) (predicting that the future of equity is good and certain because it is a flexible tradition for allowing growth in the law).

[15] Professor Henry Smith points a long finger at realists who allegedly advanced equity without bounds during the nineteenth century. Smith, *Fusing the Equitable Function*, *supra* note 9, at 186 ("Legal Realists believed in drawing upon equity to give their policy-oriented judicially-driven reform some historical pedigree."); *see* WILSON HUHN, THE FIVE TYPES OF LEGAL

might be understood as a symptom of this greater phenomenon.[16] Seen in light of a larger legal landscape, it may be expected that there would be skepticism about fusion and even a reversion to an alternative vision of equity as a self-contained system of rules.[17] With regard to remedies, it has been suggested that extending equitable doctrines to legal relief may collapse the system.[18]

Especially in an age of statutes, the legal community is suspicious of judicial discretion and skeptical of a judge's ability to weigh and balance consequences.[19] These are quintessential equitable functions.[20] Despite judicial disclaimers that equitable discretion did not grant judges a roving commission to do good,[21] some scholars claim that is exactly what happened.[22] For this reason, there are renewed efforts advocating a purpose-driven approach to equity, at least with respect to its integration into private law.[23] The emphasis is on the ends of equity in order to avoid errors in judicial reasoning and results. To be sure, Holmes admonished us to look beyond history and ethics in the application of the law.[24]

Along these lines, Professor Henry Smith recently combined the early American ideas of equity as a system and process in emphasizing its general function. Despite characterizing equity as a "system," his depiction limns the system–process dichotomy. Drawing on systems theory from institutional economics, he emphasizes

ARGUMENT 54–56 (2002) (explaining that "American courts did not formally recognize [policy] analysis as a legitimate *legal* argument until the 'legal realism' movement in the first half of the 20th century" under the influence of such legal icons as Holmes, Cardozo, Pound, and Llewellyn).

[16] *See* T. Leigh Anenson & Donald O. Mayer, *"Clean Hands" and the CEO: Equity as an Antidote for Excessive Compensation*, 12 U. PA. J. BUS. L. 947, 968–69 (2010) (surveying the Supreme Court's recent financial cases and commenting that it will discourage Congress from looking to the federal courts as a means of enforcing a national agenda); Judith Resnik, *Constricting Remedies: The Rehnquist Judiciary, Congress, and Federal Power*, 78 IND. L.J. 223, 254 (2003) (criticizing the Supreme Court's restrictive reading of its equitable remedies and noting it is part of a jurisprudential trend in other areas).

[17] Bray, *System, supra* note 9, at 551.

[18] *Id.* at 592 (indicating that it will be difficult to take apart a working system).

[19] *See generally* Jared A. Goldstein, *Equitable Balancing in the Age of Statutes*, 96 VA. L. REV. 485, 490–515 (2010) (discussing history of equitable balancing).

[20] T. Leigh Anenson, *Equitable Defenses in the Age of Statutes*, 37 REV. LITIG. 529, 542, 548 (2018) [hereinafter Anenson, *Age of Statutes*].

[21] *See* N.L.R.B. v. P*I*E Nationwide, Inc., 894 F.2d 887, 893 (7th Cir. 1990) (Posner, J.) ("[A] modern federal equity judge does not have the limitless discretion of a medieval Lord Chancellor to grant or withhold a remedy.").

[22] Smith, *Fusing the Equitable Function, supra* note 9, at 187 (explaining that realists employed equity beyond its boundaries and without its limitations).

[23] Dennis Klimchuk, *Equity and the Rule of Law, in* PRIVATE LAW AND THE RULE OF LAW 247 (Lisa M. Austin & Dennis Klimchuk, eds., 2014) (describing equity as antiopportunism in preventing the exploitation of the generality or strictness of the law).

[24] Holmes, *The Path of the Law, supra* note 6, at 464; *see* Anenson & Mark, *supra* note 4, at 1488–1526 (evaluating how the inequitable conduct defense can be shaped by considerations other than customary practice).

equity's role as a second-order safety valve in combatting opportunism.[25] Alleging that judges have not observed this goal, Smith claims that American equity has slipped its bounds and resulted in over-fusion.[26]

However, it would be remiss to reduce equity to the workings of economic forces alone. Equity also represented (and still represents) additional policies.[27] A working theory of equity should account for all of its concerns. Recall that even antiopportunism-themed equitable defenses like the clean hands doctrine have court protective purposes and enable judges, through their residual discretion, to accommodate other interests.[28] And so it seems that a conception of equity is broad enough to include many images.[29]

Moreover, many incidents of confusion over fusion in the United States occurred not (only) because courts failed to understand the general nature of equity or its goals.[30] Rather, it was because they misunderstood the meaning of the merger and otherwise lacked knowledge of the historic limits of certain equitable defenses.[31] Therefore, a general theory of equity, while necessary and helpful in suggesting

---

[25] Smith's theory offers a robust description of equity's role in relation to the common law. He underscores equity's bilevel structural quality. Smith explains that equity intervened to solve unforeseeable problems of complexity and uncertainty. *See* Smith, *Fusing the Equitable Function, supra* note 9, at 187. Smith stresses equity's transforming role in preventing the exploitation of the common law's *ex ante* formal rules. *Id.*

[26] *See* Smith, *Fusing the Equitable Function, supra* note 9, at 174.

[27] *See* discussion *supra* Chapter 2, Section 2.3.

[28] *See* discussion *supra* Chapter 2 and *infra* Chapter 6; *see also* Hila Keren, *Undermining Justice: The Two Rises of Freedom of Contract and the Fall of Equity*, 2 CANADIAN J. COMP. & CONTEMP. L. 339, 392 (2016) ("[E]quity is the insistence that judicial discretion should be applied with conscience in mind, and that the legal outcome must deter exploitation of the law while promoting fairness, moral behavior, and social justice.").

[29] Moreover, an emphasis on one picture of equity or another may depend on the question being asked. In answering questions of court power, for example, scholars will naturally examine the historical origin of equitable principles and precepts, at least as an initial inquiry. *See* Atlas Life Insur. Co. nv. W.I. Southern, Inc., 306 U.S. 563, 568 (1939) (explaining that federal courts have "authority to administer in equity suits the principles of the system of judicial remedies which had been devised and was being administered by the English Court of Chancery at the time of the separation of the two countries."); James Fullmer, Note, *The Outer Limits of Equity: A Proposal for Cautious Expansion*, 39 HARV. J.L. & PUB. POL'Y 557, 557 (2016) (explaining that understanding American equity jurisdiction by reference to the equitable powers and principles that developed in the English Court of Chancery is a good starting point); *see also* Anenson, *Statutory Interpretation, supra* note 2, at 19–39 (analyzing the authority objection to the Supreme Court's assumption of equitable defenses in statutory law). In recent times, Professor Peter Turner has turned a precise lens on equity's forgotten administrative qualities. EQUITY AND ADMINISTRATION 1, 5 (P.G. Turner ed., 2016).

[30] *See* Smith, *Fusing the Equitable Function, supra* note 9, at 195 (indicating that excessive fusion comes from not understanding equity's overall purpose).

[31] *See* discussion *supra* Chapter 4 (concluding that confusion about fusion stems from not comprehending the meaning of the merger and the failure to delineate between the defenses and their customary application).

what may be gained or lost with any union, does not provide an absolute answer to the question of fusion.[32]

Discretion is a prime example. It obviously cuts both ways.[33] Whether we take "the bitter with the sweet" or decide that the cost outweighs the benefits depends on any given fusion situation.[34] A certain degree of judicial discretion is effective to prevent misbehavior without undermining legitimate expectations and chilling desirable behavior.[35] Unlike Goldilocks and the three bears, however, it will continue to be controversial whether judges are getting the amount of discretion "just right."[36]

There are also universal rule-of-law themes at play in the integration of equitable doctrines (or vice versa) like coherence and treating like cases alike.[37] Furthermore, there are institutional issues to consider that may make integration more or less attractive. For instance, as discussed in what follows, courts could be challenged to label certain remedies law or equity, especially new theories or old theories that have changed over time.

There might be circumstances in a particular jurisdiction or subject area making judges more or less amenable to the expansion of equity as well. As an example, it may be meaningful that the law involves subject matter, such as commercial transactions, that generally has a greater need for transformation.[38] With intellectual

---

[32] Lionel Smith, *Fusion and Tradition*, in EQUITY IN COMMERCIAL LAW 19, 39 (James Edelman & Simone Degeling eds., 2005) [hereinafter Smith, *Fusion and Tradition*].

[33] *See* Doug Rendleman, *The Triumph of Equity Revisited: The Stages of Equitable Discretion*, 15 NEV. L.J. 1397, 1409 (2016) [hereinafter Rendleman, *Stages of Equitable Discretion*] ("The definition and operation of discretion will remain contested and elusive.").

[34] Stephen B. Burbank, *The Bitter with the Sweet: Tradition, History, and Limitations on Federal Judicial Power – A Case Study*, 75 NOTRE DAME L. REV. 1291, 1315 (2000).

[35] Henry E. Smith, *Why Fiduciary Law Is Equitable*, in PHILOSOPHICAL FOUNDATIONS OF FIDUCIARY LAW 278 (Andrew S. Gold & Paul B. Miller eds., 2014) [hereinafter Smith, *Fiduciary Law*] (explaining the idea is to keep the law "unpredictable enough to keep opportunists guessing but without destabilizing the law" for which it is a safety valve); Mark P. Gergen, John M. Golden & Henry E. Smith, *The Supreme Court's Accidental Revolution? The Test for Permanent Injunctions*, 112 COLUM. L. REV. 203, 237 (2012) (relating the same idea for equitable remedies).

[36] *See* Doug Rendleman, *Remedies: A Guide for the Perplexed*, 57 ST. LOUIS U. L.J. 567, 578–79 (2013) [hereinafter Rendleman, *Remedies*] (advising of his uneasiness with a high degree of equitable discretion); discussion *infra* Section 5.4.2 (discussing the debate whether equity results in a subjective versus objective inquiry); discussion *supra* Chapter 2, Sections 2.3, 2.8 (discussion discretion as a feature of equity and unclean hands).

[37] Andrew Burrows, *Remedial Coherence and Punitive Damages in Equity* (explaining that pro-fusion arguments tend to be based on rationality and consistency), in EQUITY IN COMMERCIAL LAW, *supra* note 32, at 382; *see* Smith, *Fusion and Tradition*, *supra* note 32, at 23.

[38] Grupo Mexicano de Desarrollo, S.A. v. Alliance Bond Fund, Inc., 527 U.S. 308, 337 (1999) (Ginsburg, J., dissenting) ("A dynamic equity jurisprudence is of special importance in the commercial law context."); *see also* Union Pac. Ry. v. Chi., Rock Island & Pac. Ry., 163 U.S. 564, 600–01 (1896) ("It must not be forgotten that in the increasing complexities of modern business relations equitable remedies have necessarily and steadily been expanded, and no inflexible rule has been permitted to circumscribe them.").

property law, especially, there is a strong mythology that accompanies innovation and the entrepreneurial spirit.[39] Like the great American road trip, the belief is that catharsis and salvation are attainable merely by forward momentum.[40]

Notably, the clean hands doctrine has been a success story in this general area of the law.[41] The defense has not only been expanded to bar legal relief under federal statutory law, but it also has matured into subject matter–specific species of the doctrine. These include, among others, copyright misuse, patent misuse, and inequitable conduct in the patent process.[42]

Raising the moral ideals for those seeking damages may be particularly appropriate out west in California, where the legislature has imposed the highest ethical standards in the nation in prohibiting unfair business practices.[43] Another uniquely California innovation is a provision of its Civil Code. Originally enacted in 1872, Section 3517 affirms the philosophy of unclean hands that "no one should benefit from their own wrong."[44] Courts have invoked the Code prohibition in applying unclean hands as well as many other doctrines espousing the underlying philosophy.[45]

Additionally, preventing litigants from taking advantage of their own wrong has been a theme in California's tort law.[46] Enacted by voter initiative in 1997, two

---

[39] We criticized the Federal Circuit's policy-based decision in *Therasense, Inc. v. Becton, Dickinson & Co.* as unprincipled for not equally accounting for the history of inequitable conduct. *See* Anenson & Mark, *supra* note 4, at 1502 ("Rather than synthesizing science and sociology by resorting to equitable principles, the majority in *Therasense* cemented their separation.").

[40] *See* BENJAMIN N. CARDOZO, THE NATURE OF THE JUDICIAL PROCESS 62 (1921) [hereinafter CARDOZO, JUDICIAL PROCESS] ("The great inventions that embodied the power of steam and electricity, the railroad and the steamship, the telegraph and the telephone, have built up new customs and new laws."). We previously argued that the equitable defense of unclean hands fits within Professors Lemley and Burk's idea of judicial "policy levers" that accommodate change in patent law. *See* Anenson & Mark, *supra* note 4, at 1517–18 (citing DAN L. BURK & MARK A. LEMLEY, THE PATENT CRISIS AND HOW THE COURTS CAN SOLVE IT 18 (2009)).

[41] *See* Anenson & Mark, *supra* note 4, at 1517 (explaining that literature reviewing the American patent system in historical perspective attributes its success in part to equitable principles) (citing Zorina Khan, *Innovation in Law and Technology*, *in* Vol. II, THE CAMBRIDGE HISTORY OF LAW IN AMERICA at 484, 491 495, 525–29 (Michael Grossberg & Christopher Tomlins eds. 2008)).

[42] *See* discussion *supra* Chapter 2, Section 2.1 and Chapter 3, Section 3.4.2.3 (explaining copyright misuse).

[43] WEST'S ANN. CAL. BUS. & PROF. CODE 17200 et seq.

[44] *See* Harvey v. General Tire & Rubber Co., 200 Cal. Rptr. 722, 727 (Cal. App. 1984) ("This code section provides: 'No one can take advantage of his own wrong.' It thus essentially re-states the so-called 'clean hands' doctrine").

[45] *See* Weisman v. Johnson, 183 Cal. Rptr. 792, 796 (Cal. Ct. App. 1982) (citing Code Section 3517 in support of finding that the defendant had waived arbitration rights by petitioning for arbitration with the bad-faith intent to avoid the arbitral forum if the petition was sustained); *see also* WEST'S ANN. CAL. CIV. CODE § 3517 (annotations listing cases citing the section in support of fraud, illegality, estoppel, contributory negligence, and many more).

[46] The language of the Proposition that lead to the enactment of two statutes into California law stated a purpose parallel to that of unclean hands defense: "[C]riminal felons are law breakers,

statutes establish an unlawful conduct defense to negligence claims.[47] Another California law provides that owners of real property shall not be liable for injuries that occur upon the property during or after the injured person's commission of any certain felonies.[48] The statute has been held to bar not only suits for negligent conduct but also claims for intentionally injurious acts that were justifiable under the circumstances.[49]

Perhaps, too, California's cyber roots favor fusion. The home of start-ups, global technology companies, and other technology-infused institutions in its Silicon Valley, the region's technocentric brain pool are not slaves to the status quo.[50] Seen in this light, it may not be realism but a particular kind of American idealism that is

---

and should not be rewarded for their irresponsibility ..." 1996 Cal. Legis. Serv. Proposition 213 (West). The complete text of the Proposition is as follows:

> Insurance costs have skyrocketed for those Californians who have taken responsibility for their actions ... [C]riminal felons are law breakers, and should not be rewarded for their irresponsibility ... However, under current laws, ... criminals have been able to recover damages from law-abiding citizens for injuries suffered during the commission of their crimes ... Californians must change the system that rewards individuals who fail to take essential personal responsibility to prevent them from seeking unreasonable damages or from suing law-abiding citizens.

The state of California is not alone in recognizing the unlawful conduct defense under certain circumstances. *See* Vincent R. Johnson, *Unlawful Conduct Defense in Legal Malpractice*, 77 UMKC L. REV. 43, 45 (2008–2009) (providing evidence in case and statutory law that the outlaw doctrine is alive and well in tort law despite scholarly and judicial pronouncements that it is dead); *see also* Joseph H. King, Jr., *Outlaws and Outlier Doctrines: The Serious Misconduct Bar in Tort Law*, 43 WM. & MARY L. REV. 1011, 1016 (2002) (offering a comprehensive history, description, and critique of the doctrine).

[47] *See* Quackenbush v. Super. Court, 70 Cal. Rptr. 2d 271, 273–74 (Cal Ct. App. 1997) ("On November 5, 1996, the voters approved Proposition 213, the Personal Responsibility Act of 1996, adding sections 3333.3 and 3333.4 to the Civil Code, applicable to trials commencing after January 1, 1997."). One statute precludes the case in its entirety if the claim arises from felonious conduct. CAL. CIV. CODE § 3333.3 (West 2008): "In any action for damages based on negligence, a person may not recover any damages if the plaintiffs' injuries were in any way proximately caused by the plaintiffs' commission of any felony, or immediate flight therefrom, and the plaintiff has been duly convicted of that felony." *See also* Gage v. Network Appliance, Inc., 2005 WL 3214954, at *4 (Cal. Ct. App. 2005) (holding that the initiative presupposes that the defendants may have been negligent in expressly barring negligence claim). Another statute addresses automobile accidents and precludes certain types of damages. Specifically, it bars recovery of damages to compensate for noneconomic losses such as pain and suffering or other nonpecuniary damages if the plaintiff was operating a vehicle under the influence of drugs or alcohol or owned or operated the vehicle without proper insurance or proof of financial responsibility. *See* CAL. CIV. CODE § 333.4 (West 2008).

[48] CAL. CIV. CODE § 847 (West 2008).

[49] Calvillo-Silva v. Home Grocery, 968 P.2d 65, 69 (Cal. 1998).

[50] Historians know all too well it is easier to describe *how* something came to be than to determine *why* it came to be. Deterministic theories are, of course, more satisfying because they attempt to bring order out of chaos and chance. Whether or not tech-savvy Californians had anything to do with integrating equitable principles like unclean hands into legal relief, the industry's appreciation of constant change is at least congruent with it.

responsible for fusion.[51] What is more, intellectual property law is the basis for many legal obligations in the computer technology field.

On occasion, arguments against fusion may prevail if an equitable doctrine is considered duplicative and redundant.[52] In the Commonwealth, there appears to be a dispute about the correlation of the defenses of unclean hands and illegality that share certain features.[53] The United States has statutory causes of action for illegality in tort in addition to the common law, yet the clean hands doctrine covers a wider range of conduct.[54] Chapter 6 will also show that the unclean hands defense and other kindred defenses like estoppel or *in pari delicto* are not a complete match.[55]

Last, the integration of equity into the law underscores the age-old tension between equity's recognition of continuity and change.[56] Translated into jurisprudential terms, a decision on the extension of doctrines previously exclusive to equity requires judges to consider the legal reasoning principles of tradition and public policy.[57] How far to push one mode or the other may depend on the doctrine being absorbed and its surrounding jurisprudence. After all, history does not always produce wisdom, and change is not always for the better.[58] It is not a question best resolved in the abstract. Unsurprisingly, an attempt to identify a single approach to equity from early United States Supreme Court decisions was not successful.[59]

Equity and the issue of fusion has been admittedly undertheorized.[60] But the fusion debate is *over*theorized as well. Many scholars and courts are talking past

---

[51] *Cf.* Smith, *Fusing the Equitable Function*, *supra* note 9, at 185–86.

[52] *See* Burrows, *Remedial Coherence and Punitive Damages in Equity*, *supra* note 37, at 386 (outlining his disagreement with other scholars about the similarities between common law and equitable defenses); *id.* (explaining that Meagher, Heydon, and Leeming insist that Burrows is "utterly wrong" that there are common law doctrines that mirror in nature if not in scope the equitable defenses of laches, unclean hands, and hardship).

[53] *Id.*; *see* Chafee I, *supra* note 53, at 896 (commenting that "[t]he real objection is not to one man's clean hands, but to the whole enterprise" in discussing the application of unclean hands in suits to enforce illegal contracts).

[54] *See* discussion *supra* 45–48 and Chapter 2 note 245.

[55] *See* discussion *infra* Chapter 6.

[56] Anenson, *Age of Statutes*, *supra* note 20, at 531; Zechariah Chafee, Jr., *Foreword* to SELECTED ESSAYS ON EQUITY iv (Edward D. Re ed., 1955) [hereinafter Chafee, SELECTED ESSAYS ON EQUITY] (discussing law and equity as eternal conflict between certainty and progress).

[57] *See generally* T. Leigh Anenson, *From Theory to Practice: Analyzing Equitable Estoppel Under a Pluralistic Model of Law*, 11 LEWIS & CLARK L. REV. 633, at 642–43 (2007) [hereinafter Anenson, *Pluralistic Model*] (analyzing equitable estoppel in light of jurisprudential principles of tradition, precedent, and policy).

[58] *See* Smith, *Fusion and Tradition*, *supra* note 32, at 20 n.9 (noting that even Oliver Wendell Holmes, one of the Supreme Court's most accomplished legal historians, never countenanced the blind adherence to history for history's sake but approached it with a balanced view (citing several of Holmes's writings)).

[59] *See generally* John R. Kroger, *Supreme Court Equity, 1789–1835, and the History of American Judging*, 34 HOUS. L. REV. 1425, 1427 (1998).

[60] *See, e.g.,* Lionel Smith, *Common Law and Equity in R3RUE*, 68 WASH. & LEE L. REV. 1185, 1187 (2011) [hereinafter, Smith, *Equity in R3RUE*] ("The law that comes from Equity has not been as thoroughly theorized as the common law.").

each other in claiming that *all* fusion is either valid or invalid.[61] It appears the best way to understand fusion is to look at the specifics – that is, the doctrine or, even more narrowly perhaps, the situation at issue. In fact, scholars across the common law world are arriving at a consensus that fusion, so long as it is principled, is acceptable.[62] No one is now attempting to subject equity to paralysis and put it "in a glass case."[63] Concomitantly, almost everyone would agree that unthinking, automatic fusion should be avoided.[64] While principled fusion does not tell us much about the particulars, it does direct the discussion away from *whether* to integrate equitable doctrines to *when*. Specifically, under what circumstances is fusion appropriate?

This chapter critiques fusion by focusing on the integration of unclean hands at law. Even assessing the integration of *all* equitable defenses may be too broad an inquiry and yield disagreements over one defense or another.[65] Approaching the issue of fusion at a doctrinal level enables an analysis of how the extension of unclean hands to bar damages relates to perceived problems associated with the equitable integration of our common and statutory law. In this way, the chapter aims to contribute to the larger debate about how to conceive of equity in a merged system and improves upon the current state of equity and fusion theory.

The analysis that follows examines the main points for and against fusion that concern the extension of unclean hands defense to legal relief.

---

[61] *See, e.g.,* David Morgan, Harris v. Digital Pulse: *The Availability of Exemplary Damages in Equity,* 29 MONASH U. L. REV. 377, 382–84 (2003). (It is a "showdown between old school orthodoxy and the fusion fallacy heretics."); *see also* Smith, *Fusing the Equitable Function, supra* note 9, at 181 (noting that the debate between fusionists and antifusionists does not take place on the same plane).

[62] *See* Smith, *Fusion and Tradition, supra* note 32, at 27 (calling for a balanced approach to the fusion of law and equity); *see also* James Edelman, A *"Fusion Fallacy" Fallacy,* 119 L.Q. REV. 375, 379–80 (2003) (discussing the possible grounds for supporting fusion by analogy and the academic justifications for such an approach); Keith Mason, *Fusion: Fallacy, Future or Finished?* (Justice Keith Mason, New South Wales Court of Appeals) (relating his view that "the accumulated wisdom of the ages remains a starting (and usually a finishing) point for decision-making, even at the appellate level"), *in* EQUITY IN COMMERCIAL LAW, *supra* note 32, at 41, 72.

[63] Smith, *Fusion and Tradition, supra* note 32, at 38–39 ("And no legal tradition, equity included, has reached such a state of perfection that it must be placed in a glass case and preserved from further change, on the ground that any change must necessarily be worse."); *see also id.* at 22 n.15 (defining a "fusion fallacy" as a belief in substantive fusion).

[64] *See* Bray, *System, supra* note 9, at 590 (comparing merger of courts and procedures that was transformed by statute and rule making with incremental approach taken for equitable remedies in which one doctrine or another might be integrated).

[65] The fact that the equitable defense of laches may have a substitute in the statute of limitations, for instance, is one example. *See supra* Chapter 2 note 137 and *infra* note 318.

5.3.2 Pro-Fusion School of Thought

After the union of law and equity, commentators debated the ongoing adoptability of equitable defenses in actions at law.[66] The considerations at issue provide context for the incorporation of unclean hands and bear reconsidering in the twenty-first century in light of case law developments concerning the defense.[67]

5.3.2.1 Overview

The following discussion justifies the universal consideration of unclean hands in law *and* equity cases pursuant to the principle of coherence as well as on logical and practical grounds. First, it criticizes the continued discrimination against unclean hands on the basis of an alleged historical impediment, especially given the similarities of the defense to legal and other fully incorporated equitable defenses. Second, it exposes the lack of any meaningful distinction between legal and equitable remedies that would merit different treatment of unclean hands. Third and finally, it offers the proposed case-by-case approach, which abdicates conditioning unclean hands on equitable jurisdiction, as an institutional advantage, by comparing it with the traditional test of parceling legal and equitable remedies that have largely eroded over time.

5.3.2.2 Historical Accident of Equity

In a unified system there is no reason to deny the application of unclean hands on historical grounds. The difference between law and equity is not based in theory or philosophy but rather only in historical development.[68] As explained by the

---

[66] *See generally* Charles E. Clark, *Trial of Actions Under the Code,* 11 CORNELL L.Q. 482, 492–93 (1926); Walter Wheeler Cook, *Equitable Defenses,* 32 YALE L.J. 645, 657 (1923); John L. Garvey, *Some Aspects of the Merger of Law and Equity,* 10 CATH. U. L. REV. 59 (1961); E.W. Hinton, *Equitable Defenses Under Modern Codes,* 18 MICH. L. REV. 717 (1920); Robert S. Stevens, *A Plea for the Extension of Equitable Principles and Remedies,* 41 CORNELL L.Q. 351 (1956).

[67] *See* Thomas O. Main, *Traditional Equity and Contemporary Procedure,* 78 WASH. L. REV. 429, 432 (2003) ("People need not so much to be told as to be reminded.") (quoting Melvin M. Johnson, Jr., *The Spirit of Equity,* 16 B.U. L. REV. 345, 345 (1936)).

[68] *See* RALPH A. NEWMAN, EQUITY AND LAW: A COMPARATIVE STUDY 30 (1961) [hereinafter NEWMAN, EQUITY AND LAW] ("Enough has been said to show that the reason why the body of law administered in the common law courts was the familiarity of the early chancellors with canon and Roman law, and consideration of prudence which encouraged the reduction of interference with the work of the common law courts to a minimum."); Stevens, *supra* note 66, at 351 (explaining that the distinction between law and equity was not necessary or essential – but historical).

Honorable Robert Megarry of the Chancery Division of the High Court of England: "There is much truth in the view that equity is a historical accident."[69]

Certainly, "[j]udicial terminology and its continual reference to an obsolete system of judicial organization helps to preserve the illusion."[70] Yet Oliver Wendell Holmes reminds us that "history sets us free and enables us to make up our minds dispassionately whether the survival of what we are enforcing answers any new purpose when it has ceased to answer the old."[71] According to Professor Ralph Newman:

> [W]e have no reason to suppose that the Chancellor felt that such standards were inapplicable to the kinds of cases which came before the common law courts ... The difference in principles and procedures had nothing whatever to do with any notion that the rich ethical contributions which were developed in the Chancery and were so sorely needed to make the law an instrument of justice could not be incorporated into the general law and used whenever they might be needed.[72]

Newman additionally noted in his comparative work on equity: "In all surviving legal systems except our own, equity in the course of time became absorbed into the general law."[73] The application of unclean hands in legal cases, in particular, has been traced to ancient times as apprised in Chapter 2.[74] It was recognized in creditor cases in the Roman law during the second century.[75] Early examples of unclean hands have also been found in Chinese customary law in the tenth and eleventh centuries.[76]

Even in England, equitable principles were originally used at law before the separation of law and equity.[77] With the merger in both England and America, there is no longer any reason to continue a distinction. To be sure, the absurdity of courts climbing over a barrier built by historical accident is amplified now that the barrier no longer exists. As discussed in Chapter 4, the integration of law and equity eliminated it. Courts can consider whether to incorporate unclean hands into the law like they did with other equitable defenses before the merger.

---

[69] SNELL'S PRINCIPLES OF EQUITY 7 (Robert Megarry & P.V. Baker eds., 27th ed. 1973) (explaining that law and equity both sought the same end of justice, but that the equitable body of rules appeared at a later stage of development); *accord* James Edelman & Simone Degeling, *Introduction* to EQUITY IN COMMERCIAL LAW, *supra* note 32, at 2 (explaining that Australian Justice Keith Mason denies any particular characteristic of equitable doctrine apart from historical development); *cf. id.* at 2 (noting that Sir Anthony Mason and Professor Lionel Smith accept there are unique characteristics of equity that may limit analogies to the common law in certain cases).

[70] NEWMAN, EQUITY AND LAW, *supra* note 68, at 41.

[71] Oliver W. Holmes, *Law in Science and Science in Law*, Coll. Leg. Papers 210, 225 (1921).

[72] NEWMAN, EQUITY AND LAW, *supra* note 68, at 30.

[73] *Id.* at 30; *see also id.* at 250 (noting that a version of unclean hands applied in creditor cases stems from Roman law and is recognized in most civil law legal systems).

[74] *See* discussion *supra* Chapter 2, Section 2.4.

[75] *Id.* at 31.

[76] *Id.* at 250 n.19.

[77] *See* discussion *supra* Chapter 4, Section 4.1.

In applying equitable principles, courts recognize that each party bears responsibilities.[78] This concept is not peculiar to equity but has been acknowledged in damage actions as well as suits for specific relief.[79] Equity is still ethical, but law has also become ethical.[80] By statutory authorization as well as by judicial innovation, the adoption of equitable doctrines and defenses into the law has been occurring for centuries.[81]

Moreover, the combining of the courts of equity and law severely diminished the differences in the application of equity or ethical-based principles.[82] As Chafee logically concluded more than fifty years ago: "[T]he factors which divide judicial action from moral judgments seem to me the same whether the particular suit resembles what used to go on in chancery or what used to go on in the courts of common law."[83]

---

[78] See CHAFEE, SOME PROBLEMS, *supra* note 1, at 94.

[79] See Hynes v. New York Central R.R. Co., 131 N.E. 898 (1921) (Cardozo, J.) (discussing equitable principles in damages case). In discussing the use of equitable estoppel in actions at law, the United States Supreme Court reasoned: "The doctrine of equitable estoppel is, as its name indicates, chiefly, if not wholly, derived from courts of equity, and as these courts apply it to any species of property, there would seem no reason why its application should be restricted in courts of law." Kirk v. Hamilton, 102 U.S. 68, 78 (1880).

[80] See DOUGLAS LAYCOCK, THE DEATH OF THE IRREPARABLE INJURY RULE 11–16, 29–30, nn. 27–43 (1991) [hereinafter LAYCOCK, IRREPARABLE INJURY RULE] (collecting examples of legal features in equity and equitable features at law); *see also* 1 FREDERICK W. MAITLAND, EQUITY 1 (2nd ed. 1936) (noting the difficulty of generalization about what concepts derive from equity as opposed to law because there is no pattern); Douglas Laycock, *The Scope and Significance of Restitution*, 67 TEX. L. REV. 1277, 1278–79 (1989) (explaining the law of restitution has origins in law (quasi-contract) and equity (constructive trust)).

[81] See discussion of once exclusively equitable contract defenses *supra* Chapter 4. Recent theoretical work in contract law would move remedial and contract defenses closer still. *See* Nicholas Cornell, *A Complainant-Oriented Approach to Unconscionability and Contract Law*, 164 U. PA. L. REV. 1131 (2016) (recasting contract law, including its defenses, based on an inability to complain rather than a lack of voluntary agreement). For examples of equitable integration beyond defenses, see 1 DAN B. DOBBS, DOBBS LAW OF REMEDIES: DAMAGES-EQUITY-RESTITUTION 44 (2nd ed. 1993) [hereinafter DOBBS LAW OF REMEDIES]; Douglas Laycock, *The Triumph of Equity*, 56 LAW & CONTEMP. PROBS. 53, 67–71 (1993) [hereinafter Laycock, *Triumph of Equity*] (listing trusts, mortgages, servitudes, and restitution as examples of integration); *see also* USH Ventures v. Global Telesystems Group, Inc., 796 A.2d 7, 16 (Del. Super. Ct. 2000) (citing cases and treatises) (explaining the prevalence of incorporation by the fact that "[a]ssignees can sue on contracts; recording recognizes equitable servitudes; the law of mortgages is largely statutory").

[82] See Hinton, *supra* note 66, at 718. *See generally* Simpson, *supra* note 14, at 179–80 (discussing the coalescence of law and equity in the state and federal court systems); Charles E. Clark & James W.M. Moore, *The New Federal Civil Procedure*, 44 YALE L.J. 387, 387 (1935) (same).

[83] Chafee I, *supra* note 53, at 877–906; Zechariah Chafee, Jr., *Coming into Equity with Clean Hands*, 47 MICH. L. REV. 1065, 1096 (1949) [hereinafter Chafee II]; *see also* Rosalind Poll, Note, "*He Who Comes into Equity Must Come with Clean Hands*," 32 B.U. L. REV. 66, 74 (1952) (reasoning that there should be no differentiating between legal and equitable principles of justice because of the union of equity and law).

5.3.2.2.1 IN PARI DELICTO Courts have also used the terms *in pari delicto* and *unclean hands* interchangeably or relied on the similarity between unclean hands and this kindred equitable defense in applying the defense and resolving a dispute.[84] *In pari delicto* applies to relief and perhaps best illustrates Professor Chafee's statement that the defense of unclean hands "ought not be called a maxim of equity because it is by no means confined to equity."[85] It is not surprising that *in pari delicto* was first used by Lord Mansfield, who was overheard commenting that he never liked law so much as when it resembled equity.[86]

Comparable to unclean hands, the doctrine of *in pari delicto* prevents litigants from benefiting from their own wrong.[87] It similarly serves such diverse purposes as preserving the dignity of the courts, expressing a moral principle, and enforcing public policy.[88] It stands for the idea that "courts should not lend their good offices to mediating disputes among wrongdoers."[89] This equitable defense "derives from

---

[84] *See* discussion *supra* Chapter 3, Section 3.5; *see also* DOBBS LAW OF REMEDIES, *supra* note 81, § 2.4(2) at 68 n.6 (explaining that judges often use the terms "unclean hands" and "*in pari delicto*" interchangeably).

[85] Chafee I, *supra* note 53, at 878 (quoted in Messick v. Smith, 69 A.2d 478, 481 (Md. 1949)).

[86] Smith v. Bromley, 2 Doug. 696, 99 Eng. Rep. 441n (N.P. 1760); *see* Harold Greville Hanbury, *The Field of Modern Equity, in* ESSAYS IN EQUITY 28 (1934) (citing Lord Dursley v. Lord Fitzhardinge, 6 Ves. 251, 260 (1827) (per Lord Eldon)). *See generally* NEWMAN, EQUITY AND LAW, *supra* note 68, at 12–20 (discussing how the ethical content of the common law became greatly enriched with the awakening of social consciousness at the time of Lord Mansfield); Anenson & Mayer, *supra* note 16, at 1008 ("Lord Mansfield was once labeled a heretic for introducing ethics-based equity principles into common law decision-making in commercial cases. History proved him a hero."); Henry Ingersoll, *Confusion of Law and Equity*, 21 YALE L.J. 58, 59 (1911) (commenting on how Lord Mansfield "opened the common law courts to equity"). *See also* Anthony Mason, *Fusion* (explaining that Mansfield was a member of the equity bar prior to becoming a judge), *in* EQUITY IN COMMERCIAL LAW, *supra* note 32, at 11, 17.

[87] Similar to unclean hands, the doctrine of *in pari delicto* preserves the dignity of the courts and deters illegal behavior. *See* Bateman Eichler, Hill Richards, Inc. v. Berner, 472 U.S. 299, 306 (1985). But the defenses are not an exact match. *See* discussion *infra* Chapter 6 (explaining how *in pari delicto* requires common scheme and imposes a guilt differential between the parties (i.e., that the claimant's guilt be less than the respondent)).

[88] *See* Feld & Sons, Inc. v. Pechner, Dorfman, Wolfee, Rounick, & Cabot, 458 A.2d 545, 551–52 (Pa. Super. Ct. 1983) (explaining that the failure to apply the broader principle of which *in pari delicto* is an application would aid the confessed perjurers, thwart the criminal law, and "suffer [the law] to be prostituted"); J.K. Grodecki, *In Pari Delicto Potior Est Conditio Defendentis*, 71 L.Q. REV. 254, 265–273 (1955) (advising that *in pari delicto* preserves the dignity of the courts, expresses a moral principle, and enforces public policy); John W. Wade, *Restitution of Benefits Acquired Through Illegal Transactions*, 95 U. PA. L. REV. 261, 268–81 (1947) (discussing conditions and circumstances that courts consider in applying *in pari delicto*).

[89] Bateman Eichler, Hill Richards, Inc. v. Berner, 472 U.S. 299, 306 (1985) (stating that "courts should not lend their good offices to mediating disputes among wrongdoers; and . . . denying judicial relief to an admitted wrongdoer is an effective means of deterring illegality"); *see also* BLACK'S LAW DICTIONARY 794 (7th ed. 1999) ("a plaintiff who has participated in wrongdoing may not recover damages resulting from the wrongdoing").

the Latin, *in pari delicto potior est conditio defendentis*: 'In a case of equal or mutual fault . . . the position of the [defending] party . . . is the better one.'"[90]

In *Smith v. Long*,[91] a New York appellate court found unclean hands applicable to legal relief by reference to the defense of *in pari delicto*.[92] It used the defenses interchangeably without discussion of any difference between them.[93]

Courts have additionally bolstered their conclusion that unclean hands applies at law with precedent concerning the kindred defense of *in pari delicto*. In Maryland, for instance, an intermediate appellate court in *Manown v. Adams*[94] applied unclean hands to an action at law despite its equitable roots.[95] It relied on two cases from the high court in Maryland that relied on the defense of *in pari delicto* as authority for the rule that unclean hands may be invoked to bar suits "at law and in equity."[96] The appellate court reasoned that *in pari delicto* is "merely a cognate principle to the clean hands doctrine," which justified the analogy.[97]

Similarly, as discussed in Chapter 3, Judge Posner compared unclean hands and *in pari delicto* in *Byron v. Clay*.[98] He noted in dicta that unclean hands should no longer be limited to equitable suits in light of the merger of law and equity.[99] He reasoned that even before the merger, there was a counterpart doctrine to unclean hands – *in pari delicto* – that forbade a plaintiff to recover damages if his fault was equal to the defendant's.[100]

---

[90] *Bateman Eichler*, 472 U.S. at 306.

[91] 281 A.D.2d 897 (N.Y. App. Div. 2001).

[92] *Id.* at 898 (declaring unclean hands available in "law or equity").

[93] *Smith*, 281 A.D.2d at 898; *see also Mallis*, 615 F.2d at 75–76 (applying New York law) (unclean hands considered to bar legal relief for state law claims and *in pari delicto* considered to bar the same conduct under the federal securities law claim); *cf.* Furman v. Furman, 178 Misc. 582, 586–87 (N.Y. Sup. Ct. 1941), *aff'd*, 262 A.D. 512, *aff'd*, 40 N.E.2d 643 (holding that res judicata bars subsequent legal action based upon adjudication of unclean hands in prior equity suit because unclean hands has element of equal guilt and corresponds to *in pari delicto* defense at law).

[94] 598 A.2d 821 (Md. Ct. Spec. App. 1991), *rev'd on other grounds*, 615 A.2d 611, 612 (Md. 1992).

[95] *See id.* at 825.

[96] *Id.* at 825 (citing Messick v. Smith, 69 A.2d 478 (Md. 1949); Shirks Motor Express Corp. v. Forster Transfer & Rigging Co., 133 A.2d 59 (Md. 1957)).

[97] *Id.* at 825 n.6 (equating the two defenses); *see also* Blain v. Doctor's Co., 272 Cal. Rptr. 250 (Cal. Ct. App. 1990) (recognizing unclean hands at law by relying on the Pennsylvania case of Feld and Sons, Inc. v. Pechner, Dorfman, Wolfee, Rounick, & Cabot, 458 A.2d 545, 551–52 (Pa. Super. Ct. 1983), which applied a general legal principle of *in pari delicto*). *But see* Truitt v. Miller, 407 A.2d 1073, 1079–80 (D.C. 1979) (denying unclean hands defense in action at law despite noting its similarity to *in pari delicto*); Ellwood v. Mid States Commodities, Inc., 404 N.W.2d 174, 184 (Iowa 1987) (same); Adams v. Manown, 615 A.2d 611, 623 (Md. 1992) (Chasanow, J., joined by Bell, J., dissenting) (finding the similarities between the defenses not sufficient to invoke unclean hands).

[98] 867 F.2d 1049, 1052 (7th Cir. 1989); discussion *supra* Chapter 3, Section 3.4.2.4.

[99] *Id.*

[100] *Id.* (citing Holman v. Johnson, 1 Cowp. 341, 98 Eng. Rep. 1120 (K.B.1775) (Mansfield, C.J.)). Judge Posner made a similar observation in another case considering the application of the purely equitable defense of laches at law: See Maksym v. Loesch, 937 F.2d 1237, 1248 (7th

In the jurisdiction of the Eleventh Circuit, the fact that *in pari delicto* is allowed at law seemed to be the sole basis of one court's decision. In *Boca Raton Community Hosp., Inc. v. Tenet Healthcare Corp.*,[101] the district court for the Southern District of Florida denied the plaintiff's renewed motion for class certification due in part to the potential availability of unclean hands as a defense to legal relief.[102] The district court relied on *Official Committee of Unsecured Creditors v. Edwards*,[103] in which the Eleventh Circuit Court of Appeals held that the related defense of *in pari delicto* applies to the same cause of action.[104]

5.3.2.2.2 EQUITABLE ESTOPPEL Courts have similarly justified the application of unclean hands to legal claims by analogy to the availability of the equitable defense of estoppel. As discussed in Chapter 4, there is no barrier to the application of estoppel defenses that are not dependent on the assertion of equitable relief.[105] In adopting equitable estoppel at law even prior to the procedural union of law and equity,[106] the United States Supreme Court eschewed its equitable origins and declared that "there would seem no reason why its application should be restricted in courts of law."[107]

The American-made doctrine of judicial estoppel also serves the same court protection policy as unclean hands.[108] The Supreme Court of Maryland in *Win-Mark Ltd. P'ship v. Miles & Stockbridge*[109] made the comparison: "The policy underlying judicial estoppel and underlying the clean hands doctrine is the same. 'The clean hands doctrine is not applied for the protection of the parties nor as a

---

Cir. 1991) (ultimately determining that laches would not apply to legal relief under Illinois law); discussion *supra* Chapter 3, Section 3.4.2.4.

[101] No. 0580183CIV-SEITZ, 2006 WL 3716908 (S.D. Fla. Dec. 07, 2006).

[102] *See id.* at *15.

[103] 437 F.3d 1145 (11th Cir. 2006).

[104] *See Boca Raton Community Hosp.*, 2006 WL 3716908 at *16 (citing Official Committee of Unsecured Creditors of PSA, Inc. v. Edwards, 437 F.3d 1145, 1155–56 (11th Cir. 2006)).

[105] *See* Horn v. Cole, 51 N.H. 287, 1868 WL 2290, at *4 (N.H. 1868) (stating that equitable estoppel is "habitually administered at law" but that the practice formerly was different in that common law courts did not give effect to equity and "were often enjoined"); Barnard v. German Amer. Seminary, 13 N.W. 811, 811 (Mich. 1882) ("It is never necessary to go into equity for the mere purpose of obtaining the benefit of an equitable estoppel .... "); Poksyla v. Sundholm, 106 N.W.2d 202, 204 (Minn. 1960) ("While originally the creature of equity, [equitable estoppel] is now thoroughly incorporated into the law, and is as available in a legal action as in an equitable one[.]" quoting Dimond v. Manheim, 63 N.W. 495, 497 (Minn. 1895))).

[106] *See* USH Ventures v. Global Telesystems Group, Inc., 796 A.2d 7, 17 (Del. Sup. Ct. 2000) (discussing "historical trend" of allowing equitable defenses to be heard at law); *see also supra* Chapter 4, Section 4.3.

[107] *See* Kirk v. Hamilton, 102 U.S. 68, 78 (1880) (adopting estoppel into the common law); *see also* Wehrman v. Conklin, 155 U.S. 314, 327 (1894); Dickerson v. Colgrove, 100 U.S. 578, 582 (1879).

[108] *See* T. Leigh Anenson, *The Role of Equity in Employment Noncompetition Cases*, 42 Am. Bus. L.J. 1, 32 (2005) [hereinafter Anenson, *Role of Equity*].

[109] 693 A.2d 824 (Md. 1997).

punishment to the wrongdoer; rather, the doctrine is intended to protect the courts from having to endorse or reward inequitable conduct.'"[110]

The district court for the District of South Carolina in *Buchanan Home & Auto Supply Co., Inc. v. Firestone Tire & Rubber Co.*,[111] recognized that the same conduct that qualifies as an estoppel may also constitute unclean hands.[112] The district court applied unclean hands to deny claimed damages for warranty, tort, and contract violations.[113] The court relied on the Fourth Circuit Court of Appeals decision in *Tempo Music, Inc. v. Myers*,[114] which invoked unclean hands against a claim for equitable relief and equitable estoppel to estop a claim for damages.[115] Citing *Tempo Music*, the court concluded that unclean hands applies "whether designated as the principle underlying clean hands or as equitable estoppel."[116]

5.3.2.2.3 FRAUD ON THE COURT Finally, similar to the jurisdictions drawing analogies to the defense of *in pari delicto* and the fully incorporated equitable defense of estoppel, the Supreme Court of Michigan's recent recognition at law of litigation misconduct as a form of unclean hands in *Maldonado v. Ford Motor Co.*[117] mirrors the doctrine of "fraud on the court" frequently found in legal cases. Like unclean hands, this doctrine is concerned primarily with the integrity of the judicial process.[118] It "is applied by courts to preserve the fair administration of justice against deception, and to protect against interference with courts' ability to adjudicate matters impartially and litigants' ability to present claims and defenses for fair adjudication."[119]

---

[110] *Id.* at 830 (quoting Adams v. Manown, 615 A.2d 611, 616 (1992)).

[111] 544 F. Supp. 242 (D.S.C. 1981).

[112] *Id.* at 245; *see also* Anenson, *Role of Equity*, *supra* note 108, at 47–53 (comparing equitable and other estoppels with unclean hands).

[113] 544 F. Supp. at 245.

[114] 407 F.2d 503, 507–08 (4th Cir. 1969).

[115] *Id.* at 508 n.8.

[116] 544 F. Supp. at 245; *see also* discussion *supra* Chapter 3, Section 3.4.2.2.2. (reviewing the case) and *infra* Chapter 6, Section 6.4.2 (contrasting estoppel and unclean hands).

[117] 719 N.W.2d 809 (Mich. 2006); *see also id.* at 817 n.15. *Contra* Russell v. Casebolt, 348 S.W.2d 548, 553 (Mo. 1964) (refusing to recognize unclean hands in a damages action and reversing trial court dismissal based on perjury).

[118] *See, e.g.,* Aoude v. Mobil Oil Corp., 892 F.2d 1115, 1118–19 (1st Cir. 1989) (commenting on the importance of the fraud on the court doctrine because "[c]ourts cannot lack the power to defend their integrity against unscrupulous marauders; if that were so, it would place at risk the very fundament of the judicial system"); Tri-Cran, Inc. v. Fallon (*In re Tri-Can Inc.*), 98 B.R. 609, 615–16 (D. Mass. 1989) (quoting Bulloch v. United States, 721 F.2d 713, 718 (10th Cir. 1983) (explaining that fraud on the court is "a subcategory of fraud, misrepresentation or other misconduct in which the fraud, misrepresentation, or other misconduct . . . 'is directed to the judicial machinery itself'")); Eppes v. Snowden, 656 F. Supp. 1267, 1281 (E.D. Ky. 1986).

[119] Eugene R. Anderson & Nadia V. Holober, *Preventing Inconsistencies in Litigation with a Spotlight on Insurance Coverage Litigation: The Doctrines of Judicial Estoppel, Equitable Estoppel, Quasi-Estoppel, Collateral Estoppel, "Mend the Hold," Fraud on the Court," and Judicial and Evidentiary Admissions,* 4 CONN. INS. L.J. 589, 707 (1997–98). Many courts around

The *Maldonado* court upheld the dismissal of a legal action alleging employment discrimination based on a party's and her counsel's pretrial publicity intended to taint the jury pool.[120] Following lower-court decisions in the state, the Michigan Supreme Court announced: "The authority to dismiss a lawsuit for litigant miscon-duct is a creature of the 'clean hands doctrine' and, despite its origins, is applicable to both equitable and legal damages claims . . ."[121]

Although equitable and legal defenses had different pleading practices and may have developed during different epochs in the evolution of equity, all equitable defenses and certain legal defenses evolved from common ethical precepts that have an esteemed place in our system of justice.[122] The acceptance of certain defenses and rejection of others based on historical happenstance has created divergent streams of precedent that are distinctive only in their outcomes rather than on the basis of any principled theory or policy.[123]

---

the country have remedied various kinds of litigation misconduct regardless of the relief requested. *See, e.g.,* Rockdale Management Co. v. Shawmut Bank, 418 Mass. 596, 598 (1994) (citing Hazel-Atlas Glass Co. v. Hartford-Empire Co., 322 U.S. 238, 246 (1944)); *see also* W. R. Grace & Co., v. Western U. S. Industries, Inc., 608 F.2d 1214 (9th Cir. 1979) ("That fraud on the Patent Office is also a defense to an action for damages caused by patent infringement is indicated by Hazel-Atlas Glass Co. v. Hartford-Empire Co., 322 U.S. 238, 64 S. Ct. 997, 88 L.Ed. 1250 (1944), *overruled on other grounds,* Standard Oil of California v. United States, 429 U.S. 17, 18, 97 S. Ct. 31, 50 L.Ed.2d 21 (1976)."). Rather than applying unclean hands, however, these courts have reached the same result under the doctrine of "fraud on the court." *See* Kupferman v. Consolidated Research & Mfg. Corp., 459 F.2d 1072, 1074 n.1 (2d Cir. 1972); Sun World, Inc. v. Lizarazu Olivarria, 144 F.R.D. 384, 389– 90 (E.D. Cal. 1992); *see also In re* Marriage of Lazaro, No. A107473, 2005 WL 1332102, at *3 (Cal. Ct. App. June 6, 2005) (indicating fraud on the court is unclean hands) (citing Katz v. Karlsson, 191 P.2d 541, 541 (Cal. Ct. App. 1948) (fraud on the court)).
[120] *See Maldonado,* 719 N.W.2d at 818.
[121] *Id.* at 818 (internal citations omitted) (quoting Cummings v. Wayne Co., 210 Mich. App. 249, 252 (1995) (citing Buchanan Home & Auto Supply Co., Inc. v. Firestone Tire & Rubber Co., 544 F. Supp. 242, 244–245 (D.S.C. 1981))).
[122] Anenson, *Role of Equity, supra* note 108, at 47–49.
[123] *See* discussion *supra* Chapter 4. While remedies may be less fused than the substantive law, equitable estoppel is an example of a completed fused general defense that operates across subjects. *See* Bray, *System, supra* note 9, at 592 (suggesting that the substantive law rather than remedies better align with the coherence goal).
      There are differences about fusion in many jurisdictions between the purely equitable defenses of laches and unclean hands. Kansas adopted laches into the common law but has not yet incorporated unclean hands. *See* Moore v. Phillips, 627 P.2d 831, 835 (Kan. Ct. App. 1981) (citing McDaniel v. Messerschmidt, 382 P.2d 304 (Kan. 1963) (allowing equitable defense of laches in law actions)). Illinois also absorbed the purely equitable defense of laches but denied unclean hands. *Compare* American National Bank & Trust v. Levy, 404 N.E.2d 946, 948 (Ill. App. Ct. 1980) (equitable defense of unclean hands unavailable in legal claim) *with* Villiger v. City of Henry, 362 N.E.2d 120 (Ill. App. Ct. 1977) (equitable defense of laches applies to both law and equity). Conversely, courts in Maryland have adopted unclean hands at law but rejected laches. *Compare* Smith v. Gehring, 496 A.2d 317, 322–23 (Md. Ct. Spec. App. 1985) (laches denied in legal action), *with* Manown v. Adams, 598 A.2d 821 (Md. Ct. Spec. App. 1991) (allowing unclean hands in damages case), *rev'd on other grounds,* 615 A.2d 611, 612

While there will be situations where *in pari delicto*, estoppel, fraud on the court, or other defenses conclude the case, the fact that there is more than one means of resolving a dispute has never been a reason to deny recognition to some of them and not others.[124] Indeed, multiple claims and defenses are pled daily in the "cauldron" of our courts.[125]

In addition, unclean hands is potentially more expansive in application than the defense of *in pari delicto*, fraud on the court, or the equitable defenses of estoppel.[126] For this reason, Justice Brandeis sought to extend unclean hands to damages before the merger of law and equity in the federal system. In *Olmstead v. United States*,[127] he reasoned, "The governing principle has long been settled. It is that a court will not redress a wrong when he who invokes its aid has unclean hands. The maxim of unclean hands comes from courts of equity. *But the principle prevails also in courts of law.*"[128] In the absence of any legislative obstacles created by the merger as discussed in Chapter 4, it is time to make Justice Brandeis's theory a reality.

The primary character of equity persists today as the complement of legal jurisdiction.[129] To preclude unclean hands outright threatens this time-honored tradition. It also undermines the expressed purposes of our modern judicial system and the paramount policy of justice underlying the law.[130]

(Md. 1992). Similarly, California courts have unanimously adopted unclean hands, but laches remains confined to equity actions. *Compare* County of Los Angeles v. City of Alhambra, 165 Cal. Rptr. 440, 449 (Cal. 1980) (finding laches available only in equity) *with* Fibreboard Paper Prods. Corp. v. East Bay Union of Machinists, 39 Cal. Rptr. 64, 69 (Cal. Ct. App. 1964). However, these seemingly incongruous results would be consistent to the extent the reason for the denial of laches was not an interpretation of the merger, but rather due to the statute of limitations. *See, e.g.,* Unilogic, Inc. v. Burroughs Corp., 12 Cal. Rptr. 2d 741, 744 (Cal. Ct. App. 1992).

[124] *See* FED. R. CIV. P. 8(e)(2); *see also* William Gummow, *Conclusion* to EQUITY IN COMMERCIAL LAW, *supra* note 32, at 516 [hereinafter Gummow, *Conclusion*] (quoting S. M. WADDAMS, DIMENSIONS OF PRIVATE LAW: CATEGORIES AND CONCEPTS IN ANGLO-AMERICAN LEGAL REASONING (2003)) ("Often several concepts have worked concurrently and cumulatively, so that competing explanations and categories are not so much alternatives, of which only one can be correct, as different dimensions of a complex phenomenon, of which several may be simultaneously valid and necessary." (emphasis omitted)). *But see* DOBBS LAW OF REMEDIES, *supra* note 81, § 2.4(2) at 68 (claiming use of unclean hands is "spurious" when a comparable legal rule will reach the same result).

[125] CARDOZO, JUDICIAL PROCESS, *supra* note 40, at 10.

[126] *See* discussion *infra* Chapter 6.

[127] 277 U.S. 438 (1928) (Brandeis, J., dissenting).

[128] *Id.* at 483–84 (emphasis added).

[129] *See* 27A AM. JUR. 2D *Equity* § 3 (1996).

[130] Equity was considered critical to the existence and legitimacy of law by ensuring that the law would achieve its overriding purpose – justice. *See, e.g.,* Clark v. Teeven Holding Co., 625 A.2d 869, 878 (Del. Ch. 1992) ("The use of the term 'equitable principles' ... is merely equivalent to the words 'principles of fairness or justice.'"); Anton-Hermann Chroust, *Aristotle's Conception of "Equity" (Epieikeia)*, 18 NOTRE DAME L. REV. 119, 125–26 (1942–43) (explaining the meaning

5.3.2.3 Fallacy of a Remedial Hierarchy

Not only do the similarities between unclean hands and the legal or other equitable defenses that are routinely used at law provide grounds to give unclean hands equal treatment under the law, but the lack of any real difference between legal and equitable remedies also advances this position.[131] Damages are often as severe as equitable remedies,[132] and equally harsh remedies require equal treatment.[133] Even if damages are less harmful in a particular case, such severity does not derive from any purported difference between law and equity.[134] Judges can parcel such states of affairs in each case.

Courts should prevent those who have acted unconscionably from benefiting from their own misconduct. Thus, judges should *not* require better behavior of plaintiffs simply because they are seeking an equitable remedy. The assumption that the enforcement of equitable rights is not a matter of right but rather a privilege "has long since become obsolete."[135] Indeed, the district court in *Buchanan Home & Auto Supply Co., Inc. v. Firestone Tire & Rubber Co.*[136] and the Northern District of California in *Metro Publ'g, Ltd. v. San Jose Mercury News, Inc.*[137] declared unclean

---

of equity as a component of justice); William Searle Holdsworth, *The Early History of Equity*, 13 MICH. L. REV. 293, 293 (1915).

[131] *See generally* Douglas Laycock, *The Death of the Irreparable Injury Rule*, 103 HARV. L. REV. 687 (1990) [hereinafter Laycock, *Death*]; Laycock, *Triumph of Equity*, *supra* note 81. *See also* SARAH WORTHINGTON, EQUITY 26 (2003) (explaining that many of the rules governing damages are similar to equitable relief in that they are meant to prevent unconscionable behavior); *cf.* Stephen A. Smith, *Form and Substance in Equitable Remedies*, *in* DIVERGENCES IN PRIVATE LAW 321, 330–31 (Andrew Robertson & Michael Tilbury, eds. 2016) (explaining that there is a cost advantage to the legal system to award damages since equitable relief tends to be nonmonetary, which is not executable by third parties, and enforcement entails more litigation and potentially incarceration of the defendant).

[132] CHAFEE, SOME PROBLEMS, *supra* note 1, at 29; Garvey, *supra* note 66, at 67–68; *cf.* Edward Yorio, *A Defense of Equitable Defenses*, 51 OHIO ST. L.J. 1201, 1208 (1990) (noting that successful plaintiffs may not recover their full monetary remedies due to judicial discretion in the process of measuring damages).

[133] William J. Lawrence, III, Note, *The Application of the Clean Hands Doctrine in Damage Actions*, 57 NOTRE DAME L. REV. 673, 681 (1982).

[134] *Id.*; *see* Smith, *Form and Substance in Equitable Remedies*, *supra* note 131, at 339 (delineating why granting specific relief to plaintiffs who have delayed may cause a special kind of prejudice not normally suffered when plaintiffs seek monetary damages to explain why laches is applied exclusively to equitable relief).

[135] ANDREW BURROWS, REMEDIES FOR TORT AND BREACH OF CONTRACT 457 (3rd ed. 2004); NEWMAN, EQUITY AND LAW, *supra* note 68, at 38; RAFAL ZAKRZEWSKI, REMEDIES RECLASSIFIED (2005). *But see* DOBBS LAW OF REMEDIES, *supra* note 81, § 2.4(2) at 69 (endorsing rights versus privilege dichotomy in denying unclean hands at law).

[136] 544 F. Supp. 242 (D.S.C. 1981).

[137] 861 F. Supp. 870, 880 (N.D. Cal. 1994) (finding that unclean hands barred claims for damages on trademark infringement and dilution claims).

hands a viable defense to the legal claims at issue because "rights not suited for protection at equity should not be protected at law."[138]

The court itself is also deserving of protection regardless of remedy. Indeed, in accepting the defense of unclean hands to ban the legal claims of tortious interference with contact and unfair trade practices, the Connecticut Superior Court in *First Fairfield Funding, LLC v. Goldman*[139] reasoned that "[t]he integrity of the court is no less worthy of protection in actions at law, than in actions in equity."[140]

For these reasons, Chafee and other twentieth-century commentators had called for the end to any distinction between law and equity after the integration.[141] Justice Brandeis also explained the policies underlying unclean hands that are promoted in cases seeking legal *and* equitable relief in *Olmstead v. United States:*[142] "Then aid is denied despite the defendant's wrong. It is denied in order to maintain respect for law; in order to promote confidence in the administration of justice; in order to preserve the judicial process from contamination."[143] Therefore, continuing to condition the consideration of unclean hands on the assertion of equitable relief after the merger yields inconsistent outcomes and impairs the legitimacy of law.[144]

The classic cases of *Carmen v. Fox Film Corp.*[145] highlight how the same circumstances result in conflicting judgments under the doctrine of unclean hands.[146] In the first *Carmen* case, a minor plaintiff who misrepresented her age in entering an employment contract was denied the right to sue in equity to enjoin interference with a subsequent contract she made with another employer upon disaffirming the initial contract.[147] However, after dismissal from the second job, she was allowed in the second *Carmen* case to recover a verdict at law for damages against the same defendant for having caused the breach of the second contract.[148]

The modern version of the *Carmen* cases is found in Oregon. In *N. Pacific Lumber Co. v. Oliver*,[149] the Supreme Court of Oregon precluded the enforcement

---

[138] *Buchanan Home*, 544 F. Supp. at 245; *see also Metro Publ'g*, 861 F. Supp. at 880 (quoting the foregoing passage from *Buchanan Home*).

[139] No. CV020465799S, 2003 WL 22708882, at *1 (Conn. Super Ct. Nov. 3, 2003).

[140] *Id.* at *1.

[141] CHAFEE, SOME PROBLEMS, *supra* note 1, at 94; Chafee I, *supra* note 53, at 906.

[142] 277 U.S. 438 (1928).

[143] *Id.* at 484 (Brandeis, J., dissenting).

[144] NEWMAN, EQUITY AND LAW, *supra* note 68, at 48 (listing the failure to consider the unconscientious conduct of the plaintiff to bar the recovery of damages but to consider such conduct to bar specific relief as one of the three major deficiencies in Anglo-American law); Yorio, *supra* note 132, at 1206–07 (summarizing the economic criticisms due to case outcome inconsistencies).

[145] Carmen v. Fox Film Corp., 269 F. 928 (2d Cir. 1920), *reversing,* 258 F. 703 (S.D.N.Y. 1919) (equity); Carmen v. Fox Film Corp., 198 N.Y.S. 766 (N.Y. App. Div. 1923) (law).

[146] DOBBS LAW OF REMEDIES, *supra* note 81, § 2.4 at 46 (discussing the cases); NEWMAN, EQUITY AND LAW, *supra* note 68, at 249 (same).

[147] Carmen v. Fox Film Corp., 269 F. 928 (2d Cir. 1920).

[148] Carmen v. Fox Film Corp., 198 N.Y.S. 766 (N.Y. App. Div. 1923).

[149] 596 P.2d 931 (Or. 1979).

of a noncompete agreement on the basis of unclean hands under its equitable jurisdiction.[150] In a later case seeking legal relief, an Oregon court of appeals in *Gratreak v. N. Pacific Lumber Co.*[151] refused to consider the defense of unclean hands to bar enforcement of the same covenant involving the same employer because it involved an action for damages.[152]

The Oregon appellate court and other courts acknowledge the irrationality of their decisions with respect to unclean hands.[153] Nevertheless, they continue to rely on the fictional difference in remedies to deny unclean hands even though such cases produce anomalous results. Holmes admonished long ago that "the greatest danger [in accomplishing an inaccurate legal analysis] . . . is that of being misled by ready-made generalizations, and of thinking only in phrases to which as lawyers the judges have become accustomed, instead of looking straight at things . . ."[154]

Even before consolidation of law and equity under the federal rules, the California Supreme Court looked straight at the forms of relief and declared that "[i]n reality the distinction between the two classes of remedies is more or less arbitrary and groundless."[155] In fact, "everyone agrees that the difference in the remedy has no bearing whatever on the relevance of equitable principles to the case."[156] Modern-day chancellors are in accord. In particular, Chancellor Quillen of Delaware

---

[150] *Id.* at 944. While the employer sought an injunction as well as damages in the case, the supreme court clearly stated that it was "a suit in equity." *Id.* at 934–35.

[151] 609 P.2d 375 (Or. Ct. App. 1980).

[152] *Id.* at 379. The majority justified its decision due to the nature of the requested remedy. *Id.* at 378.

[153] Judge Thornton, in dissent, noted the irregular result: "In my view, it would be anomalous to bar North Pacific from specifically enforcing a similar non-competition covenant on the ground that it had engaged in unethical conduct material to the work situation of its employe[e]. . . and then permit it to threaten to sue to enforce the identical covenant and then rely on it as a shield to liability for its threats." *Id.* at 379 (Thornton, J., dissenting); *see also* Ellwood v. Mid States Commodities, Inc., 404 N.W.2d 174, 184 (Iowa 1987) (denying unclean hands at law despite the anomalous result that the same conduct may be a legal defense by another name).

[154] Lorenzo v. Wirth, 49 N.E. 1010, 1011 (Mass. 1898), *cited in* Olson v. Synergistic Techn. Bus. Sys., Inc., 628 N.W.2d 142, 153 n.9 (Minn. 2001); *accord* NEWMAN, EQUITY AND LAW, *supra* note 68, at 41 ("Einstein has remarked that most mistakes in philosophy and logic occur because the human mind is apt to take the symbol for reality.") (citing COSMIC RELIGION 101 (Codovici Fried ed. 1931)).

[155] Philpott v. Super. Court in and for Los Angeles Cty., 36 P.2d 635, 637 (Cal. 1934).

[156] NEWMAN, EQUITY AND LAW, *supra* note 68, at 43. The irrationality of using anachronisms can also be seen when the difference between a legal and an equitable remedy depends on whether the plaintiff seeks to collect on a note versus foreclose on a mortgage. *See* Kerin v. Udolf, 334 A.2d 434 (Conn. 1973). Another specious distinction between forms of relief occurs in property cases in which the kind of remedy depends on whether the plaintiff is in possession and, accordingly, is seeking quiet title or ejectment. *See* Harsha v. Marcella, 693 P.2d 760 (Wyo. 1985); *see also* USH Ventures v. Global Telesystems Group, Inc., 796 A.2d 7, 20 (Del. Super. Ct. 2000) (explaining how law or equity depends on whether the plaintiff is in possession).

Superior Court advised in *USH Ventures v. Global Telesystems Group, Inc.* that "we need to desert the whole idea of hierarchy between law and equity."[157]

Research by Douglas Laycock supports this conclusion. After surveying more than one thousand cases, he concluded that a remedial hierarchy of legal and equitable relief no longer exists.[158] In an article published in the *Harvard Law Review* and a subsequent book on the same subject, Laycock criticized courts for continuing to cite now irrelevant conditions developed during the Middle Ages that purport to remove the remedial choices of litigants.[159] Laycock provided an exhaustive account of the formal rules announced by judges requiring an irreparable injury ("no adequate remedy at law") that disguised the many operative rules existing as the true bases for their decisions.[160] He described the continued use of the law–equity distinction as a "dysfunctional proxy" for a series of policy choices.[161] Laycock further denounced the confusing state of equity jurisprudence and detailed how such doctrinal double-talk obscured the real issues and obstructed the development of the law.[162]

Laycock's observations of equitable remedies have important implications for equitable defenses. Even though the United States Supreme Court has chosen to reestablish the law–equity line with respect to injunctions, and while fusing equitable defenses are not yet representative of the prevailing judicial climate in this country,[163] a few courts give credence to Chafee's idea that alleged differences in remedies do not require a difference in the application of unclean hands. For example, the district court in *Buchanan Home & Auto Supply Co., Inc. v. Firestone Tire & Rubber Co.*[164] declared, "the clean hands doctrine embodies a general principle equally applicable to damage actions."[165] In *Union Pac. R. Co.*

---

[157] *USH Ventures*, 796 A.2d at 15. As discussed *supra* Chapter 1 note 11, Delaware is one of six states to retain separate courts (or divisions) of law and equity.

[158] Laycock, *Death*, *supra* note 131, at 701 (reviewing 1,400 injunction cases).

[159] *See generally id.*; LAYCOCK, IRREPARABLE INJURY RULE, *supra* note 80. *See also* Laycock, *Triumph of Equity*, *supra* note 81, at 54–64 (reviewing book and article).

[160] *See* Laycock, *Death*, *supra* note 131, at 701–65 (listing seventeen proposed rules that restate the real reason for the decision without reference to the irreparable injury rule); LAYCOCK, IRREPARABLE INJURY RULE, *supra* note 80, at 265–76 (same).

[161] Laycock, *Death*, *supra* note 131, at 696, 765; *see also* Laycock, *Triumph of Equity*, *supra* note 81, at 78 (describing law and equity as a "dysfunctional proxy for a series of functional choices").

[162] *See* Laycock, *Death*, *supra* note 131, at 765–771; *accord* NEWMAN, EQUITY AND LAW, *supra* note 68, at 261 (pointing out how oblique explanations conceal rather than clarify); *see also* WILLIAM Q. DE FUNIAK, HANDBOOK OF MODERN EQUITY 123 (2nd ed. 1956) (discussing the former prerequisite to equitable jurisdiction that there be a property right in dispute by explaining that "courts of equity continue to be burdened, like Coleridge's ancient mariner, with a dead albatross hung around their necks.")

[163] *See* Gergen, Golden & Smith, *supra* note 35, at 207–08 (discussing *eBay v. MercExchange, L.L.C.*, 547 U.S. 388, 391 (2006) and its consequences across the United States).

[164] 544 F. Supp. 242 (D.S.C. 1981).

[165] *Id.* at 245. Despite diversity jurisdiction, the district court apparently viewed the question of application as a matter of federal procedural law given its references to federal decisions. *Id. passim.*

v. Chicago & N.W. Ry. Co.,[166] the District Court of Illinois also proclaimed that "The clean hands maxim is not peculiar to equity, but expresses a general principle equally applicable to damage actions."[167] The Seventh Circuit Court of Appeals had previously applied unclean hands to bar an action for damages under a federal statute in *Maltz v. Sax,*[168] declaring that the maxims of equity are available as defenses in actions at law.[169]

As discussed in Chapter 3, cases that apply unclean hands at law in reliance on precedent applying the defense to equitable relief embody the idea of equality between legal and equitable remedies.[170] Moreover, a growing number of courts have relied on the decision of the United States Supreme Court in *Precision Instrument Mfg. Co. v. Auto. Maint. Mach. Co.*[171] to extend unclean hands to legal remedies.[172]

Based on the foregoing considerations, there is no reason to elevate one remedy over another for the purposes of applying unclean hands. The defense should be considered irrespective of remedial classifications.

5.3.2.4 Institutional Advantage

The previous two sections demonstrated that the division of law and equity for the defense of unclean hands lacks a rational basis and produces anomalous results. This section explains why conditioning the availability of unclean hands on requests for equitable relief also invites other irregularities in the administration of justice.

Under the traditional test, the application of the defense of unclean hands is dependent on the assertion of an equitable remedy. As a result, lines must be drawn between legal and equitable forms of relief. Other than notable equitable remedies like injunctions, such line drawing has been and remains problematic.[173] According

---

[166] 226 F. Supp. 400 (D.C. Ill. 1964).

[167] *Id.* at 410 (citing CHAFEE, PROBLEMS, *supra* note 1, at 94). While the case concerned only equitable relief, it embodies the idea of equal application of unclean hands in principle. In making the statement, the court was attempting to justify its analogy to a case seeking damages that involved an illegal contract made in violation of the securities laws. *See id.* (citing A. C. Frost & Co. v. Coeur d'Alene Mines Corp., 312 U.S. 38, 43 (1941)).

[168] 134 F.2d 2 (7th Cir. 1943).

[169] *See id.* at 5 (citing 28 U.S.C.A. § 398 and Rule 2 of the Rules of Civil Procedure, 28 U.S.C.A. following section 723c).

[170] *See* discussion *supra* Chapter 3, Section 3.5.

[171] 324 U.S. 806 (1945); discussion *supra* Chapter 2.

[172] *See, e.g.,* Kendall-Jackson Winery, Ltd. v. Superior Court, 90 Cal. Rptr. 2d 743, 749 (Cal. Ct. App. 1999); *Cummings v. Wayne Cty.,* 533 N.W.2d 13, 14 (Mich. Ct. App. 1995); Anenson & Mark, *supra* note 4, at 1511 ("[R]elying primarily on the Supreme Court's inequitable conduct decision in *Precision Instrument,* a number of courts no longer restrict unclean hands to equitable remedies or preserve the substantive version of the defense.")

[173] To assist the modern jurist, Professor Bray has also catalogued equitable remedies and related doctrines. Bray, *System, supra* note 9, at 551–86.

to the Eighth Circuit Court of Appeals in *Ashley v. Boyle's Famous Corned Beef Co.*,[174] "Distinguishing between legal and equitable claims and remedies for purposes of applying [exclusively equitable defenses] has proven difficult."[175]

Additionally, deciphering legal from equitable remedies becomes more challenging with the passage of time.[176] As discussed in Chapter 4, many of the distinctions between law and equity are fading fast.[177] The United States Supreme Court has announced that a historical inquiry into equitable principles is not too difficult,[178] but that may not always be the case. Equity is challenging, in part because it has an extended legacy.[179] Many equitable remedies predate the nation.[180] Indeed, equitable principles and maxims are old enough to be rendered in Latin.[181] While the Court has been more careful to identify particular remedies and defenses as equitable, along with the conditions of their application,[182] there may be occasions when

---

[174] 66 F.3d 164 (8th Cir. 1995).

[175] *Id.* at 169 n.3 (laches).

[176] *See* USH Ventures v. Global Telesystems Group, Inc., 796 A.2d 7, 14 (Del. Super. Ct. 2000). The California Supreme Court explained in *Philpott v. Super. Court in and for Los Angeles Cty.*:

> Considerable confusion now exists among the bench and bar as to the proper classification of this cause of action, due to the fact that the courts of law administering this relief apply equitable principles, and to the further fact that certain expressions found in court opinion and text-books, on first impression, might seem to classify it as an action in equity.

36 P.2d 635, 639 (Cal. 1934).

[177] *See* discussion *supra* Chapter 4.

[178] *See* Great-West Life & Annuity Ins. Co. v. Knudson, 534 U.S. 204, 217 (2002) (advising that consulting current works such as *Dobbs* and the *Restatements* should make the historical answer clear (citing *id.* at 233–34 (Ginsburg, J., dissenting))).

[179] *See* Chafee, SELECTED ESSAYS ON EQUITY, *supra* note 56, at iv, xii (commenting that no other subject "offers as rich an opportunity to delve into problems of jurisprudence and the philosophy of law as does equity")).

[180] For instance, the first case articulating the principle of estoppel in the English chancery court is unknown. *See* MELVILLE M. BIGELOW, A TREATISE ON THE LAW OF ESTOPPEL, OR OF INCONTESTABLE RIGHTS 603 (6th ed. 1913) (quoting Lord Eldon's statement in *Keate v. Phillips*, (1881) 18 Ch. D. 560, 577 (Ch.), that estoppel was "a very old head of equity"). Reported decisions date from the seventeenth century. *See* SNELL'S PRINCIPLES OF EQUITY, *supra* note 69, at 561–62 (citing cases over the centuries); Walter S. Beck, *Estoppel Against Inconsistent Position in Judicial Proceedings*, 9 BROOKLYN L. REV. 245, 245 (1940) (citing early estoppel cases in equity).

[181] *See* Douglas Laycock, *How Remedies Became a Field: A History*, 27 REV. LITIG. 161, 168 (2008) ("Remedies is an ancient legal concept."). For example, the inspiration for prohibiting inconsistent conduct or conflicting allegations addressed by estoppel comes from the Latin maxim *allegans contraria non est audiendus*. T. Leigh Anenson, *The Triumph of Equity: Equitable Estoppel in Modern Litigation*, 27 REV. LITIG. 377, 384 (2008) [hereinafter Anenson, *Triumph of Equity*] (citing HERBERT BROOM, SELECTION OF LEGAL MAXIMS 139 (4th ed. 1854) ("He is not to be heard who alleges things contradictory to each other.")).

[182] In *McCutchen*, for instance, the Court cited four treatises and two of its prior decisions linking the double recovery and common fund defenses to equity and unjust enrichment. US Airways, Inc., v. McCutchen, 569 U.S. 88, 97 n.4 (2013).

it is unable to turn back the clock.[183] History can be nonexistent or inconclusive.[184] Reliance on the past is also a factual matter,[185] which means that courts and counsel (and professors) can be wrong.[186] Scholars have already accused the Supreme Court of indulging in several historical inaccuracies associated with equitable principles in its decisions.[187] A number of these claims have merit.[188] Others stem from the Court's failure to expound on the meaning of equity or acknowledge its evolutionary process.[189]

Along with defenses,[190] remedies have become so intertwined in this postmerger era that it is difficult to discern what is or was "equity" versus "law."[191] The advent of

---

[183] *See* Anenson, *Triumph of Equity, supra* note 181, at 419–21 (discussing uncertainty in the state courts concerning equitable estoppel due to its historical application in law and equity); *see also* Samuel L. Bray, *The Supreme Court and the New Equity,* 68 VAND. L. REV. 997, 1011 n.68 (2015) [hereinafter Bray, *New Equity*] (noting that there is no overview of equity in the eighteenth century).

[184] *See* Hanbury, *supra* note 86, at 50–51 ("Dean Pound has treated the history of the maxims of equity in a masterly fashion, but even his gigantic powers of research have failed to trace them to their exact sources."); *see also* Kroger, *supra* note 59, at 1471 (describing different formal and traditional conceptions of equity jurisprudence in the Founding Era that may affect the extent to which federal equity power can be justified by reference to the history of equity).

[185] PHILIP BOBBITT, CONSTITUTIONAL INTERPRETATION xiii (1991) (discussing the historical form of argument in constitutional law).

[186] *See* STEPHEN BREYER, ACTIVE LIBERTY 126 (2005) (noting that judges are not expert historians); *see generally* Matthew J. Festa, *The Useable Past,* 38 SETON HALL L. REV. 479 (2008) (proposing that historical arguments to interpret law be subject to evidentiary rules).

[187] *See* Anenson & Mark, *supra* note 4, at 1525 n.554 ("In attempting to answer questions of equity, members of the Supreme Court have disagreed over the existence or relevancy of a particular custom, been mistaken as to what it is or means, and divided when traditional principles purportedly deviate from practice.") (collecting academic writing); *see, e.g.,* Bray, *New Equity, supra* note 183, at 1001–02 (reviewing literature on the Supreme Court's historical blunders in equity jurisprudence); Chapter 3, Section 3.5. While the Court makes an easy target, there is enough blame to go around in the legal community. Practitioners lack a proper conceptual framework for equitable issues because they have not likely been educated with a holistic vision of equity and have few or no equity articles from the present generation of legal scholars outside of concerns with trusts and injunctive relief. *See* discussion *supra* Chapters 1 and 2.

[188] *See, e.g.,* Gergen, Golden & Smith, *supra* note 35, at 220, 249 (discussing the Supreme Court's disregard of the traditional equitable presumptions concerning injunctions); Bray, *New Equity, supra* note 183, at 1039–40 (citing Supreme Court cases rejecting presumptions regarding irreparable injury, balancing of hardships, the public interest, whether an injunction should issue, and the likelihood of success on the merits).

[189] *See* Anenson, *Age of Statutes, supra* note 20, at 565; *accord* Bray, *New Equity, supra* note 183, at 1017 (noting that the Court has not recognized historical change in its ERISA cases).

[190] *USH Ventures,* 796 A.2d at 14 ("[E]quitable defenses generally, a long time ago, worked their way into purely legal cases. Delaware has, however, generally failed to document, in any comprehensive fashion, the welcomed invasion.").

[191] *See* Mason, *Fusion: Fallacy, Future or Finished?, supra* note 62, at 46 ("Very few causes of action or remedies will be exclusively equitable in historical derivation and even these are now statutory in most cases."); *see also* Tiong Min Yeo, *Choice of Law for Equity* (arguing that the mixed and uncertain heritage of equitable doctrines will unduly complicate choice of law analysis for equity), *in* EQUITY IN COMMERCIAL LAW, *supra* note 32, at 147, 168. For case examples, see *USH Ventures,* 796 A.2d at 18 (describing difference in rescission at law and

statutory causes of action compounds the problem.[192] Therefore, attempts at a
reasoned distinction between legal and equitable remedies have often been exercises
in futility.[193] For example, in *Sender v. Mann*,[194] the Colorado District Court faced
the issue of whether a bankruptcy trustee's fraudulent conveyance claims against the
debtors' accomplices in a Ponzi scheme were equitable in nature under Colorado
law and subject to the defense of unclean hands.[195] The court ultimately found that
such claims fell into the category of "equitable" remedies even though the trustee
only sought money damages.[196]

   Complicating the puzzle is the state courts struggle with whether to classify claims
by their origin or nature.[197] The United States Supreme Court has also not been
clear whether the comparison is to origin, nature, or purpose.[198] Some of the

equity); Smith v. Gehring, 496 A.2d 317, 325 (Md. Ct. Spec. App. 1985) (discussing absorption
of rescission into the law courts).
[192] *See, e.g.,* Gudenau v. Bang, 781 P.2d 1357, 1363 n.9 (Alaska 1989) ("An action to enforce a
judgment may be legal or equitable in nature, depending on the relief sought."); Thompson
v. Coughlin, 997 P.2d 191, 193 (Or. 2000) (accounting under the Uniform Partnership Act
statute); Corvallis Sand & Gravel Co. v. State Land Bd., 439 P.2d 575, 578 (Or. 1968) (finding
quo warranto statute is "equity" despite tracing it to a common law writ); Norris v. United
Mineral Prods. Co., 158 P.2d 679 (Wyo. 1945) (discussing whether a statutory quiet title action
is law or equity). *Compare* Philpott v. Super. Court in and for Los Angeles Cty., 36 P.2d at 641
(tracing statutory rescission to common law forms of action), *with* Gehring, 496 A.2d at 325
(describing rescission of contract as equitable affirmative relief for purposes of applying
equitable defense of laches; *see also* Swisher v. Swisher, 124 S.W.3d 477 (Mo. Ct.
App. 2003) (statutory divorce action); *Ex parte* Payne, 598 S.W.2d 312, 318 (Tex. App. 1980)
(finding that laches is not available in statutory child support collection action), *overruled on
other grounds*, Huff v. Huff, 648 S.W.2d 286 (Tex. 1983).
[193] Chancellor Quillen describes the division of legal and equitable relief as "pretty clear-cut" with
only a small percentage of cases causing consternation and confusion.

> Law has a criminal side, equity does not. Generally, on the civil side, law litigates money
> damage suits (substitutional relief) and equity litigates suits where the Plaintiff wants
> something instead of money (relief in specie) or something in addition to money. This
> simple distinction probably takes care of over ninety-five percent of the non-statutory
> jurisdictional divide.

USH Ventures, 796 A.2d at 15.
[194] 423 F. Supp.2d 1155 (D. Colo. 2006) (applying Colorado law).
[195] *Id.* at 1167–68.
[196] *Id.*
[197] *See* discussion *supra* Chapter 3, Section 3.5 & note 279 (citing cases); *see also* Anenson,
Triumph of Equity, supra note 181, at 421 (explaining how state courts classify estoppel by its
nature rather than its origin to ascertain whether judge or jury determines the defense).
[198] Resnik, *supra* note 16, at 254 (criticizing Supreme Court remedies cases and its assessment of
equitable principles pursuant to nature rather than purpose). The controversy over certain
ancient discretionary writs is evidence of this confusion. For habeas corpus, compare Erica
Hashimoto, *Reclaiming the Equitable Heritage of Habeas*, 108 Nw. U. L. Rev. 139, 186–87
(2013) (arguing that the writ is equitable because although litigants sought the Great Writ
primarily from a common law court – the Court of King's Bench – the court's exercise of power
to issue the writ was built around equitable principles), with Bray, *System, supra* note 9, at
559–60 (arguing that habeas corpus is a legal remedy by origin). For mandamus, compare
CIGNA Corp. v. Amara, 563 U.S. 421, 440 (2011) (describing mandamus as an equitable

confusion over equitable principles presumably arises from the erroneous belief that equity, like the pastoral scene on Keats's urn, is forever frozen in time.[199] For instance, Professor Jared Goldstein's argument that the balancing process for equitable remedies lacks historical legitimacy assumes that no modernization of equity is appropriate.[200] This is surely incorrect.[201] Equity, like the tradition it is built upon, is a living thing.[202] Life is short, while art and equity are long. Although the Court may seem to be raising dead defenses, it is actually recalling rituals that are very much alive.[203] If the remedy or remedial doctrine has changed in shape or substance, there is an evaluative process of analogy that should be acknowledged to discern whether something new has been created.[204] Equally important for the application of the equitable defense of unclean hands (and the demarcation of the doctrine itself) is whether something equitable still remains.[205]

remedy), with *In re* Skinner & Eddy Corp., 265 U.S. 86, 96 (1924) (describing mandamus as a legal remedy that is subject to equitable principles).

[199] *See, e.g.,* Gummow, *Conclusion, supra* note 124, at 516 (emphasizing that "no one seriously suggests that some Ice Age descended upon equity" with the merger).

[200] *See* Goldstein, *supra* note 19, at 490–515 (questioning the historical accuracy of equitable balancing for injunctions); *cf.* David Schoenbrod, *The Immortality of Equitable Balancing*, 96 VA. L. REV. IN BRIEF 17, 18–19 (2010). The lack of clarity on this point and the Supreme Court's rote intonations of history makes Goldstein's analysis understandable. *See* Goldstein, *supra*, at 515 ("[T]he Supreme Court has falsely presented equitable balancing as an ancient judicial practice[.]"). *See generally id.* (investigating the origins of balancing the equities criterion and concluding that it is a post–Civil War phenomenon deriving from common law nuisance actions).

[201] Anenson & Mark, *supra* note 4, at 1502–05 (positing that tradition of equity includes policy analysis allowing for updating); Bray, *New Equity, supra* note 183, at 1014–15 (concluding that the Supreme Court is constructing an idealized history of equity with source materials coming from the middle to late nineteenth century).

[202] Poe v. Ullman, 367 U.S. 497, 542 (1961) (Harlan, J., dissenting) ("[T]radition is a living thing."); *see also* CARDOZO, JUDICIAL PROCESS, *supra* note 40, at 26 (commenting that there is "not a received tradition which does not threaten to dissolve").

[203] *See* Anenson, *Age of Statutes, supra* note 20, at 567; *see also* 1 POMEROY'S EQUITY JURISPRUDENCE, FIFTH EDITION, *supra* note 5, § 67 (explaining how equitable principles have an "inherent capacity of expansion" and are "essentially unlimited").

[204] *See* Anenson, *Triumph of Equity, supra* note 181, at 384–87 (explaining how estoppel originated in the law courts but that its adoption in chancery transformed it to equitable estoppel, which was then readopted in the law courts). Again, the equitable defense of unclean hands has morphed into several different doctrines, some of them used in statutory law. *See, e.g.,* Anenson, *Statutory Interpretation, supra* note 2, at 13–16 (analyzing defenses of inequitable conduct, patent misuse, and employee misconduct).

[205] *See* discussion *supra* Chapter 4 (advising how once exclusively equitable defenses like mistake or fraud have lost their equitable label after their integration into the common law). Estoppel and *in pari delicto* are available in law and equity and have a complicated history of borrowing and adaption. *See* Anenson, *Triumph of Equity, supra* note 181, at 384–87 (explaining estoppel's development in law and equity); Wade, *supra* note 88, at 268–69 (explaining the evolution of *in pari delicto* in law and equity). Estoppel has retained its equitable designation, although *in pari delicto* is often called a "common law" defense or described as unclean hands' "legal" cousin. Anenson & Mark, *supra* note 4, at 1521 n.530; Byron v. Clay, 867 F.2d 1049, 1052 (7th Cir. 1989) (Posner, J.) (discussing *in pari delicto* as unclean hands counterpart legal doctrine). Part of the difficulty stems from the different senses in which the phrase "common law" is used (i.e.,

As analyzed in Chapter 3, sometimes courts resolve the quandary by labeling the lawsuit "quasi" equitable as opposed to "purely" or "strictly" legal.[206] Similarly, in discerning judicial discretion to award or deny statutory relief, the Supreme Court has recognized an equivalency if the requested remedy "closely resembles"[207] or is "indistinguishable" from traditional equitable remedies.[208] Cases in which litigants assert two or more remedies[209] and lawsuits in which the character of the remedy changes after filing present additional dilemmas.[210]

Causes of action for promissory estoppel[211] and quasi-contract[212] as well as lawsuits seeking a declaratory judgment[213] or an accounting[214] have been particularly

common law as judge-made law in contradistinction to equity) and the issue addressed (i.e., relating to its use against damages rather than for interpretative purposes). The Supreme Court treated *in pari delicto* as an equitable defense in its statutory cases involving antitrust and securities law. *See* Anenson, *Age of Statutes, supra* note 20, at 568 n.177.

[206] *See* discussion *supra* Chapter 3, Section 3.5. On the other side of the equation is, of course, the "equitable defense." All courts agree that unclean hands was an equitable defense before the union of law and equity. Whether unclean hands is an equitable defense that can be pled at law within the meaning of the merger statute and rules is discussed *supra* at Chapter 4.

[207] CIGNA Corp. v. Amara, 563 U.S. 421, 440 (2011).

[208] Sereboff v. Mid Atlantic Medical Services, Inc., 547 U.S. 356, 368 (2006); *see* U.S. Airways Inc., v. McCutchen, 569 U.S. 88, 96 (2013) (explaining Mid Atlantic's claim to be the "modern day equivalent of an action in equity to enforce a contract-based lien – called an equitable lien by agreement").

[209] For courts looking at the remedies collectively, see C&K Engineering Contractors v. Amber Steel Co., 587 P.2d 1136, 1140–41 (Cal. 1978); Fred O. Watson Co. v. U.S. Life Ins. Co., 258 N.W.2d 776, 778 (Minn. 1977) ("incidental"); Thompson v. Coughlin, 997 P.2d 191, 195 (Or. 2000) ("ancillary"). For a case that appears to segregate the claims, see First Fairfield Funding, LLC v. Goldman, No. CV020465799S, 2003 WL 22708882, at *1 (Conn. Super Ct. Nov. 3, 2003).

[210] *See* Truitt v. Miller, 407 A.2d 1073 (D.C. 1979) (ordering equitable rescission as remedy and denying the application of unclean hands despite the complaint seeking money damages); Universal Builders, Inc. v. Moon Motor Lodge, Inc., 244 A.2d 10, 15 (Pa. 1968) (discussing how plaintiff "in effect" received a legal remedy but retained jurisdiction of equity).

Another error courts make is considering the claim (as opposed to the defense to determine whether the action is "legal" or "equitable") when unclean hands is pled as an affirmative defense to an affirmative defense. *See* Conklin v. Conklin, No. 14-77-7, 1978 WL 215763, at *9, *14 (Ohio Ct. App. Feb. 9, 1978) (wrongly classifying the plaintiff's cause of action); Tripati v. Arizona, 16 P.3d 783, 786 (Ariz. Ct. App. 2000); Billes v. Bailey, 555 A.2d 460, 462–63 (D.C. 1989).

[211] Most of the classification decisions have arisen in cases determining the right to trial by jury. *See* C&K *Engineering*, 587 P.2d at 1138–41 (holding that promissory estoppel is an equitable remedy); Olson v. Synergistic Techn. Bus. Sys., Inc., 628 N.W.2d 142, 153 (Minn. 2001) (determining that promissory estoppel is an equitable remedy); *see id.* at 154–57 (Anderson, J., Lancaster, J., concurring) (arguing that promissory estoppel is both legal and equitable remedy).

[212] *Compare First Fairfield Funding*, 2003 WL 22708882, at *1 (holding that quasi-contract is equity) *with* Karpierz v. Easley, 68 S.W.3d 565, 570 (Mo. Ct. App. 2002) (holding that quasi-contract is law); *see also* The Fischer Org., Inc. v. Landry's Seafood Restaurants, Inc., 792 A.2d 349, 357–58 (Mich. Ct. App. 2002) (applying unclean hands because unjust enrichment is equitable relief).

[213] *See* Jones v. Douglas, 418 S.E.2d 19, 22–23 (Ga. 1992) (denying laches because declaratory judgment action is legal remedy); *see also* Villiger v. City of Henry, 362 N.E.2d 120 (Ill. App. Ct. 1977) (holding that declaratory judgment action is neither legal nor equitable remedy); Beldt v. Leise, 60 P.3d 1119, 1121 (Or. Ct. App. 2003) (indicating that declaratory judgment action is legal or equitable depending on the nature of the case and relief).

[214] *See infra* notes 216–23.

troublesome. Judge Posner offered illustrative comments in an opinion that determined whether a lower court's refusal to stay a lawsuit seeking an accounting was appealable. In *Medtronic, Inc. v. Intermedics, Inc.*,[215] he declared that "the historical analysis appears to be well-nigh indeterminate in regard to whether Medtronic is seeking a legal or equitable accounting."[216] The Fifth Circuit Court of Appeals likewise had a difficult time classifying whether an accounting was equitable or legal in a case in which it attempted to determine the application of laches.[217] In *Clark v. Amoco Prod. Co.*,[218] administrators and heirs of an estate brought an action against several oil companies to establish mineral rights in an oil field and requested an accounting of all minerals extracted from the property.[219] Seventy years had passed since the deceased had allegedly received the deed. Thus, the oil companies asserted that laches barred the claim.[220] Because Texas law limits laches to suits in equity, the court contemplated whether the case fell into the category of "law" or "equity."[221] It explained the dilemma:

> [T]he prayer for an accounting is certainly a matter within the jurisdiction of equity. A dispute with regard to title to property, however, is not ordinarily a matter in equity. Under Texas law, a property right vested in possession is not properly the subject of a suit in equity. Conversely, a property right not vested in possession but which needs "to obtain the peculiar relief afforded by courts of equity in order to investigate plaintiff with the right claimed" is.[222]

Ultimately, the court of appeals sidestepped the issue by deciding the case on other grounds.[223]

Courts have grappled with the same law–equity categorical issue under federal statutory law. In discerning the employer's use of after-acquired evidence of an employee's misconduct under the discrimination laws, the district court in *Miller v. Beneficial Mgmt. Corp.*[224] equated the defense with the equitable doctrine of

---

[215] 725 F.2d 440 (7th Cir. 1984).
[216] *Id.* at 443.
[217] As explained *supra* Chapters 1 and 3, laches, like unclean hands, is a "pure" or "true" equitable defense pled during premerger days only in response to an application for equitable affirmative relief.
[218] 794 F.2d 967 (5th Cir. 1986).
[219] *See id.* at 969.
[220] *See id.* (citing City of Fort Worth v. Johnson, 388 S.W.2d 400, 403 (Tex. 1964)) ("Laches under Texas law rests on two elements: (1) an unreasonable delay in bringing a claim although otherwise one has the legal or equitable right to do so, and (2) a good faith change of position by another, to his detriment, because of this delay.").
[221] *See id.* at 971. Texas is considered by some commentators to have been the first state in the country to merge law and equity. *See* Leonard J. Emmerglick, *A Century of New Equity*, 23 TEX. L. REV. 244, 244–45 (1945) (discussing how Texas constitutional provisions provided for a blended procedure of both law and equity upon its admission to the Union in 1845).
[222] *Clark*, 794 F.2d at 971–72 (internal citations omitted).
[223] *See id.* at 972.
[224] 855 F. Supp. 691 (D.N.J. 1994).

unclean hands.[225] Because it presumed the availability of unclean hands was restricted to equitable remedies, the court proceeded to analyze whether the employee's request for back pay was legal or equitable in nature.[226] Apparently finding no precedent to be of assistance on this precise issue, the court resorted to reviewing conflicting cases that characterized back pay as either legal or equitable for other purposes.[227] Notwithstanding an absence of any agreement, the court inevitably classified an award of wages lost due to unlawful discrimination as an equitable remedy.[228]

While such mental gymnastics will continue to be constitutionally compelled in considering the right to trial by jury,[229] the availability of unclean hands to defeat actions at law can be handled separately.[230] Eliminating law–equity labels as solely determinative of the reach of the unclean hands defense would not only be consistent with the meaning of the merger but also would alleviate the need to forge fine distinctions that are, at best, ambiguous and would avoid any negative impact on the legitimacy of the law.

Another advantage of fusion, including applying unclean hands in legal actions, is that it allows judges to state directly what other courts are already doing indirectly. Recognizing equitable estoppel without the critical component of reliance can amount to unclean hands.[231] Once upon a time, even the United States Supreme Court coined a new theory of *quasi*-estoppel.[232] It employed estoppel in another context while reciting the rationale associated with unclean hands that the law

---

[225] *Id.* at 712–13.

[226] *See id.* at 712–13.

[227] *See id. Compare* Tyree v. Riley, 783 F. Supp. 877, 880 (D.N.J. 1992) (noting that the Supreme Court has held that "back pay [under Title VII] is most accurately characterized as equitable in nature"), *with* Sailor v. Hubbell, Inc., 4 F.3d 323, 325–26 (4th Cir. 1993) ("[A] back pay award under the ADEA is a legal remedy" and not an equitable one.).

[228] *Miller*, 855 F. Supp. at 712–13. For scholarly criticism of the Supreme Court's assumption that back pay is an equitable remedy, see Colleen P. Murphy, *Money as a "Specific" Remedy*, 58 ALA. L. REV. 119, 155–56 (2006) and Doug Rendleman, *Chapters of the Civil Jury*, 65 KY. L.J. 769, 772–78 (1977) (analyzing Albamarle Paper Co. v. Moody, 422 U.S. 405, 408–10 (1975)).

[229] Anenson, *Triumph of Equity, supra* note 181, at 411–22 (discussing differing standards in the states regarding when an equitable defense must be decided by a jury).

[230] *See* Unilogic, Inc. v. Burroughs Corp., 12 Cal. Rptr. 741, 745 (Cal. Ct. App. 1992); Maksym v. Loesch, 937 F.2d 1237, 1248 (7th Cir. 1991); Laycock, *Triumph of Equity, supra* note 81, at 78.

[231] Anenson, *Pluralistic Model, supra* note 57, at 663–64; Anenson, *Triumph of Equity, supra* note 181, at 390–91; discussion *infra* Chapter 6.

[232] Simmons v. Burlington, Cedar Rapids & N. Ry. Co., 159 U.S. 278 (1895) (recognizing that "[equity] may operate by analogy to estoppel – may produce a quasi-estoppel – upon the rights of remedy"). State courts also recognize the doctrine. *See, e.g.*, Fast v. Fast, 496 P.2d 171, 175 (Kan. 1992) ("'Quasi-estoppel' ... must be based on the previous assertion of a position so inconsistent with the one now taken as to make the present claim unconscionable."); Brooks v. Hackney, 404 S.E.2d 854, 858 n.3, 859 (N.C. 1991) (Quasi-estoppel is also referred to as "estoppel by acquiescence," "estoppel by election," or "estoppel by acceptance of benefits"); Keesee v. Fetzek, 723 P.2d 904, 906 (Idaho Ct. App. 1986) (describing quasi-estoppel as a "broadly remedial doctrine, often applied ad hoc to specific fact patterns").

should prevent those from benefiting from their own wrong.[233] Courts have also created confusion by extending the doctrine of *in pari delicto* in a way that amounts to unclean hands and using the terms as substitutes.[234] Instead of contorting other theories beyond their usual boundaries, addressing unclean hands in damages actions enables judges to document the real reasons for their decisions. Understanding the true premises of judgments is an important feature of our system of judge-made law. It allows those reasons to be empirically tested over time.[235]

Without a doubt, the availability of the clean hands doctrine at law raises the costs of decision making. By assessing case-by-case fusion, this chapter is endorsing the removal of the "rule" that the "standard" of unclean hands remains restricted to equity. "The resilience of equity ... allows for legitimate legal change."[236] Judges, rather than legislatures, are in the best position to accommodate equitable incursions into legal remedies. For better or worse, the choice between continuity and change has largely lain in the judicial method.[237] Courts have played a valuable and complementary role in this development of American law.[238]

Accordingly, whatever the difficulties of application, it is better than perpetuating the dichotomy that has become an obstacle to the application of unclean hands rather than a guide.[239] As Chafee stated fifty years ago: "One of the chief troubles

---

[233] *See* R. H. Stearns Co. v. United States, 291 U.S. 54, 61–62 (1934) (explaining that "the disability has its roots in a principle more nearly ultimate than either waiver or estoppel, the principle that no one shall be permitted to found any claim upon his own inequity or take advantage of their own wrong"); discussion *supra* Chapter 2; *see also* Anenson, *Age of Statutes, supra* note 20, at 558 (analyzing Supreme Court tax refund cases).

[234] *See* discussion *supra* Chapter 3.

[235] *See* HUHN, *supra* note 15, at 63 ("The disclosure of the true reasons for a decision performs a valuable function: the state premises of the law will over time be empirically tested."); Karl Llewellyn, *The Standardization of Commercial Contracts in English and Continental Law,* 52 HARV. L. REV. 700, 703 (1939) (book review) (emphasizing that "[c]overt tools are never reliable tools"); Frederick Schauer, *Do Cases Make Bad Law?,* 73 U. CHI. L. REV. 883, 889–90 (Summer 2006) (discussing how the reasons for rules announced in decisions may have normative weight and constrain future decisions).

[236] Anenson & Mark, *supra* note 4, at 1516.

[237] Mason, *Fusion: Fallacy, Future or Finished?, supra* note 62, at 41 ("Over the centuries, judges at common law and in equity moulded principles whereby the two 'systems' acted in aid of each other where appropriate, recognised and applied each other's rules when necessary to do so, and borrowed ideas from time to time."); Mason, *Fusion, supra* note 86, at 17 (listing examples of judges who "fashioned new principles applicable at common law or equity by drawing upon the companion body of law"); *see* Steve Hedley, *Rival Taxonomies Within Obligations: Is There a Problem?* (noting that the equitable method is still useful and indeed vital to the law), *in* EQUITY IN COMMERCIAL LAW, *supra* note 32, at 77, 87.

[238] *See* Anenson & Mayer, *supra* note 16, at 199 ("[I]t was the flexibility and discretionary nature of equity that allowed courts to incorporate ethical standards of business into the law in a way that reflected prevailing social mores."); James Barr Ames, *Law & Morals,* 22 HARV. L. REV. 97, 108–09 (1908) (asserting that discretion in shaping equitable remedies made English and American law more perfect than other countries).

[239] Laycock, *Death, supra* note 131, at 693 (noting that law–equity jurisdictional "rules have become obstacles to decision instead of guides").

with the frequent preoccupation of judges with the question of jurisdiction is that it makes them slide over the more important questions of wisdom and fairness that ought to receive careful attention."[240] Even courts complain that changes involved in the absorption of equity should come on a practical basis and not be burdened by outmoded concepts of "law" and "equity."[241]

In sum, justice should not depend on the arbitrary nature of the remedy requested or the irrational attempt to parcel ethos-based equitable and legal defenses. Rather, courts should invoke equitable defenses uniformly to prevent inconsistent outcomes in actions at law and equity. The notion of equality before the law has been called "the most basic principle of jurisprudence."[242] It is synonymous with justice. Consequently, unclean hands should be equal to legal defenses or other equitable defenses that have been absorbed into the common law. The defense should at least be considered in actions seeking legal relief and should not be denied solely based on premerger practices.

5.3.3 *No-Fusion School of Thought*

5.3.3.1 Overview

Those against fusion fear that equity's celebrated flexibility and emphasis on values like good faith will be lost if exclusively equitable doctrines expand into law.[243] The thought is that equitable theories may harden into absolute rules or be woodenly applied in a way that will lose the fight against the unconscientious use of rights, or more narrowly, opportunism, that equity was designed to avert and deter.[244] Others argue that fusion caused the opposite problem; that is, judges integrated equity without its own limits intact.[245] This argument will be put aside for now and

---

[240] CHAFEE, SOME PROBLEMS, *supra* note 1, at 303–04.

[241] *See, e.g.*, USH Ventures v. Global Telesystems Group, Inc., 796 A.2d 7, 14 (Del. Super. Ct. 2000).

[242] Henry J. Friendly, *Indiscretion About Discretion*, 31 EMORY L.J. 747, 758 (1982); NEWMAN, EQUITY AND LAW, *supra* note 68, at 19–20 (citing "equality" as one of the necessary virtues of justice) (quoting FREDERICK POLLOCK, JURISPRUDENCE 37 (5th ed. 1923)); Main, *supra* note 67, at 444 ("[T]here is no more fundamental social interest than that law should be uniform and impartial").

[243] Smith, *Fusion and Tradition*, *supra* note 32, at 26–29 (outlining antifusionist concerns).

[244] *See* R.P. MEAGHER ET AL., MEAGHER, GUMMOW AND LEHANE'S EQUITY: DOCTRINES AND REMEDIES 451–54 (4th ed. 2002) [hereinafter MEAGHER, GUMMOW AND LEHANE'S EQUITY, FOURTH EDITION] (noting that one of the reasons jurists resist the fusion of equity into the law is the fear that modern equity will lose its inherent flexibility and capacity to adjust to new situations).

[245] Smith, *Fusing the Equitable Function*, *supra* note 9, at 174 ("Fusion is the occasion for equity to slip its bounds – to die and to triumph at the same time."). While Smith's structural description of equity advanced here is agnostic to fusion, Smith denounces the excessive integration of equity in some areas of the law. He condemns fusion without function, which, as discussed in this book, is not a concern with the clean hands doctrine.

addressed later in analyzing the defense of unclean hands. Still others suggest that equity is a system that will somehow unravel if a uniquely equitable maxim crosses over the edge of equity and purportedly trespasses into legal claims.[246]

5.3.3.2 Equity Unraveled

The last concern simply does not exist in American law. Courts did not "pull out" unclean hands as a consideration in granting equitable relief.[247] The fear of a domino effect is inconsistent with systems theory it purports to support and the idea that private law (including equity) is modular.[248] Parts of the system may change without the entirety of equity needing to be fused. Judges simply added the condition of clean hands to litigants seeking legal relief under certain circumstances. In this way, courts actually unified case law across remedies, resulting in more data for better decision making.

5.3.3.3 Loss of Discretion, Values, and Function

The former concern about unclean hands becoming fixed and rigid has not happened either. The defense applies to a range of conduct and claims.[249] It is fair criticism that sometimes courts have been too careful with seeking a prior case before extending the defense to damages, but many would applaud a conservative judiciary that is not too carefree in creating new law.[250] Nor has the defense lost its emphasis on good-faith conduct. State and federal jurisdictions consistently find that the presence of good faith means the absence of unclean hands.[251]

[246] *See generally* Bray, *System, supra* note 9.
[247] Bray, *System, supra* note 9, at 589–90; Bray, *New Equity, supra* note 183, at 1051–52.
[248] Smith, *Fusing the Equitable Function, supra* note 9, at 176.
[249] *See* discussion *supra* Chapter 3.
[250] *See* East West Bank v. Rio School Dist., 185 Cal. Rptr. 3d 676, 683 (Cal. Ct. App. 2015) ("That finding alone is sufficient to warrant the denial of the defense."); Cross Talk Prods., Inc. v. Jacobson, 76 Cal. Rptr. 2d 615, 621 (Cal. Ct. App. 1998) (holding unclean hands inapplicable because there was no authority applying the defense to similar claims).
[251] *See, e.g.*, Le Fevre v. Borwick, 254 P.2d 626, 627–28 (Cal. Ct. App. 1953) (defense of unclean hands inapplicable even though the plaintiff failed to give certain heirs actual notice of the filing of a petition when the plaintiff made several unsuccessful efforts to locate the heirs and give notice); A.I. Gage Plumbing Supply Co. v. Local 300 of the Internat. Hod Carriers, Building & Common Laborers Union of America, 20 Cal. Rptr. 860, 866 (Cal. Ct. App. 1962). As stated in People v. Nunn, 296 P.2d 813, 818 (Cal. 1956):

> The phrase "good faith" in common usage has a well-defined and generally understood meaning, being ordinarily used to describe that state of mind denoting honesty of purpose, freedom from intention to defraud, and, generally speaking, means being faithful to one's duty or obligation. Plaintiff here, after being advised by competent labor personnel, selected the union which it considered was entitled to the work and in that respect it was being faithful to its duty.

Moreover, courts in the United States have retained the residual discretion in refusing the defense even when its conditions are satisfied.[252] American judges are sensitive to the reasons behind the maxim as well as countervailing concerns of public policy. Judges sometimes call this the "public interest exception" to unclean hands.[253] Hence, they have taken and are undertaking what scholars advocate as a "functional approach" to fusion.[254]

While the United States Supreme Court has yet to fuse the clean hands doctrine, its jurisprudence on the scope of equitable defenses is instructive. To continue the objective of equitable defenses in combatting strategic behavior in statutory law, the Court has retained its standard-like qualities and the corresponding discretion of the district court.[255] In particular, the Supreme Court has allowed for escape valves that direct judges to case-specific considerations informed by existing decisional law.[256] Once the Supreme Court determines whether and when equitable defenses are reserved under the statute, the decision to apply them is largely accomplished at the trial level on a case-by-case basis.[257]

In *McKennon v. Nashville Banner Publ'g Co.*, it emphasized that the trial court can deviate from the general rule of employee misconduct, a defense derived from unclean hands, by considering any "extraordinary equitable circumstances that affect the legitimate interests of either party."[258] When balancing the employer and employee interests, the Court advised that determining the proper parameters of equitable defenses is a particularized inquiry.[259] It stated that reconciling the employer's discrimination with the employee's own wrongdoing "must be addressed by the judicial system in the ordinary course of further decisions, for the factual

---

[252] *See, e.g.,* Yu v. Signet Bank/Virginia, 126 Cal. Rptr. 2d 516, 531 (Cal. Ct. App. 2002) (refusing to apply unclean hands defense due to strong public interest in claim of distant forum abuse); Health Maint. Network v. Blue Cross of So. Cal., 249 Cal. Rptr. 220 (Cal. Ct. App. 1988):

> The doctrine of unclean hands is not necessarily a complete defense ... It is well settled that public policy may favor the nonapplication of the doctrine as well as its application. Whenever an inequitable result would be accomplished by application of the clean hands doctrine, the courts have not hesitated to reject it.

(internal quotations and citations omitted).

[253] *See* DeBurgh v. DeBurgh, 250 P.2d 598, 605 (Cal. 1952) (recognizing a public interest exception to the application of unclean hands); discussion *infra* Chapter 2.

[254] Anenson, *Age of Statutes, supra* note 20, at 538 (showing that the Supreme Court employs a functional approach to the fusion of equitable defenses in legislation). *See generally* Smith, *Fusing the Equitable Function, supra* note 9 (calling for a functional approach to fusion).

[255] *See generally* Anenson, *Age of Statutes, supra* note 20 (identifying a method that the Supreme Court uses to define and provide the scope of equitable defenses, including unclean hands, in statutory law).

[256] *Id.* at 19.

[257] *Id.* at 24–30 (showing how the Supreme Court is developing a supervisory role with respect to equitable defenses).

[258] McKennon v. Nashville Banner Publ'g Co., 513 U.S. 352, 362 (1995).

[259] *Id.* at 362.

permutations and the equitable consideration they raise will vary from case to case."[260] Likewise, for the application of laches in *Petrella v. Metro-Goldwyn-Mayer, Inc.*, the Court provided examples of exceptional cases from lower court decisions of the defense's application at the outset of the litigation in situations resulting in an almost total destruction of the property right.[261] It further referenced the trial court decision to account for delay at the remedial stage in adjusting relief and provided a nonexclusive list of factors to assist judges in making that decision.[262]

Consequently, since Congressionally endorsed values press in more than one direction, the Court's jurisprudence indicates that it finds the virtue of ancient equitable accordion-like standards more attractive than all or nothing rules to better account for the purposes of each statute. As such, in incorporating equitable defenses into statutory law, the Court begins with the defense's traditional test and rationale, which may be further refined in light of statutory objectives.[263] These goals also enter into the district court's discretion to apply equitable defenses under the case-specific facts.[264] The public-interest criterion either is inserted as an express element of the defense or is implicit in the discretionary nature of the doctrines as shown in the Court's other cases.[265]

Just as Lord Selden's metaphor of the Chancellor's foot forever engrained in our memories the perils of equity on the rule of law,[266] Professor Stephen Burbank

---

[260] *Id.* at 361. Similarly, in *Pinter v. Dahl*, with respect to the equal fault criterion of unclean hands' cousin *in pari delicto*, the Supreme Court acknowledged that the trial court's assessment of the relative responsibility of a plaintiff will vary depending on the facts of the case. Pinter v. Dahl, 486 U.S. 622, 637 (1988). Nevertheless, to assist district courts in the exercise of their discretion, the Court pointed out that other judges had focused on the extent of cooperation between the parties in carrying out the illegal scheme. *Id.* (citing lower federal courts). The Court suggested that if the plaintiff was found to have induced the issuer not to register, he may be precluded from obtaining rescission. *Id.* To help assess the criterion of public policy, the Supreme Court provided a list of nonexclusive factors, derived from prior court decisions, to aid district courts in determining the plaintiff's status as a promoter or an investor. *Id.* at 639.

[261] Petrella v. Metro-Goldwyn-Mayer, Inc., 134 S. Ct. 1962, 1978 (2014) (describing the lower court decisions as "illustrative").

[262] *Id.* at 1978–79 (citing Haas v. Leo Feist, Inc., 234 F. 105, 107–08 (S.D.N.Y. 1916)). The Court emphasized that the factors were to help examine detrimental reliance on the delay but also explained that reliance or its absence is not the "*sine qua non* for adjustment of injunctive relief or profits." *Id.* at 1978 n.22. Courts sitting in equity often articulated a hard and soft version of delay-based inequity. However, to the extent the Court labels the adjustment version, "laches" may be confusing. *See* W.M.C. GUMMOW & J.R.F. LEHANE, EQUITY: DOCTRINES AND REMEDIES 804–05 (3d ed. 1992) (explaining that the word is used in different senses in the cases and has an ambulatory connotation); *cf. id.* at 801 (commenting on the novelty of delay short of laches denying equitable relief).

[263] Anenson, *Age of Statutes*, *supra* note 20, at 552.

[264] *Id.*

[265] *Id.*; *see* Pinter v. Dahl, 486 U.S. 622, 633–36 (1988) (extending the two-part test of equal fault and public policy for the application of *in pari delicto* to all securities cases); *see also* Anenson & Mark, *supra* note 4, at 1521 n.533 (listing federal and state cases recognizing public policy exception to doctrine of unclean hands).

[266] *See* JOHN SELDEN, TABLE TALK OF JOHN SELDEN 43 (Frederick Pollock ed., 1927).

reminds us that with equitable doctrines, as with life, we must take the bitter with the sweet.[267] In attempting to tie up all the loose ends and get everything together, we lose much of our life experience. So it is with equity. Over the centuries, equity has defied academic notions of tidiness and symmetry. State and federal judges are well aware that equity operates in the real world, where results, not simply rationales, rule the day. Litigants rarely care about the adoption of any particular theory of law. They want justice as measured by case outcomes.[268] Despite its many flaws, it is here where the value of equity endures.[269]

5.3.3.4 Amorphous Equity

Finally, probably the greater criticism of equity in America and elsewhere is the opposite problem of it being (or becoming) too amorphous.[270] This concern dovetails nicely into issues with the unclean hands defense itself that will be addressed in what follows.

5.4 APPRAISING UNCLEAN HANDS

5.4.1 *Introduction*

Regardless of the merits and legitimacy of applying equitable defenses universally to law and equity actions, issues with the clean hands doctrine itself may make it a poor choice for fusion. Chafee found the clean hands doctrine one of the most amusing maxims of equity.[271] He even added his own sense of humor when he linked the defense's popularity with the invention of the modern bathroom.[272] All kidding aside, though, preventing opportunism is a serious matter. Equally if not more

---

[267] *See* Burbank, *supra* note 34, at 1317.

[268] *See* Gary L. McDowell, *Joseph Story's Science of Equity*, 1979 Sup. Ct. Rev. 507 153, 158 (explaining that Story "viewed Equity as a system of moral machinery, whose principles were at once enlarged and elevated, yet practical."); *see also* William N. Eskridge, Jr., *Dynamic Statutory Interpretation*, 135 U. Pa. L. Rev. 1479, 1531 (1987) (asserting that legitimacy of judicial lawmaking in statutory interpretation is defined not solely by the process but by results that respond to societal needs). This is not to endorse the realist position that only results count. The entire study is premised on the idea that reasons are important as well.

[269] *See* Emily L. Sherwin, *Introduction: Property Rules as Remedies*, 106 Yale L.J. 2083, 2087–88 (1997) [hereinafter Sherwin, *Property Rules*] (remarking on the judicial preference for standards and the psychological importance of tailoring remedies to particular cases).

[270] *See* Hedley, *supra* note 237, at 87 (advocating the continued use of equity but noting that there will be legitimate concerns over the degree of flexibility that should be allowed (citing articles on debate about "discretionary remedialism")); Alastair Hudson, *Conscience as the Organising Concept of Equity*, 2 Canadian J. of Comp. & Contemp. L. 261 (2016) (noting that the real problem of equity is vagueness and uncertainty).

[271] Chafee I, *supra* note 53, at 877.

[272] Chafee, Some Problems, *supra* note 1, at 12 ("It may only be a coincidence that extensive judicial insistence on clean hands began after the advent of the modern bathroom.").

important is upholding judicial integrity. Recollect that the clean hands doctrine embodies both rationales.[273]

For these reasons, John Pomeroy found the concept of clean hands to be "one of the elementary and fundamental conceptions of equity jurisprudence."[274] American courts agree.[275] As discussed in the next chapter, it is so valuable that judges may apply it *sua sponte*.[276] The criticisms of unclean hands, however, do not denigrate its underlying principle that those seeking justice should be prevented from taking advantage of their own wrong. Rather, critics have concluded that the defense does not accomplish its purpose very well or that its application inserts other irregularities into the judicial process. These concerns are addressed next.

5.4.2 *Clarity and Consistency*

First, a criticism is that unclean hands is too vague even in the discretionary world of equity.[277] As such, its application could infringe on rule-of-law norms like clarity and consistency.[278] Neither concern, however, appears relevant in the United States.[279]

Clarity and consistency concerns arise from the failure of the law to provide adequate notice and predictability.[280] It is anxiety over these matters that fuels criticisms of equity's amorphousness.[281] Fears of uncertainty and inconsistency are

---

[273] *See* discussion *supra* Chapter 1.

[274] Anenson & Mark, *supra* note 4, at 1450 (quoting 1 POMEROY'S EQUITY JURISPRUDENCE, FIFTH EDITION, *supra* note 5, § 398).

[275] *See* Katz v. Karlsson, 191 P.2d 541, 544 (Cal. Ct. App. 1948) (declaring the unclean hands defense "the most important rule regarding the administration of justice").

[276] *See* discussion *infra* Chapter 6, Section 6.4.3.

[277] Rendleman, *Remedies*, *supra* note 36, at 578–79 (advising of his discomfort with discretionary equitable defenses like unclean hands); *see also* DOUG RENDLEMAN, COMPLEX LITIGATION: INJUNCTIONS, STRUCTURAL REMEDIES, AND CONTEMPT 270–71 (2010) [hereinafter RENDLEMAN, COMPLEX LITIGATION] (noting that remedial coherence could be achieved by removing the doctrine of unclean hands from equity).

[278] Smith, *Fusion and Tradition*, *supra* note 32, at 24 (identifying general criticisms of the fusion of equitable doctrines and emphasizing that clarity and consistency raise separate concerns); *accord* Anenson & Mark, *supra* note 4, at 1512 (explaining concerns with uncertainty and inconsistency for the discretion defense of unclean hands).

[279] No doubt one can find cases representative of this phenomena. Chafee certainly did circa 1950. *See generally* Chafee I, *supra* note 53; Chafee II, *supra* note 83. Sections 5.4.2.1 (California) and 5.4.2.2 (United States Supreme Court) *infra* provide a contrary picture today.

[280] *See* Irit Samet, *What Conscience Can Do for Equity*, *in* JURISPRUDENCE: AN INTERNATIONAL JOURNAL OF LEGAL AND POLITICAL THOUGHT 13, 20 (2012) (noting that clarity and predictability are of crucial importance in certain areas of private law).

[281] *See* Hudson, *supra* note 270, at 261 (advising it is the central debate for equity); *see also* GEORGE W. KEETON, THE NATURE OF EQUITY 2 (3rd ed. 1984) (discussing the opposing virtues of certainty and justice).

usually based on an assumption that judges derive decisions on their own subjective beliefs.[282] There is an alternative and better view that equitable doctrines are (or at least can be) objective, meaningful inquiries.[283]

Certainly, the concept of clean hands will never be as clear and constant as other legal precepts that take the form of "rules" as opposed to "standards."[284] But strict legal precepts are not always better than dynamic ones; rules are not always better than standards.[285] Indeed, if the clean hands doctrine were to take the shape of a formal legal precept, it would fail in its essential purpose.[286] Recall the defense's correlation to equitable constructive fraud.[287] The whole point was to prevent fraudsters and charlatans from securing a roadmap for how to get around the law.[288] Somewhat shadowy rules and subsequent discretion are necessary to accomplish that goal.[289] In an English equity opinion approved by Chief Justice Marshall, Lord Chancellor Eldon declared, "The Rule is clear enough; but the application in

---

[282] *See, e.g.*, Goldstein, *supra* note 19, at 538 (equating discretion with the whim of judges); Mary Siegel, *The Dangers of Equitable Remedies*, 15 STAN. J.L. BUS. & FIN. 86, 88 (2009) ("[E]-quitable doctrines allow courts not only to create law, but also to empower that law to supersede statutes that legislatures have created.").

[283] *See generally* Samet, *supra* note 280, at 13–35 (arguing that the conscience-based categories of equity are not a threat to the rule of law); Hudson, *supra* note 270, at 264–65 (arguing that conscience is an objective, workable inquiry).

[284] *See* Gail L. Heriot, *A Study in the Choice of Form: Statutes of Limitations and the Doctrine of Laches*, 1992 B.Y.U. L. REV. 917, 918 (discussing potential difference in outcomes given the form of the legal precept as a rule or standard). Legal precepts can also vary between rules and standards. *See* James G. Wilson, *Surveying the Forms of Doctrine on the Bright Line–Balancing Test Continuum*, 27 ARIZ. ST. L.J. 773, 825 (1995) (describing various forms of legal commands such as multifactor tests and totality-of-the-circumstances tests).

[285] *See* MindGames, Inc. v. Western Pub. Co., Inc., 218 F.3d 652, 656 (7th Cir. 2000) (Posner, J.) ("No sensible person supposes that rules are always superior to standards, or vice versa."); Smith, *Fusion and Tradition, supra* note 32, at 38 (discussing the relationship between equity and law and noting that discretion is not "necessarily injustice").

[286] *See, e.g.*, KENNETH C. DAVIS, DISCRETIONARY JUSTICE: A PRELIMINARY INQUIRY 107 (1969) ("Turning all discretion into law would destroy the individualizing element of equity and discretion."); *see also* Smith, *Fusion and Tradition, supra* note 32, at 38 (noting the impossibility of making the law absolutely certain in advance). For examples of equitable doctrines in U.S. law, see Anenson & Mark, *supra* note 4, at 1516 (demonstrating that the Federal Circuit's restriction of unclean hands qua inequitable conduct demonstrates in attempting to achieve certainty in an area inherently uncertain was counterproductive) and Camilla E. Watson, *Equitable Recoupment: Revisiting an Old and Inconsistent Remedy*, 65 FORDHAM L. REV. 691, 787–88 (1996) (analyzing doctrinal development in the defense of equitable recoupment in federal tax law and showing how a narrow construction can also produce inconsistent results). Moreover, given the importance of particularized findings of facts and circumstances, attempts to quantify discretion for equitable remedies have been ineffective. *See* Amer. Hosp. Supply Corp. v. Hospital Prods., Ltd., 780 F.2d 589, 593 (7th Cir. 1986) (Posner, J.) (adopting paradigm for preliminary injunctions proffered in John Leubsdorf, *The Standard for Preliminary Injunctions*, 91 HARV. L. REV. 525, 525 (1978) albeit quantifying the formula).

[287] *See* discussion *supra* Chapter 2.

[288] *Id.*; *see* Anenson & Mayer, *supra* note 16, at 974–79.

[289] T. Leigh Anenson, *Public Pensions and Fiduciary Law: A View from Equity*, 50 U. MICH. J.L. REF. 261, 262–63 (2017) [hereinafter Anenson, *A View from Equity*].

each particular case must depend on the discretion of the judge."[290] The clean hands doctrine operates as a safety valve for litigants seeking to take an unfair advantage or otherwise abuse their rights.[291] Of course, the defense is not the only area of private law to do so. But it is an important one.

A certain amount of ambiguity is not only essential in cases of unclean hands, but opacity also has other virtues. It provides for richer forms of moral and democratic relations and adds analytical power and normative force.[292] Along similar lines, one might picture the elasticity of the elements of unclean hands as garden walls that create space for the garden.[293] Whether or not the doctrine operates efficiently is beside the point as well.[294] What is important is that, as a legal standard, the defense of unclean hands is a workable one.

Judicial practice shows that it is. Two examples that follow illustrate the point.

5.4.2.1 California

Take the integration of unclean hands at law in California. As developed in Chapter 3, California is the first state in the country to apply the defense regardless of the remedy requested.[295] It is also the only jurisdiction with a developed jurisprudence invoking the doctrine to preclude a wide variety of common law and statutory claims.[296]

California courts continue to use the defense's traditional elements,[297] rely on historical authorities such as John Pomeroy and Joseph Story,[298] and consult a mixture of federal as well as state cases to inform the defense's scope and

---

[290] Motluck v. Buller, 10 Ves. Jun. 292, 305 (1804), *cited in* Cathcart v. Robinson, 30 U.S. 264, 276–77 (1831) (discussing clean hands as a condition of equitable relief).

[291] *See* discussion *supra* Chapter 2.

[292] Seana Valentine Shiffron, *Inducing Moral Deliberation: On the Occasional Virtues of Fog*, 123 Harv. L. Rev. 1214, 1214 (2010) (asserting that ambiguity provides for richer forms of moral and democratic relations). As noted by Canadian equity scholar Lionel Smith, "[c]omplexity is not always worse than simplicity, if the complexity adds analytical power or permits the enforcement of additional normative standards." Smith, *Fusion and Tradition, supra* note 32, at 19, 38.

[293] Bobbitt, *supra* note 185, at 177 (using metaphor to express the idea of conscience and constraints despite the incommensurability of the modes of legal reasoning).

[294] *See* Yorio, *supra* note 132, at 1225–26 (refuting economic argument that equitable defenses are inefficient).

[295] *See* discussion *supra* Chapter 3.

[296] *See id.* (reviewing the adoption of unclean hands to cases seeking legal relief in California and other states).

[297] *See, e.g.*, Harvey v. General Tire & Rubber Co., 200 Cal. Rptr. 722, 727 (Cal. Ct. App. 1984) (restating the classic unclean hands criteria of "inequitable conduct" and a "sufficient nexus between this inequitable conduct and the nature of the relief sought").

[298] Thirty cases in California cite Pomeroy. *See, e.g.*, Jaramillo v. County of Orange, 133 Cal. Rptr. 3d 751, 757 (Cal. Ct. App. 2011) (citing Pomeroy); Brown v. Grimes, 120 Cal. Rptr. 3d 893, 908 (Cal. Ct. App. 2011) (same). For cases citing Story, see, for example, DeBurgh v. DeBurgh, 250 P.2d 598, 602 (Cal. 1952).

application.[299] The test set forth by the court in *Blain v. Doctor's Co.* also predominates. The added focus on an "analogous case" ensures that the defense's elements are applied contextually.[300] True, certain courts only pay lip service to it.[301] But other cases show it has teeth.[302]

By way of background, repeated application has generated an acknowledgment that the clean hands doctrine is not favored in domestic relations disputes.[303] Conversely, because malicious prosecution is a disfavored claim, courts have held that the bar of unclean hands applies with more force.[304] Other applications of unclean hands have yielded more concrete rules in discreet contexts such as situations involving mortgages and foreclosures.[305]

Like any judge-made doctrine deriving from the collective experience of courts over time, unclean hands law is not perfect. Courts could do better about identifying the degree of misbehavior rather than collapsing the entire analysis into the

---

[299] *See, e.g.*, DeBurgh, 250 P.2d at 598 (citing United States Supreme Court decisions). Like other state courts, most citations are to the Supreme Court's decision in *Precision Instrument. See* Salas v. Sierra Chem. Co., 327 P.3d 797, 812 (Cal. 2014), *cert. denied*, 135 S. Ct. 755 (2014) (citing *Precision Instrument*); Burton v. Sosinsky, 250 Cal. Rptr. 33, 41 (Cal. Ct. App. 1988) (same). California judges also resort to other state decisions when helpful. *See, e.g.*, Miller & Lux v. Enterprise Canal & Land Co., 75 P. 770, 772 (Cal. 1904) (citing state supreme court cases from New York, Indiana, and Vermont); Blain v. Doctor's Co., 272 Cal. Rptr. 250, 256 (Cal Ct. App. 1990) (citing Pennsylvania and Oregon decisions); In re Brandie W., 203 Cal. Rptr. 537, 539–40 (Cal. Ct. App. 1984) (considering and distinguishing New York cases).

[300] *See* Kendall-Jackson Winery, Ltd. v. Superior Court, 90 Cal. Rptr. 2d 743, 749 (Cal. Ct. App. 1999) ("Whether the defense of unclean hands applies in a particular case depends on (1) analogous case law, (2) the nature of the misconduct, and (3) the relationship of the misconduct to the claimed injuries." (citing Blain v. Doctor's Co., 272 Cal. Rptr. 250, 256 (Cal Ct. App. 1990))).

[301] *See* Burton v. Sosinsky, 250 Cal. Rptr. 33, 41 (Ct. App. 1988) ("Although no case directly on point has been located, we see no reason why a successful defense of unclean hands should not bar the foreclosure of the mechanics' lien."); discussion *supra* Chapter 3.

[302] *See, e.g.*, East West Bank v. Rio School District, 185 Cal. Rptr. 3d 676, 683 (Cal. Ct. App. 2015) ("That finding alone is sufficient to warrant the denial of the defense."); Cross Talk Prods., Inc. v. Jacobson, 76 Cal. Rptr. 2d 615, 621 (Cal. Ct. App. 1998) (holding unclean hands inapplicable because there was no authority applying the defense to similar claims); In re Brandie W., 203 Cal. Rptr. 537 (Cal. Ct. App. 1984) (refusing to apply unclean hands defense in part due to the lack of analogous case law).

[303] *See, e.g.*, DeBurgh v. DeBurgh, 250 P.2d 598, 605 (Cal. 1952) (citing Chafee for a public interest exception to the clean hands doctrine in the domestic relations case); Ruiz v. Ruiz, 85 Cal. Rptr. 674 (Cal. Ct. App. 1970) (reversing trial court application of unclean hands in domestic relations matter relying on Chafee's recommendation that the defense should be restricted in this area).

[304] *See Kendall-Jackson Winery, Ltd.*, 90 Cal. Rptr. 2d at 755.

[305] For instance, "[i]t is settled in California that a mortgagor cannot quiet his title against the mortgagee without paying the debt secured." Shimpones v. Stickney, 28 P.2d 673, 683 (Cal. 1934); *see also* Stebley v. Litton Loan Servicing, LLP, 134 Cal. Rptr. 3d 604, 607 (Cal. Ct. App. 2011) ("Allowing plaintiffs to recoup the property without full tender would give them an inequitable windfall, allowing them to evade their lawful debt.").

connection component.[306] Another area of improvement is when courts conflate the connection component with their residual discretion in ensuring a just application of the defense.[307] Judges should focus on party and court protection purposes to satisfy the requisite connection.[308] They should resort to residual discretion when those aims are fulfilled, but there are other considerations that trump the defense's application.[309] California courts have not seemed to settle on a standard of review either.[310] Yet these criticisms amount to no more than any other doctrine.

While the clean hands doctrine crossed the law–equity border fifty years ago, the defense has not run amok in preventing, willy-nilly, an unwarranted number of claims. Many, if not most, cases refuse to apply the defense.[311] This result runs counter to conventional wisdom that judges will continue to expand equitable defenses.[312] Courts have also hewed to the tradition of allowing a party to purge or cure the unclean conduct.[313] Similar to its classic definition, it remains an

---

[306] *See* Agricola Baja Best., S. De. R. L. de C.V. v. Harris Moran Seed Co., 44 F. Supp.3d 974, 995 (S.D. Cal. 2014) (applying California law) (indicating that the conduct was not sufficiently unclean because there was no evidence that it impacted the issues in the case).

[307] In declining unclean hands, judges can better clarify whether the defense was not satisfied or whether, despite its existence, they have declined to apply it. Health Maint. Network v. Blue Cross of So. Cal., 249 Cal. Rptr. 220, 232 (Cal. Ct. App. 1988). In some early cases, it is difficult to discern whether judges are actually applying unclean hands or simply declining equitable relief. Cathcart v. Robinson, 30 U.S. 264, 276–77 (1831).

[308] One equity judge and scholar explains how the private purpose of unclean hands assists in the maxim's application: "One way of testing for the application of the maxim is to consider whether the right the claimant seeks is one which, if protected, would allow the claimant to take advantage of their wrong." *See, e.g.,* PETER W. YOUNG ET AL., ON EQUITY, 180–84 (2009); MEAGHER, GUMMOW AND LEHANE'S EQUITY, FOURTH EDITION, *supra* note 244, at 98–102. In analyzing the purpose of court protection, the next chapter demonstrates that courts can consider the defense along a four-part continuum to aid its application. *See* discussion *infra* Chapter 6.

[309] Anenson & Mark, *supra* note 4, at 1503. Scholars also agree that unclean hands should be analyzed in light of the purposes and policies of the areas of law to which it intervenes. Professor (now judge) Finn reached the same conclusion examining equitable doctrines and rules in the private law of contract and tort. *See* Finn, *Unconscionable Conduct, supra* note 5, at 41, 44; *see also* Peter Birks, *Equity in the Modern Law: An Exercise in Taxonomy,* 26 W. AUST. L. REV. 1, 3 (1996) (explaining that Judge Finn, along with Australian Justices Meagher, Gummow, and Lehane, are "widely acknowledged to be among the greatest masters of equity in the modern world").

[310] *See* Jaramillo v. County of Orange, 133 Cal. Rptr. 3d 751, 757 (Cal. Ct. App. 2011) (citing Brown v. Grimes, 120 Cal. Rptr. 3d 893, 908 (Cal. Ct. App. 2011) (noting differences across cases).

[311] *See, e.g.,* Garcia v. World Sav., FSB, 107 Cal. Rptr. 3d 683, 694–95 (Cal. Ct. App. 2010) (holding that inequitable conduct in misrepresentation on loan application that the plaintiffs would reside in the property held unrelated to their claim for promissory estoppel based on lenders promise to postpone foreclosure sale).

[312] *See* Heriot, *supra* note 284, at 968 (judges favor discretionary standards because they are close to the outcome).

[313] *See, e.g.,* Jade Fashion & Co., Inc. v. Harkham Indus. Co., 177 Cal. Rptr. 3d 184, 200 (Cal. Ct. App. 2014) (finding that connection component fails when litigant asserting unclean hands got the amount credited despite earlier fraudulent inducement of a $30,000 overpayment); Chapter 2, Section 2.7.2 (citing authorities).

affirmative defense that cannot be used to seek affirmative relief,[314] although the defense applies to preclude the assertion of other equitable defenses.[315]

In addition, as developed in Chapter 2, California decisions assess the defense piecemeal on a claim-by-claim basis.[316] California (and other) courts also constrict the defense to a particular remedy or use the doctrine to diminish (but not disallow) the remedy.[317] As a result, the risk of overbreadth has not materialized because the unclean hands analysis is particularized.

5.4.2.2 United States Supreme Court

The United States Supreme Court has not integrated equitable defenses since recognizing equitable estoppel at law in the nineteenth century.[318] Nevertheless, its approach to equitable doctrines illustrates that they satisfy rule of law norms like clarity and consistency. The Court has determined the scope of equitable defenses through a deeper and wider frame of analysis. An equitable perspective permits a

---

[314] *See* Brown v. Grimes, 120 Cal. Rptr. 3d 893, 908 (Cal. Ct. App. 2011) (ruling that the clean hands doctrine cannot be used to secure affirmative relief). The doctrine of unclean hands is an affirmative defense invoked by defendants to prevent a plaintiff from obtaining relief. Giraldo v. Cal. Dep't of Corr. & Rehab., 85 Cal. Rptr. 3d 371, 393 (Ct. App. 2008) (citing Kendall-Jackson Winery, Ltd. v. Super. Ct., 90 Cal. Rptr. 2d 743, 746 (Ct. App. 1999)); *cf.* De Garmo v. Goldman, 123 P.2d 1, 6 (Cal. 1942) (("The burden is on the one coming into a court of equity for relief to prove not only his legal rights but his clean hands, and he may not rely on any deficiencies that may be laid at the door of the defendants."); Green v. Brow, 224 P.2d 476, 478 (Cal. Ct. App. 1950) (ruling that it is the plaintiff's burden to show his or her hands are clean).

[315] Typically, both plaintiffs and defendants may use unclean hands to block claims and defenses. It is an affirmative defense or an affirmative avoidance in response to an affirmative defense. *See* Jonathan M. Stern, *Untangling a Tangled Web Without Trial: Using the Court's Inherent Powers and Rules to Deny a Perjuring Litigant His Day in Court*, 66 J. AIR L. & COM. 1251, 1261 n.50 (2001) (citing cases). *But see* Alcatel USA, Inc. v. DGI Techs., Inc., 166 F.3d 772, 794–95 (5th Cir. 1999) (finding clean hands are not necessary to raise an equitable defense in a copyright infringement case).

[316] *See* discussion *supra* Chapter 2, Section 2.7.2.

[317] *See* discussion *supra* Chapter 2, Section 2.7.2; *infra* Section 5.4.2.2.

[318] Kirk v. Hamilton, 102 U.S. 68, 78 (1880) (equitable estoppel). The Court limited laches to its historical setting of equitable relief and refused the opportunity to fuse laches to legal relief for the first time. Petrella v. Metro-Goldwyn-Mayer, Inc., 134 S. Ct. 1962, 1967, 1977 (2014) (recognizing laches as a defense to equitable relief and acknowledging estoppel as a defense to legal and equitable relief); *see also* SCA Hygiene Prods. v. First Quality Baby Prods., 137 S. Ct. 954, 957, 959 n.2 (2017) (extending *Petrella*'s refusal to extend laches to damages in patent law but not ruling on the defense's application to equitable relief). In prior cases, the Court had indicated that it may be reticent to extend laches to legal claims brought within a prescriptive period. *Petrella*, at 1973–74 (citing cases); *see also* Anenson, *Triumph of Equity*, *supra* note 181, at 407–08 (contrasting the Supreme Court's cautious approach to the fusion of laches versus equitable estoppel). The Court either interpreted the statute to preclude laches or declined to exercise its discretion to extend the defense due to the specific policy issues in copyright law. *See* discussion *supra* Chapter 3 note 323.

weightier analysis by drawing meaning from equity's five-hundred-year history in addition to its operation across multiple subjects.

More precisely, the Supreme Court's decisions consider precedent associated with unclean hands outside a particular field of law at issue in the case.[319] Its unclean hands cases additionally cited historical sources, including the treatise authored by Sir Richard Francis credited with the idea of the maxim,[320] the original English case to recognize unclean hands in *Dering v. Earl of Winchelsea*,[321] and seminal treatises on equity jurisprudence written by Pomeroy and Story.[322] There-fore, in setting the scope of the equitable defenses, there is an identifiable pattern in the Supreme Court's decisional history of equitable defenses to assist in building a body of cases along principled lines.[323]

The starting point for defining these doctrines, including unclean hands, is their historic definition and rationale.[324] The substance is being supplied in part by state (private) law.[325] It appears that the Court is distilling the governing rules of equitable defenses from the overlapping practices of many jurisdictions rather than the idiosyncratic rules of any particular state.[326] The Supreme Court's composition in creating equitable defenses supports Professor Caleb Nelson's thesis of the post-*Erie* persistence of general federal common law.[327] It also places federal equity jurispru-dence within a broader experience concerning the relation between written statutes and unwritten law.[328]

---

[319] Bein v. Heath, 47 U.S. 228 (1848) (cited by Kitchen v. Rayburn, 86 U.S. 254, 263 (1874) and Keystone Driller Co. v. Gen. Excavator Co., 290 U.S. 240 (1933)).

[320] Milwaukee R.R. Co. v. Soutter, 80 U.S. 517, 523–24 (1872) ("He that hath committed iniquity shall not have equity.").

[321] Peoria Gas & Electric Company v. Peoria, 200 U.S. 48 (1906).

[322] *See, e.g.*, Keystone Driller Co. v. Gen. Excavator Co., 290 U.S. 240, 244–45 (1933) (citing JOSEPH STORY, COMMENTARIES ON EQUITY JURISPRUDENCE AS ADMINISTERED IN ENGLAND AND AMERICA § 98 (W.H. Lyon ed., 14th ed. 1918) and 2 JOHN NORTON POMEROY WITH JOHN NORTON POMEROY, JR., A TREATISE ON EQUITY JURISPRUDENCE, AS ADMINISTERED IN THE UNITED STATES OF AMERICA § 397 (Bancroft-Whitney 4th ed. 1918)); Simmons v. Burlington, Cedar Rapids, & N. Ry. Co., 159 U.S. 278, 291 (1895) (citing Pomeroy and justifying its decision under rationale associated with unclean hands).

[323] *See* Anenson, *Age of Statutes, supra* note 20, at 537–38.

[324] *Id.* at 538–41, 563.

[325] Anenson, *Age of Statutes, supra* note 20, at 554, 571 (explaining that the Supreme Court rested its analysis of equitable defenses on private law decisions (citing U.S. Airways, Inc. v. McCutchen, 569 U.S. 88, 98–99 (2013), Bateman Eichler, Hill Richards, Inc. v. Berner, 472 U.S. 299, 306 (1985), and Precision Instrument Mfg. Co. v. Auto. Maint. Mach. Co., 324 U.S. 806, 814 (1945))).

[326] *Id.*

[327] Caleb Nelson, *The Persistence of General Law*, 106 COLUM. L. REV. 503, 503 (2006) [herein-after Nelson, *General Law*].

[328] *Id. See generally* Caleb Nelson, *State and Federal Models of the Interaction Between Statutes and the Unwritten Law*, 80 U. CHI. L. REV. 657 (2013) (showing how federal courts read statutes to encompass more issues than state courts do, with the result that federal courts handle those issues under the rubric of statutory interpretation while state courts resort to the unwritten general common law).

History is full of live and dead things, some destined for resurrection. Because history presents an image of the continuity of mankind, its content turns up in the social sciences. Law is, after all, a past-dependent institution.[329] It is not surprising then that the Supreme Court begins constructing these defenses in statutory law out of the foundation of history in the same way as houses in medieval Rome were constructed out of stones taken from the Coliseum.[330]

But the historical definition of a defense is just the beginning. It is not merely learning that makes a historian but also discernment. One studies history, like law, to acquire judgment.[331] The tradition of equity allows for such judgment through its emphasis on public policy and equitable discretion.[332] In equity's so-called concurrent jurisdiction, equity operated in relation to the common law.[333] The pendulum-like dependency between law and equity cannot be overlooked. While the law without equity would have been "barbarous, unjust, and absurd," equity without the law would have been a "'castle in the air.'"[334] Equity's guiding role was to follow the law.[335]

The Supreme Court's commitment to equitable defenses demonstrates that equity also follows the statute.[336] The Supreme Court is observing legislative signals as a source of policy. The Court is engaging in a dual-purpose analysis in

---

[329] *See* Richard A. Posner, *Past-Dependency, Pragmatism, and Critique of History in Adjudication and Legal Scholarship*, 67 U. CHI. L. REV. 573, 573 (2000).

[330] *See* HUHN, *supra* note 15, at 49 ("Tradition often exerts a silent influence on legal reasoning. Our traditions establish baselines which are background assumptions that favor the status quo and place the burden of proof on any person who seeks to change the existing order.").

[331] *See* Holmes, *The Path of the Law, supra* note 6, at 469 (criticizing a rule that "simply persists from blind imitation of the past"). Similarly, Holmes said that "[h]istory must be part of the study, because without it we cannot know the precise scope of rules which it is our business to know. It is a part of the rational study, because it is the first step towards an enlightened skepticism, that is, toward a deliberate reconsideration of the worth of those rules." *Id.*

[332] Anenson & Mark, *supra* note 4, at 1502–03.

[333] Smith, *Equity in R3RUE, supra* note 60, at 1194–95 (explaining the tripartite classification of equity jurisdiction (exclusive, concurrent, auxiliary) that originated with Fonblanque's notes that was adopted and popularized by Story and others); *see also id.* at 1195 ("The classification has not been a particularly successful one and little is heard of it today …").

[334] Laycock, *Triumph of Equity, supra* note 81, at 67 (quoting MAITLAND, *supra* note 80, at 19).

[335] *See, e.g.,* JAMES W. EATON, HANDBOOK OF EQUITY JURISPRUDENCE § 14 at 47 (1901) ("Where legal rights are considered in a court of equity, the general rules and policy of the law must be obeyed."); YOUNG ET AL., *supra* note 308, §§ 3.140–3.170 at 166–69 (2009) (explaining that the maxim that equity follows the law has two meanings; the first is that equity supplemented the common law only when it went against conscience, and second, that it reflects the way that equity modeled some of its doctrines on analogous common law doctrines such as laches being given the same time period as the corresponding statute of limitations). Of course, Cardozo makes the point that equitable maxims are prudential rules. *See* Graf v. Hope Building Corp., 254 N.Y. 1, 9 (1920) ("Equity follows the law, but not slavishly nor always.").

[336] Anenson & Mark, *supra* note 4, at 1502–05 (discussing the concept involving the defense of inequitable conduct); *see also* YOUNG ET AL., *supra* note 308, § 4.680 at 255 (noting that the practice of equity "following the law" to some extent applies to legislative-made law in the Commonwealth).

considering the defense objectives along with the statutory goals.[337] The two-tiered analysis is a way of harmonizing the law.[338] It is perhaps what Professor Burbank meant when he reflected on the interdependence of law and equity and recommended that courts adopt a balanced approach to tradition.[339]

Moreover, the traditional formulation is subject to refinement in light of statutory purposes while still providing the district judge enough discretion to deviate from the rule.[340] The Court is not remaking the defenses but amending their application.[341] The Supreme Court's stewardship in setting strictures on these doctrines, which will be further outlined in Section 5.4.3, makes it unlikely that their inclusion will undermine ideals of justice that the law should be sufficiently clear.

Guidance in the application of unclean hands at law can also be found at the appellate level in the Supreme Court cases considering the defense in statutory causes of action. The Supreme Court has been increasingly cognizant of its supervisory role in relation to the lower courts in applying equitable defenses.[342] For centuries, the English Court of Chancery was "in practice as well as in theory a one-judge court."[343] As such, equitable discretion is usually seen as a normative principle of equity instead of an allocation of power between the trial and appellate courts.[344]

Judge Friendly clarified, however, that simply because the entire judicial system has discretion in certain areas of the law does not answer the question of the

---

[337] Anenson & Mark, *supra* note 4, at 1502–05.

[338] Law and equity have been borrowing from each other for centuries. *See, e.g.*, Mason, *Fusion: Fallacy, Future or Finished?*, *supra* note 62, at 41 (noting how statutory enactments are subject to the judicial method).

[339] Professor Burbank explained:

> We have been fortunate that our system has included, most of the time and in most American jurisdictions, both law and equity, each of which requires the other and both of which, in combination, have helped us over more than two hundred years to make social and economic progress. That progress has often not come easily, and there is much of it still to be made.

Burbank, *supra* note 34, at 1346.

[340] *See id. But see infra* Chapter 6 (noting that statutory purposes are not relevant when the defense is used procedurally primarily in a protect-the-court capacity).

[341] *See* Anenson, *Age of Statutes, supra* note 20, at 548.

[342] *See* discussion *supra* Section 5.3.3.3 (outlining ways that the Supreme Court is taking on a supervisory role concerning equitable defenses).

[343] Not until the nineteenth century were equity judges subordinate to the chancellor appointed. T. PLUCKNETT, A CONCISE HISTORY OF THE COMMON LAW 209–10 (5th ed. 1956); 1 W. HOLDSWORTH, A HISTORY OF ENGLISH LAW 442–44 (3rd ed. 1922). Equity became institutionalized after a long period in which the chancellor was lawmaker and law adjudicator. Heriot, *supra* note 284, at 948 (finding discretionary standards make more sense when there is a single decision maker).

[344] Friendly, *supra* note 242, at 773 n.97 (suggesting the possibility that "'the discretion of the chancellor' was intended as a normative principle of equity in general rather than an allocation of power between the trial and appellate courts." (citing OWEN M. FISS, INJUNCTIONS 74–76 (1972)).

discretionary power of the district judge *vis-à-vis* the courts of appeal.[345] Discussions of equitable discretion rarely attend to the differences in these respective spheres of judicial authority.[346]

The Supreme Court is delineating its role in three related ways. First, it is no longer eschewing formulas.[347] Second, it is providing more direction than resolving defenses under the case-specific facts.[348] Third, as discussed, its articulated parameters for equitable defenses allow for exceptions enlightened by prevailing precedent.[349] Consequently, just as Professor Abraham Chayes's celebrated research explained (and justified) the greater function of trial judges in public law litigation,[350] maturing Supreme Court jurisprudence on equitable defenses in statutory law evinces a more involved appellate role as well. Observed broadly, the Court's developing doctrine for defenses largely aligns with its other modern equity cases.[351] It has been continuing the work of equity judges as dispensers of justice as well as builders of a system of law.

Cardozo said that a system of appeals assures that "the tide rises and falls, but the sands of error crumble."[352] Such appellate supervision on federal equity jurisprudence corresponds to what Professor Sarah Cravens calls "procedural bounds" for judicial discretion.[353] The fact that the Court is sometimes synthesizing decisions

---

[345] Friendly, *supra* note 242, at 755.

[346] *See* David L. Shapiro, *Jurisdiction and Discretion*, 60 N.Y.U. L. Rev. 543, 546 (1985) ("Normative discretion is discretion delegated to a rulemaking or adjudicative body by the legislature, while allocative discretion refers to the delegation of decision-making authority within the particular hierarchy (here, the judiciary)."); Maurice Rosenberg, *Judicial Discretion of the Trial Court, Viewed from Above*, 22 Syracuse L. Rev. 635, 637 (1971) (distinguishing primary from secondary discretion).

[347] Anenson, *Age of Statutes*, *supra* note 20, at 556.

[348] *Id.* at 28–29.

[349] *Id.* at 28–29.

[350] Abram Chayes, *The Role of the Judge in Public Law Litigation*, 89 Harv. L. Rev. 1281, 1283–84 (1976).

[351] Anenson & Mark, *supra* note 4, at 1507 (explaining the Court's approach in *eBay v. MercExchange, L.L.C.*, 547 U.S. 388, 391 (2006) as developing mandatory reasoning requirements for the exercise of lower court discretion); Bray, *New Equity*, *supra* note 183, at 1025, 1048 (discussing how state and federal courts had used very similar considerations and tests to the four-prong format outlined in *eBay*) (citing Rachel M. Janutis, *The Supreme Court's Unremarkable Decision in* eBay v. MercExchange, L.L.C., 114 Lewis & Clark L. Rev. 597, 618–624 (2010)); *see also* Heriot, *supra* note 284, at 952 (suggesting that trial judges undervalue rules in favor of standards such that appellate courts should provide a shorter discretionary leash).

[352] Cardozo, Judicial Process, *supra* note 40, at 177.

[353] *See* Sarah M. R. Cravens, *Judging Discretion: Contexts for Understanding the Role of Judgment*, 64 U. Miami L. Rev. 947, 983 (2010) (reviewing remedial discretion and concluding that procedural rather than substantive bounds are the most practically useful for constraining both the original discretion determinations and the appellate review of those determinations).

across state lines in defining equitable defenses further confines judicial discretion.[354] Not unlike the Supreme Court's method of determining equitable remedies, it provides district courts with reasoning requirements derived from decisional law to exercise their discretion in assessing equitable doctrines that may prevent statutory relief.[355] These firm yet flexible tests for equitable defenses provide an intelligible body of doctrine that affords accordion-like outlets for district courts to dispense justice.[356] Arguably, in this way, the Court has taken advantage of the epistemic and institutional virtues of the analogical reasoning process.[357] However, it is still providing a measure of predictability to justify the inclusion of equitable defenses in statutory law.[358]

Accordingly, the Supreme Court's jurisprudence reflects its commitment to the accretive change characteristic of judge-made law.[359] Benjamin Cardozo used the metaphor of a glacier – an eon's worth of snow compressed to ice – to describe the incremental modification process of the common law.[360] Rather than blasting ahead in new terrain in a manner that might result in shallow and unsettled decisions,

[354] Nelson, *General Law, supra* note 327, at 503, 568; *see* Caleb Nelson, *The Legitimacy of (Some) Federal Common Law*, 101 VA. L. REV. 1, 36 (2015) (discussing the idea that courts can identify coherent themes in American common law).

[355] Anenson & Mark, *supra* note 4, at 1505–07 (finding procedural bounds prevalent in equitable remedies and the discretionary defenses). Empirical assessments of other judge-made doctrines demonstrate the probability of more predictable decisions when there is clear precedent and effective judicial oversight. Emerson H. Tiller & Frank B. Cross, *What is Legal Doctrine?*, 100 Nw. U. L. REV. 517, 520 (2006) (citing Nancy C. Staudt, *Modeling Standing*, 79 N.Y.U. L. REV. 612, 612 (2004)).

[356] *See* Richard L. Marcus, *Slouching Toward Discretion*, 78 NOTRE DAME L. REV. 1561, 1561 (2003) ("We have to give the judge some elbow room, objectively, individually, contextually."); Rosenberg, *supra* note 346, at 662 ("Many questions that arise in litigation are not amenable to regulation by rule because they involve multifarious, fleeting, special, narrow facts that utterly resist generalization . . . "); *see also* Wilson, *supra* note 284, at 836 (describing various forms of legal commands such as multifactor tests and totality-of-the-circumstances tests and claiming that they all should exist).

[357] *See* Marcus, *supra* note 356, at 1561 (discussing relation between judicial discretion and social legitimacy); Emily Sherwin, *A Defense of Analogical Reasoning in Law*, 66 U. CHI. L. REV. 1179 (1999) (defending analogical reasoning for its epistemic and institutional advantages); *see also* Emily Sherwin, *Judges as Rulemakers*, 73 U. CHI. L. REV. 919 (2006) (proposing that the use of precedent and analogical reasoning broadens perspective and leads to better assessments of potential consequences); *cf.* Jeffrey J. Rachlinski, *Bottom-Up Versus Top-Down Lawmaking*, 73 U. CHI. L. REV. 933, 953 (2006) (noting the pros and cons of both legislative and judicial lawmaking).

[358] *See* Rendleman, *Stages of Equitable Discretion, supra* note 33, at 1444 (explaining how appellate decisions limit a trial judge's equitable discretion by refining and clarifying the law) (citing Anthony Mason, *The Place of Equity and Equitable Remedies in the Contemporary Common Law World*, 110 L. QUAR. REV. 238, 258 (1994)).

[359] *See, e.g.*, Birks, *supra* note 309, at 13 ("Interpretative change depends on continuity. It cannot ignore the intervening centuries.").

[360] CARDOZO, JUDICIAL PROCESS, *supra* note 40, at 25 (noting the "effects must be measured by decades and even centuries."). "Thus measured," Cardozo advised, "they are seen to have behind them the power and the pressure of the moving glacier." *Id.*

the Court is equipping the lower courts with gear, or a method, for a deep and steady backcountry experience. Thus far, statutory equitable defenses have a unique blend of hard-shell protection and soft-shell breathability. Beneath interlocking private and public interests, there lies a slow, deep accumulation of unglamorous practice, the shared wisdom of many, which anticipates an infinite loop of new applications. In short, the Supreme Court has maintained a method of judicial discretion, allowing paradoxically for continuity and change in a way that exalts rather than degrades statutory law. "Many statutory regimes would not have functioned effectively without a leavening of equity."[361]

5.4.3 *Separation of Powers*

Second, when the unclean hands defense is raised to preclude recovery for statutory violations, a related reproach is that it gives judges too much power at the expense of the legislature. This is particularly true in the federal courts, where a recent survey reveals that the Supreme Court employs an equitable discretion default directive that includes equitable defenses when interpreting statutory equitable remedies.[362] As a result, an assortment of indeterminate defenses may stand in the way of remedying statutory violations.

The authority of federal judges to fashion remedies, unlike many of their state counterparts who may be popularly elected, is a check upon democracy by a branch of government not subject to popular control.[363] Even more troublesome, perhaps, in terms of an intolerable usurpation of power, is that a corollary to equity is choice. Yet combatting opportunism is no simple task. It requires equitable doctrines to be malleable.[364] It also means that judges need discretion to apply (or even update) defenses in the context of the case.[365] It is this discretionary power – and its potential abuse – that is difficult to reconcile with legislative deference in the state and especially the federal courts under silent statutes. Such discretionary decision making risks the expansion of the judicial office in relation to other equal branches of government. From a separation-of-powers perspective, denying relief despite a violation of statutorily proscribed conduct can be seen as the zenith of the judiciary's institutional authority.[366] Therefore, scholars are understandably uneasy about the

[361] Gummow, *Conclusion, supra* note 124, at 517.

[362] *See generally* Anenson, *Statutory Interpretation, supra* note 2.

[363] *See, e.g.,* Nicholas S. Zeppos, *Judicial Candor and Statutory Interpretation,* 78 GEO. L.J. 353, 389–90 (1989) ("[J]udicial interpretation of statutes raises a problem of legitimacy, i.e., justification for unelected and unrepresented judges making law in a representative democracy.").

[364] Anenson, *A View from Equity, supra* note 289, at 263; Smith, *Fiduciary Law, supra* note 35, at 264–65; *see also* discussion *supra* Chapter 2, Section 2.8.

[365] *See* discussion *supra* Chapter 2, Section 2.8.

[366] *See, e.g.,* Leubsdorf, *supra* note 286, at 549–50 (asserting that courts must honor the law of liability in determining remedies); Rendleman, *Remedies, supra* note 36, at 579 (cautioning against too much judicial discretion in statutory cases).

ability of the judiciary to weaken substantive statutory protections in the name of adjusting remedies.[367]

The constitutionally-derived doctrine of separation of powers makes government more efficient through an effective division of labor and disperses power to reduce the risk of tyranny.[368] The equitable defense axiom can be envisioned as advancing both goals. The equity-observing exegesis of the statute's meaning enables the judicial branch leeway to perform its primary function and curbs that power through an effective arrangement of checks and balances. In particular, equitable remedies and defenses provide protection against the over- (or under-) inclusiveness of statutory rules.[369] While scholars have lamented the inability to adequately explain the assortment of equitable principles and doctrines as a unified theory, collectively, they evince equity's primary cleansing function in preserving the legitimacy of the law.[370] Even scholars critical of equitable discretion to qualify statutory relief admit to the necessity of a judicial safety valve of some kind.[371]

A quintessential area of equity jurisprudence is remedies. The need for statutory discretion at the rights implementation stage dates to Aristotle.[372] The Greek philosopher's idea of *epikeia* recognized that laws made by legislative enactment

---

[367] *See, e.g.*, Eric R. Claeys, *The Conceptual Relation Between IP Rights and Infringement Remedies*, 22 GEO. MASON L. REV. 825 (2015) (critiquing the constriction of remedies as potential subterfuge for restricting rights); Tracy Thomas, *eBay Rx*, 2 AKRON INTELL. PROP. J. 187, 189–90 (2008) (questioning whether the Supreme Court right-remedy distinction facilitated its decision to restrict the remedy).

[368] Cass R. Sunstein, *Constitutionalism after the New Deal*, 101 HARV. L. REV. 421, 432–33 (1987). For a discussion of the competing purposes of the separation of powers doctrines, see W.B. GWYN, THE MEANING OF SEPARATION OF POWERS 127–28 (1965); Paul R. Verkuil, *Separation of Powers, The Rule of Law and the Idea of Independence*, 30 WM. & MARY L. REV. 301, 303–04 (1989).

[369] *See* Gergen, Golden, & Smith, *supra* note 35, at 233 (explaining model of equitable decision making); *see also* Anenson & Mark, *supra* note 4, at 1514 (concluding that the Federal Circuit's failure to follow Supreme Court doctrine on ensuring equitable principles are flexible made its former law of inequitable conduct overinclusive and its new law underinclusive).

[370] *See* Anenson & Mayer, *supra* note 16, at 974 (commenting that the application of equitable defenses reinforces equity's function in maintaining law's integrity); Anenson, *Role of Equity*, *supra* note 108, at 63 (analyzing equitable defenses in the context of unfair competition that highlight equity's forgotten role in maintaining the integrity of the law); Emily L. Sherwin, *Law and Equity in Contract Enforcement*, 50 MD. L. REV. 253, 304–05 (1991) [hereinafter Sherwin, *Contract Enforcement*].

[371] *See, e.g.*, Michael T. Morley, *Enforcing Equality: Statutory Injunctions, Equitable Balancing under eBay, and the Civil Rights Act of 1964*, 2014 CHI. LEGAL F. 177, 214–15.

[372] The association between equity and Aristotelian philosophy in the enforcement of statutes has been recognized repeatedly both here and abroad. *See, e.g.*, RENDLEMAN, COMPLEX LITIGATION, *supra* note 277, at 143–44. The relationship has been acknowledged by judges and scholars. *See, e.g.*, Petrella v. Metro-Goldwyn-Mayer, Inc., 134 S. Ct. 1962, 1979 (2014) (Breyer, J., dissenting) ("'[T]he nature of the equitable,' Aristotle long ago observed, is 'a correction of law where it is defective owing to its universality.'" (citation omitted)); McDowell, *Story's Science of Equity*, *supra* note 268, at 157–58 (explaining Story's efforts toward regeneration of an original understanding of equity that was begun with Aristotle). For an extensive treatment of the historical and conceptual development of equity from Greek to Roman to English, see Max

required remedy-tailoring discretion.[373] Without judicial discretion, attempts to lay down rules in advance could yield situations not envisaged by the rule-maker.[374] Accordingly, allowing the decision maker a "space of justice" is necessary to effectively administer statutes.[375] The spacious dimension to adjudicating equitable issues is a salient feature of classic equity.[376] It is also one that the Supreme Court accepted in its statutory task concerning equitable remedies and defenses.[377]

Discretionary decision making for equitable principles has long been understood to be within the special competence of the judiciary.[378] As a result, the fact that Congress did not mention equitable defenses or other discretionary denials of relief in a statute has not been and should not be taken as an implied repeal of these longstanding principles. Therefore, the equity canon of construction and its implicit background assumption of equitable defenses recognize the importance of maintaining the existing relationship between the legislature and the courts. As a practical matter, courts have been historically better equipped to deal with the intricacies involved in the implementation of the law.[379]

Radin, *A Juster Justice, a More Lawful Law, in* LEGAL ESSAYS IN TRIBUTE TO ORRIN KIP McMURRAY 537, 541 (Radin ed. 1935).

[373] *Magna Moralia* and *Nicomachean Ethics, in* THE WORKS OF ARISTOTLE (W.D. Ross trans., Oxford at the Clarendon Press 1925); *Art of Rhetoric, in* 2 THE WORKS OF ARISTOTLE (W. Roberts trans., Encyclopedia Britannica 1952).

[374] *See id.; see also* William N. Eskridge, Jr., *Spinning Legislative Supremacy*, 78 GEO. L.J. 319, 323–27 (1989) (explaining how judges must deal with gaps in the law); Felix Frankfurter, *Some Reflections on the Reading of Statutes*, 47 COLUM. L. REV. 527, 529 (1947) (explaining that the ambiguities of language along with unanticipated situations arising after enactment of a statute compel judicial construction).

[375] JOHN GLOVER, EQUITY, RESTITUTION & FRAUD, § 1.6, at 8 (2004) (using term to describe the application of equitable principles); *see also* William M. Landes & Richard A. Posner, *The Independent Judiciary in an Interest-Group Perspective*, 18 J.L. & ECON. 875, 879 (1975) ("[T]he limits of human foresight, the ambiguities of language, and the high cost of legislative deliberation combine to assure that most legislation will be enacted in a seriously incomplete form, with many areas of uncertainty left to be resolved by the courts.").

[376] *See, e.g.,* KENNETH C. DAVIS, DISCRETIONARY JUSTICE: A PRELIMINARY INQUIRY 107 (1969) ("Turning all discretion into law would destroy the individualizing element of equity and discretion."); *see also* Smith, *Fusion and Tradition, supra* note 32, at 24–25 (discussing how equitable principles are context specific "liability conclusions"); GLOVER, *supra* note 375, at 8 (advancing the idea of a "hermeatic circle" in resolving equitable issues).

[377] Anenson & Mark, *supra* note 4, at 1520–21 (discussing the retention of equitable discretion in remedies and defenses); Bray, *New Equity, supra* note 183, at 1036 (same).

[378] Anenson & Mark, *supra* note 4, at 1450–53, 1515; William N. Eskridge, Jr., *Public Values in Statutory Interpretation*, 137 U. PA. L. REV. 1007, 1023 (1989) [hereinafter Eskridge, *Public Values*] (discussing how interpretation to preserve the traditional separation of responsibilities in government has been understood in institutional competence terms).

[379] *See* Shapiro, *supra* note 346, at 548–49 (justifying judicial discretion in equitable remedies); *see also* Cass R. Sunstein, *Interpreting Statutes in the Regulatory State*, 103 HARV. L. REV. 405, 482 (1989) (advocating for a canon of construction to avoid irrationality and injustice on the ground that courts are better able to focus upon concrete and unforeseeable effects of statutory provisions).

Judges here and abroad are intimately familiar with this perennial problem of justice. Australian High Court Justice William Gummow, writing extracurially, explained: "Much of the difficulty which the courts continually encounter with statutory interpretation reflects an unsettling need to accommodate what one might call a socially directed rule, expressed as an abstraction, to the infinite variety of human conduct revealed by the evidence in one case after another."[380] The Supreme Court has echoed similar sentiments in its commitment to equitable discretion concerning remedies and defenses that focuses concern on "the fact that special circumstances, often hard to predict, could warrant special treatment in an appropriate case."[381] These expressions of the judicial function reflect Aristotle's awareness that the problem of justice "is always pressing for solution."[382]

Moreover, while the Supreme Court has not addressed the source of its authority to craft limitations on legislation through equitable defenses or announced a tradition-tipping technique of statutory interpretation, the previous section disclosed that the Court is allowing for change at a gradual pace through trial court decisions and structured in light of legislative aims.[383] The Court begins with a baseline of history and ends by assessing statutory objectives in a way that usually limits the scope of the defense.[384] We see the same phenomena in some of the states, including the California fusion cases concerning the clean hands doctrine.[385] In particular, federal and state courts have disallowed the defense against favored litigants that the statute was meant to protect, and the courts have otherwise keyed the defense's application to statutory purposes.[386]

---

[380] William Gummow, Change and Continuity: Statute, Equity, and Federalism 18 (1999) [hereinafter Gummow, Change and Continuity].

[381] Holland v. Florida, 560 U.S. 631, 650 (2010) (citing, *e.g.*, Hazel-Atlas Glass Co. v. Hartford-Empire Co., 322 U.S. 238, 248 (1944) (discussing equity's flexibility to relieve hardships that accompany "hard and fast adherence" to absolute legal rules).

[382] Chafee, Selected Essays on Equity, *supra* note 56, at iii–iv.

[383] *See* discussion *supra* Section 5.4.2.2; Anenson, *Age of Statutes, supra* note 20, at 562; *see also* Eskridge, *Public Values, supra* note 378, at 1042 (concluding that statutory evolution encourages the development of statutory policy through its implementation in trial courts, which promotes "orderly change and measured continuity").

[384] *See* discussion *supra* Section 5.4.2.2; Anenson, *Age of Statutes, supra* note 20, at 562–63.

[385] *See* Mendoza v. Ruesga, 86 Cal. Rptr. 3d 610, 619 (Cal. Ct. App. 2008) (ruling that unclean hands is not a defense to an action for violation of the immigration consultants act because "[a]pplication of the doctrine would allow unscrupulous immigration consultants to go unpunished and undermine the protective purposes of the legislation.").

[386] *Id.; see, e.g.*, Whittemore v. Owens Healthcare-Retail Pharmacy, Inc., 111 Cal. Rptr. 3d 227, 229 (Cal. Ct. App. 3d Dist. 2010), citing Health & Safety Code §§ 11700 et seq. ("The doctrine of unclean hands does not preclude recovery in circumstances covered by the Drug Dealer Liability Act because the very purpose of the Act is to permit recovery of damages by the user and others damaged by the use of prohibited drugs in the specified circumstances prescribed in the Act.").

In fact, the clear statement rule with respect to remedies can be considered a remnant of the Equity of the Statute doctrine.[387] While the doctrine's demise has been announced by scholars here and abroad, it may have simply been relocated in interpreting provisions for equitable relief.[388] When equity is *in* the statute, the words carry with them a method of analysis. The Supreme Court has consistently defined equitable defenses according to their historical descriptions and rationales as well as confined them to their customary contexts.[389] But it has also subjugated them to case and other consequences, including statutory goals.[390] Equity's historic connection to the public interest has been used in the service of legislative object- ives.[391] In this way, these discretionary doctrines remain retrospective and retroactive phenomena fixed to their function. The cases show that it is a method of history moderated by policy analysis pursuant to statutory purposes and bound down by precedent.[392] In other words, there is no equity "in the air."[393] It is grounded in law. Moreover, as explored in the previous section, the Court is building a federal equity jurisprudence out of the general common law reflecting the shared consensus across the several states.[394]

Modernization, of course, is tricky. To reiterate, the Supreme Court's current mode of modification in permitting judge-made equity to survive in the face of a silent statute is one of restraining application rather than redefinition.[395] It has usually chosen to impose restrictions on a doctrine's use rather than adopt it

---

[387] GUMMOW, CHANGE AND CONTINUITY, *supra* note 380, at 20 (commenting that interpretative presumptions are a remnant of the Equity of the Statute doctrine); *see also* Amy Coney Barrett, *Substantive Canons and Faithful Agency*, 90 B.U. L. REV. 109, 127 (2010) (explaining that the Equity of the Statute doctrine was inherited from the English common law).

[388] Scholars have noted the rise and fall of the Equity of the Statute doctrine allowing for policy analysis in statutory interpretation. John F. Manning, *Textualism and the Equity of the Statute*, 101 COLUM. L. REV. 1, 125 (2001); *cf.* Andrew Burrows, *The Relationship between Common Law and Statute in the Law of Obligations*, 128 L. QUAR. REV. 232, 241 (2012) ("[T]he medieval idea of the 'equity of the statute' fell out of favour in the 18th century.") (English context); *see also* YOUNG ET AL., *supra* note 308, at 254 (surmising that the legacy of the Equity of the Statute doctrine is purposive construction); Frederick J. de Sloovere, *The Equity and Reason of a Statue*, 21 CORNELL L.Q. 591, 595 (1937) (same).

[389] *See* Anenson, *Age of Statutes, supra* note 20, at 538–42; Anenson, *Statutory Interpretation, supra* note 2, at 42 (analyzing cases of unclean hands defense, unclean hands–derived defenses, and other equitable defenses).

[390] *Id.* at 34–35; Anenson, *Age of Statutes, supra* note 20, at 542–48.

[391] Anenson, *Statutory Interpretation, supra* note 2, at 43.

[392] Anenson, *Age of Statutes, supra* note 20, at 554–55 (calling the Supreme Court a medieval modernist in its approach to equitable defenses because it relies on history to define a defense but also considers the policy objectives to amend its application).

[393] Finn, *Unconscionable Conduct, supra* note 5, at 43.

[394] *See* discussion *supra* Section 5.4.2.2. *See generally* Nelson, *General Law, supra* note 327 (describing how federal courts continue to draw rules of decision from general American jurisprudence).

[395] Anenson, *Age of Statutes, supra* note 20, at 553; *see also* Anenson & Mark, *supra* note 4, at 1515 ("Guidance in application, rather than continual re-interpretation, is more appropriate for lower court instruction [on equitable defenses].") (citing state and federal courts).

wholesale or deny its existence altogether.[396] The Court has narrowed equitable defenses either by limiting their application to certain kinds of relief, to particular plaintiff classes, or through heightened criteria like exceptionalism.[397]

In layering equity over legislation, the Court has also relied on lower court cases to build change-allowing criteria into the defenses.[398] In *Petrella*, the Court even sought shared ground in deciding laches in copyright law by inserting statutory words into the relevant circumstances confining lower-court discretion in evaluating the effect of delay to adjust equitable relief at the remedial stage of the litigation.[399] The Supreme Court's textualization of tradition may explain other areas of its equity jurisprudence.[400] From this vantage, equitable defenses are sticky *and* spongy.[401] They are not dislodged easily, yet they also absorb the underlying values (and sometimes the actual language) of the statute at issue.

Despite the many references to the historical tradition of equity and the appearance of antiquarianism, the United States Supreme Court has been a medieval modernist in its approach to equitable defenses.[402] Methodologically, it has taken a middle path. It has chosen reformation rather than revolution. The Court's approach to equitable defenses may even be perceived as a renaissance in the sense that it is searching for new learning in earlier legal traditions.

England and its chancellors did not just invent equity as a political, administrative, and judicial system. They invented the *idea* of equity, an idea that American

---

[396] Specifically, the Court has been constrained in supplying the substance of equitable defenses by external sources of custom and internal sources of precedent in alignment with statutory purposes. Anenson, *Age of Statutes, supra* note 20, at 554 (describing the Supreme Court's method of making equitable defenses). The Court has been hesitant to allow exclusively equitable defenses to cross the law–equity border. *Id.* at 568.

[397] *Id.* at 546; Anenson, *Statutory Interpretation, supra* note 2, at 37.

[398] *See* Anenson, *Age of Statutes, supra* note 20, at 553. *Petrella*, for example, relied on "illustrative" lower federal copyright decisions for what constitutes "extraordinary circumstances" amounting to laches as a bar to equitable relief. Petrella v. Metro-Goldwyn-Mayer, Inc., 134 S. Ct. 1962, 1978 (2014).

[399] Petrella v. Metro-Goldwyn-Mayer, Inc., 134 S. Ct. at 1979 (listing, among other considerations, the authority "to order injunctive relief 'on such terms as it may deem reasonable.' Sec. 502(a)").

[400] Scholars have questioned whether *eBay's* criteria that include an adequate remedy at law and irreparably injury constitute different inquiries. *Compare* LAYCOCK, IRREPARABLE INJURY RULE, *supra* note 80, at 8–9 (finding the two criteria equivalent), *with* Gene R. Shreve, *Federal Injunctions and the Public Interest,* 51 GEO. WASH. L. REV. 382, 392–93 (1983) (locating differences between the doctrines). Notably, no adequate remedy at law was part of the statutory language of jurisdiction under the Judicature Act. *See* Shapiro, *supra* note 346, at 548–49 (concluding that the adequate remedy requirement was jurisdictional, whereas irreparable injury was a consideration for courts in exercising their discretion).

[401] Samuel L. Bray, *A Little Bit of Laches Goes a Long Way: Notes on Petrella v. Metro-Goldwyn-Mayer, Inc.,* 67 VAND. L. REV EN BANC, 1, 15 (2014) (using the term "sticky" in relation to whether courts will recognize traditional equitable principles in federal statutes).

[402] Anenson, *Age of Statutes, supra* note 20, at 554–55. As discussed earlier, California jurisprudence tracks the U.S. Supreme Court in charting a middle path in integrating equitable defense like unclean hands into legislation.

courts have carried into statutory construction. Judges could have abandoned equitable defenses not because they are wrong or deficient but because they are old. Instead, they are using history to translate equity's meaning in the present day. Therefore, statutory cases concerning equitable defenses, including the clean hands doctrine, have been sensitive to separation-of-powers concerns.

5.4.4 *Good Judgment*

A third and final critique is that judges may not use good judgment and fail to weigh and balance the appropriate policies at stake. In other words, the fear is that courts will overlook their discretion to refuse the defense or neglect to use their discretion appropriately. This criticism stems from Chafee's iconoclastic analysis of unclean hands cases that judges in the United States have taken to heart.[403] A review of the cases does not support that judges regularly abuse or inadvertently misapply the defense.[404]

The fact that the defense is available does not necessitate its application in every case. Courts have discretion to apply unclean hands in the interests of justice. The "power of discretion" has been considered the "great contribution of equity" to the judicial system.[405]

But the *wise* exercise of discretion is no easy undertaking. In applying unclean hands, courts are often caught between Scylla and Charybdis such that by refusing to aid one party, the court may aid the other.[406] To be sure, the application of unclean hands admittedly leaves courts in a pickle. Preventing a litigant from

---

[403] The court of appeals in *Blain v. Doctor's Co.*, rejected counsel's argument for the reason that these kinds of "boilerplate generalities" are "precisely the sort of overgeneralization that Chafee cautions against." 272 Cal. Rptr. 250, 257 (Cal. Ct. App. 1990). The court then synthesized Chafee's critique of unclean hands to outline a case-specific approach to its application. *Id.; see also* Messick v. Smith, 69 A.2d 478, 481 (Md. 1949) ("We have no occasion to pursue the details of Professor Chafee's interesting iconoclastic discussion, which is revolutionary in classification and nomenclature, not in application, of legal principles.").

[404] *See* discussion *infra* Section 5.4.

[405] HENRY L. MCCLINTOCK, HANDBOOK OF THE PRINCIPLES OF EQUITY v (2nd ed. 1948) (preface). Equity appeared as the priestly or royal dispensation as a matter of grace from the rigor of the strict law. NEWMAN, EQUITY AND LAW, *supra* note 68, at 14, 37.

[406] The controversy played out to its final conclusion in *Manown v. Adams*, in which the Maryland Court of Appeals ultimately avoided the issue of the application of unclean hands at law. 615 A.2d 611, 617 (Md. 1992). St. Thomas Aquinas had perhaps the best, albeit unworkable, solution in modern litigation. He argued that "the giver deserves to lose what he gave, wherefore restitution should not be made to him; and, since the receiver acted against the law in receiving, he must not retain the price but must use it for some pious object." AQUINAS, *supra* note 288, II-II Q. 62, Art. 5. Of course, the same perils of public policy apply to other defenses that apply to damages like *in pari delicto. See* Feld and Sons, Inc. v. Pechner, Dorfman, Wolfee, Rounick, & Cabot, 458 A.2d 545, 551–52 (Pa. Super. Ct. 1983) (avoiding resort to the doctrine of *in pari delicto* due to ambiguity in application); discussion *supra* Chapter 3.

benefiting from their own wrong allows another wrong to stay in place.[407] The defense's application permits a party to violate the law. Presumably, it is for this reason that Doug Laycock considers the clean hands doctrine immoral because "two wrongs don't make a right."[408] But they do make a valid defense. The connection component explains why. Bear in mind that unclean hands does not apply unless there is a connection between the conduct and the case.[409] This rule of relatedness provides a reasonable prescription for its application.[410] As emphasized by Judge Posner, "The linguistically fastidious may shudder at 'nexus,' that hideously overworked legal cliché, but there can be no quarrel with the principle."[411]

Professor Laycock may accept the original doctrinal setting that described a situation in which the plaintiff's fault contributed to their own harm.[412] As illustrated in Chapter 2, the court in *Dering v. Earl of Winchelsea* denied the defense but suggested that it may be satisfied if the applicant for relief had bored a hole in the side of a ship that caused his goods to be thrown overboard to save the ship.[413] Such a person could not claim contribution from his fellow cargo owners because he had unclean hands.[414] Recall that even as applied (more controversially) to similar conduct, in which there are a few fusion cases,[415] the doctrine is said to have normative virtues.[416]

In addition to the risk that the scope of the disablement may be defined too indiscriminately, consideration of the unclean hands defense (along with many other legal and equitable doctrines)[417] also calls for the identification and reconciliation of other competing interests at stake in the case.[418] Due to the risks of a

---

[407] *See* Clemens v. Clemens, 28 Wis. 637, 655, 9 Am. Rep. 520 (1871) (discussing the idea that no one should take advantage of their own wrong and advising that "[t]he very working of this principle, this one-sided and uneven justice, suggests great caution in its application.").

[408] *See* Douglas Laycock, Modern American Remedies 933 (4th ed. 2010) [hereinafter, Laycock, Remedies]; *id.* at 936 (questioning the basic premise of the doctrine). *Contra* Ori J. Herstein, *A Normative Theory of the Clean Hands Defense*, 17 Legal Theory 171, 195–96, 199–200 (2011) (arguing that unclean hands embodies *tu quoque* and retribution norms associated with fairness and justice).

[409] *See* discussion *supra* Chapter 2.

[410] *See* discussion *supra* Chapter 2; *see also* discussion *supra* Chapter 6 (providing four-phase procedural model of incorporation of unclean hands at law to further clarify the doctrine); *see also* Anenson, *Role of Equity, supra* note 108, at 49–50 (noting that "it is difficult to reconcile those cases determining if misconduct is related to the lawsuit or merely collateral.").

[411] Shondel v. McDermott, 775 F.2d 859, 869 (7th Cir. 1985).

[412] *See* discussion *supra* Chapter 2, Section 2.7.2.

[413] 1 Cox Eq. 318, 320, 29 Eng. Rep. 1185 (1787).

[414] *Id.* (announcing that such a person would be the author of the loss).

[415] *See* discussion *supra* Chapter 2, Section 2.7.2, and Chapter 3.

[416] *See* discussion *supra* Chapter 2, Section 2.3. *See generally* Herstein, *supra* note 408 (developing a normative theory of the clean hands doctrine).

[417] *See, e.g.,* Laycock, *Triumph of Equity, supra* note 81, at 73 ("Discretion and flexibility pervade the system and are not limited to the historic confines of equity.").

[418] *See* discussion *supra* Chapter 2. The indeterminacy associated with the range of choice, including the selection of policy goals and the process of balancing the competing policies,

mechanical application, Chafee called unclean hands a "mischievous" doctrine capable of causing harm.[419] In assessing the application of unclean hands in twentieth-century equity cases, Chafee also described the clean hands doctrine as "really bundles of rules relating to diverse subjects."[420] The discrete application of the defense is not surprising given its standard-like quality that courts will give meaning to in individual cases.[421] Indeed, the only way to achieve a more unified rule of unclean hands is through the collaborative efforts of judicial precedent.[422]

Equitable issues have been subject to precedent since the eighteenth century.[423] While federal and state courts have intimated otherwise on certain occasions,[424] it is axiomatic that the principle of *stare decisis* is alive and well in the tradition of equity

makes policy analysis the most subjective type of argument. *See* Anenson, *Pluralistic Model, supra* note 57, at 655 (citing HUHN, *supra* note 15, at 68).

[419] Chafee I, *supra* note 53, at 878–90. He further concluded that the use of "the clean hands maxim sometimes does harm by distracting [a judge's] attention from the basic policies which are applicable to the situation before them." CHAFEE, SOME PROBLEMS, *supra* note 1, at 94–95.

[420] Chafee I, *supra* note 53, at 878. This is not necessarily bad and, in any event, is similar to other equitable defenses. *See* Anenson, *Pluralistic Model, supra* note 57, at 646 (describing equitable estoppel as a chameleon that takes its color from the surrounding circumstances).

[421] *See, e.g.,* Larry Alexander, *Incomplete Theorizing: A Review Essay of Cass R. Sunstein's Legal Reasoning and Political Conflict,* 72 NOTRE DAME L. REV. 531, 541 (1997) (book review) ("Rules are often described as 'bright line' (clear and easy to follow), 'formal' (to be applied without regard to substance of the results but only with regard to the rule's terms) and 'opaque' (to the rules' background justifications) ... Standards are norms that have the opposite characteristics ... Standards are thus vague, substantive (as opposed to formal), and transparent (to background values)."); Kathleen M. Sullivan, *The Justices of Rules and Standards,* 106 HARV. L. REV. 22, 58 (1992) ("Rules aim to confine the decisionmaker to facts ... A legal directive is 'standard' – like when it tends to collapse decisionmaking back into the direct application of the background principle or policy to a fact situation.").

[422] Like any standard, equity experienced periods of growth and crystallization. *See, e.g.,* Anenson, *Pluralistic Model, supra* note 57, at 643–44 ("[T]he English Court of Chancery during the eighteenth and nineteenth centuries came to be called a court of 'crystallized conscience.'") (citing Hanbury, *supra* note 86, at 35); Patrick S. Atiyah, *From Principles to Pragmatism: Changes in the Function of the Judicial Process and the Law,* 65 IOWA L. REV. 1249, 1251–59 (1980) (describing how English equity and the common law lost flexibility in the nineteenth century followed by a resurgence of discretion after the merger of law and equity in the twentieth century); Hanbury, *supra* note 86, at 32 (describing the "golden age" of equity as beginning during the time of Lord Nottingham, who began the transformation of equity "from a heterogeneous medley of isolated, empirical beliefs into a stable and increasingly rigid system of rules" until the first years of the nineteenth century).

[423] *See* Pierpont v. Fowle, 19 F. Cas. 652, 658 (D. Mass. 1846) ("Precedents are to govern conscience in chancery as well as at law."); JOSEPH STORY, COMMENTARIES ON EQUITY JURISPRUDENCE AS ADMINISTERED IN ENGLAND AND AMERICA § 18 (Melville M. Bigelow ed., 13th ed.) (asserting that the system of equity is bound by precedent); W.H.D. Winder, *Precedent in Equity,* 57 L. Q. REV. 245, 247 (1941) ("Before the opening of the eighteenth century precedent was rapidly superseding conscience as the foundation of practical equity.").

[424] Anenson, *Pluralistic Model, supra* note 57, at 129 (noting that there is "precedent paradoxically pronouncing there is no precedent"); *see also* NEWMAN, EQUITY AND LAW, *supra* note 68, at 28 ("[R]elief in the court of the Chancellor was granted according to criteria which were not confined by rules of strict logic or by analogy to prior decisions.").

in America.[425] For instance, in copyright cases, unclean hands has developed into a distinct defense of "copyright misuse."[426] The progression of precedent applying unclean hands to legal claims in California is also representative of this phenomenon.[427] The initial decision made the defense available to preclude a claim for tortious union activities.[428] It was then extended to bar malicious prosecution,[429] the foreclosure of a mechanic's lien,[430] and conversion,[431] as well as many other causes of action for damages.[432]

The California Court of Appeals decision in *Blain v. Doctor's Co.*[433] also provides an excellent demonstration of how the underlying policies of unclean hands are evaluated in resolving a concrete dispute. In attempting to discern whether unclean hands should be available in a legal malpractice action, the appellate court was clearly not satisfied by the lack of insight from existing authorities in applying the defense.[434] It complained that Chafee "offers no detailed exposition of the case law"[435] and found the comments to Section 889 of the *Restatement of*

---

[425] *See, e.g.,* Gergen, Golden, & Smith, *supra* note 35, at 205 (concluding that "the *eBay* opinion has had cataclysmic effect" by becoming "the test for whether a permanent injunction should issue, regardless of whether the dispute in question centers on patent law, another form of intellectual property, more conventional government regulation, constitutional law, or state tort or contract law").

[426] *See* discussion *supra* Chapter 3, Section 3.4.2.3; *supra* Section 5.3.1 (discussion other intellectual property defenses that grew from the clean hands doctrine).

[427] For a more detailed analysis of California's incorporation of unclean hands, see discussion *supra* Chapter 3, Section 3.4.1.1.

[428] Fibreboard Paper Prods. Corp. v. East Bay Union of Machinists, 39 Cal. Rptr. 64 (Cal. Ct. App. 1964). The appellate court, however, did not apply the defense of unclean hands due to the absence of a relevant connection between the bad conduct and the substance of the case. *See id.* at 97.

[429] Pond v. Insur. Co. of N. America, 198 Cal. Rptr. 517, 522 (Cal. Ct. App. 1984).

[430] Burton v. Sosinsky, 250 Cal. Rptr. 33, 41 (Cal. Ct. App. 1988) ("California has taken the position that this defense is available in a legal action."); *see also id.* ("Although no case directly on point has been located, we see no reason why a successful defense of unclean hands should not bar the foreclosure of the mechanics' lien.").

[431] Unilogic, Inc. v. Burroughs Corp., 12 Cal. Rptr. 741, 745 (Cal. Ct. App. 1992); Gen-Probe, Inc. v. Amoco Corp., 926 F. Supp. 948, 952 (S.D. Cal. 1996) (applying California law) (finding no connection between the conduct constituting unclean hands and lawsuit).

[432] *See* Kendall-Jackson Winery, Ltd. v. Superior Court, 90 Cal. Rptr. 2d 743, 749 (Cal. Ct. App. 1999) ("The defense is available in legal as well as equitable actions."); Alan Klarik Enterprises, Inc. v. Viva Optique, Inc., No. B179607, 2006 WL 2423552, at *5 (Cal. Ct. App. Aug. 23, 2006) ("[U]nclean hands applies not only to actions seeking equitable relief, but applies as well today as a defense to legal actions . . . "); Travel America, Inc. v. Camp Coast to Coast, Inc., Nos. G028513, G028738, 2003 WL 558563, at *4 (Cal. Ct. App. Feb. 27, 2003) (holding that unclean hands operates as a bar to an entire lawsuit asserting legal and equitable claims).

[433] 272 Cal. Rptr. 250 (Cal. Ct. App. 1990).

[434] *Id.* at 256 (noting the "sparse product" of authorities such as Chafee, Wigmore, and the Restatement).

[435] *Id.*

Torts addressing unclean hands "unilluminating."[436] Despite these perceived inadequacies, the court reached a reasoned and fair solution that invoked unclean hands and barred the legal claim.[437]

More specifically, it precluded a legal malpractice action against counsel who advised his client to lie at a deposition.[438] The court found committing perjury constituted unclean hands regardless of the requested remedy.[439] The court emphasized that the injury stemmed from a criminal conviction attributable to the ill-advised perjury, and recovery might soften the effect of the penal sanction.[440] Again, California courts have used the paradigm provided in *Blain* to resolve subsequent cases involving unclean hands.[441]

Additionally, aware that equitable defenses are a powerful psychological component in equity jurisprudence, the Supreme Court has consistently cautioned lower courts against overemphasizing the moral worth of the parties to the exclusion of the private and public purposes of the defense and the rights involved.[442] While there has been an endorsement of the view that the application of discretionary defenses like unclean hands have no adverse effect on conduct rules aimed at party behavior,[443] this is not necessarily always the case.[444]

---

[436] *Id.* It was also not satisfied with Wigmore's synopsis of the defense. *Id.* ("What cases would lie in the first of Wigmore's categories is not self-explanatory.").

[437] *Id.* at 258; *cf.* 2 RONALD E. MALLEN & JEFFREY M. SMITH, LEGAL MALPRACTICE § 17.4 (3d ed. 1989) (denying relief to clients engaged in misconduct in legal malpractice cases).

[438] *See* 272 Cal. Rptr. at 258–59.

[439] *See id.*

[440] *Id.* at 258.

[441] *See* discussion *supra* Section 5.4.2.1.

[442] Perma Life Mufflers, Inc. v. Int'l Parts Corp., 392 U.S. 134, 139 (1968), *overruled on other grounds by* Copperweld Corp. v. Indep. Tube Corp., 467 U.S. 752 (1984); *see also* Craig M. Boise, *Playing with Monopoly Money: Phony Profits, Fraud Penalties, and Equity*, 90 MINN. L. REV. 144, 189–92 (2006) (asserting that the unclean hands defense is a powerful psychological component in statutory law). The warning was repeated in *McKennon*. McKennon v. Nashville Banner Publ'g Co., 513 U.S. 352, 361 (1995) ("In determining appropriate remedial action, the employee's wrongdoing becomes relevant not to punish the employee or out of concern 'for the relative moral worth of the parties,' but to take due account of the lawful prerogative of the employer in the usual course of its business and the ... corresponding equities that it has arising from the employee's wrongdoing.") (citing *Perma Life Mufflers, Inc.*, *supra*).

[443] *See* Sherwin, *Property Rules*, *supra* note 269, at 2086–88 (claiming equitable defenses do not operate as conduct rules because they remain uncertain until the dispute is adjudicated (citing Sherwin, *Contract Enforcement*, *supra* note 370, at 300–14)).

[444] *See* Anenson & Mayer, *supra* note 16, at 979–83 (describing the concept of acoustic separation, in which conduct and decision rules can operate in tandem and fulfill the policy functions of both precepts, but rejecting the theory in public or quasi-public claims) (citing Meir Dan-Cohen, *Decision Rules and Conduct Rules: On Acoustic Separation in Criminal Law*, 97 HARV. L. REV. 625, 630–34 (1984)).

A standard approach in considering the common law incorporation of unclean hands is to evaluate the defense's application based on its dual purposes of party and court protection.[445] As explained in Chapter 2, some courts require a heightened state of mind to satisfy the defense that may narrow the scope of judgment.[446] Finally, consider that some courts resolve doubts in applying the defense against it.[447] The presumption-like phraseology limits the defense to "extraordinary," "disfavored," or "exceptional" cases.[448]

The point is not to put the defense back on the pedestal that Chafee knocked it off sixty-five or so years ago.[449] Further study of the unclean hands defense (along with mapping the margins of related defenses) would be a fruitful endeavor and lead to better judicial reasoning. The important indication is that it is yielding sound outcomes and is not anathema to the law.

In justifying the case law system in America, Karl Llewellyn explained how judicial decisions provide congruence between legal rules and "real-life" norms.[450] While discretionary doctrines such as unclean hands may be criticized by lawyers as lacking predictability and providing too many opportunities for error, they paradoxically provide legal certainty for laypersons and foster legitimacy in our courts.[451] From Llewellyn's perspective, certainty to the layperson potentially means changes in the law to reflect ever-evolving social norms, which brings the law closer to life and increases law's utility to society.[452] Law is about life and its infinite complexities. And life never stops. In this way, the discretionary application of unclean hands is

---

[445] For a discussion of the doctrinal development of unclean hands at law based on the doctrine's dual purposes of court protection and deterrence, see *infra* Chapter 6; *see also* Wilson R. Huhn, *The Stages of Legal Reasoning: Formalism, Analogy and Realism*, 48 VILL. L. REV. 305, 317–18 (2003). Professor Huhn portrays the policy argument as a five-step process.

> First, one must imagine the hypothetical consequences of interpreting the law one way or another. Second, one must identify the interest or abstract principle that a rule serves. Third, one must evaluate the weight of that interest or principle. Fourth, one must estimate the likelihood that the rule will accomplish its goal and serve this interest or principle. Finally, one must simultaneously balance the weight and likelihood of all the competing interest and principles.

HUHN, *supra* note 15, at 131.

[446] *See* discussion *supra* Chapter 2, Section 2.7.3.

[447] *See* discussion *supra* Chapter 2, Section 2.8.

[448] *See* discussion *supra* Chapter 2, Section 2.8.

[449] Chafee I, *supra* note 53, at 878 ([I]t is a pity to take this beautiful statue off its lofty pedestal . . .").

[450] Karl N. Llewellyn, Paul Gewirtz, & Michael Ansaldi, *The Case Law System in America*, 88 COLUM. L. REV. 989, 991 (1988).

[451] *See id.* The conflict between fairness and certainty is a version of the rules–standards debate. To argue the debate in the abstract tends to oversimplify it. Naturally, it is the *relative* uncertainty that counts in the context of the circumstances of a case.

[452] *See id.; see also* Anenson & Mark, *supra* note 4, at 1509–10 ("[T]he accumulated legacy of court work will provide guidance in the nature of Llewellyn's 'situation sense' for the district courts to conduct a contextual normative inquiry.").

the beauty of the defense.[453] "Human diversity has been equity's lock and stock as well as its *raison d'être*."[454]

Like Shakespeare's rose, the power of unclean hands lies in its name. While historically the subject of poor jokes,[455] the defense has served as a significant safety valve in equity cases for more than two hundred years. Be it law or equity, then, the moral authority of the doctrine provides courts a legitimate reason to do the right thing.

In summary, equitable defenses like unclean hands present a fascinating study in contradictions. They require reflection on the relationship between judicial power and legislative deference, the correlation between principle and practice, the reconciliation of private and public interests, and the connection of past to present. The concept of fusion addresses all of these concerns. It is no wonder the debate has been so vigorous and intractable.

5.5 CONCLUSION

American equity has been a model of fluidity and diversity – a true melting pot. In what was once an outpost of the British Empire, a showdown over the idea of fusion is taking place. State and federal courts are pioneering the expansion of the unclean hands defense to damages actions. Perhaps it is not so surprising that in a country that promises transformation, its courts would effectuate a major change in the law of equity. "Where there is an open mind, there will always be a frontier."[456]

The movement of unclean hands across the law–equity divide provides evidence upon which to analyze the fusion debate. This chapter has shown that equitable principles like unclean hands can be equally appropriate in curtailing damages. Opportunities for opportunism arise regardless of the form of relief. Courts of law, no less than courts of equity, deserve protection when unconscionable conduct taints the administration of justice. Drawing attention to the use of unclean hands in the United States also provides an in-depth look at a defense that has fallen into disrepair and not a little disrepute. This chapter has attempted to rehabilitate the doctrine by demonstrating its continued importance in the modern age.

---

[453] *See* Roscoe Pound, *Do We Need a Philosophy of Law?*, 5 COLUM. L. REV. 639, 650 (1905) (concluding that "the rise of the court of chancery preserved [our legal system] from medieval dry rot").

[454] Anenson & Mark, *supra* note 4, at 1515.

[455] Chafee I, *supra* note 53, at 877.

[456] *Profile of America: An Autobiography of the U.S.A.* (Emilie Davie ed. 1960) (attributing quotation to Charles F. Kettering).

6

Thinking Procedurally

The governing principle has long been settled. It is that a court will not redress a wrong when he who invokes its aid has unclean hands. The maxim of unclean hands comes from courts of equity. But the principle prevails also in courts of law ... Then aid is denied despite the defendant's wrong. It is denied in order to maintain respect for law; in order to promote confidence in the administration of justice; in order to preserve the judicial process from contamination ... It is sometimes spoken of as a rule of substantive law. But it extends to matters of procedure as well.

– Louis D. Brandeis[1]

6.1 INTRODUCTION

This chapter builds a theoretical foundation for the adoption of the equitable defense of unclean hands in legal cases. It suggests a process-based approach that would assist courts in deciding whether to incorporate unclean hands in a particular case. It then justifies the proffered analytical framework on doctrinal and normative grounds.

Unclean hands tends to be viewed as a means of protecting individual litigants. Seen through the lens of its court protection purpose, however, the doctrine's institutional benefits come into focus. In outlining this process-based theory, the chapter asserts that preserving the integrity of the justice system is a paramount purpose of unclean hands.[2] It orients the criteria of evaluation around this core value by segregating the conduct at issue in the cases according to the degree of causal connection or contribution to achieving this goal.[3] The considerations are as

---

[1] Olmstead v. United States, 277 U.S. 438, 483–85 (1928) (Brandeis, J., dissenting). For further discussion of the case and its implications, see *infra* Section 6.3.4.

[2] *See* discussion *infra* Section 6.3.4.

[3] *See* discussion *infra* Section 6.3.5.

follows: litigation misconduct with the potential to interfere with the adjudication process (tainting the jury pool), other misconduct that may interfere with the process (falsifying documents during commercial transaction later necessary as evidence), misconduct in prior litigation that has no potential to disrupt the process (perjury in a prior case that is relevant to the existing case), and finally, nonlitigation misconduct that has no effect on the adjudication process (illegal, unethical, or other wrongful conduct outside the litigation process in the current or any former case).[4]

These four phases of consideration are listed in order of importance in serving the court protection policy of unclean hands. Hence, the nature and amount of interference with the judicial process influences the defense's availability at law and potential application. For instance, conduct that interferes with the judicial mission by tainting the jury pool or obstructing witness testimony (Phase One) would be the highest priority in considering case dismissal for unclean hands. By contrast, prelitigation misconduct such as fraud during a commercial transaction (Phase Four) would be the lowest priority and would require, at minimum, a consideration of the policies of the claim before dismissal pursuant to the defense.

The proposed process-based theory follows from the idea that the law–equity merger in federal and state civil procedure allows courts to adopt the defense in lawsuits seeking legal remedies on a case-by-case basis.[5] Previous chapters argued that the exclusive use of the labels "law" and "equity" to determine the application of unclean hands after the integration stands on flawed premises.[6] By exposing those flaws regarding the meaning of the merger, this research revealed that the union in state and federal civil procedure neither mandated nor forbade the reception of unclean hands.[7] Rather than an "all or nothing" proposition, the union did not prevent courts from choosing to accept or reject the equitable defense in each case.[8] Because a number of jurisdictions have yet to take a position on the common law incorporation of unclean hands, the merger methodology suggested in this chapter has the potential for a substantial impact on the resolution of future cases.

---

[4] *See* discussion *infra* Section 6.3.5.
[5] *See* discussion *supra* Chapters 3–5; *accord* Anthony Mason, *Fusion, in* EQUITY IN COMMERCIAL LAW 11, 12 (James Edelman & Simone Degeling eds., 2005) (discussing merger in England and Australia) ("[I]t is also clear that the [Judicature] Acts did not require the courts to treat the rules of common law and equity as if they must forever remain unchanged in frozen isolation."); Keith Mason, *Fusion: Fallacy, Future or Finished?* (Justice Keith Mason, New South Wales Court of Appeals) ("[I]t ... [is] equally clear that the *Judicature Act* did not forbid the continuing development of law and equity, including development in the direction of integration of principles, if the single Court otherwise considered this an appropriate application of earlier precedents."), *in* EQUITY IN COMMERCIAL LAW, *supra*, at 41, 56.
[6] *See* discussion *supra* Chapters 3–5.
[7] *Id.*; *accord* Mason, *Fusion* (commenting that there is no support for a view that the Judicature Acts in England substantively and instantly merged law and equity), *supra* note 5, at 12; Mason, *Fusion: Fallacy, Future or Finished?* (same) (citing cases), *supra* note 5, at 56.
[8] *See* discussion *supra* Chapter 4.

The process-based theory may also be utilized by courts to consider the application of unclean hands to legal remedies regardless of their reading of the consolidation of law and equity.[9] It can clarify the current doctrine in those jurisdictions that have ruled the merger mandated the adoption of unclean hands at law.[10] It is additionally applicable in those courts that declare the merger dictates the denial of the defense.[11] Courts generally reject the defense at law for the reason that the legislature limited the consolidation of law and equity to the courts and their procedures.[12] As such, they read the *procedural* union to exclude the *substantive* reception of unclean hands that was pled under premerger practice only against equitable remedies.[13] Because the process-based theory proposed in this chapter is based on the kind of unclean conduct and its connection to the case from a procedural perspective, it will help courts classify the defense under the conventional notion of a consolidation of procedures.

Moreover, the fact that certain courts have fused unclean hands at law as a function of their inherent judicial power suggests that a process-based theory of unclean hands may have even broader implications for the power of courts to resolve issues of civil procedure.[14] Consequently, whether courts accept, deny, or have yet to decide the availability of unclean hands at law after the merger of law and equity, the process-based theory proposed in this chapter will help separate what unclean hands is (or should be) from what it is not.

6.2 OVERVIEW

Section 6.3 articulates the process-based theory and justifies its use under existing doctrine and the defense's purpose of court protection. Section 6.4 discusses the theory's universal application to legal or equitable remedies notwithstanding the conflict in the cases concerning the interpretation of the integration. Since the merger, scholars and courts alike have sought to change the conversation about law and equity.[15] Previous chapters illustrated that the labels "law" and "equity" are problematic when used exclusively to reject or accept fusion. Nevertheless, a number of courts continue to adhere to these antiquated abstractions in considering

---

[9] *See* discussion *infra* Section 6.4.1.
[10] *See* discussion *infra* Section 6.4.1; *see also* discussion *supra* Chapter 3, Section 3.4 (describing courts in state and federal jurisdictions that now allow the defense of unclean hands in law and equity cases).
[11] *See* discussion *infra* Section 6.4.1; *see also* discussion *supra* Chapter 3, Section 3.3 (outlining courts in state and federal jurisdictions that have refused to extend the defense of unclean hands to legal remedies).
[12] *See* discussion *supra* Chapter 4.
[13] *See* discussion *supra* Chapter 4.
[14] *See* discussion *infra* Section 6.3.4 (discussing source of authority for unclean hands and its implications for separation of powers and federalism).
[15] *See* discussion *supra* Chapters 3 and 5.

unclean hands and its status in the law.[16] Section 6.4 demonstrates that the foregoing process-based theory can nevertheless endure either within or without these orthodox categories. This section additionally highlights the importance of unclean hands as a procedural tool by distinguishing the defense from other potential theories of dismissal. The chapter concludes that the recommended framework will not only clarify unclean hands but also will advance the assimilation of this equitable defense into the law.

6.3 PROCESS-BASED THEORY OF UNCLEAN HANDS

6.3.1 *Introduction*

Despite the rhetoric of completing the union of law and equity, procedural reform was initially interpreted by many courts to foreclose this presumably substantive defense of unclean hands in legal cases.[17] As shown in the previous chapters, however, American jurisdictions no longer limit the doctrine to equitable remedies. This chapter analyzes how the courts are also not sustaining the substantive version of the defense. Indeed, they are invoking unclean hands at law to protect their own procedural interests in a fair outcome.[18]

Despite these changes, there has been little commentary on unclean hands since the work of Zechariah Chafee, Jr.[19] The late Professor Chafee categorized the defense by the subject matter of the case.[20] But Chafee's commentary and classification scheme do not invariably fit the cases today. The interests of the parties are being supplanted by the courts' interest in protecting the litigation process as

---

[16] *See* discussion *supra* Chapters 3.
[17] *See* discussion *supra* Chapter 2.
[18] *See* discussion *infra* Sections 6.3.3 and 6.3.4.
[19] *See* discussion *supra* Chapter 2.
[20] Chafee examined a total of eighteen different groups of cases considering unclean hands: (1) suits to enforce illegal or immoral trusts; (2) suits to undo deeds and other executed transactions for such reasons as fraud and mistake, where A is himself a wrongdoer; (3) suits to undo completed transactions in fraud of creditors or for evading taxes; (4) suits to undo an executory transaction growing out of wrongful conduct in which both parties have shared; (5) suits to remove cloud on title; (6) suits for specific performance of contracts where A has engaged in fraud, sharp practice, or other unethical conduct; (7) suits to enforce illegal contracts; (8) miscellaneous tort suits by a person charged with a crime; (9) suits to protect copyrights and literary property; (10) patent suits; (11) suits to protect trade-marks or trade-names; (12) labor litigation; (13) suits to enjoin torts of various kinds, where A has committed similar torts against B or otherwise wronged him; (14) suits to enforce building restrictions and other equitable servitudes; (15) matrimonial litigation; (16) suits concerning corporate and stock transactions; (17) suits for contribution, subrogation, and other remedies of a surety; and (18) miscellaneous proceedings in equity. *See generally* Zechariah Chafee, Jr., *Coming into Equity with Clean Hands*, 47 MICH. L. REV. 1065 (1949) [hereinafter Chafee II] (listing ten different groups of cases); Zechariah Chafee, Jr., *Coming into Equity with Clean Hands*, 47 MICH. L. REV. 877, 885–906 (1949) [hereinafter Chafee I] (listing eight different groups of cases).

substantiated by the growing number of cases incorporating the defense into the law.[21] As a result, the historical stereotype of unclean hands as a substantive defense invoked only against claims for equitable relief is unreliable.

One court explained: "[I]t would be strange if a court of equity had power—because of public policy for its own protection—to throw out a case because it *entered* with unclean hands and yet would have no power to act if the unconscionable conduct occurred while the case was in court."[22] Moreover, before dismissing a damages action for unclean hands predicated on its own procedural interests, another court specifically complained that Chafee's analysis was not helpful and otherwise noted the lack of literature assisting in the application of the defense.[23] Consequently, there is dissatisfaction with existing scholarship, a fifty-plus-year gap since Chafee's claim-based analysis of unclean hands as a substantive defense, and an accumulating legacy of court decisions now invoking the defense to defend the litigation process.

The use of the defense to secure primarily the procedural aims of court protection rather than the substantive aims of party protection bears further consideration. Current court practice challenges the traditional assumptions of Chafee and others who viewed unclean hands solely as a substantive defense.[24] For this reason, there is a need to re-examine the premises of the defense to aid its correct application at law.

This chapter provides a process-based conception of the defense. It integrates the defense across claims by focusing on its court protection purpose as well as unifies the disparate treatment of the defense across jurisdictions by providing a procedural paradigm of incorporation. In short, it presents a legal decision-making framework

---

[21] *See* discussion *infra* Section 6.3.4; *see also* Douglas Laycock, *The Triumph of Equity*, 56 LAW & CONTEMP. PROBS. 53, 81 (1993) [hereinafter Laycock, *Triumph of Equity*] ("[E]quitable innovations have been carried well beyond what either common law or equity was doing before the merger, and no foreseeable retrenchment is likely to change that.").

[22] Am. Ins. Co. v. Lucas, 38 F. Supp. 896, 921 (W.D. Mo. 1940), *aff'd sub nom.* Am. Ins. Co. v. Scheufler, 129 F.2d 143 (8th Cir. 1942); Gaudiosi v. Mellon, 269 F.2d 873, 881–82 (3d Cir. 1959) ("No principle is better settled than the maxim that he who comes into equity must come with clean hands and keep them clean throughout the course of the litigation, and that if he violates this rule, he must be denied all relief whatever may have been the merits of his claim."); Aris-Isotoner Gloves, Inc. v. Berkshire Fashions, Inc., 792 F. Supp. 969, 972 (S.D.N.Y. 1992) (finding unclean hands in case seeking equitable relief based on party perjury and reasoning that "we are not here limited by a purported requirement that forces us to separate wrongdoing that occurs prior to the instigation of legal proceedings from that which occurs during legal proceedings").

[23] Blain v. Doctor's Co., 272 Cal. Rptr. 250, 256 (Cal. Ct. App. 1990).

[24] *See* Laycock, *Triumph of Equity*, *supra* note 21, at 70 (placing the equitable defense of unclean hands in the section entitled "Substance" and not the section entitled "Procedure"); Aleksandr Shapovalov, *Should a Requirement of "Clean Hands" Be a Prerequisite to the Exercise of Diplomatic Protection? Human Rights Implications of the International Law Commission's Debate*, 20 AM. U. INT'L L. REV. 829, 845 (2005) (arguing unclean hands is "substantive" law, not procedure).

for the incorporation of unclean hands into the common law and uses judicial opinions to illustrate its application and interpretation.

The process-based theory detailed in the following sections is designed to assist courts in the incorporation process. It is relevant in all cases considering unclean hands to block legal relief regardless of their view of the merger and its impact on unclean hands.

6.3.2 *Overview*

This section develops methodological guidelines for courts in deciding whether to make the defense of unclean hands available against a particular legal claim or claims. The proposed analytical construct has interpretative and prescriptive aspects. It has an interpretative aspect that attempts to make sense of unclean hands cases. It also has a prescriptive aspect, arguing that the defense ought to serve the central interest of court protection and outlining four criteria to achieve that purpose. The four criteria are: (1) misconduct in the present litigation that potentially interferes with the process, (2) misconduct outside the present litigation that potentially interferes with the process, (3) misconduct in prior litigation with no potential to interfere with the process, and (4) nonlitigation misconduct with no potential to interfere with the process.

The following sections more fully articulate the process-based theory. Section 6.3.3 justifies the form of the test as a metatheory. Section 6.3.4 endorses the primacy of the court protection policy. Sections 6.3.5 and 6.3.6 explain the four degrees of separation from that policy under existing doctrine and its relation to the elements of the defense.

6.3.3 *The Approach: Form and Function*

To develop a test that will reliably determine whether to apply or deny the defense of unclean hands is an admittedly difficult task. The difficulty lies in the recognition that the desirability of the defense depends on context and on the particular claims or issues at stake. Specifically, the applicability of unclean hands depends on the nature of the alleged unclean conduct, its relation to the case, the consistency of the defense with the claim asserted, and other circumstances.[25] The proffered theory of incorporation is a metatheory in the sense that it is meant to resolve first-order conflicts among the considerations bearing on the application of unclean hands.[26]

---

[25] *See* Chafee II, *supra* note 20, at 1091–92 (noting that "[i]t is largely shaped by the human practices and public policies involved in the situation"); *infra* Section 6.3.6.; *supra* Chapter 2 (discussing elements).

[26] *See* Philip Wang, Pragmatism and Consequentialism 4 (May 25, 2007), available at SSRN: https://ssrn.com/abstract=996260 or http://dx.doi.org/10.2139/ssrn.996260 (unpublished manuscript, on file with author) ("A metatheory occurs at a higher level of generality—it describes

Put differently, the proposed construct identifies and prioritizes criteria to help courts reach the best legal outcome.

Any framework for unclean hands must cover numerous contexts, which in turn limits its normative ambitions. One approach could be to develop a highly abstract theory to apply to such a wide range of circumstances. From one perspective, the abstractions of "law" and "equity" can be seen as such broad classifications. Take into account that the debate over the application of unclean hands turns on whether, as an equitable defense, it is restricted in application against an "equitable" remedy or whether it may be used to defeat "legal" remedies as well.

Previous chapters have demonstrated that looking solely at the division of law and equity for the defense of unclean hands not only answers the wrong question (in terms of the meaning of the merger) but also lacks a rational basis, produces anomalous results, and invites other irregularities in the administration of justice.[27] Therefore, even assuming these classifications will live to die another day in this postmerger world, such grand levels of generality without more do not assist the absorption of unclean hands into the common law.[28] Classifications are analytical conveniences meant to aid understanding. If they cease to serve their purpose, they should be abandoned.

There are many reasons to support or oppose the application of unclean hands in a particular case, but none of those issues are resolved by the labels "law" and "equity." In fact, this taxonomy has become a counterproductive distraction to the extent that courts are losing sight of the reasons for the doctrine of "clean hands."[29] Because the availability of the defense depends on context and on the particular issues at stake, focusing on its objectives fosters a more effective use of the defense.[30]

---

the considerations that go into choosing a normative theory and it helps us to select a normative theory that is best according to that metatheory.").

[27] *See* discussion *supra* Chapter 5.

[28] *See* discussion *supra* Chapter 5. The danger of labels in the fusion debate was expressed by Justice Mason (Australia) as follows: "Labels can operate as signposts, but they can also be misleading either because they may conflate separate concepts or (when different labels are seized upon as automatic indicators of distinctive legal concepts) because they may impede parallels or analogies being drawn (that is, principled fusion)." Mason, *Fusion: Fallacy, Future or Finished?*, *supra* note 5, at 70.

[29] *See* Chafee I, *supra* note 20, at 878, 892, 895; *see also* Chafee II, *supra* note 20, at 1095 (suggesting that "a thoughtful consideration of the defense of plaintiff's fault in connection with the policies of various branches of substantive law might lead to several improvements on the present situation").

[30] *See* discussion *supra* Chapter 5 (outlining purposeful theory of equity); *see also* Walter Wheeler Cook, *Equitable Defenses*, 32 YALE L.J. 645, 657 (1923) (concluding that clear legal analysis is "absolutely essential if we are ever to blend common law and equity law into a single, harmonious, and self-consistent system"). Reasoning from purposes, or policy analysis, is a proper topic of judicial inquiry and particularly appropriate to equitable defenses. *See* T. Leigh Anenson, *The Triumph of Equity: Equitable Estoppel in Modern Litigation*, 27 REV. LITIG. 377, 390–91 (2008); *cf.* T. Leigh Anenson, *From Theory to Practice: Analyzing Equitable Estoppel Under a Pluralistic Model of Law*, 11 LEWIS & CLARK L. REV. 633, 660 (2007) [hereinafter

Those goals are emphasized and prioritized in the suggested solution and more fully explained in subsequent sections of this chapter.

Another approach in considering the application of unclean hands at law could be to highlight various factors that matter and embrace them all.[31] This would leave judges to exercise judgment by achieving an ineffable balance among assorted and sometimes antithetical considerations. To be sure, it is a typical task in the nature of common law judging.[32] Nevertheless, classic commentary casts doubt on the defense's conceptual underpinnings even before the border wars between "law" and "equity."[33] Indeed, in assessing the application of unclean hands in twentieth-century equity cases, Chafee complained that unclean hands was a rascally doctrine due to its diversity of application.[34] Accordingly, while perhaps appropriate as an antidote to the dogmatism against the defense at law, different theoretical insights should inform analysis of the doctrine in different contexts.

In particular, as more fully discussed in what follows, first-order concerns should be with court protection. Second-order concerns should be with the relations between the parties where correcting past injustices and future deterrence are at stake. The designated purposive approach best captures the difficulty of evaluating judicial action concerning the incorporation of unclean hands.[35] It is a compromise position in that it does not continue rigid conceptual categories like "law" and "equity." Nor does it offer maximum judicial flexibility and innovation for a defense

Anenson, *Pluralistic Model*] (arguing that policy analysis should be a preferred method of interpretation in analyzing equitable estoppel).

[31] *See* Mason, *Fusion, supra* note 5, at 14 (outlining various considerations in determining whether equity should adopt a particular common law rule or remedy or vice versa); *see also* John C.P. Goldberg, *Twentieth-Century Tort Theory*, 91 Geo. L.J. 513, 578–80 (2003) (calling this model of decision-making "congenial pluralism").

[32] *See, e.g.*, Antonin Scalia, *The Rule of Law as a Law of Rules*, 56 U. Chi. L. Rev. 1175, 1187 (1989) ("We will have totality of the circumstances tests and balancing modes of analysis with us forever—and for my sins, I will probably write some of the opinions that use them."); *see also* H.L.A. Hart, Problems of Philosophy of Law, *in* 6 The Encyclopedia of Philosophy 271 (Paul Edwards ed., 1967) (discussing the multiplicity of diverse considerations that courts are required to balance in the common law method of analysis).

[33] As discussed in previous chapters, the federal system and most state systems gradually integrated law and equity within one court but allowed for their administration by separate procedural rules.

[34] Chafee I, *supra* note 20, at 878; discussion *supra* Chapters 2 and 5.

[35] *See* Sara Sun Beale, *Reconsidering Supervisory Power in Criminal Cases: Constitutional and Statutory Limits on the Authority of the Federal Courts*, 84 Colum. L. Rev. 1433, 1474 (1984) (defining the federal courts' implied judicial power to regulate procedure by using the purpose of the ruling to distinguish substance from procedure and noting that "a ruling should be regarded as procedural and thus within the implied authority of the federal courts only if its purpose is to enhance the fairness, reliability, or efficiency of the litigation process"); William Powers, Jr., *Border Wars*, 72 Tex. L. Rev. 1209, 1223 (1994) ("Standard doctrinal analysis resolves ambiguities and conflicts by referring to the overarching purposes reflected in the doctrine."); Judith Resnik, *Constricting Remedies: The Rehnquist Judiciary, Congress, and Federal Power*, 78 Ind. L.J. 223, 254 (2003) (criticizing making equitable relief available based on its nature rather than its purpose because "nature does not create categories but human judgment does").

already criticized for its weak unifying properties.[36] The proffered process-based position facilitates the correct choice and weight among arguably relevant criteria to assist courts and counsel in incorporating unclean hands in a given case or against a given claim.

A certain amount of vagueness stems from the nature of its object,[37] but the model aspires to coherence at the core of adjudication.[38] Moreover, this more structured type of balancing process is by now familiar to modern American attorneys and judges.[39]

The next section explains why the foundation for the incorporation of unclean hands into the common law should involve an overriding interest in safeguarding the justice system.

6.3.4 *Unclean Hands as Protector of the Process*

The emphasis on the integrity of the court and its procedures explained in this section is both a normative recommendation and a restatement of the law with respect to unclean hands. The process-based theory reinforces the policy of court protection as the preferential doctrinal home for the defense under our jurisprudence.

The defense of unclean hands serves two policies in our law. It applies for the protection of the parties and for the protection of the court.[40] The doctrine protects

---

[36] *See* Chafee I, *supra* note 20, at 878.

[37] *See* discussion *supra* Chapters 2 and 5. Leon Green explains the nature of judicial decision making as follows:

> The ultimate question in any particular case is: how does the court value the respective interests subject to its power? This is beyond the range of arbitrary rules and formulas and colorful phrases, and in the realm of what we like to call "reason and justice." Reason and justice are, of course, not always safe guides for the settlement of disputes, but historically they have been the best we have had.

Leon Green, *Relational Interests*, 29 U. ILL. L. REV. 1041, 1049 (1935); *cf.* Anenson, *Pluralistic Model, supra* note 30, 642–51 (discussing difficulty in application of equitable estoppel for the same reasons).

[38] *See* Jeffrey J. Rachlinski, *Bottom-Up Versus Top-Down Lawmaking*, 73 U. CHI. L. REV. 933, 960–62 (2006) (arguing that the ability to make categories is a benefit of an analogical adjudication process); *cf.* Goldberg, *supra* note 31, at 580 (proposing that one method to help tort law become more coherent and still accept multiple and diverse tort theories is to identify a set of meta-principles).

[39] *See* WILSON HUHN, THE FIVE TYPES OF LEGAL ARGUMENT 137 (2002) (describing combined categorical and balancing approaches in constitutional law); James G. Wilson, *Surveying the Forms of Doctrine on the Bright Line–Balancing Test Continuum*, 27 ARIZ. ST. L.J. 773, 825 (1995) (describing various forms of legal commands such as multifactor tests and totality of the circumstances tests).

[40] *See, e.g.*, Gaudiosi v. Mellon, 269 F.2d 873, 881 (3d Cir. 1959); Kendall-Jackson Winery, Ltd. v. Super. Ct., 90 Cal. Rptr. 2d 743, 749 (Cal. Ct. App. 1999); Manown v. Adams, 598 A.2d 821, 824 (Md. Ct. Spec. App. 1991), *vacated on other grounds*, 615 A.2d 611, 612 (Md. 1992); Maldonado v. Ford Motor Co., 719 N.W.2d 809, 818 (Mich. 2006); *supra* Chapter 2.

the parties by preventing a claimant from benefiting from his or her own misconduct in the action.[41] As such, like other defenses applicable to damages, courts considering unclean hands acknowledge the culpabilities of both parties in resolving cases.[42]

The policy of court protection, however, distinguishes unclean hands from other equitable maxims and defenses.[43] Scholars and courts alike have consistently acknowledged judicial integrity as an important feature of the doctrine.[44]

---

[41] *See* discussion *supra* Chapter 2.

[42] *Id.*

[43] For example, the doctrine of clean hands is distinguishable from the equitable maxim that "one seeking equity must do equity." T. Leigh Anenson, *The Role of Equity in Employment Noncompetition Cases*, 42 AM. BUS. L.J. 1, 47–48 (2005) [hereinafter Anenson, *Role of Equity*]. The latter principle is concerned primarily with the rights and duties of the parties. Hall v. Wright, 125 F. Supp. 269, 273–74 (S.D. Cal. 1954), *aff'd* 240 F.2d 787 (9th Cir. 1957). Unclean hands is concerned primarily with protecting the integrity of the judicial process from improper action by a party. *Id. But see* Hill v. Estate of Allred, 216 P.3d 929, 936 (Utah 2009) (positing that unclean hands is based on the maxim "he who seeks equity must do equity"). The district court in *American Ins. Co. v. Lucas*, explained:

> These arguments are not convincing and the cases cited are not applicable. The underlying defect in the arguments is that counsel confuse two maxims of equity. They seem to be considering the maxim "He who seeks equity must do equity." That maxim is not involved here. These proceedings rest upon the maxim as to "unclean hands." While situations arise where either or both maxims, as well as other maxims, might apply; and therefore some confusion is present in the decisions, nevertheless, these two maxims have cardinal differences . . . The vitality of each, since ancient times, undeniably proves some differences. The difference of importance here is as follows. In applying the maxim requiring equity from one seeking equity the court is concerned primarily with the rights and duties of the parties inter sese. In applying the "clean hands" maxim the court is concerned primarily with protecting its own integrity from improper action by a party.

38 F. Supp. 926, 934 (W.D. Mo.1940) (internal citations omitted). *Compare* Chafee II, *supra* note 20, at 1095 (calling the two maxims "fairly close" although noting that "the clean hands maxim relates to the past and the doing equity maxim relates to the future"). Nevertheless, as discussed *supra* Chapter 5, unclean hands shares the court protection purpose of the narrower defenses of *in pari delicto*, fraud on the court, and estoppel.

[44] *See* U.S. v. Any and All Assets of That Certain Business Known As Shane Co., 816 F. Supp. 389, 400 (M.D.N.C. 1991) ("The court applies the clean hands doctrine, 'not for the protection of the parties, but for its own protection.'" (quoting Mas v. Coca-Cola Co., 163 F.2d 505, 507 (4th Cir. 1947))); *In re* Hathaway, 364 B.R. 220, 244 (Bankr. E.D. Va. 2007) ("The clean hands doctrine was designed to safeguard the judicial process, not to protect the parties.") (citation omitted); Gratreak v. N. Pacific Lumber Co., 609 P.2d 375, 378 (Or. Ct. App. 1980) ("The doctrine of clean hands is applied for the protection of the integrity of the court and not for the benefit of the parties."). Herstein hedges on the court protection point of the unclean hands defense. Ori J. Herstein, *A Normative Theory of the Clean Hands Defense*, 17 LEGAL THEORY 171, 208 (2011) (recognizing that the moral norms of *tu quoque* and retribution may be relatively low and that the main force behind the justification of the clean hands doctrine may derive from the doctrine's role in furthering other values such as deterrence, judicial efficiency, or court legitimacy).

This virtue has been extolled in treatises and early equity opinions by the United States Supreme Court.[45]

The primacy of the court protection policy of unclean hands was underscored by Justice Brandeis in *Olmstead v. United States*[46]: "Then aid is denied despite the defendant's wrong. It is denied in order to maintain respect for law; in order to promote confidence in the administration of justice; in order to preserve the judicial process from contamination."[47] A principal interest in court protection is also corroborated by the many courts that have relied on that purpose to consider unclean hands in fusion cases of first impression.[48] These courts determined that policy rather than pedigree should prevail and applied the doctrine to legal claims pursuant to prevailing interests in deterring fraud and safeguarding the administration of justice.[49] In particular, a number of courts were persuaded to extend unclean hands to legal remedies by the United States Supreme Court decision in *Precision Instrument Mfg. Co. v. Auto. Maint. Mach. Co.*[50] In *Precision Instrument*, the Supreme Court held that where an applicant for a patent suppressed facts that

---

[45] *See, e.g.,* Precision Instrument Mfg. Co. v. Auto. Maint. Mach. Co., 324 U.S. 806, 814 (1945); 2 JOHN NORTON POMEROY, A TREATISE ON EQUITY JURISPRUDENCE AS ADMINISTERED IN THE UNITED STATES OF AMERICA § 397 (Spencer W. Symons ed., Bancroft-Whitney 5th ed. 1941).

[46] 277 U.S. 438 (1928). In *Olmstead*, the majority of the Court found no constitutional violation and refused to suppress evidence gathered by telephone taps that were illegal under state law. *See generally id. Olmstead* was overruled in *Katz v. United States*, 389 U.S. 347 (1967), which held wiretapping subject to the constraints of the Fourth Amendment of the U.S. Constitution. *Id.* at 353. Brandeis's dissents in *Olmstead* and other cases were later adopted by the majority of the United States Supreme Court under the so-called supervisory power doctrine. *See* Beale, *supra* note 35, at 1443–45 (citing, *e.g.,* McNabb v. United States, 318 U.S. 332 (1943)). Under this doctrine, the Court accepted Brandeis's view that litigation misconduct principally harms judicial integrity. *Id.* at 1452; *see also id.* at 1442–43 & n.56 (noting the court's change of position was influenced by a report publishing objectionable federal and state investigative practices written by consultants that included Zechariah Chafee).

[47] *Olmstead*, 277 U.S. at 484 (Brandeis, J., dissenting) (explaining the policies underlying unclean hands that are promoted in cases seeking legal *and* equitable relief); *see also* Beale, *supra* note 35, at 1443 ("Justice Brandeis' primary concern was not the parties' rights, but rather the protection of the government, particularly 'the purity of its courts.'" (quoting Casey v. United States, 276 U.S. 413, 425 (1928) (Brandeis, J., dissenting))).

[48] *See, e.g.,* Manown v. Adams, 598 A.2d 821, 826 (Md. Ct. Spec. App. 1991), *vacated on other grounds*, 615 A.2d 611, 612 (Md. 1992) (ruling that the judge must determine the application of unclean hands because the doctrine's "purpose is to protect institutional interests"); Maldonado v. Ford Motor Co., 719 N.W.2d 809, 818 (Mich. 2006) ("The 'clean hands doctrine' applies not only for the protection of the parties but also for the protection of the court.") (citation omitted).

[49] *See* discussion *supra* Chapter 2 (discussing equity jurisdiction based upon fraud); *see also* Mason, *Fusion: Fallacy, Future or Finished?*, *supra* note 5, at 41 ("Investigation of pedigree is being eclipsed by the greater need to have regard to the function served by a particular right or remedy and to the overlap of the parallel or discordant strands suggested by historical enquiries about 'legal' and 'equitable' rules.").

[50] 324 U.S. 806 (1945). As discussed in Chapter 2, *Precision Instrument* is the leading case in the country on the clean hands doctrine. *Supra* Section 2.5; *see also supra* Chapter 2 note 100 and *infra* note 55 (listing cases relying on this decision to apply the defense to bar damages).

should have been brought to the attention of the Patent Office, the party did not "display[] that standard of conduct requisite to the maintenance of [an equitable action]."[51]

The precedential legacy of the federal district court decision in *Buchanan Home & Auto Supply Co., Inc. v. Firestone Tire & Rubber Co.*[52] has also extended unclean hands at law in other state and federal courts.[53] The District Court of South Carolina in this seminal case emphasized the main reason for the defense is to protect the integrity of the court and its ability to ascertain the truth.[54] In cases of first impression, Michigan courts applied unclean hands at law, relying on the court protection grounds and following *Precision Instrument* and *Buchanan.*[55] The Supreme Court of Michigan found its procedural prerogatives so important, in fact, that it seemed to create an exception of constitutional stature to the reading of the merger rule limiting unclean hands to equitable remedies.[56]

---

[51]   *Id.* at 819. As explained in Chapter 3, other courts have also relied on the application of unclean hands in equity actions to incorporate the defense into the common law.

[52]   544 F. Supp. 242 (D.S.C. 1981).

[53]   *See* Cummings v. Wayne County, 533 N.W.2d 13, 14 (Mich. Ct. App. 1995) (citing *Buchanan*, 544 F. Supp. at 244); Bartlett v. Dunne, No. C.A. 89–3051, 1989 WL 1110258, at *3 (R.I. Super. Ct. Nov. 10, 1989) (citing *Buchanan*, 544 F. Supp. at 244).

[54]   *Buchanan*, 544 F. Supp. at 244. The court additionally declared:

> No court of equity [or court of law in this instance] ought to listen to a man whose very presence suggests danger to the administration of justice and whose past conduct affecting the matter in litigation would cast doubt upon the ability of the court to ascertain from him the truth with respect thereto.

Id. at 247 (quoting Mas v. Coca-Cola Co., 163 F.2d 505, 511 (4th Cir. 1947)).

[55]   Maldonado v. Ford Motor Co., 719 N.W.2d 809, 818 (Mich. 2006) (citing Cummings v. Wayne County, 533 N.W.2d 13, 14 (1995) (citing *Buchanan*, 544 F. Supp. at 244–45)). The Michigan appellate court in *Cummings v. Wayne Cty.*, 533 N.W.2d 13 (Mich. Ct. App. 1995), cited to *Precision Instrument* to extend unclean hands to legal claims. *Id.* at 14. Other courts confirm the court protection sentiment in extending unclean hands to damages actions. *See, e.g.*, First Fairfield Funding, LLC v. Goldman, No. CV020465799S, 2003 WL 22708882 at *2 (Conn. Super. Ct. Nov. 3, 2003) ("The integrity of the court is no less worthy of protection in actions at law, than in actions in equity.").

[56]   *See* discussion *supra* Chapter 3. Remember that the Supreme Court of Michigan justified its power to dismiss the case pursuant to unclean hands as follows: "The authority is rooted in a court's fundamental interest in protecting its own integrity and that of the judicial process." *Maldonado*, 719 N.W.2d at 818 (internal citations omitted). Michigan otherwise follows the traditional view that the merger of law and equity precludes unclean hands in cases seeking legal remedies. *See* Clarke v. Brunswick Corp., 211 N.W.2d 101, 102–03 (Mich. Ct. App. 1973) (holding that the defense of unclean hands did not apply because the substantive differences remain after the merger of law and equity).

The source of power for unclean hands in most opinions has not been explored, but most state courts appear to base their dismissals under their common law or equity powers, which perhaps allows them to shape legal standards more cautiously than under the state constitution. *See, e.g.*, Judith S. Kaye, *State Courts at the Dawn of the New Century: Common Law Courts Reading Statutes and Constitutions*, 70 N.Y.U. L. REV. 1, 17 (1995); Hans A. Linde, *Are State Constitutions Common Law?*, 34 ARIZ. L. REV. 215, 227 (1992) (discussing how the common law basis for judicial decisions leaves "lawmakers every opportunity to clarify, to amend, or to reject

State courts may have an advantage over federal courts in the scope of their powers *vis-à-vis* the legislative branch.[57] Nevertheless, there is also scholarly and doctrinal support for the notion that federal courts have inherent authority to regulate procedure by adjudication that is ancillary to the judicial function.[58] Sara Sun Beale's analysis of the supervisory power decisions of the federal courts[59] and

the court's understanding of the state's policy before freezing it into constitutional law"). Nevertheless, Judge Judith Kaye reminds us that "state courts move seamlessly between the common law and state constitutional law, the shifting ground at times barely perceptible." Kaye, *supra*, at 15; *see also* Robert F. Williams, *In the Supreme Court's Shadow: Legitimacy of State Rejection of Supreme Court Reasoning and Result*, 35 S.C. L. REV. 353, 382 (1984) ("One could argue that because state constitutions are relatively easy to amend, thereby correcting 'mistakes,' state courts should be willing to render more expansive or controversial state constitutional interpretations.").

[57] *See* Helen Hershkoff, *State Courts and the "Passive Virtues": Rethinking the Judicial Function*, 114 HARV. L. REV. 1833, 1888 (2001) ("State power, by contrast [to federal power], is plenary and inherent, and the theory of state judicial power is correspondingly expansive."). State courts may be able legitimately and overtly to make state policy and even procedural rules in the course of adjudication, despite complaints of "judicial activism," but the federal courts' common law and constitutional powers are more circumscribed. *See* Kaye, *supra* note 56, at 20; *see also* Hershkoff, *supra*, at 1842 (calling for empirical research on the relation between existing state institutional structures and the scope of the judicial function). For state cases formulating procedural decisions as a matter of inherent power, see Amy Coney Barrett, *Procedural Common Law*, 94 VA. L. REV. 813, 873–74 (2008) [hereinafter, Barrett, *Procedural Common Law*] (citing cases from Pennsylvania, New York, Kentucky, and the colonies). *See also* A. Leo Levin & Anthony G. Amsterdam, *Legislative Control over Judicial Rulemaking: A Problem in Constitutional Revision*, 107 U. PA. L. REV. 1, 30 (1958) (discussing and providing an example of state courts invalidating legislative attempts to regulate judicial procedure); Mark H. Zitzewitz, Comment, State v. Krotzer: *Inherent Judicial Authority—Going Where No Court Has Gone Before*, 81 MINN. L. REV. 1049, 1060 (1997) (explaining that state "courts also have 'inherent powers' that arise from the judiciary's historic powers of equity and its oversight role in the courtroom").

[58] For inherent authority to dismiss for unclean hands, see Am. Ins. Co. v. Lucas, 38 F. Supp. 896, 921–22 (W.D. Mo. 1940) (declaring the court's authority to dismiss case seeking injunction pursuant to unclean hands rested with its inherent procedural power), *aff'd sub nom.* Am. Ins. Co. v. Scheufler, 129 F.2d 143 (8th Cir. 1942). For cases asserting inherent power over procedure or the progress of the lawsuit generally, see Barrett, *Procedural Common Law*, *supra* note 57, at 844 nn. 90–91 (cataloguing U.S. Supreme Court cases). Along with Professors Beale and Barrett, other scholars also support a constitutional source of authority in federal courts to adjudicate procedure. *See* David E. Engdahl, *Intrinsic Limits of Congress' Power Regarding the Judicial Branch*, 1999 BYU L. REV. 75, 83–86; Thomas W. Merrill, *The Common Law Powers of Federal Courts*, 52 U. CHI. L. REV. 1, 24 (1985). Debate continues, however, as to the scope of that authority. *See* Barrett, *Procedural Common Law*, *supra* note 57, at 833 (surveying literature).

[59] Professor Beale's justification for the source of authority of the federal courts' supervisory power cases depends on the reason for the ruling and uses a similar definition of procedure to the one proposed herein, which is guided by the purpose of the ruling. *See* Beale, *supra* note 35, at 1474–75, 1513. She argues that procedure should include only matters relating to the efficiency and reliability of the litigation that are intrinsic to the judicial process in which the courts have special competence. *Id.*; *accord* Barrett, *Procedural Common Law*, *supra* note 57, at 823 (explaining that procedural decisions are "primarily concerned with the regulation of court processes and in-courtroom conduct"). In her view, rulings meant to promote policies extrinsic to the judicial

Amy Coney Barrett's account of procedural common law[60] may also support a constitutional source of authority for the defense when federal courts exercise their protective function.[61]

Court sensitivity to its own administration can be seen as well in the willingness to invoke the defense *sua sponte*.[62] Safeguarding courts' integrity may also be the reason why so many federal courts sitting in diversity instinctively apply federal law without an *Erie* analysis to determine the applicability of unclean hands in cases seeking legal relief.[63]

process, like the conditions under which a legal right exists, would be considered substantive and not justified under Article III. Beale, *supra* note 35, at 1490–91; *see also id.* at 1513.

[60] Barrett, *Procedural Common Law, supra* note 57, at 879–88. Professor Barrett explains her theory as follows: "Federal procedural common law is supported by the twin justifications that federal courts can develop uniform common law rules in enclaves of constitutional preemption and that Article III impliedly grants each federal court power to regulate its procedure in the course of adjudicating cases." *Id.* at 888. She identifies dual strands of federal procedural common law with different sources of power and constraints. *See id.* at 879–88. "Uniform doctrines" produce binding precedent under a court's common law power and are subject to Congressional abrogation. *See id.* (citing preclusion and abstention as examples). "Discretionary doctrines" are limited to the locality of the court, arise under its constitutional power, and are not subject to legislative abrogation. *See id.* (citing a decision dealing with service of process and time limitation issues as examples). Some doctrines seem to spring from both strands of authority. *See id.* (citing remittitur, stare decisis, and forum non conveniens as examples).

[61] Sorting out substance from procedure is imperative in striking an appropriate balance between the powers of the federal and state governments and between the branches. *See* Stephen B. Burbank, *The Bitter with the Sweet: Tradition, History, and Limitations on Federal Judicial Power – A Case Study*, 75 NOTRE DAME L. REV. 1291, 1292–93 (2000) (advising that neglecting procedure is a mistake because "procedure is power" that can "implicate dilemmas, in particular separation of powers and federalism, that loom large in constitutional law, and because consideration of judicial responses to those dilemmas may cast light on the broader landscape"). In contrast to federal substantive common law, Congress's ability to abrogate procedural common law can be called into question. Barrett, *Procedural Common Law, supra* note 57, at 816 ("[T]here is likely some small core of inherent procedural authority that Congress cannot reach."); *see also id.* at 817, 882–83 (noting such inherent procedural power would be limited to the federal court location).

[62] *See* Gaudiosi v. Mellon, 269 F.2d 873, 881 (3d Cir. 1959); Am. Ins. Co. v. Lucas, 38 F. Supp. 896, 921 (W.D. Mo. 1940) ("A court of equity is so jealous in guarding itself against such misuse that it will, sua sponte, apply the maxim whenever it discovers the unconscionable conduct."), *aff'd sub nom.* Am. Ins. Co. v. Scheufler, 129 F.2d 143 (8th Cir. 1942); Katz v. Karlsson, 191 P.2d 541, 545 (Cal. Ct. App. 1948); Stachnik v. Winkel, 230 N.W.2d 529, 532 (Mich. 1975); In re Estate of Richardson, 903 So.2d 51, 55 (Miss. 2005); Skirvin v. Sigler, 83 P.2d 530, 532 (Okla. 1938); Gratreak v. N. Pacific Lumber Co., 609 P.2d 375, 378 (Or. App. Ct. 1980); *see also* Welch v. DiBlasi, 289 A.D.2d 964, 964–65 (N.Y. App. Div. 2001) (finding no waiver of unclean hands for failure to plead it (citing Richards v. Levy, 40 A.D.2d 1055, 1056 (N.Y. App. Div. 1972) (reasoning that because unclean hands protects the public interest, it "need not be pleaded at all as the court may raise it sua sponte")); *cf.* Anenson, *Pluralistic Model, supra* note 30, at 666–67 (explaining that courts have raised the equitable defense of estoppel of their own accord and have considered it for the first time on appeal to protect the integrity of the judicial process).

[63] *See, e.g.*, Smith v. Cessna Aircraft Co., 124 F.R.D. 103, 105–07 (D. Md. 1989); discussion *supra* Chapter 3 (analyzing certain cases).

The application of unclean hands pursuant to the court protection purpose defends the judicial process in two ways. First, it protects judicial integrity, "because allowing a plaintiff with unclean hands to recover in an action creates doubts as to the justice provided by the judicial system."[64] The Supreme Court of the United States has described wrongdoing that has a similar negative effect on the judicial process as "a 'flagrant affront' to the truth-seeking function of adversary proceedings"[65] by placing the court in the position of being "the abetter of iniquity."[66] Second, the doctrine of unclean hands is applied to defend against misconduct that actually interferes with the court process in the present case.[67] This kind of unclean conduct has a more tangible relation to court procedure and is exemplified in myriad forms of litigation misconduct. Used in this way, the defense serves a real as opposed to a representative role in protecting the judicial function. Notably, both its concrete and symbolic aspects preserve the forgotten function of ancient equity in maintaining the sanctity of law and its processes.[68]

The former split systems of law and equity were not seen as conflicting, but as complementary, in the sense that equity cured defects in the law or prevented its abuse.[69] The inherently variable value of "justice" was obviously a beacon of equity,

---

[64] Kendall-Jackson Winery, Ltd. v. Super. Ct., 90 Cal. Rptr. 2d 743, 749 (Cal. Ct. App. 1999); *see also* Mas v. Coca-Cola Co., 163 F.2d 505, 511 (4th Cir. 1947). The unwillingness to endorse injustice was aptly expressed by the court in *Gaudiosi*, which noted:

> [C]ourts are concerned primarily with their own integrity in the application of the clean hands maxim. Courts in such situations act for their own protection and not as a matter of "defense" to the defendant. Public policy not only makes it obligatory for courts to deny a plaintiff relief once his "unclean hands" are established but to refuse to even hear a case under such circumstances.

Gaudiosi, 269 F.2d at 882.

[65] ABF Freight Sys., Inc. v. NLRB, 510 U.S. 317, 323 (1994) (considering the doctrine of fraud on the court and stating: "False testimony in a formal proceeding is intolerable. We must neither reward nor condone such a 'flagrant affront' to the truth-seeking function of adversary proceedings."); *cf.* John C.P. Goldberg, *Rethinking Injury and Proximate Cause*, 40 SAN DIEGO L. REV. 1315, 1335–43 (2003) (advocating that proximate cause should turn on whether the defended was "affront[ed]" or "wronged").

[66] Precision Instrument Mfg. Co. v. Auto. Maint. Mach. Co., 324 U.S. 806, 814 (1945) (quoting Bein v. Heath, 47 U.S. 228 (1848)); discussion *supra* Chapter 2, Section 2.5.

[67] *See Smith*, 124 F.R.D. at 105–07; Buchanan Home & Auto Supply Co., Inc. v. Firestone Tire & Rubber Co., 544 F. Supp. 242, 244–45 (D.S.C. 1981); Maldonado v. Ford Motor Co., 719 N.W.2d 809, 818 (Mich. 2006); Cummings v. Wayne Cty., 533 N.W.2d 13, 14 (Mich. Ct. App. 1995).

[68] Anenson, *Role of Equity*, *supra* note 43, at 63; *see* Mason, *Fusion: Fallacy, Future or Finished?*, *supra* note 5, at 53, 75 (noting the judicial power to prevent abuse of process); Wesley Newcomb Hohfeld, *The Relations between Equity and Law*, 11 MICH. L. REV. 537, 556, 560–61 (1913) (citing examples); *supra* Chapter 2, Section 2.3.

[69] *Compare* FREDERICK W. MAITLAND, A COURSE OF LECTURES (J. Brunyate ed., Cambridge Univ. Press 1947) (emphasizing general absence of conflict between law and equity), *with* Hohfeld, *supra* note 68, at 543–45 (answering Maitland by pointing out the recurring conflict between equitable and legal rules and equity's supremacy). *See* Philip A. Ryan, *Equity: System or Process?*, 45 GEO. L.J. 213, 215–16 (1957) (explaining "the classical jurisprudence debate

in comparison to the strict common law.[70] Courts advocate "justice" in applying unclean hands, although it is not a matter on which they typically reflect in any depth.[71]

Because the overall purpose of the law is now said to be justice, it is instructive to look at the meaning of unclean hands from a principles-of-justice perspective.[72] In that vein, the defense can be considered to have a substantive justice component (party protection) and a procedural justice component (court protection).[73] Substantive justice for the sake of unclean hands includes individualistic notions of corrective justice that aim to restore equilibrium between the parties as a matter of moral responsibility.[74] In addition to correcting past wrongs, the deterrence of future behavior is a related substantive, albeit instrumental, aim of unclean hands.[75]

Procedural justice under the auspices of unclean hands advances the social interest in judicial integrity.[76] There are related instrumental concerns for the deterrence of future deviance during the litigation process or, correspondingly, the

between Langdell-Ame-Maitland and Spence-Pomeroy-Hohfeld on whether equity did or did not conflict with the common law").

[70] *See* Darien Shanske, Note, *Four Theses: Preliminary to an Appeal to Equity,* 57 STAN. L. REV. 2053, 2054 (2005) ("Aristotle's account of equity has been received into the legal tradition many times and this reception is ongoing today.").

[71] *See, e.g.,* Am. Ins. Co. v. Lucas, 38 F. Supp. 896, 921 (W.D. Mo. 1940) (noting that lack of precedent does not restrict a court of equity from dismissing cases for unclean hands as a matter of "justice" or "natural justice"), *aff'd sub nom.,* Am. Ins. Co. v. Scheufler, 129 F.2d 143 (8th Cir. 1942); Kendall-Jackson Winery, Ltd. v. Superior Court, 90 Cal. Rptr. 2d 743, 749 (Cal. Ct. App. 1999) (declaring that unclean hands promotes justice).

[72] *See* Roscoe Pound, *The Theory of Judicial Decision,* 36 HARV. L. REV. 641, 654 (1923) (discussing the impact of our ideas about the end of law such as philosophical, political, ethical as "phenomena of the highest significance for the understanding of the actual functioning of judicial justice"). *See generally* Richard W. Wright, *The Principles of Justice,* 75 NOTRE DAME L. REV. 1859 (2000) (using natural law theory to understand and evaluate the positive law's goal of justice).

[73] *See* Wright, *supra* note 72, at 1859–60 (describing procedural justice as "formal").

[74] *See, e.g.,* W. Jonathan Cardi, *Reconstructing Foreseeability,* 46 B.C. L. REV. 921, 941 (2005) (discussing the concept of corrective justice and its use in tort theory to justify the correction of past wrongs as a matter of moral responsibility); Goldberg, *supra* note 31, at 570 (explaining the goal of corrective justice in tort law theory is to restore equilibrium between the victim and the one who caused harm).

[75] *Cf.* Goldberg, *supra* note 31, at 565–67 (detailing other tort theories besides individual justice to include social justice, compensation-deterrence, enterprise liability, and economic deterrence); Michael L. Wells, *Proximate Cause and the American Law Institute: The False Choice Between the "Direct-Consequences" Test and the "Risk Standard,"* 37 U. RICH. L. REV. 389, 406 (2003) (calling deterrence of future behavior in tort law utilitarian). Courts seldom distinguish between the utilitarian and moral duty aspects of corrective individual justice theory in addressing unclean hands. *But see* Buchanan Home & Auto Supply Co., Inc. v. Firestone Tire & Rubber Co., 544 F. Supp. 242, 246 (D.S.C. 1981) (noting the plaintiff's contractual and moral duty to maintain accurate records).

[76] *See* Wright, *supra* note 72, at 1859–60 (describing procedural justice as equality, such as like cases being treated alike); Barrett, *Procedural Common Law, supra* note 57, at 827–29 (placing precedent within procedural common law).

encouragement of candor and correct behavior by litigants and ethical conduct by their attorneys.[77] A more targeted societal goal is court control over its own proceedings.[78]

The policies of procedural and substantive justice (court and party protection) are not entirely separable in the situation of unclean hands. A wrong perpetrated on the system, like perjury[79] or corrupting the jury,[80] if unchecked, may have grave consequences to the opposing litigant.[81] Nevertheless, the view is that interference with the ability of the judicial system to adjudicate a matter constitutes a more direct harm to the court as opposed to the parties.[82] As one court explained in applying unclean hands: "It is a power inherent in every court of justice so long as it retains

[77] *See* Maldonado v. Ford Motor Co., 719 N.W.2d 809, 819 (Mich. 2006) (commenting on the trial court's "gate-keeping obligation" to sanction misconduct to deter others in the future). There is ample authority for the regulation of procedure in cases holding that federal courts have implied authority to prevent misuse of their own processes, such as whether to punish contempt of court or to allow jurors to impeach their own verdict. *See, e.g.*, Anderson v. Dunn, 19 U.S. (6 Wheat.) 204, 227–28 (1821); McDonald v. Pless, 238 U.S. 264, 266 (1915) (recognizing inherent judicial power of courts "to enforce their own self-preserving rules").

[78] *But see* Barrett, *Procedural Common Law, supra* note 57, at 845–46 (placing the court's authority to vacate judgments for fraud outside the context of procedure and akin to the power to punish and control those who serve the court). For articles mapping the inherent power of the judiciary, including those that concern core adjudicative activities, see Daniel J. Meador, *Inherent Judicial Authority in Civil Litigation*, 73 Tex. L. Rev. 1805, 1819 (1995); Robert J. Pushaw, Jr., *The Inherent Powers of Federal Courts and the Structural Constitution*, 86 Iowa L. Rev. 735 (2001).

[79] *See* case discussion *infra* at Section 6.3.5.1.

[80] *Id.*

[81] Depending on the kind and degree of interference, government inaction in failing to dismiss could infringe the opposing litigant's constitutional rights to due process of law. *See Maldonado*, 719 N.W.2d at 824 (discussing trial court duty to dismiss the case and noting that "few, if any, interests are more fundamental than the right to a fair trial by an impartial jury" (citing Gentile v. State Bar of Nevada, 501 U.S. 1030, 1075 (1991))); *see also* Mona v. Mona Elec. Group, Inc., 934 A.2d 450, 472–74 (Md. Ct. Spec. App. 2007) (holding there was no abuse of discretion for the trial court to reduce a jury award for unclean hands in equity case for potential perjury based on finding that the judge has some responsibility to ensure the integrity of the judicial process). Similarly, the judicial response to unclean hands will benefit the wrongdoer's opponent and provide a costly lesson of how not to behave as a litigant and/or counsel.

[82] *See* Jonathan M. Stern, *Untangling a Tangled Web Without Trial: Using the Court's Inherent Powers and Rules to Deny a Perjuring Litigant His Day in Court*, 66 J. Air L. & Com. 1251, 1254 (2001) (viewing conduct interfering with the litigation process as a wrong perpetrated on the system rather than an individual litigant (citing Hazel-Atlas Glass Co. v. Hartford-Empire Co., 322 U.S. 238, 246 (1944) (describing fraud on the court as "a wrong against the institutions set up to protect and safeguard the public") and other cases)); Rockdale Management Co. v. Shawmut Bank, N.A., 638 N.E.2d 29 (Mass. 1994) (manufacturing evidence and perjury constitutes fraud on the court by improperly influencing the trier or unfairly hampering the presentation of the opposing party's claim or defense); Stern, *supra*, at 1254 n.10 (explaining that fraud on the court, "[u]nlike the defense of spoliation of evidence, . . . is not recognized as an independent cause of action because it is a wrong against the judicial system" and citing cases for support). *See generally* Fed. R. Civ. P. 60(b) (providing grounds for relief from judgment).

control of the subject-matter and of the parties, to correct that which has been wrongfully done by virtue of its process."[83] Injury to the process in this manner provides the court the right and sometimes the duty to dismiss for unclean hands.[84]

In an advocacy system in which incentives to game the system are an acknowledged and acceptable risk, the supposed guardian against such shenanigans is the judge.[85] Empowering the judge through the invocation of unclean hands is an essential institutional check. In the absence of such protection, it is no overstatement that the danger to the individual litigant could be one of constitutional dimension. And, perhaps most important, the allowance or endorsement of such litigation or other misconduct could cost the court credibility with the interest group to which it is accountable – the public.[86] Accordingly, the ability

[83] Am. Ins. Co. v. Lucas, 38 F. Supp. 896, 921 (W.D. Mo. 1940) (quoting United States v. Morgan, 307 U.S. 183, 197 (1939) (internal quotations and citation omitted)) (dismissing case pursuant to unclean hands), aff'd sub nom., Am. Ins. Co. v. Scheufler, 129 F.2d 143, 148 (8th Cir. 1942) (a party "must keep his hands clean throughout the litigation" or his action will be subject to dismissal).

[84] A court's right to dismiss for unclean hands becomes a duty if the parties' constitutional rights to due process or otherwise would be infringed should the court do nothing. See Beale, supra note 35, at 1469 n.235 (noting that "[i]n most if not all such cases" where a procedural rule would "deprive one of the litigants of due process of law," the judicial power to promulgate procedural rules would be indispensable to the judicial function and would override a Congressionally prescribed rule (citing Chambers v. Mississippi, 410 U.S. 284 (1973) (rule prohibiting party's impeachment of his own witness violates due process))); id. at 1494–1501 (discussing valid remedial authority of courts in the event of a constitutional rights violation). In addition to considering the defendant's right to due process if it fails to dismiss for unclean hands, a court must also consider the plaintiff's right to due process if it does dismiss without an adequate connection to the case. See Beale, supra note 35, at 1453 (discussing that the U.S. Supreme Court declined to use its supervisory power "as a punitive measure against unrelated wrongdoing . . . or as an indirect mode of disciplining misconduct" (citing U.S. v. Mitchell, 322 U.S. 65, 70 (1944))); Stern, supra note 82, at 1290 (discussing outer limits of authority to dismiss if wrongdoing does not relate to the matter in controversy and citing, for example, Wyle v. R.J. Reynolds Indus., Inc., 709 F.2d 585, 589, 591 (9th Cir. 1983) (citing Ins. Corp. of Ireland, Ltd. v. Compagnie des Bauxites de Guinee, 456 U.S. 694 (1982))).

[85] Cf. T. Leigh Anenson, Creating Conflicts of Interest: Litigation as Interference with the Attorney–Client Relationship, 43 Am. Bus. L.J. 173, 205 (2006) [hereinafter Anenson, Interference with the Attorney–Client Relationship] (discussing new litigation tactic of filing lawsuits against opposing counsel to interfere with the attorney–client relationship of the opposing party and the case); T. Leigh Anenson, Absolute Immunity from Civil Liability: Lessons for Litigation Lawyers, 31 Pepp. L. Rev. 915 (2004) [hereinafter Anenson, Lessons for Litigation Lawyers] (discussing absolute immunity from civil liability of litigators who engage in bad behavior or other nefarious tactics against an opposing party related to the lawsuit in order to further the advocacy system interest in zealous representation).

[86] The premise of the court protection policy is that the effective functioning of the judicial system requires public respect for and acceptance of court rulings that would be undermined directly if courts could not ascertain the truth of the matter before them or indirectly by ratifying illegal or unethical behavior. Cf. Amy Coney Barrett, Stare Decisis and Due Process, 74 U. Colo. L. Rev. 1011, 1021 (2003) (explaining Llewellyn's view that "the public nature of decision-making works strongly against any impulse to engage in unreasoned or willful decisionmaking" (citing Karl N. Llewellyn, The Common Law Tradition: Deciding Appeals 19–61 (1960))). Judicial legitimacy is a particularly sensitive subject at the federal

of the court to invoke unclean hands as a matter of procedural justice is not only acceptable but essential.

In light of the foregoing, safeguarding the administration of justice is an important feature of unclean hands that has been and should continue to be a fundamental value in its application.

6.3.5 *Four Phases of Unclean Hands*

Previous chapters discussed a series of cases in which courts moved from formalistic law and equity distinctions to a more functional approach to determine the application of unclean hands at law.[87] The preceding sections provided background support for the insight that the incorporation issue is now ripe for a realistic analysis revolving around the court protection principle.[88] This section aims to evaluate the absorption of unclean hands pursuant to a process-based theory in an effort to develop a better understanding of the theory and the defense it purports to define.

The proposed procedural approach establishes when the considerations brought to bear in one context ought to apply and trump those of another. When litigants use underhanded means to advance their legal claim, like providing false testimony or destroying evidence, the causal connection between such unclean conduct and its interference with the judicial function plays prominently into the availability of unclean hands at law.[89]

The legal community has long debated the metaphysics of causation in just about every area of the law.[90] A recurring and difficult question is who should shoulder responsibility from an empirical and normative standpoint.[91] The normative questions, in particular, are necessarily contestable and therefore laden with interesting issues. This chapter cannot resolve those debates. Nevertheless, it does suggest that spatio-temporal proximity of the alleged unclean conduct to

---

level. *See* Craig Green, *Repressing Erie's Myth*, 96 Cal. L. Rev. 595, 598 (2008) (noting that "American legal culture has long worried over undue judicial power").

[87] *See* discussion *supra* Chapters 3–5.

[88] *See* discussion *supra* Sections 6.3.3 and 6.3.4.

[89] *See* Wilson R. Huhn, *The Stages of Legal Reasoning: Formalism, Analogy and Realism*, 48 Vill. L. Rev. 305, 317–18 (2003) (describing the policy argument as a five-step process that includes estimating "the likelihood that the rule will accomplish its goal and serve this interest or principle"); Huhn, *supra* note 39, at 138 (noting that this step is "essentially a causation requirement") (emphasis omitted).

[90] *See, e.g.*, H.L.A. Hart & Tony Honoré, Causation in the Law (2nd ed. 1985).

[91] *See* Heidi M. Hurd & Michael S. Moore, *Negligence in the Air*, 3 Theoretical Inquiries in Law 333, 336 (2002) (explaining tests for proximate causation as "elusive, multiple, and often conflicting in their implications for cases"); Richard W. Wright, *Once More into the Bramble Bush: Duty, Causal Contribution, and the Extent of Legal Responsibility*, 54 Vand. L. Rev. 1071, 1072 (2001) (describing legal cause as "opaque and confused" both in America and abroad). *See generally* Wright, *supra* (examining the empirical issue of causal contribution as distinguished from the normative issue of the extent of legal responsibility).

interference with the case is a rough but good proxy for this progressive diminishment in causal contribution.[92]

The circumstances are divided into four phases. The first phase begins with litigation misconduct in the existing case, and the last phase ends with nonlitigation misconduct that does not disrupt the litigation. Conduct fitting within the first three phases should be a better basis for the application of unclean hands than actions in the fourth and final phase. The last criterion, in particular, has the most tangential connection to safeguarding the administration of justice. Hence, this framework would direct courts to be most sensitive to other factors, like whether the application of the defense defeats the purposes of the asserted claim.

6.3.5.1 Phase One: Misconduct in the Present Litigation that Potentially Interferes with the Process

Litigation misconduct in an existing case like the Michigan cases of *Maldonado v. Ford Motor Co.*[93] and *Cummings v. Wayne Cty.*[94] provides the closest nexus to satisfying the goal of court protection. *Cummings* involved witness tampering.[95] The intermediate appellate court explained that the death threats by the plaintiff "permanently deprived the court of the opportunity to hear the testimony of witnesses who would be able to testify openly and without fear."[96]

---

[92] Commentators have described it as follows:

> On a plausible theory of causation, causal relations peter out gradually by transmission through events. This is because causation is a scalar relation (more-or-less affair) and because the degree of causal contribution by some act to some harm becomes less and less as successively larger groups of other events join the act in causing the harm.

Hurd & Moore, *supra* note 90, at 410; *see also* Michael S. Moore, *Causation and Responsibility*, 16 Soc. Phil. & Pol'y 1, 15–17 (Summer 1999) ("Our liability doctrines thus presuppose that causation is the kind of relation that can 'peter out.'"); *cf.* Anenson, *Lessons for Litigation Lawyers, supra* note 85, at 932–46 (using a spatio-temporal relationship between litigator misconduct and the litigation to assess the doctrine of absolute immunity from civil liability for litigators).

[93] 719 N.W.2d 809 (Mich. 2006).

[94] 533 N.W.2d 13 (Mich. Ct. App. 1995).

[95] *Id.* at 14.

[96] *Id.; accord* Gaudiosi v. Mellon, 269 F.2d 873, 881 (3d Cir. 1959) (attempts to intimidate stockholders in action for equitable relief relative to proxy contest sustained due to finding of unclean hands). The now infamous case that settled the primacy of equity over the law in seventeenth-century England arose when the Court of Chancery enjoined a common law judgment secured by fraud via witness tampering. *See* Earl of Oxford's Case (1615), 21 Eng. Rep. 485 (Ch.); *see also* Frederick T. White & Owen D. Tudor, A Selection of Leading Cases in Equity, Vol. II, Part 2, at 1298 (1877) (discussing an account of the common law case in which the plaintiff lost the verdict in the law court because one of the witnesses was "artfully kept away"). *See generally* Peter W. Young et al., On Equity, § 1.220, at 23 (2009) (discussing the dispute between Chief Justice Coke and Chancellor Ellesmere and its resolution in favor of equity by King James I).

The litigation misconduct in *Maldonado* occurred when both the party and her attorney improperly attempted to influence the jury through the repeated pretrial publicity of evidence ruled inadmissible at the trial.[97] In affirming the dismissal, the Michigan Supreme Court ruled that a showing of actual prejudice to the jury pool in the case was not necessary.[98] It held that a substantial likelihood of such harm was enough. That likelihood was established by the premeditated misconduct "designed to taint the potential jury pool, deny defendants a fair trial, and frustrate the due administration of justice."[99] It emphasized the trial court's "gate-keeping obligation ... to impose sanctions [for misconduct] that will not only deter the misconduct but also serve as a deterrent to other litigants."[100]

The Michigan Supreme Court located the source of its dismissal power under the doctrine of unclean hands.[101] It found the power to dismiss to be inherent in its judicial authority under the state constitution.[102] As the court noted, its constitutional power in any case would be superior to purported legislative prerogatives that Code pleading could take away.[103]

Witnesses tampering and tainting the jury pool directly affect the court's truth-seeking mission. Such dirty tactics interfere with the provider and adjudicator of the facts at trial. Under these circumstances, not even the quintessential method of achieving accuracy and sincerity through cross-examination would remedy the situation.

Additionally, a finding of unclean hands due to a party's perjury or when a party has fabricated, destroyed, or suppressed evidence would each also fall into Phase One.[104] The Rhode Island Superior Court decision in *Bartlett v. Dunne*[105] and the district court of Maryland decision in *Smith v. Cessna Aircraft Co.*[106] both found that

---

[97] *Maldonado*, 719 N.W.2d at 814.

[98] *Id.* at 822.

[99] *Id.* n.25; *see also id.* at 818–19 (reasoning that the substantial likelihood standard comported with First Amendment jurisprudence and the Code of Professional Responsibility).

[100] *Maldonado*, 719 N.W.2d at 819.

[101] *Id.* at 818.

[102] *Id.*

[103] *Id.* For further discussion of the case, see Chapter 3, Section 3.4.1.5 (analyzing Michigan cases fusing unclean hands into damages actions).

[104] *See* Aoude v. Mobil Oil Corp., 892 F.2d 1115, 1118 (1st Cir. 1989) (describing fabrication of evidence and perjury as "near-classic" examples of an abuse of the judicial process); Aris-Isotoner Gloves, Inc. v. Berkshire Fashions, Inc., 792 F. Supp. 969, 972 (S.D.N.Y. 1992) (applying unclean hands to preclude equitable relief on the basis of perjured testimony in instant proceedings or original contempt proceedings). The violation of a court order would satisfy this criterion as well. *See Maldonado*, 719 N.W.2d at 819–22 (avoiding issue of whether plaintiff violated court order and finding warning issued in open court sufficient to invoke duty to the trial court). Note that the violation of a court order or other duty to the court transforms what might be nonlitigation misconduct outlined as Phase Two into the litigation misconduct of Phase One.

[105] No. C.A. 89–3051, 1989 WL 1110258 (R.I. Super. Ct. Nov. 10, 1989) (dismissing negligence complaint due to plaintiff's perjury at trial regarding alcohol consumption prior to accident).

[106] 124 F.R.D. 103 (D. Md. 1989) (dismissing damages claim related to lost income).

perjury warranted dismissal of damages claims pursuant to unclean hands. In *Smith v. Cessna Aircraft Co.*, the court emphasized how plaintiff's perjury hindered the court's ability to ascertain the truth.[107] It explained:

> It can hardly be disputed that Mr. Garner's hands are unclean with respect to a matter at issue in this litigation. Mr. Garner has filed suit, seeking damages resulting from the crash of his plane. As part of those damages, he seeks compensation for the income he lost while recuperating from his injuries. His tax returns are critical to allowing the defendants to assess accurately their potential liability for these damages. By providing the defendants with tax documents that were admittedly false, and by lying in his deposition and answers to interrogatories, Mr. Garner has abused the discovery system and has deprived the defendants of essential information.[108]

Because discovery as to economic damages is relevant to evaluate demands and offers in the pretrial stage, the court held that "the fact that the fraud and perjury are discovered before trial does not vitiate the taint upon the litigation process as a whole."[109]

Due to its close relation with the purpose of court protection, cases in this phase need not consider the claim at issue or its consistency with the assertion of unclean hands.

6.3.5.2 Phase Two: Misconduct Outside the Present Litigation that Potentially Interferes with the Process

The next phase in the approach would be nonlitigation misconduct prior to or during the litigation that has the potential to affect the court's ability to control the proceedings or ensure a fair outcome. Using previously manufactured documents as evidence, as in *Buchanan Home & Auto Supply Co., Inc. v. Firestone Tire & Rubber Co.*,[110] or filing contemporaneous collateral proceedings,[111] each falls within this second phase.[112]

---

[107] *Id.* at 105–07.

[108] *Id.* at 107.

[109] *Id.*

[110] 544 F. Supp. 242 (D.S.C. 1981).

[111] A Michigan Court of Appeals, in a case of first impression, also extended the *Cummings* line of precedent to include procedural interference by means of collateral proceedings. *See* Prince v. MacDonald, 602 N.W.2d 834, 836 (Mich. Ct. App. 1999) (sanctioning defendant under the authority of *Cummings* without mentioning "unclean hands," for filing bad-faith bankruptcy petition to delay proceedings). For another application of unclean hands based in part on interference through collateral proceedings, see Hall v. Wright, 240 F.2d 787, 796 (9th Cir. 1957) (affirming the application of unclean hands in part on grounds that the parties' other frivolous lawsuits adversely affected the current case involving alleged patent infringement and unfair competition).

[112] Note that if the misconduct does not involve the violation of a court order or other duty to the court (as opposed to the parties to each other), the case moves from Phase One to Phase Two,

In *Buchanan*, the District Court of South Carolina commented that the dealership's prior scheme to defraud Firestone by doctoring documents affected Firestone's ability to present a defense.[113] The court invoked unclean hands to dismiss the dealership's claims for monetary relief because the dealership's actions were a risk to the administration of justice.[114]

Prior to suing Firestone for tort, contract, and warranty claims, the dealership had falsified and forged adjustment forms necessary for it to obtain the handling fee and billing credit for replaced Firestone tires.[115] While the plaintiff did not manufacture the evidence for the purpose of interfering with the litigation,[116] the court found that "[t]he essence of plaintiff's cause of action is based on evidence which it admits having forged and falsified for its own benefit."[117] It explained:

> Firestone is now prevented from cross-checking these forged and falsified adjustment forms because of plaintiff's failure to collect and maintain accurate information about the adjustments . . . Essential to recovery on all of plaintiff's claims is a determination of the number of legitimate warranty claims plaintiff had to process. The plaintiff's fraud discussed above hopelessly obscures any possibility of accurately resolving this question.[118]

For this reason, the district court found the application of unclean hands advanced its court protection purpose regardless of remedy.[119]

The *Buchanan* case incorporating unclean hands into the common law involved actual interference with the case before the court. Misdeeds with the potential to disrupt the process or its outcome should also be included in Phase Two.[120] Again, like Phase One, given the direct relation between the misconduct and the interest in

---

dealing with nonlitigation misconduct that otherwise has the potential to interfere with the current case.

[113] *Buchanan*, 544 F. Supp. at 246.

[114] *Id.* at 247; *see also* Stratton v. Sacks, 99 B.R. 686, 694 (D. Md. 1989) ("Although the clean hands doctrine is an equitable principle, it has been applied by a district court in this Circuit [in *Buchanan*] to defeat an action at law." (internal citation omitted)).

[115] *Buchanan*, 544 F. Supp. at 243–44. Plaintiff admitted that approximately 600 adjustment forms were forged or otherwise falsified. Each form was worth $40 to $50. *Id.* at 244.

[116] If plaintiff had fabricated evidence for purposes of defrauding the court, it would be considered Phase One misconduct under the schema outlined previously.

[117] *Buchanan*, 544 F. Supp. at 245.

[118] *Id.* at 246

[119] *Id.* at 247.

[120] The degree of causal connection required could vary, for instance, from foreseeability to knowledge with substantial certainty. *See* discussion *supra* Chapter 2, Section 2.7.1. As discussed *supra* Section 6.3.5.1, the Michigan Supreme Court held that the substantial likelihood of harm to the litigation process was sufficient to dismiss for unclean hands. Maldonado v. Ford Motor Co., 719 N.W.2d 809, 822 (Mich. 2006). The court was drawing from First Amendment jurisprudence (and professional ethics standards) because the plaintiff claimed her constitutional rights were violated by the trial judge's gag order. *Id.* at 823–25. In the 4–3 decision, three judges agreed with the plaintiff. *Id.* at 826–841. Four judges upheld the dismissal on the basis of unclean hands. *Id.* at 826.

the integrity of the process, a court need not consider the policies of the asserted claim or whether the application of unclean hands comports with it.

6.3.5.3 Phase Three: Misconduct in Prior Litigation with No Potential to Interfere with the Process

An even more attenuated connection bearing on the court protection purpose is misconduct or fraud perpetrated in another court that does not interfere with the court's ability to hear and decide the case. Nevertheless, without the bar of unclean hands, claimants would somehow benefit from their prior unclean conduct in the current action. Courts invoke unclean hands to deter future misdeeds against the judicial system and not to dirty themselves by seemingly endorsing such misbehavior.[121] In contrast to the tangible harm to court procedures in Phase One and Two cases, Phase Three cases involve intangible harm to the process.[122]

Because Phase Three cases concern the public perception of legitimacy, courts should consider other public policy interests in the prior lawsuit as well as the current lawsuit. This was exactly the scenario in the early equity cases from the United States Supreme Court. These decisions applied the doctrine of unclean hands to ban perjury and other evidentiary misconduct in the patent process against plaintiffs seeking equitable relief.[123] In *Precision Instrument Mfg. Co. v. Auto. Maint. Mach. Co.*,[124] for example, the Court refused to assist the wrong and allow the abuse of the patent privilege with deleterious consequences to the public.[125] These rulings are so closely aligned with the policies of the claim that they are considered part of the substantive law that patents procured by fraud are unenforceable.[126]

---

[121] *See* Adams v. Manown, 615 A.2d 611, 616 (Md. 1992).

[122] *See* Halverson v. Hardcastle, 163 P.3d 428, 440 (Nev. 2007) (distinguishing the inherent power to dismiss for "litigation abuses" from the inherent power to "prevent injustice and to preserve the integrity of the judicial process").

[123] *See, e.g.*, Precision Instrument Mfg. Co. v. Auto. Maint. Mach. Co., 324 U.S. 806, 816–17 (1945); Hazel-Atlas Glass Co. v. Hartford-Empire Co., 322 U.S. 238, 246 (1944) (fraud on the public and the court), *overruled on other grounds sub nom.*, Standard Oil Co. v. United States, 429 U.S. 17 (1976); SEC v. U.S. Realty & Improvement Co., 310 U.S. 434, 455 (1940); United States v. Morgan, 307 U.S. 183, 194 (1939).

[124] 324 U.S. 806 (1945).

[125] *Id.* at 814 (quoting Bein v. Heath, 47 U.S. (6 How.) 228, 247 (1848)); *see also* Goldman, *supra* note 318, at 46 (noting that the Supreme Court's prior decisions in *Keystone Driller Co. v. Gen. Excavator Co.*, 290 U.S. 240 (1933) and *Hazel-Atlas Glass Co. v. Hartford-Empire Co.*, 322 U.S. 238 (1944), also dealt with fraud on the Patent Office, but focused on its effect on the judicial process).

[126] *See* DOUGLAS LAYCOCK, MODERN AMERICAN REMEDIES 933 (4th ed. 2010) (noting that the application of unclean hands in *Precision Instrument* ultimately became a rule of patent law that patents procured by fraud are invalid); T. Leigh Anenson & Gideon Mark, *Inequitable Conduct in Retrospective: Understanding Unclean Hands in Patent Remedies*, 62 AM. U. L. REV. 1441, 1451–53 (2013) (explaining the genesis of the "inequitable conduct" defense in patent law stemming from the Supreme Court's unclean hands decisions in cases such as *Precision Instrument*).

The state appellate court decisions finding unclean hands available in legal claims in *Blain v. Doctor's Co.*,[127] *Kirkland v. Mannis*,[128] *Manown v. Adams*,[129] and *Pond v. Insur. Co. of N. America*[130] fall into this third phase. These cases dealt with perjury or other litigation misconduct in prior court proceedings.[131]

The California Court of Appeals decision in *Blain* affirmed the dismissal of a legal malpractice action against counsel who advised his client to lie at a deposition.[132] The court found committing perjury constituted unclean hands to bar a claim for damages.[133] The Oregon Court of Appeals decision in *Kirkland* also affirmed the dismissal of a legal malpractice action pursuant to the plaintiff's unclean hands in providing perjured testimony.[134] The former client alleged malpractice because his attorney manufactured a story for his defense, which he then incorporated in his testimony before the judge and jury in his criminal trial.[135]

The plaintiff in the Maryland appellate decision *Manown* was seeking repayment of a loan that he had previously failed to list as a transfer of assets in his bankruptcy proceeding and divorce action.[136] While the claim was breach of contract and not tort as in *Blain* and *Kirkland*, the unclean hands claimed in *Manown* was also perjury, albeit in a prior bankruptcy and divorce proceeding. Emphasizing that the defense served to protect the court and to suppress illegal and fraudulent transactions, a Maryland appellate court found unclean hands applicable to this action at law despite its equitable roots.[137]

Similarly, in *Pond*, an insurance agent withheld documents in the insurer's indemnity suit against him. That allowed the agent to escape liability and served as the basis of his subsequent malicious prosecution case.[138] The California Court of

---

[127] 272 Cal. Rptr. 250 (Cal. Ct. App. 1990).

[128] 639 P.2d 671 (Or. Ct. App. 1982). As discussed *supra* Chapter 3, the same court in a later case disavowed the decision to apply the defense to damages actions. *See* McKinley v. Weidner, 698 P.2d 983, 985 n.1 (Or. Ct. App. 1985).

[129] 598 A.2d 821 (Md. Ct. Spec. App. 1991), *vacated on other grounds*, 615 A.2d 611, 612 (Md. 1992).

[130] 198 Cal. Rptr. 517, 522 (Cal. Ct. App. 1984).

[131] *See also* Smith v. Long, 281 A.D.2d 897, 898 (N.Y. App. Div. 2001) (declaring unclean hands available in "law or equity" to bar enforcement of an agreement entered into to perpetrate a fraud on the Small Business Administration).

[132] *Blain*, 272 Cal. Rptr. at 258–59.

[133] *Id.*

[134] *Kirkland*, 639 P.2d at 671–73. *But see* McKinley v. Weidner, 698 P.2d 983, 985 (Or. Ct. App. 1985) (criticizing *Kirkland* for applying unclean hands in an action at law but otherwise approving the result as "right in substance").

[135] *Kirkland*, 639 P.2d at 673 ("[P]laintiff and defendant cooperatively presented a perjurous tale at plaintiff's criminal trial, and the tale did not sell. Because of his acknowledged perjury, plaintiff brings his complaint with unclean hands and may not recover.").

[136] Manown v. Adams, 598 A.2d 821, 823 (Md Ct. Spec. App. 1991), *vacated on other grounds*, 615 A.2d 611, 612 (Md. 1992).

[137] *Id.* at 824–25.

[138] Pond v. Insur. Co. of N. America, 198 Cal. Rptr. 517, 521–23 (Cal. Ct. App. 1984).

Appeals characterized the agent's conduct in bringing the malicious prosecution action as "classic 'chutzpah'" and affirmed the dismissal for unclean hands.[139]

All of these cases involved some form of misconduct in a prior proceeding: written or oral testimony or the withholding or manufacturing of evidence. The misconduct occurred at various times, whether during pretrial discovery procedures or during the trial itself. *Pond* and the federal patent cases concerned litigants attempting to capitalize on a prior fraud that was successful. The state malpractice cases, by comparison, involved parties seeking to recoup their losses when the misconduct failed to achieve their nefarious ends. In these cases, the parties were trying to blame their attorneys for something the court found to be their own fault. Viewed from this perspective, the facts constituting the unclean hands defense also could rebut the requisite causation element of the asserted claim.[140] Along with *Manown*,[141] the two malpractice cases also involved parties suing each other in the subsequent lawsuit who had jointly committed the misconduct.[142]

Like the Supreme Court's consideration of patent policy, the state courts also considered the respective claims and interests in the former proceedings. For instance, perjury during a former bankruptcy proceeding was considered in *Manown*, which was further appealed to Maryland's highest court.[143] It ultimately avoided the intermediate appellate court's decision to apply unclean hands by ruling that the bankruptcy trustee was the real party in interest.[144] Because dismissing the case pursuant to unclean hands would have deprived the bankrupt's creditors of an asset, the court determined that the interests of the bankruptcy creditors outweighed any procedural interest of the court in being manipulated by litigants.[145]

[139] *Id.* at 523 (citations omitted). The court emphasized that dismissal as a matter of law for unclean hands did not require a finding that the agent was guilty of perjury, concealment, or other illegal conduct. *Id.* Instead, it held "[a]ny *unconscientious* conduct upon his part which is connected with the controversy will repel him from the forum whose very foundation is good conscience." *Id.* For further discussion of the elements of unclean hands, see Chapter 2, Section 2.7.

[140] *See* Blain v. Doctor's Co., 272 Cal. Rptr. 250, 258–59 (Cal. Ct. App. 1990) (dismissing attorney malpractice case on basis of unclean hands on the grounds that the claims of emotional distress and loss of ability to practice medicine were attributable to litigant's own misbehavior in lying under oath). For discussion of California cases fusing unclean hands, see Chapter 3, Section 3.4.1.1.

[141] Manown, plaintiff Adams's former girlfriend, participated in his scheme to hide assets. *Manown*, 598 A.2d at 824.

[142] *See Blain*, 272 Cal. Rptr. at 255; Kirkland v. Mannis, 639 P.2d 671, 673 (Or. Ct. App. 1982).

[143] Adams v. Manown, 615 A.2d 611 (Md. 1992).

[144] *Id.* at 617–18; *see also id.* at 622–23 (Chasanow, J., dissenting) (criticizing the majority's refusal to rule on the issue of applying unclean hands at law and finding the defense applies only against claims seeking equitable relief).

[145] *Id.* at 617–18. The Maryland Court of Appeals in *WinMark Ltd. P'ship v. Miles & Stockbridge*, 693 A.2d 824 (Md. 1997), characterized the dilemma it had faced in *Adams v. Manown*:

Indeed, there, liability of the defendant in the civil action to the discharged bankrupt had been determined by judgment. To the extent that the judgment was collectible,

In contrast, the appellate court in *Kirkland* approved the use of unclean hands by leveraging its own interests with that of the underlying claim. Allowing the legal malpractice claim based on the unethical advice to lie under oath during criminal proceedings would have detracted from the criminal sanction.[146] While *Kirkland* did not address the dismissal's potential encouragement of unethical attorney behavior, the appellate court in *Blain* considered the issue before permitting the operation of unclean hands in a similar claim. The court found that the attorney gained no personal benefit in advising his client to lie and noted the existence of other means to deter or punish professional ethics violations besides the risk of civil liability.[147]

Accordingly, Phase Three cases place the second court in the unique position of vindicating the general judicial interest in integrity, assuming such procedural interests comport with the concerns of the substantive law. If the application of unclean hands will nevertheless undermine those incentives or interests, the subsequent court should weigh and balance the need for judicial protection before making unclean hands available.[148]

6.3.5.4 Phase Four: Nonlitigation Misconduct with No Potential to Interfere with the Process

The most remote relation to judicial integrity is misconduct independent of the violation of duties during the advocacy process that does not disrupt the pending case. In comparison to the other three phases, neither the nature of the misconduct nor its effect is connected to court procedure. There is no litigation misconduct in

---

> extinguishing it by applying the clean hands doctrine would have resulted in a windfall to the judgment debtor and would have deprived the bankrupt's creditors of an asset from which they should have benefited.

WinMark, 693 A.2d at 830. Notably, Maryland's highest court in *Adams v. Manown* could have held that unclean hands applied at law but refused to use it in the case for the reason that the perjury was "unrelated" to the claim or not supported by policy reasons. For discussion of Maryland cases fusing unclean hands, see Chapter 3, Section 3.4.1.3.

[146] *Kirkland*, 639 P.2d at 673; *see also Blain*, 272 Cal. Rptr. at 256, 258 (reviewing *Kirkland* with approval and noting that "the injury stemmed from a criminal conviction, attributable to the ill-advised perjury, and recovery might have softened the effect of the penal sanction").

[147] *Blain*, 272 Cal. Rptr. at 258–59; *see also* Anenson, *Interference with the Attorney–Client Relationship, supra* note 85, at 218 (discussing professional sanctions that supplement the civil and criminal law). Nevertheless, a cause of concern to the legal profession has been the inability of codes of ethics or disciplinary sanctions to deter attorney misconduct. *See, e.g.,* Peter Megargee Brown, *The Decline of Lawyers' Professional Independence, in* THE LAWYER'S PROFESSIONAL INDEPENDENCE: PRESENT THREATS/FUTURE CHALLENGES 23, 25–26 (1984) (citing perceived failure to discipline lawyers for myriad abuses—to each other, the courts, to the client, to the public interest—as a cause of decline of professional independence).

[148] *See* Adams v. Manown, 615 A.2d 611 (Md. 1992). A second case under state law could be complicated by concerns of federalism if the prior court and source of law is federal law. *See* WinMark Ltd. P'ship v. Miles & Stockbridge, 693 A.2d 824, 831 (Md. 1997) (analyzing issue of federal preemption).

the present case (Phase One) or in another case (Phase Three). The nonlitigation misconduct also does not interfere with the existing litigation (Phase Two).

The disputes in this phase usually involve illegal or unethical business practices prior to the legal dispute involving the commercial transaction. These kinds of misdeeds have the most tenuous relationship to procedural justice and the policy of court protection. It is only in the enforcement of such unclean claims that a court figuratively dirties itself, which may adversely impact its public perception.

Phase Four cases are most closely aligned with the substantive justice component of party protection. For this reason, the invocation of unclean hands can be seen most clearly as a substantive (as opposed to procedural) defense to the legal claim. This situation requires the fullest consideration of the policies of the claim, whether they derive from common law or legislative enactment. It is in this instance that Chafee's description of unclean hands is truest: "this vague single principle gets most of its qualities in a given group of cases from the substantive law of the particular subject."[149]

Many of the federal cases allowing unclean hands in damages actions in this fourth phase involve the abuse of statutory rights or the violation of duties dealing with intangible personal property such as intellectual property and securities litigation.[150] The availability of unclean hands under a particular legislative enactment will depend on additional considerations of legislative text and intent, especially the public interest.[151]

The Fifth Circuit Court of Appeals decision in *Kuehnert v. Texstar Corp.*,[152] for instance, focused on whether unclean hands would advance the policies of the securities law as opposed to law–equity labels in applying the defense.[153] In fact, the court focused so much on the policy issues that it failed even to mention the merger.[154] In reviewing the divided *Kuehnert* decision on an analogous issue,

[149] In reviewing the application of unclean hands, Professor Chafee concluded that the maxim was transformed into the substantive law and that any principle derived from those cases would be suspect without also considering the nature of the lawsuit. See Chafee II, *supra* note 20, at 1071, 1074–75, 1092; *see also* Sprenger v. Trout, 866 A.2d 1035, 1045 (N.J. Super. Ct. App. Div. 2005) (searching for precedent concerning the particular kind of action before the court in considering the application of unclean hands at law).

[150] *See, e.g.,* Supermarket of Homes, Inc. v. San Fernando Valley Bd. of Realtors, 786 F.2d 1400, 1408 (9th Cir. 1986) (intellectual property); Kuehnert v. Texstar Corp., 412 F.2d 700, 704 (5th Cir. 1969) (securities law).

[151] T. Leigh Anenson, *Statutory Interpretation, Judicial Discretion, and Equitable Defenses*, 79 Univ. Pitt. L. Rev. 1, 15–19 (2017) [hereinafter Anenson, *Statutory Interpretation*]; discussion *supra* Chapter 5.

[152] 412 F.2d 700 (5th Cir. 1969) (invoking unclean hands to bar a tippee from recovering losses against an insider/tipper for providing false information in federal securities litigation).

[153] *Id.* at 704; *see also* case discussion *supra* Chapter 3, Section 3.4.2.6.

[154] For other cases ignoring the issue of incorporation in applying unclean hands to damages but otherwise observing the competing interests at stake, see discussion *supra* Chapter 3, Section 3.4.1.1 (citing Blain v. Doctor's Co., 272 Cal. Rptr. 250, 255–59 (Cal. Ct. App. 1990) and Kirkland v. Mannis, 639 P.2d 671 (Or. Ct. App. 1982)).

the district court in *Nathanson v. Weis, Voisin, Cannon, Inc.* called the policy analysis "a close one."[155] The court explained:

> The basic question, as this court views it, centers not about the claims asserted by plaintiffs against the defendant or the defense advanced in resistance to those claims, but rather about third parties not involved in the litigation—the investing public and what policy with respect to the allowance or disallowance of the defense would best serve to carry out the prime purpose of the securities laws to protect the investing public.[156]

Other Phase Four cases applied unclean hands to legal claims under the following statutes: Sherman Antitrust Act,[157] Lanham Act[158] for copyright[159] and trademark[160] infringement, and civil RICO.[161] Given the importance of aligning unclean hands with the policies of the claim, it makes sense that in copyright cases (like the equity cases involving patents), unclean hands has developed into the defense of "copyright misuse."[162]

Circumstances falling into Phase Four under state common law also involved business activities. For example, *Fibreboard Paper Prods. Corp. v. East Bay Union of Machinists*[163] concerned employment and union activities; *Jesperson v. Ponichtera*,[164] corporate governance issues; *First Fairfield Funding, LLC v.*

---

[155] 325 F. Supp. 50, 52–53 (S.D.N.Y. 1971).

[156] *Id.*

[157] Maltz v. Sax, 134 F.2d 2, 5 (7th Cir.1943) ("As to unclean hands: The maxims of equity are available as defenses in actions at law (28 U.S.C.A. § 398; Rule 2 of the Rules of Civil Procedure, 28 U.S.C.A. following section 723c).").

[158] Energizer Holdings, Inc. v. Duracell, Inc., No. 01 C 9720, 2002 WL 1067688, at *3 (N.D. Ill. May 28, 2002) (applying Urecal Corp. v. Masters, 413 F. Supp. 873, 875 (N.D. Ill. 1976); *see also* discussion *supra* Chapter 3, Section 3.4.2.4 (citing cases).

[159] Tempo Music, Inc. v. Myers, 407 F.2d 503, 507 (4th Cir. 1969); *see also* discussion *supra* Chapter 3, Section 3.4.2.2.

[160] Metro Publ'g, Ltd. v. San Jose Mercury News, Inc., 861 F. Supp. 870, 880–81 (N.D. Cal. 1994); *see also* discussion *supra* Chapter 3, Section 3.4.2.3.

[161] Boca Raton Community Hosp., Inc. v. Tenet Healthcare Corp., 238 F.R.D. 679, 693–94 (S.D. Fla. 2006); *see also* discussion *supra* Chapter 3, Section 3.4.2.1.

[162] *See* discussion *supra* Chapter 3, Section 3.4.2.3. The copyright misuse cases involve an abuse of right similar to the patent misuse cases. Anenson, *Statutory Interpretation, supra* note 151, at 13–14 (analyzing Supreme Court patent decisions involving unclean hands). They are also like the Phase Three malpractice cases in that the court is essentially finding that the infringement is the plaintiff's own fault and providing an alternative ground of dismissal that could be an absence of causation.

[163] 39 Cal. Rptr. 64, 97–98 (Cal. Ct. App. 1964); *see also* discussion *supra* Chapter 3, Section 3.4.1.1.

[164] No. CV88 0096615 S., 1990 WL 283884, at *1 (Conn. Super. Ct. July 16, 1990) (addressing shareholder derivative action alleging wrongful conversion and breach of fiduciary duty by officer and director who asserted the defense of unclean hands of the shareholders by participating in and benefiting from any wrongdoing); *see also* discussion *supra* Chapter 3,

Goldman,[165] *Big Lots Stores, Inc. v. Jaredco, Inc.,*[166] and *Unilogic, Inc. v. Burroughs Corp.,*[167] failed business project and deals. Various tort and contract claims were pled for damages, as well as advanced in defense as unclean hands.[168]

Courts in these cases did not necessarily engage in an overt policy analysis of whether the purposes of the defense are consistent with those of the claim or any other interests at stake.[169] Due to the primary interests of party protection in Phase Four cases, the four-phase framework would direct courts to balance these interests against the interests of the claim. Such balancing should make it progressively less likely that the defense will be available at law as compared to cases within Phases One, Two, and Three. As will be discussed in the next section, certain Phase Four cases found the defense available at law but ultimately did not use it.

In sum, the suggested model or metatheory is motivated by the underlying idea that the two policies of unclean hands provide good heuristics to assess the availability of the defense against legal remedies. By emphasizing the doctrine's procedural over its substantive ends (court protection over party protection), the four-phase analysis obligates litigants to come into court with clean hands and keep them clean during the litigation process. The next section discusses the four stages and their relation to the elements of the defense.

6.3.6 Relation to Elements

The four-phase model aims to theorize unclean hands in a way that explicitly incorporates the need for more specific inquiries, thereby leaving the ultimate question of application for resolution by the diverse factors that can affect such determinations. There are two inquiries. First, where does the case fall under the four phases? Second, are the elements of unclean hands satisfied? In other words, is

---

Section 3.3 (advising that the Supreme Court of Connecticut has since ruled unclean hands is not available to bar damages).

[165] No. CV020465799S., 2003 WL 22708882, at *1 (Conn. Super. Ct. Nov. 3, 2003) (dealing with third-party defendant alleging unclean hands on the part of the plaintiff in connection with the plaintiff's initial acquisition of a contract in a common law interference and statutory unfair trade practices action with contract to purchase property); *see also* discussion *supra* Chapter 3, Section 3.3 (advising that the Supreme Court of Connecticut has since ruled unclean hands is not available to bar damages).

[166] 182 F. Supp. 2d 644, 652–53 (S.D. Ohio 2002); *see also* discussion *supra* Chapter 3, Section 3.4.2.5.

[167] 12 Cal. Rptr. 2d 741, 743 (Cal. Ct. App. 1992); *see also* discussion *supra* Chapter 3, Section 3.4.1.1.

[168] *See, e.g., Fibreboard,* 39 Cal. Rptr. 64 (tortious union activities); *Unilogic,* 12 Cal. Rptr. 2d 741 (conversion).

[169] Given the procedural posture of the Connecticut cases, in which the trial courts ruled on motions to strike answers asserting unclean hands, it is possible that the court was reserving such policy analysis for a later dispositive ruling. *See Jesperson,* 1990 WL 283884, at *2; *First Fairfield,* 2003 WL 22708882, at *2.

the conduct sufficiently unclean and connected to the case to merit dismissal of the legal claim in light of the public policies at stake?

The two-level inquiry poses some conceptual complications. It would be simpler and, therefore, seem desirable to have the application of unclean hands measured only by its elements. In a perfect world, a single-level analysis should aid courts and facilitate a correct and consistent outcome.[170] Yet the elements in their current configuration have not done the heavy lifting that the doctrine requires. Indeed, Chafee criticized the defense for its mischievousness around 1950.[171] Given its standard-like qualities, there seems to be little prospect for complete clarification by focusing solely on the elements.[172]

As discussed in Section 6.4.1, and as outlined in earlier chapters, the problem of unclean hands resists simple definition, simplistic generalization, and simple-minded theory. As a result, the four-pronged overlay provides more specific guidance to courts in their decision-making process.

While this chapter cannot explore the full potential of the four-phase model of unclean hands or offer detailed examples of its interrelation to the elements of the defense, some general comments are in order. Cases falling into certain phases almost always guarantee that the "relevancy" or "unclean conduct" element is met.[173] For instance, litigation misconduct in the current case (Phase One) or even the former case (Phase Three) is probably sufficiently soiled to constitute "unclean" hands.

Assume, however, that the misconduct is perjury about an unrelated matter during a deposition that has no legal relevance to the lawsuit.[174] Assume further

---

[170] *See* Cardi, *supra* note 74, at 933–36 (noting that the reasons for separate and distinct elements of a claim are to avoid duplication, serve as an analytical blueprint so that like cases can be treated alike, and help analysis to further a correct and consistent outcome).

[171] Chafee I, *supra* note 20, at 878. He also stated "that insofar as it is a principle it is not very helpful but it is at times capable of causing considerable harm." *Id.*

[172] *See* discussion *supra* Chapter 5, Section 5.4.4 (discussing ways of narrowing the defense including requiring intent); *see also* discussion *supra* Chapter 2, Section 2.7.1 (analyzing conflict in the cases on any state-of-mind requirement).

[173] *See* Smith v. Cessna Aircraft Co., 124 F.R.D. 103, 105–07 (D. Md. 1989) (finding perjury in deposition and interrogatory responses regarding filing tax returns, when claim included damages for lost income, amounted to unclean hands as to lost earnings claim, but not the entire complaint); *see also* Derzack v. County of Allegheny, 173 F.R.D. 400, 415 (W.D. Pa. 1996) (dismissing entire case for fraud on the court and rejecting plaintiffs' "no harm, no foul" argument that because their fraudulent scheme of manufacturing income tax returns that drastically inflated their business income to support their business loss claim and subsequently covering up their scheme was found out before any real damage had been done to the merits of the case or defendants' ability to prosecute same, and because they "voluntarily" withdrew their business loss claim).

[174] *See* Rodriguez v. M & M/Mars, No. 96 C 1231, 1997 U.S. Dist. LEXIS 9036, at *5–6 (N.D. Ill. June 18, 1997) (dismissing sexual harassment case under inherent powers for plaintiff's attempt to "conceal relevant information bearing directly upon her credibility"); Stern, *supra* note 82, at 1257 n.30 ("A witness' credibility is always relevant and litigants almost always are witness in

that the perjury can be sufficiently checked by cross-examination or sanctions.[175] In this circumstance, a judge may conclude that the perjury lacked the requisite relation to the case if the false testimony did not foreseeably interfere with the case or its outcome. A court may also require actual harm or a more stringent connection, like substantial certainty of interference, before finding unclean hands. Again, the intent of the wrongdoer or a pattern of misbehavior may influence the court's decision to dismiss.[176]

The connection element of the defense may also be met in Phase Three cases concerning litigation misconduct in another court, where the litigant abused the right or privilege in the underlying case stemming solely from the dirty deed. Assuming no other interests were at stake,[177] the second lawsuit would be tainted in the attempt to benefit or recoup losses from the prior dishonesty and would satisfy the requisite connection component.

Phase Four cases will probably provide the least overlap between the elements and the availability of unclean hands at law. Indeed, courts that found the defense available in damages actions did not necessarily apply it.[178] The first case to recognize the defense against legal remedies in the United States, *Fibreboard Paper Prods. Corp. v. East Bay Union of Machinists*,[179] was such a situation. In *Fibreboard*, the California Court of Appeals determined there was no connection between the plaintiff's claim in tort and the defendant's alleged breach of contract and fraudulent misrepresentation.[180] The court reasoned, "It would amount to a straining of the doctrine to hold that defendants could escape liability for tort because Fibreboard breached its contract or because it was guilty of fraudulent misrepresentations."[181] Thus, while the conduct component is broad enough to extend beyond illegality and include unethical business activities, courts are not likely to dismiss when those activities amount to a counterclaim. Rather, they will consider the allegation of

---

their own cases."). Typically, the misconduct need not be legally relevant from an evidentiary perspective. *See id.*

[175] *See* Bower v. Weisman, 674 F. Supp. 109, 112 (S.D.N.Y. 1987) (denying dismissal for fraud on the court and taxing plaintiff with costs, fees, and expenses of additional depositions that were necessitated by the perjury); Stern, *supra* note 82, at 1257–58 (discussing case in which counsel made a tactical decision to save the perjury for cross-examination at trial rather than seek dismissal when misrepresentation was about a matter peripheral to the claim).

[176] *See* discussion *supra* Chapter 2, Section 2.7 (analyzing elements of the unclean hands defense).

[177] *See* discussion *supra* Chapter 2 (discussing third-party interests, such as when the fraud is perpetrated on the bankruptcy court and creditors).

[178] *See, e.g.*, Gen-Probe, Inc. v. Amoco Corp., 926 F. Supp. 948, 952 (S.D. Cal. 1996) (applying California law) (finding no connection between the conduct constituting unclean hands and the lawsuit); *see also* discussion *supra* Chapter 3, Section 3.4.1.1.

[179] 39 Cal. Rptr. 64, 96 (Cal. Ct. App. 1964) (noting it was a question of "first impression" whether the equitable defense of unclean hands applied as a defense to a legal action); *see also* discussion *supra* Chapter 3, Section 3.4.1.1.

[180] *Id.* at 98.

[181] *Id.* at 97.

unclean hands as a damages issue.[182] Under the cases considering unclean hands against statutory claims for damages, it appears that the connection component is more likely met when the alleged unclean conduct is in violation of the same statute.[183]

The process of judging requires courts to undertake the unenviable task of bridging the gap between the law and the ever-changing circumstances of life it is trying to capture.[184] The process-based theory is being offered as a preferred solution to some aspects of this intractable problem concerning the defense of unclean hands. There will be overlap between the four phases and the elements. It will be messy. But just because the framework does not satisfy an academic desire for tidiness and symmetry does not mean it cannot offer some improvement in the application of unclean hands. The risk of removing a popular and effective—if not optimal or efficient—tool in equitable remedies from the bulk of legal cases is too great.[185] When the assault is on the dispute resolution processes, we need all the weapons we can get. Our very justice system is at stake.

In addition, the reality is that lawyers are asserting unclean hands in legal cases, and some courts are listening. The doctrine was first sanctioned at law by a state supreme court in 2006.[186] That court, moreover, appeared to resurrect the defense as a constitutional principle.[187] A multitude of lower courts in the state and federal

[182] Courts applying unclean hands generally give the remedy of dismissal or partial dismissal of the related claim. No court appears to have considered the defense's use for lesser sanctions such as when there has been litigation misconduct.

[183] *See, e.g.,* Mallis v. Bankers Trust Co., 615 F.2d 68, 75–76 (2d Cir. 1980) (declining to apply unclean hands because the basis of the misconduct was not a violation of the same statute as the claim), *abrogated in part on other grounds by* Peltz v. SHB Commodities, Inc., 115 F.3d 1082, 1090 (2d Cir. 1997); Kuehnert v. Texstar Corp., 412 F.2d 700, 703–05 (5th Cir. 1969); Boca Raton Community Hosp., Inc. v. Tenet Healthcare Corp., 238 F.R.D. 679, 693–94 (S.D. Fla. 2006) (asserting unclean hands pursuant to the same conduct of unlawful charging practices in violation of the same civil RICO statute).

[184] *See* discussion *supra* Chapter 5, Section 5.4.4.

[185] There are times when dismissal for unclean hands may be an efficient remedy. *Cf.* Anenson, *Interference with the Attorney–Client Relationship, supra* note 85, at 235 (noting the efficiency of removing potential satellite litigation due to litigation misconduct within the same case); Stern, *supra* note 82, at 1252 n.3 (noting that "it is more difficult to obtain relief from a judgment for fraud than it is to avoid a judgment in the first instance for fraud on the court").

[186] Maldonado v. Ford Motor Co., 719 N.W.2d 809 (Mich. 2006); *see also* discussion *supra* Chapter 3, Section 3.4.1.5.

[187] *See Maldonado,* 719 N.W.2d at 818. Placing the authority to dismiss on constitutional grounds potentially elevates the defense above statutory abrogation and makes the merger debate irrelevant. *See* Kaye, *supra* note 56, at 15–17 (explaining how deciding issues on state common law as opposed to state constitutional grounds allows—rather than forecloses—later correction by the court and the legislature). *But see* Hershkoff, *supra* note 57, at 1852 (noting the "conditional nature of [] state constitutional decisions, which are easily amended and frequently experimental in approach" (citing Helen Hershkoff, *Positive Rights and State Constitutions: The Limits of Federal Rationality Review,* 112 Harv. L. Rev. 1131, 1162–63 (1999))). While focusing on constitutional rights and not power, Judge Kaye discussed how state courts are answering Justice Brennan's call to "step into the breach" and interpreting their state

systems are following suit and applying unclean hands to damages.[188] To paraphrase Oliver Wendell Holmes, it is time to pull the dragon out of the cave and count its teeth.[189]

The foregoing four-pronged framework identifies a set of metaprinciples to help establish when considerations brought to bear by one situation ought to apply and trump those of others for the purpose of applying unclean hands in legal cases. The organizing principle is the assurance of public confidence in the integrity of the judicial process. The thesis was tested, at least in its general form, by examining cases that showed it is coherent and determinate enough to perform the task successfully. The procedural paradigm is not intended to define conclusively the evolving role of unclean hands at law as a defender of the legal process but rather to open other opportunities for further investigation.

The next section discusses the implications of the foregoing four-pronged analysis on the application of unclean hands in legal cases.

6.4 IMPLICATIONS

The procedural framework outlined already has potentially far-reaching consequences. First, in the courts that considered unclean hands at law, the majority denies the defense due to its substantive nature. Segregating cases into four levels relative to their ability to accomplish the court protection policy helps courts identify when the defense becomes "procedure" sufficient for incorporation at law. Second, despite the coincidence of unclean hands and other defenses in certain cases, it still plays a valuable and unique role in the common and statutory law.

6.4.1 *Universal Use*

There are three approaches to the incorporation of unclean hands in cases seeking legal remedies. The two case-based views of the merger reach different conclusions in applying the defense at law.[190] The third and newer approach reconciles the

constitutions more expansively than the federal constitution. *See* Kaye, *supra* note 56, at 11–13 (quoting William J. Brennan, Jr., *State Constitutions and the Protection of Individual Rights*, 90 HARV. L. REV. 489, 503 (1977)).

[188] *See* discussion *supra* Chapter 3, Section 3.4.

[189] Holmes commented on the history behind "why a rule of law has taken its particular shape":

> When you get the dragon out of his cave on to the plain and in the daylight, you can count his teeth and claws, and see just what is his strength. But to get him out is only the first step. The next is either to kill him, or to tame him and make him a useful animal.

O.W. Holmes, *The Path of the Law*, 10 HARVARD L. REV. 457, 469 (1897).

[190] *See* discussion *supra* Chapters 3–4. Recall that, at one point, scholars also took an all-or-nothing position on fusion. *See* discussion *supra* Chapter 5.

opposing rationales regarding the merger by proposing a new method to resolve the incorporation question.[191] The compromise position suggests a case-by-case consideration of unclean hands for the overwhelming number of jurisdictions that have not yet determined its status in damages actions.[192]

The foregoing framework offers a unified theory of judicial work in which the boundary problem between "law" and "equity" is no longer decisive. As such, it has ramifications regardless of the merger rationale. In particular, it facilitates the application of unclean hands in those courts that have not automatically accepted or rejected the defense.[193] The suggested mode also helps refine the analysis of unclean hands in those dozen or so state and federal jurisdictions that automatically apply the defense at law.[194]

Moreover, the process-based paradigm delineates what is "substance" from "procedure" for purposes of applying the defense against legal remedies under the prevailing view of the union of law and equity.[195] As Justice Brandeis explained long ago, "[Unclean hands] is sometimes spoken of as a rule of substantive law. But it extends to matters of procedure as well."[196] On the substance–procedure continuum, Phases One and Two would certainly be "procedure," as they directly impact the litigation process. The indirect impact on the judicial system in Phase Three is a gray area that could also be considered "procedure." Phase Four would clearly be "substantive."[197]

Consequently, classifying cases in terms of court protection has theoretical and practical implications. It is relevant regardless of the continuing conflict in the cases regarding the meaning of the merger and its effect on the defense of unclean hands.

---

[191] *See* discussion *supra* Chapter 4.

[192] *See* discussion *supra* Chapter 4–5.

[193] *See* discussion *supra* Chapter 3.

[194] *See* discussion *supra* Chapter 3–4.

[195] It must be emphasized that the law–equity merger is considered procedural and not meant to affect substantive rights. To the extent that "substantive" is defined in the sense that it means to change the result, *see* Lionel Smith, *Fusion and Tradition* (outlining different concepts of fusion, including terminological, procedural, and substantive), *in* Equity in Commercial Law, *supra* note 5, at 19, 21–22, then the procedural paradigm offered herein would not compromise the merger debate. Courts are dismissing cases and, hence, changing results by invoking unclean hands (albeit for purportedly procedural reasons).

[196] Olmstead v. United States, 277 U.S. 438, 484–85 & n.20 (1928) (Brandeis, J., dissenting) (citing cases).

[197] The four-pronged paradigm may have import as well for federal courts sitting in diversity jurisdiction and choosing state or federal law for defining unclean hands in an *Erie* analysis. *See* David Crump, *The Twilight Zone of the* Erie *Doctrine: Is There Really a Different Choice of Equitable Remedies in the "Court a Block Away"?*, 1991 Wis. L. Rev. 1233, 1234 ("The knottiest questions deal with the distinction between substantive law and procedure, which in turn determines the reach of the *Erie* doctrine . . . ."); Allen R. Stein, Erie *and Court Access*, 100 Yale L.J. 1935, 1941 (1991) (arguing to end the substance–procedure distinction).

6.4.2 *Parallel Theories*

Unclean hands shares important similarities and critical differences with other defenses regularly recognized at law. The similarities suggest that it is possible for unclean hands to overlap with theories like *in pari delicto*, estoppel, and fraud on the court. In these situations, one or more of these other defenses may reach the same result as unclean hands, raising the question of whether it is even necessary in legal cases.[198]

The differences, however, demonstrate that unclean hands is indispensable. While it is difficult to draw sharp lines around each separate defense, comparisons between them have reached a consensus that unclean hands is more expansive in application.[199]

Similar to unclean hands, the doctrine of *in pari delicto* preserves the dignity of the courts and deters illegal behavior.[200] *In pari delicto*, however, forbids a plaintiff to recover damages only if his or her fault is at least equal to the defendant's.[201] A court may dismiss a case for unclean hands notwithstanding the equality or mutuality of the fault between the parties.[202] "Since the clean hands principle [was] being applied . . . to protect the integrity of the courts and the judicial process," the district court in *Buchanan Home & Auto Supply Co., Inc. v. Firestone Tire & Rubber Co.* refused to balance the respective misconduct between the parties.[203]

---

[198] *See* Laycock, *Triumph of Equity, supra* note 21, at 70 ("Unclean hands has its legal counterpart, *in pari delicto*, and as Chafee showed, a host of narrower doctrines serve the same purpose.").

[199] *See* Anenson, *Role of Equity, supra* note 43, at 51–52 (explaining that unclean hands is broader in application than the defenses of equitable estoppel and waiver); William J. Lawrence, III, Note, *The Application of the Clean Hands Doctrine in Damage Actions*, 57 NOTRE DAME L. REV. 673, 676, 683–84 (1982) (distinguishing unclean hands from the narrower doctrine of *in pari delicto*).

[200] *See* discussion *supra* Chapter 5.

[201] *See* Bateman Eichler, Hill Richards, Inc. v. Berner, 472 U.S. at 306 (noting that the common law defense "derives from the Latin, *in pari delicto potior est conditio defendentis*: 'In a case of equal or mutual fault . . . the position of the [defending] party . . . is the better one.'") (citation omitted).

[202] *See, e.g.*, Precision Instrument Mfg. Co. v. Auto. Maint. Mach. Co., 324 U.S. 806, 814 (1945) (explaining that a dismissal under the clean hands doctrine follows regardless of the conduct of the defendant); Buchanan Home & Auto Supply Co., Inc. v. Firestone Tire & Rubber Co., 544 F. Supp. 242, 247 (D.S.C. 1981) (rejecting plaintiff's request to balance the equities between the parties for the doctrine of unclean hands); N. Pacific Lumber Co. v. Oliver, 596 P.2d 931, 938 (Ore. 1979) ("The maxim is applied for the protection of the court and not for the benefit of the defendant, who may in fact be equally affected with the improper transaction." (quoting HENRY L. MCCLINTOCK, HANDBOOK OF THE PRINCIPLES OF EQUITY 60 (2nd ed. 1948))). The refusal to balance the conduct of the parties is technically correct in terms of meeting the elements of unclean hands, yet it is not uncommon for courts to compare such conduct in exercising their discretion. *See* discussion *supra* Chapter 2, Section 2.8.

[203] *Buchanan*, 544 F. Supp. at 247.

The defense of *in pari delicto* also requires a common scheme, which is not a component of unclean hands.[204]

Many but not all of the Phase Three cases incorporating unclean hands into the law involve misconduct by the parties targeting a third party as opposed to each other, which is suggestive of an *in pari delicto* situation. The legal malpractice cases of *Blain v. Doctor's Co.*[205] and *Kirkland v. Mannis*[206] could have constituted *in pari delicto*, as both attorney and client in each case allegedly engaged in a common scheme to defraud the court by perjured testimony.[207]

In *Manown v. Adams*,[208] the parties engaged in a common scheme when the plaintiff's former girlfriend accepted an asset transfer as a loan to hide the money from the divorce and bankruptcy courts.[209] Nonetheless, the parties would not likely have been found in equal fault. The debtor husband owed legal duties to the courts in his former proceedings; his girlfriend did not. Additionally, in the Phase Four case of *Boca Raton Community Hosp., Inc. v. Tenet Healthcare Corp.*,[210] both parties were engaging in the same illegal activities in violation of RICO but did so separately and not jointly.[211]

Courts have similarly justified the application of unclean hands to legal claims by analogy to the availability of the equitable defense of estoppel.[212] In dismissing the case because the plaintiff falsified reimbursement forms that would be needed as evidence, the district court in *Buchanan Home & Auto Supply Co., Inc. v. Firestone*

---

[204] See *Bateman Eichler*, 472 U.S. at 307, 310–11 (confining the application of *in pari delicto* under federal antitrust laws and federal securities laws to the doctrine's traditional limitations, which require that the plaintiff bear "at least substantially equal responsibility for the violations he seeks to redress"); Perma Life Mufflers, Inc. v. Int'l Parts Corp., 392 U.S. 134, 138 (1968), *overruled on other grounds by* Copperweld Corp. v. Independence Tube Corp., 467 U.S. 752, 766 (1984); Nathanson v. Weis, Voisin, Cannon, Inc., 325 F. Supp. 50, 53 n.11 (S.D.N.Y. 1971) (explaining under the securities laws that *in pari delicto* is narrower than unclean hands, as it "contemplates equal and simultaneous participation by the parties in the same illegal activity").

[205] 272 Cal. Rptr. 250 (Cal. Ct. App. 1990).

[206] 639 P.2d 671 (Or. Ct. App. 1982).

[207] *Blain*, 272 Cal. Rptr. at 258–59 (perjury at deposition); *Kirkland*, 639 P.2d at 671–73 (perjury during trial). Whether the attorney's advice to lie would be equivalent to or less than his client's actual lie could be an issue in considering equal fault; however, the same Oregon appellate court disagreed with its decision in *Kirkland* and declared that the decision should have been dismissed pursuant to *in pari delicto*. McKinley v. Weidner, 698 P.2d 983, 985 (Or. Ct. App. 1985). The *in pari delicto* criterion was met as well in *Smith v. Long*, 281 A.D.2d 897, 898 (N.Y. App. Div. 2001), where both parties allegedly transferred stock ownership to defraud the SBA.

[208] 598 A.2d 821 (Md. Ct. Spec. App. 1991), *vacated on other grounds*, 615 A.2d 611, 612 (Md. 1992).

[209] *Id.* at 823–24.

[210] 238 F.R.D. 679 (S.D. Fla. 2006).

[211] *Id.* at 693–94.

[212] See discussion *supra* Chapter 5. Judicial estoppel also serves the same court protection policy as unclean hands. *Id.* Judicial estoppel, however, is narrower than unclean hands in that it generally requires reliance by the court on a prior position during the litigation. See Anenson, *Triumph of Equity*, *supra* note 30, at 394–96.

Tire & Rubber Co.,[213] recognized that the same conduct that qualifies as an estoppel may also satisfy unclean hands.[214] Yet equitable estoppel regularly requires reliance on an inconsistency that was not clearly present in *Buchanan*.[215] The dealership admitted that the customer forms used to verify the replacement tires were forged but contended that it did replace the tires.[216] Therefore, these defenses were not an exact match on the facts of *Buchanan Home & Auto Supply Co., Inc.* except in their equitable origin.

Finally, the Supreme Court of Michigan's recognition at law of litigation misconduct as a form of unclean hands in *Maldonado v. Ford Motor Co.*[217] is similar to the doctrine of "fraud on the court," frequently found in legal cases.[218] Like unclean hands, this doctrine is concerned primarily with the integrity of the judicial process.[219]

Nevertheless, fraud on the court typically involves fabrication of evidence or perjury by the parties to help their cause.[220] It does not usually include attempts to

[213] 544 F. Supp. 242 (D.S.C. 1981).
[214] *Id.* at 245; *see also* Anenson, *Role of Equity, supra* note 43, at 47–53 (comparing equitable and other estoppels with unclean hands); discussion *supra* Chapter 5, Section 5.3.2.2.2, and Chapter 3, Section 3.4.2.2.2.
[215] Some courts have removed the reasonable reliance requirement in furtherance of other policies. Anenson, *Pluralistic Model, supra* note 30, at 663–64; Anenson, *Triumph of Equity, supra* note 30, at 390–91. Even so, estoppel is narrower than unclean hands in its requirement of inconsistent or contradictory conduct. *See* Anenson, *Role of Equity, supra* note 43, at 47–53.
[216] *Buchanan*, 544 F. Supp. at 245. As discussed *supra* in Chapter 3, Section 3.4.2.2, and Section 6.3.5.2, the dealership attempted to justify the forgeries by explaining that they had insufficient forms. *Id.* The court did not believe the explanation and indicated that it could have found an estoppel. *Id.; see also id.* at 244 (noting admission by dealership of filing adjustment forms when the replacement tire was manufactured by one of Firestone's competitors). If the tires had not been replaced, there would have been an inconsistency in the dealership's conduct in falsifying forms that Firestone relied upon in paying the handling fees and crediting the dealership account. The court also suggested, however, that even if the tires were replaced, it was the dealership's duty under the contract "to maintain and keep accurate records of the replacements and adjustments it made." Its failure to do so warranted dismissal. *Id.* at 246.
[217] 719 N.W.2d 809, 818 (Mich. 2006); *see also id.* at 817 n.15.
[218] *See* discussion *supra* Chapter 5, Section 5.3.2.2.3. The seminal U.S. Supreme Court case on the subject of fraud on the court is *Hazel-Atlas Glass Co. v. Hartford-Empire Co.*, 322 U.S. 238 (1944), *overruled on other grounds sub nom.*, Standard Oil Co. v. United States, 429 U.S. 17 (1976). In *Hazel-Atlas*, the applicant's officials and attorneys prepared and arranged for the publication of an article, purportedly written by a disinterested expert, which was then used to influence favorable treatment by the Patent Office and, subsequently, the circuit court of appeals in the infringement case. *Id.* at 240–41. This constituted fraud on the court, cost the patent holder the case, and effectively perhaps the patent. *Id.* at 251. *See generally* Anenson & Mark, *supra* note 126 (analyzing the case in the context of the inequitable conduct defense derived from unclean hands).
[219] *See* discussion *supra* Chapter 5.
[220] *See* Stern, *supra* note 82, at 1254 (discussing cases in which the fabrication, destruction, or suppression of evidence and related perjury led to dismissal or default judgment under the doctrine of fraud on the court). Unlike unclean hands, a determination that there has been fraud on the court does not necessarily result in the remedy of dismissal.

harm the opposing side by interference with the jury or adverse witnesses, as found in the cases of *Maldonado* and *Cummings*, which fall within Phase One. While fraud on the court may correspond with Phase Three cases,[221] it would not normally include nonlitigation misconduct that still interferes with the judicial process, as in Phase Two or Phase Four cases that have no impact on court procedure. Even if these doctrines are used simultaneously, the availability of unclean hands in addition to another means of protection—such as fraud on the court, perjury prosecutions, or Rule 11 sanctions—raises the cost of lying or other bad behavior to curb such behavior in the future.

Consequently, while all of these defenses may be pled alternatively or separately in any given situation,[222] the doctrine of unclean hands provides broader (or at least different) coverage against the mischief that seems inherent in our adversary system.[223] It is this protective feature of unclean hands that should provide it a place within our law.

Attempts to garner improper litigation leverage by instigating known or new tricks of the litigation trade is a disease that can infect individual cases or an entire docket.[224] It cannot be emphasized too many times that when litigants and their counsel begin gaming the system, we all lose.[225]

---

[221] The unclean hands case of *Precision Instrument Mfg. Co. v. Auto. Maint. Machinery Co.*, 324 U.S. 806, 815 (1945), relied on the fraud-on-the-court case of *Hazel-Atlas*, 322 U.S. at 246. The Court in *Precision Instrument* concluded that the application of unclean hands was justified because "[o]nly in that way can the Patent Office and the public escape from being classed among the 'mute and helpless victims of deception and fraud.'" *Id.* at 818 (quoting *Hazel-Atlas*, 322 U.S. at 246).

[222] *See* Anenson, *Role of Equity*, *supra* note 43, at 23 n.124 (discussing a case in which attorneys advocated three alternative theories of equity—unclean hands, estoppel, and waiver—and court decided on the basis of estoppel); *cf.* T. Leigh Anenson, *Litigation Between Competitors with Mirror Restrictive Covenants: A Formula for Prosecution*, 10 STAN. J.L. BUS. & FIN. 1, 20 (2005) (discussing additional strategies to preclude competitor challenge to validity of employment noncompete agreement).

[223] *See* R.J. Gerber, *Victory vs. Truth: The Adversary System and Its Ethics*, 19 ARIZ. ST. L.J. 3, 4 (1987) (inquiring whether the adversary system "may exalt trickery and victory over ethics and truth"); *see also* MARTIN MAYER, THE LAWYERS 20 (Dell Publishing Co., Inc. 1968) (quoting Judge Learned Hand: "[A]s a litigant, . . . I should dread a lawsuit beyond almost anything else short of sickness and death."); Burnele V. Powell, *Open Doors, Open Arms, and Substantially Open Records: Consumerism Takes Hold in the Legal Profession*, 28 VAL. U. L. REV. 709, 713 (1994) (noting that the legal profession is not self-regulated but rather is regulated by the judiciary).

[224] *See* Gerber, *supra* note 224, at 6–20 (listing examples of the "tricks of the litigation trade" as the shotgun complaint, the tactical counterclaim, delay pettifoggery, discovery abuses, harassing and coaching witnesses, dumb shows, bushwhacking, and lying). *See generally* Anenson, *Interference with the Attorney–Client Relationship*, *supra* note 85 (discussing new attempt to garner improper litigation leverage by suing the opposing advocate).

[225] *See* Eugene R. Anderson & Nadia V. Holober, *Preventing Inconsistencies in Litigation with a Spotlight on Insurance Coverage Litigation: The Doctrines of Judicial Estoppel, Equitable Estoppel, Quasi-Estoppel, Collateral Estoppel, "Mend the Hold," Fraud on the Court," and*

A system without the safeguard of unclean hands and other protective measures would simply surrender the legal process to the least restrained and worst-behaved litigants. Removing such defensive doctrines:

> would create a world in which legal questions come increasingly to be decided, not by a fair and rational search for truth, but by bullying and uncivil behavior, personal abuse, one-upmanship, and public exhibitionism on the part of those who are custodians of this system, the bar. Justice under the law cannot flourish within such a system.[226]

Neither can it seemingly flourish, at this juncture, without unclean hands.

In summary, unclean hands continues to bear the birthmark of an equitable defense to the extent that it is contained in cases seeking equitable remedies. Chapters 4 and 5 rejected the preoccupation with the merger of law and equity as a barrier to the application of unclean hands under the common law. This chapter focused on specific, contextual issues in which unclean hands can and should be decisive in real-world disputes, especially those with grave consequences to the administration of justice. As a result, it sketched an account of unclean hands that can help explain why it has a legitimate role to play in cases asserting legal (as well as equitable) remedies.

6.5 CONCLUSION

The clean hands doctrine has been known to be a challenge, burdened by conflicting results and judicial discord. The uncertainty over its postmerger status in cases at law has added to the confusion. Previous chapters suggested a modest doctrinal shift in interpreting the merger as continuing to allow the pleading of unclean hands in damages actions on a case-by-case basis. This chapter advances that analysis by providing guidance for courts to evaluate the defense under the common and statutory law.

The proposed process-based theory preserves the core intuition that the conduct constituting unclean hands must primarily have the potential to interfere with the interests of the justice system and only secondarily with the interests of the parties. As

---

Judicial and Evidentiary Admissions, 4 CONN. INS. L.J. 589, 622 (1997–98) (explaining that courts applying equitable canons such as unclean hands have shown an unwillingness to "countenance the devolution of the judicial system into a forum of 'mere gamesmanship'") (citation omitted); Anenson, *Interference with the Attorney–Client Relationship, supra* note 85, at 241 ("Just as markets cannot operate on self-seeking opportunism and strategic behavior by using schemes unrelated to business excellence and efficiencies, the advocacy system depends on participants that are committed to maintaining the legal framework with a system in place to correct institutional failures.").

[226] Maldonado v. Ford Motor Co., 719 N.W.2d 809, 825 n.26 (Mich. 2006) (quoting Grievance Adm'r v. Fieger, 719 N.W.2d 123, 144 n.34 (Mich. 2006)).

a practical matter, it requires litigants to come into court with clean hands and not dirty them during the litigation process.

The importance of understanding the equitable defense of unclean hands is evidenced by its use in thousands of cases decided in recent years. Yet scholarship concerning unclean hands has been virtually nonexistent since the integration of law and equity in the United States. Zechariah Chafee's influential study of the substantive aspects of the defense is incomplete. The foregoing exposition extends beyond Chafee's examination to formulate a procedural paradigm. It discussed where we are, where we are going, and how we should get there. It is a new front in the "fusion wars" being waged in the rest of the common law world regarding the relationship between common law and equity and the question of integration.[227]

The chapter does not purport to account for every decision regarding the incorporation of unclean hands into the common law. Nor does it identify a universal test for when unclean hands should bar a legal claim in a particular case, although it has implications for that analysis. The chapter does demonstrate some of the under-appreciated complexities that attend the idea of unclean hands and attempts to articulate a coherent conception of the defense. It suggests an analytical blueprint that explains and defends the defense on doctrinal and theoretical grounds in the hopes of laying the groundwork for its future in the twenty-first century.

---

[227] *See* discussion *supra* Chapter 1 and Chapter 5, Section 5.3.1.

7

Conclusion

It has been seventy-five years since the Federal Rules of Civil Procedure unified law and equity. In the states, fusion began even earlier in the late nineteenth century. During this time period, state and federal courts have been grappling with whether and under what circumstances equitable defenses – including unclean hands – bar legal relief.

This book analyzed the legal status of unclean hands in the United States. It is one of many issues of law–equity integration being addressed by judges across the commonlaw world. To answer this query, it suggested that courts consider the fusion of law and equity as part of a larger historical and analytical framework.

Fusion is just one example of how the law evolves through the centuries. And it is an example that exemplifies Oliver Wendell Holmes's refusal to perpetuate a legal rule after the historical reason for the rule no longer existed.[1] In this vein, courts should be encouraged to exercise their discretion on a case-by-case basis when considering the viability of an equitable defense – whether it be unclean hands or any other equitable defense – to actions seeking damages.

---

[1] O.W. Holmes, *The Path of the Law*, 10 HARVARD L. REV. 457, 469 (1897).

Index

accommodation, 107
accounting, 144–45
acquiescence, 14, 36, 108
American Law Institute, 8–9, 29
Aquinas, Thomas, 170
Aristotle, 17, 52, 165, 167. *See also epikeia*
Ashley v. Boyle's Famous Corned Beef Co., 140
Australia, 3, 5, 10, 29, 44, 102–3, 127, 157, 167

bankruptcy law, 26, 72–73, 142, 201–2, 213
Barrett, Amy Coney, 189
Bartlett v. Dunne, 79, 197
Beale, Sara Sun, 189
Bein v. Heath, 35
Big Lots Stores, Inc. v. Jaredco, Inc., 87, 206
Blackstone, 17, 102, 109
Blain v. Doctor's Co., 46, 57, 70–71, 76, 156, 170,
   173–74, 201, 203, 213
*Boca Raton Community Hosp., Inc. v. Tenet
   Healthcare Corp.*, 79, 131, 213
Brandeis, Justice Louis, 35, 40, 134, 136, 177, 187, 211
*Buchanan Home & Auto Supply Co., Inc.
   v. Firestone Tire & Rubber Co.*, 77, 79, 81,
   83–84, 94, 132, 135, 138, 188, 198, 212, 214
Burbank, Stephen, 151, 161
Byron v. Clay, 86, 93, 130

California, 67–71, 155–58
Canada, 5, 10
Cardozo, Benjamin, 94, 96, 160, 162–63
Carmen v. Fox Film Corp., 136
Cathcart v. Robinson, 35
Chafee, Zechariah, 11, 13–14, 18, 21, 28, 41, 44, 46,
   59, 65, 70, 82, 95–96, 102, 104–5, 116, 128–29,
   136, 138, 147, 152–53, 170, 172–73, 175, 180–81,
   184, 204, 207, 217

Chayes, Abraham, 162
Chinese customary law, 23, 127
Clark v. Amoco Prod. Co., 145
clean hands doctrine
   ability to cure, 50
   attempt, 43
   causal relation, 38–45
   claim specific application, 48, 158
   harm, 42
   presumption against, 54
   public interest criterion, 44
   purposes of, 20–22
   state of mind, 31–38
   underlying values, 21
Commentaries on Equity Jurisprudence, 26.
   See also Story, Joseph
Commonwealth, 4, 30, 57. *See also* Australia,
   Canada, England, New Zealand
constructive fraud, 36, 45, 154
contribution, 36, 40, 171
conversion, 47, 67, 69, 87, 173
copyright misuse defense, 13, 84, 122, 173, 205
Cornell, Nicholas, 21
Corpus Juris Secundum, 29, 34, 61
Cravens, Sarah, 162
Cummings v. Wayne Cty., 76–78, 90, 188, 196, 198,
   215

declaratory judgment, 68, 71, 144
Dering v. Earl of Winchelsea, 23, 25, 31, 39–40, 46,
   68, 159, 171
Deweese v. Reinhard, 42
discretion, judicial. *See* subject heading
   effect of alternative sanction, 54
   factors, 53
   legitimacy of, 121